Remaking
New
Orleans

THOMAS JESSEN ADAMS
& MATT SAKAKEENY, *editors*

Remaking

New Orleans

Beyond Exceptionalism and Authenticity

DUKE UNIVERSITY PRESS
Durham and London | 2019

Printed in the United States of America on acid-free paper ∞
Designed by Julienne Alexander
Typeset in Garamond Premier Pro by Westchester
Publishing Services

Library of Congress Cataloging-in-Publication Data
Names: Adams, Thomas Jessen, editor. | Sakakeeny, Matt, [date]
editor.
Title: Remaking New Orleans : beyond exceptionalism and
authenticity / Thomas Jessen Adams and Matt Sakakeeny, editors.
Description: Durham : Duke University Press, 2019. | Includes
bibliographical references and index.
Identifiers: LCCN 2018040997 (print)
LCCN 2018053730 (ebook)
ISBN 9781478003328 (ebook)
ISBN 9781478001829 (hardcover : alk. paper)
ISBN 9781478002871 (pbk. : alk. paper)
Subjects: LCSH: New Orleans (La.)—Social conditions—21st
century. | New Orleans (La.)—Politics and government—
21st century. | New Orleans (La.)—Social life and
customs—21st century. | New Orleans (La.)—In popular culture. |
Ethnology—Louisiana—New Orleans.
Classification: LCC F379.N54 (ebook) | LCC F379.N54 R46 2019
(print) | DDC 976.3/35—dc23
LC record available at https://lccn.loc.gov/2018040997

Cover art: Tavares Strachan, *You Belong Here*, Prospect 3, New
Orleans, 2014. Blocked-out neon, 30′ × 80′. Courtesy of the artist.

Contents

Part Two Producing Authentic New Orleans

Part Three What Is New Orleans Identity?

Part Four   Predictive City?

Acknowledgments

THIS BOOK GREW OUT of a 2014 conference held at Tulane University titled "New Orleans as Subject: Beyond Authenticity and Exceptionalism." Funding for the conference was provided by the New Orleans Center for the Gulf South, with additional support provided by the Tulane Office of Academic Affairs, the Stone Center for Latin American Studies, Newcomb College Institute, the Tulane Department of Music, the Tulane Department of Political Science, and the United States Studies Centre at the University of Sydney. We'd like to thank conference participants Vincanne Adams, Vern Baxter, Maria Casati, Joel Dinerstein, Adrienne Dixson, Rien Fertel, Megan French-Marcelin, Cedric Johnson, Yuki Kato, Alecia Long, Vicki Mayer, Marguerite Nguyen, Aaron Nyerges, Larry Powell, Adolph Reed, Helen Regis, Kodi Roberts, Heidi Schmalbach, Felipe Smith, Randy Sparks, Steve Striffler, Christien Tompkins, and Bryan Wagner as well as the numerous audience members who helped make the event full of stimulating and lively discussion.

Sue Mobley joined in helping to organize the conference and brought her deep knowledge not only to the introduction but to the entire editorial process. This book would not have been the same without her contributions. Kyle DeCoste offered invaluable support during the conference, editorial input on the introduction, and formatting of the final manuscript. Ken Wissoker guided the publication with a steady hand, and we thank the entire team at Duke along with the two anonymous reviewers who provided critical and thorough feedback.

We dedicate this book to gumbo, King Rex, foggy nights on the Mississippi, and memories of Marie Laveau.

Introduction

What Lies beyond Histories of Exceptionalism and Cultures of Authenticity

THOMAS JESSEN ADAMS, SUE MOBLEY, & MATT SAKAKEENY

"New Orleans is a world apart," notes a tourism website, "in many ways its own little city-state, part of the United States but at the same time so different from every other place in the country." Could anyone familiar with the city have escaped this truism that New Orleans is a land unto itself, and could any of us who have been enchanted with this place deny experiencing its singularity in profound ways? Within the specter of American exceptionalism, in which the United States is idealized as an immigrant country of hard workers and liberal dreamers—"a special case 'outside' the normal patterns and laws of history," as Ian Tyrrell has argued—New Orleans resides as a thing apart, the exception to the exception.[1] From the beginning of its existence as a juridically American locale, those both inside and outside the city have marked it off as anathema to broader patterns of urbanity, culture, politics, economics, and, indeed, Americanness. Placed in opposition to a nation perpetually driven by progress, New Orleans is the "city that care forgot." It can also be the "Paris of the South," the "northernmost Caribbean City," and the "most African city in the United States." That New Orleans can be all of these is what makes this place different from any other place, or the United States as a whole. Or so the story goes.

The response to Hurricane Katrina in August 2005 is a useful barometer of exceptionalism discourse and the importance it plays in the city's identity vis-à-vis the nation. "Only a sadist would insist on resurrecting this concentration of poverty, crime, and deplorable schools," wrote veteran journalist Jack Shafer, while Speaker of the House Dennis Hastert observed from Washington, "it looks like a lot of that place could be bulldozed."[2] To be sure, the overwhelming response to the devastation in New Orleans was an outpouring of assistance, with thousands of volunteers and donors supporting rebuilding efforts and contributing their dollars and sweat to the process of bringing a major American city back from the brink. Affective cases for rebuilding were packaged under titles like *Why New Orleans Matters* and *What Can't Be Lost*. Testifying on Capitol Hill about the "strategy necessary to rebuild Louisiana," then Lieutenant Governor Mitch Landrieu, who would be elected mayor in 2010, explained to Congress, "Louisiana has an economic asset that other states can only dream of: a multifaceted, deeply rooted, authentic, and unique culture."[3] Though the calls for support ran directly counter to the desires of the conservative bulldozers, both relied upon a broadly shared perception of an inimitable city set apart from a normative America.

How is it possible that the justification given for saving New Orleans and southeastern Louisiana was not that it's a major metropolitan area, home to 1.3 million people, or the nation's busiest port system, or perhaps the key nodal point in North America's oil and gas infrastructure? From the other perspective, would senior politicians and influential opinion makers have called for the abandonment of the Bay Area following the Loma Prieta earthquake in 1989, or of lower Manhattan and northern New Jersey after Hurricane Sandy struck in 2012, or of the Houston metropolitan area inundated by Hurricane Harvey in 2017? Whether sinful or soulful, post-Katrina New Orleans was to live or die by the sword of exceptionalism, by how those in power assessed the value—not least in monetary terms—of its culture.

New Orleans exceptionalism, its raison d'être, is grounded in notions of cultural authenticity embodied in creolized cuisine and architecture, jazz and other musical traditions, community parades and black Indian processions, voodoo queens and Mardi Gras royals, public drinking and prostitution. We should state at the outset that as residents of New Orleans, each of us participates in the city's multifaceted traditions and attends to various cultural formations in our research. This book is an attempt not only to draw out other, more neglected areas of local study but to highlight the affinities between scholars, popular historians, journalists, and tourism marketers who have narrowed in on select cultural formations, masking their incorporation into the market, and thus imbuing them with authenticity as definitively local and communitarian. This cultivated rendering of New Orleans is rooted in a nineteenth-century romantic literary tradition, continuously repackaged through the twin engines of tourism and economic development schemes, and supported by research in sectors of the humanities and social sciences that has isolated the city from comparison. Such a consensus is the result of an analytical tautology in which cultural authenticity renders New Orleans exceptional and the city's exceptionalism renders it authentic. As local musician Louis Prima observed after opening a nightclub on Bourbon Street, "People look to us for what they have been led to expect [that] New Orleans can give them."[4]

In this book we argue that the New Orleans created by this feedback loop, in which authenticity and exceptionality are perpetually reaffirmed, has obscured other possible understandings. The equation of historical exceptionalism plus cultural authenticity has been not so much imagined as conjured as an entity outside of history, outside of capital, and outside of politics. It is not our purpose to prove New Orleans's typicality or exceptionality, or demonstrate how it exists as an authentic bastion of meaning in an otherwise artificial world, or how its various social formations are in fact products of capitalist social relations, marketing constructs, or cultural appropriation. Rather, this is an attempt to move beyond these dichotomies and to ask what is hidden in their invocation. *Remaking New Orleans* is aligned with progressive scholarship in history, anthropology, political science, and urban studies that pursues how the very "New Orleansness" of New Orleans has taken root in the city's notoriously unstable terrain. The editors take inspiration from other place-based studies—Mike Davis's Los Angeles, Hal Rothman's Las Vegas, John L. Jackson's "Harlemworld"—that track the accumulative construction of cities and neighborhoods as distinctive locales.[5] The contributors go about interrogating and recontextualizing the most salient symbols of New Orleans exceptionalism (Congo Square, Creole literature, jazz, the Katrina disaster) and locating subjects that do not conform to caricatures of cultural authenticity (Vietnamese American New Orleanians, middle-class black suburbanites, pro wrestlers, philanthrocapitalists).

More than a critique of area studies or scholarship specific to the city, this book also contributes to research on exceptionalism and authenticity as theoretical concepts. When a city can exemplify nothing except itself, its uniqueness—to invoke the adjective most often applied to New Orleans—renders it an incomparable cultural island. The more holistic and inclusive New Orleans we put forth has the capacity to inform scholars working in other areas about the machinations of exceptionalism and authenticity—key concepts in the humanities and humanistic social sciences—on the ground.

The contributors in this volume show what New Orleans–as-exception can teach us about other locales, as they draw comparisons to other sites and frame specific claims to authenticity within and against legacies of intellectual thought. Ethnographic and cultural studies of New Orleans have eschewed the attendees of wrestling matches and the quotidian lives of suburban blacks in favor of Mardi Gras Indian ceremonies, Creole culinary traditions, and community parades known as "second lines" (see chapters 5, 9, 10, this volume). This focus on the supposedly authentic and relatively unmediated mirrors tendencies in anthropology and cultural studies that have been subject to sustained critique in poststructural readings. Similarly, historians of New Orleans have tended to focus on the distinctive context of the French and Spanish colonial city and its denizens, New Orleans's nodality within the American slave trade, and challenges to the black-white color line, while eliding the variety of ways in which New Orleans is part of less exceptional but no less interesting developments in urbanity, inequality, and American politics. Together, we ask what putting a city on a pedestal of distinction accomplishes in terms of civic participation, identity formation, cultural production, tourism marketing, urban planning, disaster recovery, political gamesmanship, and more.

In pursuing these themes within a discrete locale, we aim to intervene in the now robust multidisciplinary debates about New Orleans and contribute to current debates within the humanistic social sciences surrounding cultures of authenticity and histories of exceptionalism. New Orleans is a model site for tracking authenticity and exceptionalism as moving targets, seemingly rooted in place and yet ascribed to different cultural formations and subject positions over time. The individual chapters take up these and other topics, proceeding in rough chronological order from the colonial period to contemporary New Orleans. This introductory chapter is intended as a selective genealogy that tracks the accumulation of exceptionalism and authenticity over three centuries, beginning with an overview of the twin concepts as they have been theorized in the humanities and social sciences.

Theorizing Exceptionalism and Authenticity

In both scholarly and popular understandings of American urbanity, Chicago reigns as the most distinctly American city, aided in no small part through the work of the successive Chicago schools of sociology, anthropology, and political science. New York is the engine that moves the nation's finance and high culture. Boston and Philadelphia are home to that most American of events, the Revolution itself. Cincinnati, St. Louis, Denver, Salt Lake City, and San Francisco (along with Chicago as well) are all part of the Turnerian and thus intrinsically American march west. Pittsburgh, Detroit, and Cleveland stand as symbols of industrial might in the so-called American Century. Los Angeles, as one contemporary scholar put it, is the logical outcome of the values enshrined in the Constitution.[6] As we near the third decade of the twenty-first century, the megalopolises of the Sun Belt—Atlanta, Houston, Dallas, Phoenix, and Miami—increasingly stand as interchangeable representatives of an American dream grounded in the imperatives of property ownership, mass consumption, migration, and the elusive lure of multicultural opportunity.

New Orleans, on the other hand, stands utterly outside the nation's story of its urban identities. As one real estate developer and a leading light of New Urbanism put it, to understand New Orleans one must "recalibrate" to understand that "New Orleans [is] not an American city."[7] New Orleans is considered exceptional to the broader US but also to the American South and Louisiana, and to the Atlantic and the Caribbean, depending on which time and place one is writing about. This language has similarly hamstrung New Orleans itself—in politics, economics, and culture—as issues get framed around progress versus preservation, authentic versus plastic, gemeinschaft versus gesellschaft, the pastoral versus the industrial. In this way New Orleans as a city stands as the consummate other in broader narratives of modernization, development, liberalism, society, and rationality. All that makes New Orleans worthy of value and preservation is in its oppositionality to national values of progress and modernity. This antimodernism can become uneasily equated with racial primitivism, as when the performance traditions of black New Orleanians are portrayed solely as vestiges from an African past rather than complex and cosmopolitan cultural formations, or when creolism and the supposed exceptionality of interracial sex are romanticized in accounts of quadroon balls that obscure the gendered coercion inherent in *plaçage*. When a locale is so defined by such discursive idioms, it is time to interrogate the nature of those idioms within the very narratives and geopolitical flows that actualized them.

An oddly *Volksgemeinschaft* island of twenty-first-century social analysis, New Orleans continues to generate research that fetishizes collective meaning and the bonds of sociability as truly organic. The city's exceptionality rests on a vision of culture and community as authentic, making it a model site for tracking contemporary attachments to authenticity and the relationship of such attachments to changing philosophical, anthropological, and materialist theories. In her study of "salvage ethnographers" who sought to document folk cultures against the encroaching threat of industrial modernity, Regina Bendix identifies a broader tension in searches for authenticity, which are "oriented toward the recovery of an essence whose loss has been realized only through modernity, [but] whose recovery is feasible only through methods and sentiments created in modernity."[8] Historically tied to the rise of bourgeois capitalism and the attendant estrangement of individuals from (imagined) organic communities, the very effort to capture authenticity leads to its perceived loss via processes of recognition, reproduction, and especially commodification. As Lionel Trilling summarizes this deeply entrenched fetishization of the authentic, "Money, in short, is the principle of the inauthentic in human existence."[9]

As the mystical "southern Babylon," a place seemingly preserved so we might forget to care (about a Protestant work ethic, about accruing capital, about transgressing taboos, about untended levees), New Orleans is imagined as a place of pastness, somehow predating capitalist alienation and inauthentic (i.e., state-sponsored rather than community-sponsored) social welfare.[10] A demarcated zone of festivity and excess—music and dance, food and drink, sociability and sex—is imbued with authenticity in the Rousseauian sense as a fundamental, even primal, human endeavor that is idealized as antithetical to bourgeois social expectations. The ludic spaces of Mardi Gras, of Bourbon Street, or of a musical funeral procession appear as timeless, masking their incorporation into the very market forces they appear to subvert. New Orleans "performs as a simulacrum of itself," Joseph Roach observes, "apparently frozen in time, but in fact busily devoted to the ever-changing task of recreating the illusion that it is frozen in time."[11] The city's authenticity, its originality, is in its failure to fully Americanize and modernize, by preserving not only its historic buildings but also its time-honored traditions for reasons other than maximal profit making. This creates a metric, what David Grazian terms a "symbolic economy of authenticity," in which an original, authentic experience resides at the opposite end of the spectrum from a staged, overtly commodified experience that smacks of "Disneyfication."[12]

The search for authenticity as an end goal is a fool's errand, tied to a romantic vision of meaning centered on an individualistic conception of truth through personal fulfillment. In its essential antimodernism, authenticity as value becomes, paradoxically, the highest value of modernity and beyond.[13] Manufacturing authenticity for notoriety and profit has been a time-honored occupation for generations of New Orleanians and its many suitors. Authenticating New Orleans remains an imperative for musicians, chefs, and anyone else employed in a tourism industry that inflates authenticity within a highly curated experience economy. In this global marketing paradigm, business consultants discuss how "authenticity has overtaken quality as the prevailing purchase criterion, just as quality overtook cost, and as cost overtook availability."[14] So while the Starbucks corporation has cultivated a perception of authenticity through individual handcrafted service, New Orleans has a much longer history of "place-branding" and, as with all brands, the cultural meanings of this particular brand are organized by economic exchange.[15] The grounds of this actual city may not be manicured to the degree of Disneyland, but that is precisely what lends it salability as real.

A recurring yet submerged theme of New Orleans history is how image manufacturing in the domain of perception feeds back into reality to enhance the symbolic authenticity of cultural forms. Shannon Dawdy finds comparable levels of romanticized exoticism in other sites, such as Japan or the French countryside, but notes "what stands out in the New Orleans case is the extent to which this idiom came to be appropriated by locals."[16] A public secret among New Orleanians is that the mundanities of daily life are necessarily acted out on the theater stage of exceptionalism and authenticity; all the city is a stage and the locals are merely players. In *Ethnicity, Inc.*, Jean Comaroff and John Comaroff survey numerous sites where identities have increasingly become "*both* commodified, made into the basis of *value-added* corporate collectivity, and claimed as the basis of shared emotion, shared lifestyle, shared imaginings for the future."[17] Though they attribute this process of authentication to recent neoliberal incorporations of culture, the long history of marketing place-based identity in ways that reaffirm locals' lived experience—of being New Orleanians—is one of the many ways this particular city is more predictive than regressive.

Substantive critiques of contemporary political economy and culture are concentrated in "Predictive City?," the last section of the book. The first three sections—"Constructing Exceptional New Orleans," "Producing Authentic New Orleans," and "What Is New Orleans Identity?"—show that the city has long been at the forefront of national patterns of urban planning and place-branding, structural inequality and racialization. Beyond New Orleans, the authors suggest that the cutting edge of contemporary politics of demobilization, dislocation, and upward redistribution of wealth is the allure of social identity as the basis for representation and political constituency. They demonstrate how exceptionalism and authenticity—as a member of racial group, resident of a particular neighborhood, native of a particular place, and so on—are integral to the hegemony of capitalist social relations.

The attachment to exceptionalism and authenticity is at the very heart of neoliberalism, positing difference rather than exploitation as the central injustice of the contemporary world. This dislocation is the precise manner in which capitalism frees itself from opposition.

This collection is part of an accelerative force toward defamiliarizing New Orleans, moving beyond the celebratory mode of documenting the city's beloved traditions while leaving their status as markers of identity unexamined. We bring to the fore a speculative body of literature that has critically examined the city's identity and questioned how it has been constructed. Approached anew as a city on the forefront of national trends in urban development, New Orleans becomes a rich site for understanding the quintessential concerns of American cities, with implications far beyond the boundaries of Orleans Parish. The remainder of this chapter provides a detailed genealogy of the two interrelated and essentializing processes at the heart of this volume, the historicizing of the city's past as exceptional and the grounding of this exceptionalism in cultural formations deemed authentic.

The Grounds of Exceptionalism and Authenticity in the Colonial and Antebellum Eras

In most accounts, the founding of New Orleans in 1718 signals the literal and figurative arrival of the city's exceptional status, as a French and then Spanish colony contiguous with North American British colonies and, later, the United States. The city's place as a backwater in the French and Spanish empires allowed for improvisation and experimentation in social relations, while vulnerability to disease and hardship necessitated interdependence and intimacy. In this liminal milieu, the boundaries of racialization and sexuality looked decidedly more permeable than they would come to be in the Anglo-Protestant South.[18] In her study *Building the Devil's Empire*, Shannon Dawdy excavated how New Orleans gained a "special reputation in the early eighteenth century" and then traced how this status has "endured and become part of the lore of the city."[19] Because the seeds of exceptionalism and authenticity were retroactively planted in this foundational period, and because the chapters in this book deal only passingly with the colonial and antebellum eras, our formulation of New Orleans's *longue durée* starts with an extended analysis of the city's beginnings.

From the standpoint of the present, social and political dynamics of race, religion, and sexuality became imbued with an exotic character in many accounts that contrast colonial Louisiana with Anglo-Protestant governance in the United States.[20] In this dominant formulation, New Orleans appears wholly exceptional as an unruly environment that laid the foundation for the most concentrated free black population in the slave South, the burgeoning of a mixed-race Creole identity with in-between political status, Catholic social practice in a largely Protestant early republic, and the unparalleled presence of a variety of African-derived cultural practices. However, looking "seaward rather than landward," from an Atlantic perspective "where the USA is not automatically the object of comparison," as historian Mark L. Thompson suggests, New Orleans appears as but one outpost within a massive geographic and cultural swath of French and Spanish territories stretching from Granada through Florida and Mexico to California, and north to Canada.[21]

With a population just above 2,500 in 1763, early New Orleans was a relatively dense outpost of colonial elites, artisans, traders, and sailors, nestled among adjacent hinterlands of indigo and tobacco plantations.[22] Such a small city, with most interactions, economic and otherwise, taking place face to face, rendered the law of the metropole secondary to the exigencies of daily life. In her study *Race, Sex, and Social Order in Early New Orleans*, Jennifer Spear argues that eighteenth-century New Orleans was comparable to seventeenth-century South Carolina. Both sites experienced a "frontier phase," when slaves could be found in most skilled sectors of a mixed economy, before settling into a "full-blown slave society" where the master-slave dichotomy governed all social relations.[23]

With Etienne Bore's 1795 development of a technique to reliably crystallize sugar from immature cane, New Orleans entered a period of rapid and radical change. A viable cash crop led to the importation of vast numbers of enslaved people to serve the restructuring of plantations for sugarcane production. At the same time, an influx of Saint-Domingue refugees upended the demographics of the city, doubling the overall population and adding 3,102 *gens de couleur libre* to the free black population of New Orleans proper. From a population of 8,056 in 1803, New Orleans had risen to 17,242 inhabitants in its first appearance in the US decennial census in 1810, making it the seventh largest city in the country.[24] The promise of economic opportunity continued to lure "carpetbaggers" south for decades after the Louisiana Purchase. In transitioning from a colonial to an antebellum city, New Orleans gradually reinvented its political, economic, and social relations.

Prior to Americanization, New Orleans was a particular place connected to and comparable with other port cities in a sprawling intercoastal region.[25] Within an Atlantic context of cultural creolization, *mestizaje*, and ongoing negotiation between the laws of the metropole and local practices, the only aspect of the city that stood out was how exceptional this frontier slave society appeared when "refracted by an Anglo-American lens."[26] It was, of course, the emplacement of a Franco-Latin city within an Anglo-Protestant nation that juridically distinguished its development from Veracruz, Port-au-Prince, and other Atlantic hubs. Once New Orleans was accommodated into the North American context, its status as a port city further marked it as other in comparison to the frontier slave societies and well-established plantation regimes that characterized the mid-Atlantic and Deep South.

However, emphasizing the legal and cultural structure of the plantation misses the central role that New Orleans and other port cities played in the development of the nation at large. A primary motive for the Louisiana Purchase in 1803 was control of the port, a strategic nodal point that vastly increased connections between Atlantic world trade networks and internal frontier economies. The once liminal was now rendered integral to nation building, reorienting US economics and politics to include new global markets, while reaping the fruits of one of the most fertile riverine valleys of the world. Traders expanded production along routes developed over centuries by Native Americans, with dependence on indigenous populations ultimately leading to warfare, enslavement, genocide, and deterritorialization, as happened throughout the Americas.[27] Outside the city limits, the lives of the indigenous and the enslaved were further entwined by marronage, intermarriage, and collaboration in uprisings. These activities fueled New Orleans's long-standing reputation as a cultural island, literally surrounded by swampland, but again, the delineation between urban centers and liminal frontier zones was common to many Atlantic regions.

As the sources of exceptionalism strengthened in this transitional antebellum era, the first glimmerings of some notion of authenticity or, at least, oppositionality to Yankee modernity began to be seen. Speculative hordes were "swarming in from the northern states," as the last French governor of Louisiana put it, "each one turn[ing] over in his mind a little plan of speculation."[28] It was the accounts of cultural difference by travelers and shocked migrants on the make that supplied the historical record with abundant evidence of New Orleans's otherness. A recurring trope was the high concentration and visibility of black New Orleanians: enslaved and free; African, African American, and Creole. In published travelogues, essays, and diaries, events that were common throughout the Atlantic world—ring shout dances, slaves attending the opera, free people of color operating businesses, mixed-race women consorting with European men—were recontextualized as spectacles of difference within a new national context. Observers shared a sense of bewilderment that such a variegated racial structure existed on American soil, and opened a key fissure between New Orleansness and Americanness.

Much of New Orleans's reputation for transgression stems from a long-standing tension around the intersection of race and sex, specifically a fixation on intermixture, beginning with legal and cultural conflicts between the French and Spanish regimes and the Yankee interlopers who began arriving in the early nineteenth century. Spear argues it was through this interface that the city earned its reputation "as a site in which relationships between Euro-American men and non-European women were widespread and generally accepted." But she notes that interracial relationships were not uncommon elsewhere the US: "Although the eighteenth century saw an increase in the hostility directed towards racially exogamous relationships, these relationships—including those between white women and black men—continued to receive a measure of toleration, and perhaps even at times acceptance, well into the nineteenth century."[29] Emily Clark similarly finds "women whose racial ancestry would have earned them the color term quadroon lived everywhere in nineteenth-century America."[30] However, over the course of the nineteenth-centruy interracial sex, and especially its human results, were increasingly quarantined in New Orleans, as national narratives portrayed the city as an exotic other to a normative American experience. The imagined confinement to a single locale functioned to absolve the nation of both moral depravity and collective complicity in sexual violence and rape, while rendering invisible those consenting relationships between racially exogenous free people.

The romanticization of interracial sex and specifically plaçage has worked to obscure the economically and structurally coercive aspects of these arrangements, by focusing instead on the illicit allure and legendary beauty of the women involved. The persistent framing of these relations as voluntary or culturally authentic obscures the economic drivers and supports "the image of black women as promiscuous," which as Joy James indicates "was manufactured by white males, [and] deflected attention from racialized sexual violence inflicted by white men."[31] This racial imaginary drove a fancy trade in sexual slaves, the establishment and expansion of quadroon balls to include the invitation of outsiders, and the prostitution of light-skinned women and children. The city's reputation for sexual license, which would provide fodder for generations of New Orleans tourism marketers, was more than in part derived from a brutal history of enslavement, enforced prostitution, and concubinage fueled by the particularities of elite white leisure, patriarchy, and racialized sexual tourism.

Contextualizing Antebellum New Orleans

What has solidified into a narrative of relative laxity around the policing of racial boundaries ignores a political history that is at once far more structured and contested. As Joseph Roach argued, the image of New Orleans as a ludic space of vice masks how "transgression [is] carefully channeled into regulated conduits of time and space," such as Congo Square dances, Mardi Gras masquerades, and quadroon balls that remain "easily within the laws' reach."[32] Racial policing was written into the Code Noir and was central to Governor Vaudreuil's 1751 police regulations, as well as the brutal response to the German Coast slave uprising of 1811 and the manhunt for escaped slave Bras-Coupé in the 1830s, which the nascent police department used to justify its bureaucratic growth.[33] While claims to exceptionalism and cultural authenticity have largely presented the city's racialization in terms of tolerance and accommodation associated with a large population of relatively well-off free people of color, a counternarrative that encompasses a more diverse group of black New Orleanians has attended to the lived experience of racial domination and surveillance.

From 1808 to 1865, New Orleans was the site of the largest slave market in the US, with approximately one million people passing through its auction blocks from the upper South to the burgeoning cotton kingdom. The magnitude and significance of this second Middle Passage was "not only about Louisiana," argues Walter Johnson, but "the making of the antebellum South."[34] At the state level, a series of laws—beginning in 1807 with "An Act to Regulate the Conditions and Forms of the Emancipation of Slaves" and regularly recurring until the "Act to Prohibit the Emancipation of Slaves" in 1857—would close loopholes to manumission and *coartación*. The legislative and juridical enclosure of blacks brought Louisiana, and New Orleans with it, firmly into the legal and social frameworks of the plantation South.[35] This history of slave regimes, racial policing, and legal restriction not only contradicts celebratory portrayals of New Orleans as a site of transgression but also loosens the grip on a culture of authenticity that has made the city appear wholly exceptional.

In the decades preceding the Civil War, a cotton boom gripping the lower South made New Orleans a critical point of connection between urban centers of global capitalism and their peripheral hinterlands.[36] While northern cities set about consolidating juridically free labor, New Orleans's deepening investment in slave labor led to perhaps the city's least-recognized historical uniqueness. At the same time, New Orleans, unlike any other city in the future Confederacy, developed a large class of white wage laborers, including huge swaths of German and Irish immigrants. The six thousand Irish who perished digging the New Basin Canal in the 1830s were a testament to both the city's uniqueness within the Deep South and the complicated nature of costs and benefits derived from perhaps the one locale in the world that could feasibly marshal large forces of slave or free laborers. By the time of the Civil War, the city would find itself four times larger than the second largest locale in the treasonous South, with a per capita income second in the nation, literally the only city worth speaking of in the Confederacy.[37]

During this boom time New Orleans was commonly viewed as less exceptional than it would come to be seen in later periods, inviting comparisons from travelers to Boston, New York, Charleston, and Savannah and, as suited a major economic center, to London and Paris. One visitor in 1853 wrote, "The French and older portions of the city have a more bald and business-like character; but New Orleans is beyond everything else a business and trading city."[38] The expansiveness of New Orleans's capitalist infrastructure runs counter to prevailing associations with antimodernism and cultural preservation, which derive from the marketability of the city as antiquated or even retrogressive.[39]

Romanticizing New Orleans

It was the events leading up to the Civil War and its aftermath of Reconstruction and Redemption that propelled the invention of a romanticized New Orleans. The alchemic reaction of race and sex swelled further in the public imagination. The elaborate literary and commercial tropes of the quadroon and the fictionalized figure of the tragic mulatto had debuted in antebellum antislavery fiction of the 1840s and were buttressed by popular histories that singled out the city as a space of sexual taboo. This literature "created a circular feedback phenomenon," writes Clark, "that fed the invention and proliferation of activities in New Orleans designed to satisfy the market for encounters with quadroons aroused by the earliest accounts."[40] In other words, the social construction of New Orleans as a perpetual colonial space not only allowed mainstream America to define itself and its values against an other, the narrative itself fueled the very transgressive practices associated with coloniality.

It was a loose aggregate of post–Civil War authors, including George Washington Cable and Lafcadio Hearn, who positioned old, quaint, and charming New Orleans against a country relentlessly committed to moral and material progress. Whether fashioning poetic histories that glorified the city's Creole distinctiveness or exoticizing the African-derived cultural practices sustained under colonial rule, local writers cultivated a literary landscape that continues to shape the city's legibility.[41] To extrapolate from Frederick Starr's collection of Lafcadio Hearn's New Orleans writings, authors did not merely reflect perceptions of New Orleans as exceptional, they invented this very idea. Take Hearn's description in 1879 of the deep affective divide between Creole Downtown and Anglo Uptown,

> where sat, in old-fashioned chairs, good old-fashioned people who spoke the tongue of other times, and observed many quaint and knightly courtesies forgotten in this material era. Without, roared the Iron Age . . . it was the year 1878 . . . and yet some people wonder that some other people never care to cross Canal [Street].[42]

In Hearn's telling, the predominantly Creole neighborhoods below Canal Street had managed to ward off the impulses toward capitalist modernity—industrialization, rationality, and above all else inauthenticity—while Yankee values reigned supreme in the more Anglo neighborhoods Uptown (see chapter 3, this volume). Hearn's contemporaries Charles Gayarré and Grace King also brought increased recognition to local folkways, as did successors like Lyle Saxon and Robert Tallant, exoticizing and feminizing the Creole Belle on the banks of the Mighty Mississippi.[43] Writers tended to present the city's economic infrastructure as itself representative of a cultural way of life that played out as an ideological struggle between Creole traditionalists and American progressives. "Through these artistic representations," writes Dawdy, "New Orleans became a foil for the rest of the nation, an imaginary island of colonial dissipation within a country relentlessly committed to moral and material progress."[44] In contemporary New Orleans, the patina aesthetic of faded buildings and tarnished souvenirs perpetuates the impression of "the city that care forgot" while simultaneously providing the grounds for selling nostalgia in the form of French antiques, Mardi Gras memorabilia, and other uncanny commodities.

The contested figure of the Creole runs throughout diverse and sometimes competing sets of claims to New Orleans exceptionalism, and definitions of Creole identity have shifted across the colonial, antebellum, and postbellum eras.[45] After the Civil War, for instance, Gayarré and his cohort of European descendants attempted to define a white vision of Creole, declaring, "It has become high time to demonstrate that the Creoles of Louisiana . . . have not, because of the name they bear, a particle of African blood in their veins."[46]

But it was an oppositional stance to the racial purity of the Creole category, popularized by Cable, Rodolphe Desdunes, and others, that came to define New Orleans as a city of intermixture—of jazz and gumbo, of plaçage and quadroon balls—still evoked by many tour guides and historians.[47] At the close of the nineteenth century, Homer Plessy, the son of mixed-race French-speaking Haitian émigrés, was arrested for boarding a whites-only train car, and New Orleans became the nation's testing ground for the Supreme Court decision legalizing racial segregation based on the so-called one-drop rule.[48] *Plessy v. Ferguson* has become foundational for claims to the city's Creole distinctiveness. What is less discussed is how New Orleans was the battleground for remapping national racial structures into hardened categories of blackness and whiteness, and how the city itself came to adhere to those norms.

Under Jim Crow, many Creoles of color sought to retain a circumscribed cultural identity, but legally and practically their status was bound to that of African Americans. On the other side of the color line, white Catholic Creoles came to recognize common interests with Anglo-Protestants as a way of consolidating and expanding power.[49] The cultural conflict that spawned so much disagreement over the nature of Creole distinctiveness looks in practice like a papering over of an obligatory consensus about the implementation of racial, class, and political orderings.[50] Despite their antinomies, white Creole and Anglo elites colluded in their essential agreement on white supremacy and maintaining control of the expansive role New Orleans had built as the merchant city for the cotton South.

Authenticating Mardi Gras

A particularly visible example of these shared directives is the reorganization of Mardi Gras by Protestant, English-speaking white males who rose to power over French-speaking Creoles and founded what became known as the old-line Mardi Gras krewes of Comus, Momus, Rex, and Proteus around the time of the Civil War.[51] Wrapping Latin Catholic tradition in an ancestral canon of English literature and often scathing political satire, this constellation of elites would reinforce hierarchies of race, ethnicity, class, religion, and gender for over a century. It was these men who formed the central bloc that would dedicate the next decade to defeating Reconstruction via legal and political challenges and violent treason. In 1866 they were a central part of the attack on hundreds of black (and more than a few white) supporters of the Republican-backed Louisiana Constitutional Convention, killing more than fifty and injuring hundreds.[52] The Redeemers would go on to provide the penultimate salvo to defeating Reconstruction in Louisiana in their attempted overthrow of the state government and municipal police at the Battle of Liberty Place in 1874. Throughout the imposition of Jim Crow over the ensuing two and a half decades—culminating in the disenfranchising Constitution of 1898 and continuing well after—this ruling class would help enshrine Lost Cause myths in the city's cultural consciousness.[53] New Orleans was not alone in this effort, as throughout the South there emerged a conscious project of tethering a reimagined and romanticized white identity to the paramilitary arms of the southern Democracy, such as the Ku Klux Klan and the Knights of the White Camellia. Beyond what was clearly a cross-fertilization of membership, the direct link between white terror organizations and the old-line krewes is traceable in their regalia (robes, hoods, and masks) and the inordinately ritualistic and secretive practices of their meetings, processionals, and balls.[54]

For more than six decades between Redemption and the legislative victories of the civil rights movement in the 1950s, white elites continued their dominance over political and social interests. This period witnessed a brutal segregation calcifying as common practice within the city. Events like the citywide antiblack race riots in the aftermath of Robert Charles's shooting of police officers in 1900 demonstrate that New Orleans was utterly typical of the profound violence that greeted African Americans across the South as Jim Crow came to power.[55] A history of interracial labor radicalism—including the 1907 General Levee Strike and the 1929 Streetcar Strike—stand as remarkable moments within an otherwise unbroken history of disenfranchisement and segregation that exacted a brutal toll on black New Orleanians.[56] While the size of the city and its independent black economic base allowed a certain degree of daily anonymity and removal from the harshest of Jim Crow violence found in rural areas, the difference was always one of degree on a spectrum of lived and feared brutality. The political ring that ran the city for much of these decades—the Regular Democratic Organization, or Old Regulars—combined a violent enforcement of white supremacy with the patronage of an open shop system that directed public spending toward private gain. Of course, once a year many Old Regulars removed their suits and ties and donned the costumes of Comus and Rex, suggesting that cultural transgression could easily be the flip side of the coin of white supremacy and antidemocratic rule.

As a festival celebration of transgression, Mardi Gras came to represent the pinnacle of exceptionality and cultural authenticity of New Orleans.

Today the King of Rex continues his symbolic reign as honorary mayor for a day, ostensibly sharing rule with the King of Zulu since the post–civil rights era of interracial governance (see chapters 4 and 14, this volume). However, despite its place as a central locus where exceptionalism and authenticity come together, the construction of New Orleans's signature festival as authentic and the meaning of that authenticity are moving targets. As Kevin Fox Gotham argues, "In the case of New Orleans, authenticity has always been a fluid and hybrid category that is constantly being created again and again as social movements, cultural authorities, and other groups struggle to legitimate selective and idealized perceptions of the city as fixed and immutable."[57] Later, in the 1960s, ethnic whites excluded from the old-line krewes would form their own "super krewes" such as Bacchus and Endymion, demonstrating how "a cultural form that was initially viewed as inauthentic by some segments of the local population has, over time, become redefined and recognized as an authentic expression of Carnival."[58] Embedded in this authentic tradition of transgression, then, are stratified layers of struggle over power that have sedimented over time. What began as an affinity between Catholic Lenten rituals and African-derived festival traditions was reappropriated as a display of Anglo-Protestant supremacy after the Civil War. A century later, official Mardi Gras opened up to include krewes founded by those excluded from the then-traditional power bloc, and by the 1990s several old-line krewes stopped parading rather than comply with an antidiscrimination ordinance.[59] While the authenticity of the tradition rests upon its perceived timelessness as a premodern bacchanalia, the ongoing and dynamic reinvention of Mardi Gras serves as a prism for changing social identities and political machinations over several centuries.

In the same period of heightened segregation between Reconstruction and *Brown v. Board of Education*, black New Orleanians fostered their own carnival societies, parades, and cultural traditions. Middle- and upper-class Creoles and African Americans who led the ongoing legal struggle against Jim Crow formed the Prince Hall Masons (1863), Original Illinois Club (1894), and the Zulu Social Aid and Pleasure Club (1916), which still parades before Rex on Mardi Gras day. Working-class African Americans formed "tribes" of Mardi Gras Indians, marching through back-a-town neighborhoods dressed in elaborate hand-sewn suits and confronting one another in symbolic combat. Clyde Woods connects social institutions and neighborhood networks such as these to a racial politics of resistance:

The neighborhood and ward complex of large extended families, social aid and pleasure clubs, churches, healers, businesses, schools, other organizations and clubs, brass bands, musicians, artisans, workers, labor leaders, Mardi Gras Indians and second lines provided an endless supply of community-centered leadership, development initiatives, and institutionalized planning.[60]

Jazz came to be recognized as the most celebrated cultural formation to emerge from these multifaceted and complex interactions, ultimately redefining what constituted the locally authentic in explicitly racial terms. But the development of jazz also demonstrates how musical formation and innovation were linked to other constituencies and practices in these complex spaces, indicating the expansiveness of black cultural practice and the multiplicity of blackness as a category that resisted containment within the reductive strictures of racial binarism established by *Plessy v. Ferguson*.

Jazz and the Racialization of Cultural Authenticity

In the antebellum period, the city's musical identity was defined by the sheer abundance of musical offerings, representing the ethnic heterogeneity of its inhabitants, including ballroom dance and French opera, marching bands and slave dances, street criers and organ grinders.[61] Since the early twentieth century, there has developed a broad consensus that New Orleans music encompasses jazz, blues, rhythm and blues, soul, funk, brass band, and related styles that are bound together through an association not only with place but also with race. Since emancipation, changing interpretations of New Orleans culture have been linked to differing identifications with blackness, which might refer to slaves at Congo Square, mixed-race Creoles, urban migrants from rural plantations, and other social identities that bear out the claim that New Orleans is "the most African city in the Unites States."[62]

In Melville Herskovits's paradigmatic model of acculturation, which identified African cultural retentions and calculated their variability across the New World, the United States was proposed as the nation with the highest rate of assimilation to Euro-American norms. But New Orleans was an exception where "those aspects of the African tradition peculiar to this specialized region have reached their greatest development."[63] Starting in the 1930s, folklorists such as Zora Neale Hurston and Alan Lomax came to New Orleans in search of African residues that they and others found in funerals with music, voodoo and hoodoo rites, Mardi Gras Indian rituals, and more.[64] An urban counterpart to the rural sea islands of Georgia and South

Carolina, New Orleans became a primary site for locating musical and religious practices derived from an African past. But those traditions incubated in the urban contact zone of New Orleans developed into distinct formations of modern blackness and Americanness that circulated globally. When rhythm and blues singer Ernie K-Doe famously quipped, "I'm not sure, but I think all music comes from New Orleans," he captured the status of his hometown as a source of cultural origination and innovation while also reinforcing the implicit bond between New Orleans as a musical city and New Orleans as a black city.

In relation to jazz, this linkage forged an either/or dialectic in which many historians and musicians have cast the music strictly in terms of black vernacular practices, maintained from the African-derived dances of the enslaved in Congo Square up through the musical forms of Afro-Protestant worship and blues aesthetics that served as a refuge in the afterlife of slavery. Revisionists attempting to respond that jazz was the invention of white musicians have largely and rightfully been dismissed as both virulently racist and woefully inaccurate. A more complexly entwined local history has been excavated by Bruce Raeburn and other scholars identifying an "incipient jazz community" of black American, Creole, Jewish, Sicilian, and Irish performers interacting, if not always collaborating, in the formation of jazz.[65] Without questioning the primacy of black musical practices, Raeburn underscores the city's heterogeneity and cosmopolitanism by tracing, for instance, Latin rhythms and Creole repertoires incorporated into jazz as a black art form. In this formulation, the ingenuity of jazz is in its capaciousness, which contests the Jim Crow and broader American imperative of defining race as the principal arbiter of social difference. Nevertheless, in the bulk of scholarly discourse and popular accounts, New Orleans jazz continues to be invoked in terms of vernacularism, traditionality, and cultural memory in ways that do not interrogate the ingenuity of black invention or accommodate the multiplicity of blackness as both a cultural and political category.[66]

Marketing Exceptionalism and Authenticity in the Tourist City

Starting in the 1930s, city officials and business leaders in New Orleans began to expand upon and exploit the romance generated through music, literature, food, and other cultural forms, now as a tool for the emerging mass tourism market. Earlier efforts, driven by the New Orleans Association of Commerce, had focused on a progressive, business-oriented vision in keeping with the emphasis on port and railway linkages. Transport systems were central to the association's other major project of creating the city's first master zoning plan and would eventually align with efforts to fund the second stage of the Centroport project in the new Industrial Canal. At this initial stage, tourism offered diversification to an economy based primarily in shipping while marketing the benefits of that economy. The economic collapse of the Great Depression, a gradual retraction of shipping and manufacturing, and postintegration white flight all contributed to a massive disinvestment in the urban core. In the wake, tourism began assuming more and more significance in the city's overall economic infrastructure. This shift in political economy gave rise to the city's branding as a destination for authentic cultural pursuits.[67]

The historical materials for this refashioning were drawn from myriad sources, including the highly subjective historical accounts of Cable, Hearn, Gayarré, and others in the post–Civil War period; popular histories drawn from these accounts, like Herbert Asbury's *The French Quarter*; and folkloric studies by authors employed by the Works Progress Administration, such as Saxon, Dreyer, and Tallant's *Gumbo Ya-Ya*.[68] Lynnell Thomas has shown how popular histories have been shaped by contemporary tourism marketing as promoters' selective mythologizing of the past has reinforced notions of benign racial exceptionalism:

> [An] emphasis on selected features of these eras—such as European cultural influences, the relative freedom of New Orleans's black population, the city's laissez-faire attitudes regarding race, the social sanctioning of interracial unions, and a large population of free blacks—lent itself to the construction of New Orleans as benefitting from the most liberal and refined elements of southern culture while avoiding its most brutal, inhumane, and inegalitarian features. As a result, New Orleans was often portrayed by tourism promoters, artists, and even historians as a racially exceptional city that was not sullied by the racial tension and conflict affecting other southern cities.[69]

Initially, the racial reconfigurations of white supremacy that followed the defeat of Reconstruction were reified in deracinated discourse, but marketing strategies became more explicit about the racialized and creolized dimensions of culture over the second half of the twentieth century. City boosters have focused particularly on what they call the holy trinity—food, music, and architecture—each deriving from an Afro-Creole cultural matrix. Starting midcentury, institutions such as Preservation Hall, the Jazz and Heritage Festival, and the Historic Voodoo Museum began exhibiting black cultural traditions primarily for white consumption. Inclusion of a jazz band, a gumbo vendor, or a Mardi Gras Indian tribe has become virtually compulsory at local festivals, but their appearance at the 1984 Louisiana World Exposition was considered progressive at the time.[70] The incorporation of the independent Greater New Orleans Black Tourism Network into the official tourism bureau in 1990 indicated a revised strategy to acknowledge "cultural diversity and heritage [as] the city's tourism equity."[71] Here we witness not simply an emerging consensus of New Orleans as the most African city in the United States but a market-driven recognition of place- and race-based culture as a source of both cultural and monetary capital. Rebranding the city as a destination for the consumption of black culture gave New Orleans a competitive advantage over other sites. It also reordered the racial implications of cultural authenticity alongside Atlanta and other Southern cities that positioned themselves to profit from emerging black middle-class tourism.

A Model Postindustrial City

The intensified branding of New Orleans as a destination for touristic consumption paralleled a nationwide shift away from urban industrialism in the second half of the twentieth century. The decline of manufacturing employment and the outmigration of labor to the suburbs occurring throughout the nation was exacerbated locally by a drastic reduction in port employment. Poor choices in structural modernization and delays in implementing technological innovations, particularly the adoption of standardized shipping containers, drastically reduced shipping-related commerce.[72] At the same time, the city witnessed a massive growth in service industry jobs concentrated in nonunion and thus low-waged hotels, restaurants, and entertainment destinations catering to tourists. The erosion of the city's tax base was aggravated by white flight to suburban Jefferson, St. Bernard, and St. Tammany parishes in the wake of the civil rights movement, school desegregation efforts, and real estate development made possible by swamp drainage and flood abatement technology. Middle-class black residents, meanwhile, concentrated in neighborhood enclaves such as New Orleans East and the gated community of Pontchartrain Park (see chapter 9, this volume).

The battles fought in and around New Orleans at the height of the civil rights era—the anti-integration riots of 1960 and ongoing fights against Leander Perez's white supremacist political fiefdom in Plaquemines and St. Bernard parishes being the most famous among countless more quotidian struggles—stand as important and decidedly unexceptional parts of a broader

Southern whole.[73] By the late 1960s and early 1970s, with the elections of Moon Landrieu and then Dutch Morial as mayor, New Orleans joined many other cities in developing an interracial political and professional-managerial class. It was this incorporation of the liberal imperatives of the Civil Rights Act within the city's Democratic machine that both marked the end of de jure segregation and legitimated the progrowth, anti-redistributive political economic imperatives that continue to characterize municipal governance.[74]

Starting in the middle of the 1970s, New Orleans took advantage of Community Development Block Grants and Urban Development Action Grants available for the redevelopment of low-income neighborhoods. As in many other American cities, leaders used the funds primarily to develop downtown economic and entertainment districts and leverage private-sector investment.[75] As Megan French-Marcelin argues in this volume (chapter 11), the imperatives of urban competition, white flight, and inner-city blight led city leaders—black and white alike—to privatize city planning and cater to the whims of developers for the purpose of luring a tax base back to the city. Ironically, in a New Orleans where architectural distinction was a key facet of the tourism economy, this strategy replicated the modernism and aesthetic blandness of revitalization schemes common to many American cities during the period, most visibly with the Poydras Street high-rises in the Central Business District (CBD). By the last decades of the twentieth century, New Orleans was exemplary of the postindustrial neoliberal city in terms of urban planning, suburbanization, economic restructuring, housing privatization, and racialized poverty and blight.

Exceptionalism and Authenticity in Contemporary New Orleans

The upwardly redistributive, federally bankrolled policies and programs begun in the 1970s were a harbinger for a feeding frenzy of privatization and investment opportunity in the wake of Hurricane Katrina, with many of the same actors simply dusting off plans that had been shelved in the Reagan and Clinton eras. In an opportunistic acceleration of the HOPE VI program of poverty deconcentration, marginally damaged public housing was demolished, and the contracts for rebuilding, maintenance, and management were given to developers such as McCormack Baron Salazar, bankrolled by the investment firm Goldman Sachs.[76] These trends were most brazenly illustrated by President George W. Bush's suspension of the Davis-Bacon Act in September 2005 that all but guaranteed that rebuilding would be done at below living wages. As Vincanne Adams discusses in this volume (chapter 13), the rebuilding of private housing was assisted not by a WPA-style program but by thousands of volunteers, many of whom were part of a charitable economy driven by for-profit philanthropic companies. The scope of philanthrocapitalism deployed in the rebuilding efforts represented the success of George H. W. Bush's initial plan for "a thousand points of light" as a privatized alternative to a social state increasingly imagined by both left and right as inefficient and backward.[77]

Since 2005, New Orleans has more than ever revealed itself not as a cultural oddity at the periphery of the nation-state but as a prime laboratory for centralized neoliberal experimentation. For a comparative example, anyone relating Katrina to September 11, as sociologists Kevin Gotham and Miriam Greenberg have, must begin by acknowledging vast differences "in the type of disaster trigger (i.e., a terrorist strike and hurricane) and the intensity of the scale of destruction." Yet these distinctions of causality mask the reality that "policymakers and government officials responded with strikingly similar, market-oriented strategies of recovery and redevelopment," even if the effects of 9/11 on the quotidian lives of everyday New Yorkers looked nothing like the corresponding effects of Katrina on New Orleanians.[78] New York City and New Orleans resist comparison in many other ways, yet they are both paradigmatic as crisis cities, in which an event outside the business cycle prompts a recovery process that is squarely within it. If, as contributor Adolph Reed Jr. has argued (chapter 14), neoliberalism represents nothing more than capitalism freed from effective opposition, then post-Katrina New Orleans represents a national and global vanguard of social abandonment and insecurity.

Approaching contemporary New Orleans as a model neoliberal city in terms of housing, specifically the global crisis of urban real estate speculation and rent intensification, we find the historical residues of exceptionalism and authenticity at play in complex ways. The Tremé neighborhood, or the Sixth Ward, stands here as a representative example. The parts of the neighborhood between Claiborne Avenue and the French Quarter witnessed rent intensification and speculation dating back to the 1970s, following suburbanization, blight remediation, and displacement and redevelopment schemes that drained the area of many residents and resources (see chapter 5, this volume).[79] Touted as the first black neighborhood in the United States, the area became increasingly attractive to preservationists, artists, and other gentrification pioneers drawn by the area's historic housing stock and proximity to the French Quarter and CBD. When Katrina struck, only select parts of the neighborhood were flooded, but the calamity enabled the destruction and redevelopment of the neighboring Lafitte and Iberville housing projects, while a real estate frenzy for architecturally significant homes accelerated the rebuilding process in the stretch of higher elevation along the Mississippi now dubbed the "sliver by the river."

Tremé has joined Harlem, Chicago's Bronzeville, Pittsburgh's Hill District, and Washington, DC's Shaw neighborhood in what Derek Hyra calls "Black-branding," a process by which "versions of Black identity are expressed and institutionalized in a community's social and built environments" even as the neighborhoods lose black residents to displacement.[80] This hyperlocal branding passes over the disinvestment of the late twentieth century and the historical (or current) presence of low-income residents to stitch mythical golden eras together. In New Orleans, black-branding connects a romanticized rendering of antebellum free people of color to the Jim Crow self-sufficiency of the Claiborne Avenue business district and the most respectable versions of contemporary black culture into a seamless continuum. Tremé in particular exemplifies how the global sweep of urban development schemes can be enhanced by local particularities based in race and culture. By 2012, when the Tremé 200 festival celebrated the neighborhood's bicentennial with music, parades, and food, all but one of the live music venues, bars, and restaurants had been shut down through aggressive ordinances pushed by members of the Historic Faubourg Tremé Association. Tremé's cultural and economic value depends on its continual reinscription as the country's oldest black neighborhood, while it simultaneously finds itself at the cutting edge of real estate speculation and residential displacement that make it ever more wealthy and white and devoid of the spaces that nurtured the city's cultural history.

As with the aftermath of the Civil War, when a romantic literary tradition made the master narrative of exceptionalism and authenticity common sense, the aftermath of Katrina has galvanized New Orleanians into a deeper recognition and drive for preserving culture under the aegis of disappearing authenticity. The broad national and international presence of New Orleans as an icon of cultural distinctiveness—made famous by its increasingly high-profile musicians, the reception of David Simon's television series *Treme*, its celebrity chefs, and the revival of hip forms of Southern gothic centered in and around the city like *True Blood*, *True Detective*, and *Beasts of the Southern Wild*—only serves to further place New Orleans and south Louisiana in the role of alien and exotic other (see chapter 7, this volume). The exceptional status of the city, the cultivated patina of its built environment, and the endurance of local cultural traditions has helped attract tens of thousands of new transplants to neighborhoods such as the Tremé, spiking housing costs and sparking an intense (and ironic) debate about the sustainability of New Orleans's exceptionality under the threat of homogenized modernization (see chapter 6, this volume).

The city's development focus has come to include efforts to attract a Richard Florida–style creative class and a desperate hope to retain them. The young urban-rebuilding professionals, social entrepreneurs, high-tech innovators, and others entering this urban laboratory constitute a demographic raised in an age when market-based and high-technocratic solutions to social problems are hegemonic.[81] Mainstream publications, universities like Tulane, and scores of politicians thus revel in a wave of entrepreneurial efforts that have pushed the city onto Forbes lists. Coworking spaces and business incubators have proliferated, most emphasizing a social-entrepreneurship model that offers a heady appeal to the nearly half of local start-up leaders who are alums of one of the nation's dominant education reform organizations, Teach for America.[82] The majority of the post-Katrina creative class has moved into neighborhoods such as the Warehouse District, CBD, and Bywater that are not as steeped as the Tremé in discourses of historical exceptionalism or architectural authenticity. A proliferation of condominium buildings and short-term rental units accommodates a mix of transplants and tourists who may or may not share an investment in the New Orleansness of their surroundings.

Exceptionality still maintains an important allure in the aftermath of the levee failures, especially in a good deal of writing intended for mass audiences.[83] It has become somewhat of a biannual rite of passage for the nation's newspaper of record to send a travel or style reporter or, even better, enlist a recently transplanted New Yorker to parachute into New Orleans and send back exoticized dispatches with titles such as "Love among the Ruins." The formula is straightforward: interview a handful of young artists/musicians/chefs about the city's post-Katrina transformation, add in a couple of eerily lit snapshots of decaying buildings or exotic "creatures" like Mardi Gras Indians, make sure to pay homage to a different pace of life, untrammeled by the trappings of upper-middle-class work prerogatives, and above all convince the reader that New Orleans is unlike anywhere else in America.

While filming the show *Treme* in 2010, David Simon told the *New York Times Magazine*, "Lots of American places used to make things. Detroit used to make cars. Baltimore used to make steel and ships. New Orleans still makes something. It makes moments."[84] Yet, unlike the relative prosperity of the postwar steel industry in Baltimore, where Simon based his previous series *The Wire* and *Homicide*, a livable wage based on creating moments has largely eluded New Orleanians and others throughout the US. The great and telling exception is New Orleans's perceived plastic evil twin, Las Vegas, where the success of the Culinary Union Local 226 in unionizing hospitality workers has produced at least the skeleton version for what such an economy and politics might look like.[85] There is more than a little irony to the fact that New Orleans—a city that incessantly pays homage to its culture bearers—does decidedly less to ensure their prosperity than a city, also built on moments, that wears mass production, inauthenticity, and a sense that the customer is always right on its sleeve. Yet, in this regard, New Orleans completely typifies a broader American experience (above and beyond Las Vegas) that has for centuries devalued labor that does not produce material commodities. The inequalities caused by this history are especially apparent in postcontainerization, post–oil bust New Orleans, where the economic dislocations are felt primarily by those whose labor is not defined as valuable and who have no institutional mechanism to shift such definitions. This creates a conundrum whereby the primarily black, low-income culture bearers whom the city depends upon to entice tourists and their dollars are potentially priced out and pushed out of the new New Orleans. As with much of what we have presented in this admittedly sweeping and selective history of a single city, we submit that this place with an obsessive dedication to its past is uncannily predictive of the future.

Conclusion

Americanist scholarship has stubbornly clung to the idea that research into its collective endeavor illuminates some essential Americanness, that the corpus of, say, American economic history illuminates a national story and indeed a national identity.[86] In the same way that American historical and literary scholarship has often unconsciously posited an exceptional America, much scholarship and reporting on New Orleans has sought some essential essence, something that defines the city as a whole. In this way, New Orleans has existed as a singular subject unlike any other American city. We would ask if this New Orleans has been continuously reimagined in a discursive feedback loop that constantly reaffirms its exceptionality. An ethnography of brass bands in post-Katrina New Orleans does not have to be a story about

New Orleans as singular entity; it can also be a story about labor exploitation and racism in an urban environment defined by deep contingency and
context. Likewise, a social history of African Americans and working-class
whites in late nineteenth- and early twentieth-century New Orleans might
be about circular migration, political economy, interracial sociability, and
real estate development defined by a plethora of local, national, and global
currents rather than anything essentially New Orleans.

Just as New Orleans has been isolated as a singular subject, its cultural formations have frequently been frozen as fixed and timeless. A long tradition
of both scholarly and popular ethnography has produced a vision of New Orleans as containing a unique and static culture, a vision deeply informed
by marketing strategies. Because of its position as a locale defined by its exoticism, research on culture bearers within the city has called for various
iterations of classical ethnographic informancy. As Aaron Nyerges details
in this volume (chapter 3), Alan Lomax's 1938 interview of Jelly Roll Morton stands as one classic example. But the broader anthropological stance
assumes New Orleans is a place with a singular meaning that can only be
parsed by close ethnographic contact with natives (see chapter 6, this volume). It becomes a place to be either saved from the supposedly encroaching
imperatives of bourgeois values—as in so much cultural and architectural
preservation rhetoric—or, alternately, to be documented before the natives
and their practices go the way of so many premodern cultures before them.
And like classical Western ethnography, such an analytic style is intellectu-
ally predicated upon proving exceptionality and distinctiveness vis-à-vis an
imagined, modern world.

As contemporary commentators as diverse as Betty Friedan, C. Wright
Mills, and David Riesman argued, and more recent scholars ranging from
Doug Rossinow to Daniel Rodgers to David Harvey have shown, middle-
class America has searched for meaningful experience in the face of the
bogeyman of conformity, bureaucracy, and the meaninglessness of mass
culture since the atomic age. T. J. Jackson Lears writes, "Seekers of authenticity often lack any but the vaguest ethical or religious commitments. Their
obsession with 'meaning' masks its absence from any frame of reference
outside the self. . . . What begins in discontent with a vapid modern culture ends as another quest for self-fulfillment—the dominant ideal of our
sleeker, therapeutic modern culture."[87] New Orleans provides an authentic
playground for this existential crisis of modern culture and thus power-
fully replicates the broader cultural and therapeutic logic of contemporary

capitalism. The irony of so many homages to the city's authentic character is that this very notion of the city as oppositional to the standardization of contemporary life is, in fact, integral to the very success of its place-branding. New Orleans sells moments moored in individualized self-fulfillment and disconnected from any larger political or ethical constituency other than vague references to an indeterminate and singular community.

Moving beyond the dichotomous frameworks of exceptionalism and authenticity requires greater attention to the multiple temporalities of social life. As an example, how might we understand the resurgence of a self-conscious New Orleans culture after Katrina? There is the long history of invented tradition and imagined community that looks remarkably similar across space and time, especially when said imagined community is perceived as under threat. There is the meaning that New Orleanians invest in their practices and the range of cultural expressions legitimized as authentic, shaped by and increasingly in concert with the prerogatives of touristic culture (see chapter 14, this volume). There is the growing economic value in cultural distinction, not simply in regard to tourism but real estate and style, an outgrowth of the broad trend toward niche commodity production in postwar mass culture. New Orleans, as countless travelogues of the post-Katrina era make clear, represents the forefront of such distinction. That these distinctions are indicative of New Orleans does not mean they are entirely unique to New Orleans, rooted in a singular locale, or unchanging over time. Further, an analytic lens that dynamically accounts for difference is not the same as one that statically identifies exceptionality.

At a basic level, all places and cultural formations are different: they are produced by a series of contingent events and processes that occur over changing temporalities and in diverse contexts. While we can recognize that Omaha, Newark, Cleveland, Oakland, and New Orleans are all different from each other, with distinctive histories and internal cultural formations, to single New Orleans out as exceptional implies an essential similarity between the other four. Generations of scholars located in and around the city have made this precise move, either consciously or unconsciously. In so doing, a variety of other histories have become marginalized, not the least of which being the political, economic, and social processes, powers, and inequalities that exceptionality, along with its intellectual handmaiden, authenticity, have masked. The essays that follow are united in their attempt to break out of the intellectual confines of these dichotomies. They posit a city not of cultural essences and singular histories but of diverse peoples, meanings, and practices that are always contingent, rife with conflict, and grounded in social, political, and historical contexts of multiple temporal and geographic scales.

Notes

1 Tyrrell 1991, 1031.
2 Shafer 2005.
3 Mitch Landrieu to House Committee on Transportation and Infrastructure, US House of Representatives, October 18, 2005, http://www.columbia.edu/itc/journalism/cases /katrina/State%20of%20Louisiana/Office%20of%20the%20Lieutenant%20Governor /Landrieu%20Congressional%20Address%20Accountability%2010-18-2005.pdf.
4 Quoted in Campanella 2014, 138.
5 Davis 1992; Rothman 2002; J. Jackson 2001.
6 Weinstein 1996.
7 Andres Duany, quoted in Curtis 2009.
8 Bendix 1997, 8.
9 Trilling 1972, 124. See also Michaels 1998.
10 The "southern Babylon" reference is in Long 2004.
11 Roach 1996, 180.
12 Grazian 2003. On "Disneyfication," see Souther 2006.
13 Lears 1981; Halttunen 1982; Lasch 1978.
14 Gilmore and Pine 2007, 5.
15 Banet-Weiser 2012.
16 Dawdy 2016, 52.
17 Comaroff and Comaroff 2009, 2, emphasis in original.
18 On rogue colonialism, see Dawdy 2008 and Powell 2012. On racialization and sexuality, see Spear 2009.
19 Dawdy 2008, xv.
20 Hall 1992a; Powell 2012; Usner 1992.
21 Thompson 2008, 306.
22 Dawdy 2008.
23 Spear 2009, 56.
24 Census of the City of New Orleans, exclusive of seamen and the garrison, American State Papers: Miscellaneous 10:364, appears with the notation: "N.B. This census appears to be incorrect, as, by some unaccountable mistake the number of free people of color in the second district is not included; and, on the whole, the population is thought to be underrated." It is worth noting that the slave population enumeration for the second district is considerably higher than for surrounding districts.
25 Vidal 2014.
26 Clark 2013, 130.
27 The deep reliance on slave labor for nation building and capital expansion rendered New Orleans a slave society, distinct in Ira Berlin's categorical terminology from a society with slaves such as Baltimore or St. Louis. Berlin's taxonomy of slave societies and

societies with slaves allows New Orleans to be distinguished from both Baltimore and St. Louis in this regard. Nonetheless, despite the importance of slavery to the surrounding plantation economies and its centrality to the internal slave trade itself, while more important than in either of the aforementioned cities, slave labor was nonetheless an ancillary part of the internal urban economy within New Orleans. Indeed, New Orleans's exceptional character has thus seemingly foreclosed possibly fruitful urban historical comparisons between the three cities of roughly equal antebellum size.

28 Laussat (1831) 1978, 103.

29 Spear 2003, 76.

30 Clark 2013.

31 James 1996, 142.

32 Roach 1996, 252.

33 On racial legal regimes, see Gross and de la Fuente 2013. On Congo Square, see Evans 2011. On the slave uprising of 1811, see Rasmussen 2011. On Bras-Coupé, see Wagner 2009, 79–115.

34 W. Johnson 1999, 18.

35 Spear 2009, 219.

36 W. Johnson 1999; A. Rothman 2005; Marler 2013.

37 Nystrom 2010, 7.

38 Quoted in Stanonis 2006, 5.

39 See Dawdy 2016, e.g., 51.

40 Clark 2013, 149.

41 Fertel 2014. On exoticizing African-derived cultural practices, see Wagner 2009; Sakakeeny 2011b.

42 Hearn 2001, 147.

43 On literary tropes of exceptionalism, see Eckstein 2005; Lightweis-Goff 2014.

44 Dawdy 2016, 56.

45 On the history of "Creole" as a racial designation in Louisiana, see Tregle 1992. On the assimilation of Creoles, see Hirsch 2007.

46 Charles Gayarré, "Mr. Cable's Freedmen's Case in Equity," *New Orleans Times-Democrat*, January 11, 1885, 3. See Fertel 2014.

47 Yet in Ronald Walters's (1973) classic understanding of the Northern ideology of Southern eroticism, New Orleans was but one part of a long tradition of Southern exoticization that served to legitimate Northern free-labor ideology. Richard Campanella (2008, 161–67) argues that New Orleans was the only city in the US to produce its own ethnicity, Creole. Yet if we widen our gaze to south Texas (Tejano), the broader Southwest (Chicano), individual states like Hawaii and California (Hapa) as well as perhaps even other individual cities like New York (Nuyorican) and Miami (Miami Cuban), New Orleans and south Louisiana look decidedly unexceptional in regard to the production of ethnicity. John Blassingame's social history of black New Orleans life in the two decades following the victory of the US Army in New Orleans, despite being to this day the most sophisticated such history, also suffers from this romanticization of a variety of practices associated with this image of New Orleans. Ironically, his conclusions, as befits the generation of 1970s urban social historians of which he was a part, largely demonstrates New Orleans as exemplary of other urban patterns (Blassingame 1973).

48 Domínguez 1986.

49 Arnold Hirsch (2007) suggests that group identity of Creoles of color dissolved gradually from abolition until the post–civil rights period.

50 Powell 2012; Roumillat 2013.

51 Gill 1997.

52 Hollandsworth 2001; Reynolds 1964.

53 Powell 1999.

54 Parsons 2005. On the flip side of this white supremacist history, the regalia and organization of the city's black high school marching bands, prevalent in the contemporary era in nearly every traditional carnival krewe, evoke the Reconstruction-era marching companies that Julie Saville has argued "attemp[ed] to form disciplined solidarity across plantation boundaries." Indeed, for the historically attuned onlooker, watching the St. Augustine High School Marching Band lead off the Rex parade on Mardi Gras day can appear as a contemporary pageant of Reconstruction-era paramilitary conflict (see Saville 1996).

55 On Robert Charles and the riots, see Hair 1976.

56 On the general levee strike, see Arnesen 1994. On the street car strike, see Mizell-Nelson 2009.

57 Gotham 2007a, 205.

58 Gotham 2007a.

59 Gill 1997.

60 Woods 2017, 91.

61 Kmen 1966.

62 Hall 1992b, 59.

63 Herskovits 1941, 245.

64 Hurston 1931; Lomax 1950.

65 On the "incipient jazz community," see Raeburn 2009a.

66 On black vernacular music in New Orleans, see Floyd 1991 and Brothers 2006. For a revisionist claim of the white invention of jazz, see Brunn 1960.

67 Stanonis 2006.

68 Asbury 1936; Saxon, Dreyer, and Tallant 1945.

69 Thomas 2014, 7.

70 Gotham 2010.

71 Quoted in Thomas 2014, 45.

72 See Mah 2014.

73 Fairclough 1995.

74 For a sustained interrogation of the politics of race and redistribution during the Great Society era and its aftermath, see Germany 2007.

75 Brooks and Young 1991; French-Marcelin 2015; chapter 9, this volume.

76 T. Adams 2014.

77 V. Adams 2013; chapter 12, this volume.

78 Gotham and Greenberg 2014, x.

79 Crutcher 2010.

80 Hyra 2017, 75.

81 Campanella 2013.

82 Hendrix 2015.

83 See Duany 2009; Watts and Porter 2013; Solnit and Snedeker 2013; Cowen and Seifter 2014.

84 Mason 2010.

85 H. Rothman 2002. See also Orleck 2005.

86 See Tyrrell 1991.

87 Lears 1981, 306.

PART ONE

Constructing
Exceptional
New Orleans

La Catrina

The Mexican Specter of New Orleans

SHANNON LEE DAWDY

We came into an old, ailing city, filthy with the smoke of wood and coal.
It is one of those Gulf cities that all seem like sisters, but very large, very
developed. Tampico, Veracruz, and Campeche would all fit within it—
and it has something of all of them—and of Veracruz above all.

—Mexican writer JUSTO SIERRA MÉNDEZ,
on his arrival in New Orleans in 1895

Sierra, a native of Campeche, recognized something deeply familiar and
sororal about New Orleans—from its architecture, to its commercial life,
to its food. During his stay, he was ably hosted by the city's Mexican community. But his account is barely recognizable in the city's vain reflections
of itself today. What happened to the *mexicanidad* of New Orleans? What
is the place of Mexico in the history of New Orleans? Why does Mexico
seem to matter so little to New Orleans's narratives of authenticity and exceptionalism? In fact, Sierra makes New Orleans appear quite unexceptional
when viewed as an extension of Mexico rather than the United States. The
explorer of New Orleans's archives and old texts will frequently come across
references to Mexico, but without an already existing genealogical narrative,
it is hard to know where to put them.[1] Mexico comes across as a constant
but ghostly presence in the history of the city. This chapter is a descriptive
attempt to bring that historical specter forward and ask it questions. Both

CALAVERA CATRINA

Figure 1.1

La Catrina, 1913. Lithograph by José Guadelupe Posada.

Veracruz and New Orleans, after all, in the nineteenth century earned the
title City of the Dead. New Orleans likes to think this is because of its beautiful above-ground tombs. But the nickname originally referred to a shared
history of yellow fever in these two ports, a disease itself not unconnected
to their shared history as the largest slave markets on the Gulf. This spectral-
sister relation can be represented by the twin figures of Catrina and Katrina.
La Catrina is the iconic image of Day of the Dead in Mexico, a lady skeleton
wearing a pretentiously fashionable hat by which the cartoonist José Guadelupe Posada meant to parody the elite criollos (those of majority Spanish
descent) and their emulation of European styles. The lady forgets that she is
really Mexican. She is thus an apt representation for the way in which Mexico has haunted Louisiana, down to Katrina. New Orleans forgets that in
some way she is Mexican.

As the editors of this volume point out, Hurricane Katrina and its aftermath have been a worry stone for New Orleans's perennial preoccupation
with authenticity. What surged to view through the disaster provides rich
material for a reweaving of the historic fabric. In Walter Benjamin's words,
these moments are like flashes from a camera bulb: "what has been comes

together in a flash with the now to form a constellation."[2] Sudden change creates a confrontation between the past and the present, rearranging things and enabling new realizations about both. What I can see now, looking back, is that the popular imaginary has forgotten New Orleans's Mexico connections. While I will briefly outline the contours of this now-neglected history, the more important point for discussion is the contours of forgetting. Forgetting is a negative dispositive of authenticity. Attending to what drops out in public memory underscores the way in which authenticity registers are created through willful enunciation. They are not passive constructions. Paul Connerton argues that there are at least seven types of social forgetting. As I argue, the two that seem to fit best with the New Orleans–Mexico case are "forgetting that is constitutive in the formation of a new identity" and "repressive erasure."[3] More uniquely, I argue that the temporality of relations—continuous, sudden, revived, or ruptured—has a significant effect upon the ways in which they are remembered, or forgotten.

As some may recall, a rather ridiculous controversy broke out a few months after the storm during the period of cleanup and reconstruction, when the underprovisioned city was suddenly being served by a new fleet of taco trucks. The trucks plied flooded-out neighborhoods, serving day workers performing the cleanup and gut stripping of mildewed buildings. Many of these workers spoke Spanish; the majority (though not all) were Mexican. They liked tacos. Ever open to culinary possibilities, many other New Orleanians discovered they liked truck tacos too. Yet a hue and cry went out to ban the unregulated trucks. Jefferson Parish outlawed them. No parallel moves were made to outlaw unregulated fish and produce trucks, or snowball stands, which have long been fixtures of the local consumer landscape. One does not have to be an anthropologist or political analyst to realize that the undocumented trucks were serving as a proxy for the undocumented workers from Mexico and Tejas who flocked to the city in those months to provide much-needed labor. But clearly, some locals felt threatened by this new population.[4]

I admit that I was naively taken aback by this rejection of a foreign body by the local collective. Familiar with all those dusty references to Mexico in the archive, I knew that Mexicans have never been foreign to New Orleans.[5] But there are significant differences between archive and memory. Mexico could be narrated as one branch of New Orleans's deep heritage. The constant ply of goods and people back and forth between New Orleans and the Gulf Coast of Mexico formed a rhythmic undercurrent of the colonial period that continued well into the twentieth century, along with significant flows from Cuba and, later, Honduras, two Latin American connections that have received more acknowledgment in recent years. Katrina's flash of the bulb revealed that the Mexico connection was utterly forgotten and unacknowledged in the popular imagination. I am fairly certain that if the food trucks were serving shrimp po'boys, everything would have been fine. But tacos are not authentic New Orleans. Or so the story goes.

This chapter restores to view some of the connections between Mexico and New Orleans and, more importantly, tries to understand why and how they have been so actively forgotten. Once I began looking more closely at the Mexican connections from the French colonial period to the post-Katrina present, it became clear to me that the linkages were diverse and episodic. The temporality of New Orleans's relationship to Mexico resists a continuous genealogy. It is, indeed, more of a sibling than a parental relationship, but no less intimate. The history of connection has had many facets and many chapters. They do not add up to a neat teleology by which we comfortably arrive in the present.

The Catrina Archive

The connection between Mexico and New Orleans has been at its most active in times of crisis—supply and labor shortages, wartime, and revolution. In the eighteenth and nineteenth centuries, such crises were more the norm than the exception. The primary feature of this lifeline was an informal, and often illegal, flow of goods and people that provided mutual material comfort and, at times, refuge and the prospect of a new life. Thus, the fact that the crisis of Katrina sparked a revival of this flow is only the latest instance in a long pattern that I will try to briefly recapture here, from the beginning of the Louisiana colony in the early 1700s through the Mexican Revolution.[6]

Mexico was Louisiana's first raison d'être. With its patent to Antoine Crozat's Louisiana company in 1712, the French Crown explicitly sought Mexican silver emanating from the port of Veracruz, as seen in a founding document titled "Project for the Royal Company of the Indies on the Subject of Trade with Mexico."[7] The scheme represented a sanctioned form of smuggling, legitimizing a commerce that the LeMoyne brothers had already established by 1708 along the Gulf Coast. Soon, a thriving coastal trade by small boats and minor players became one of the only reliable features of the colonial economy, a condition that soon benefited the port of New Orleans (established 1718). In this system of intercolonial commerce across the Gulf-Caribbean, the general pattern was a transshipment flow of sugar, coffee, flour, cloth, tools, liquor, leather, Indian trade items (primarily firearms, beads, and blankets), and household sundries. Some of these items were local colonial products, while others were European imports being moved around by enterprising middlemen. The types of goods within this flow changed over time as Louisiana experimented with cash crops of tobacco, sugar, and indigo. In the French period, Louisiana exported tobacco to Mexico, while it imported sugar. In the Spanish period, this pattern flipped. Louisiana indigo had been intended for the European market, but the industry failed, to be replaced by a lucrative middleman trade in Mexican cochineal (a red dye extracted from beetle juice). Some of the more enduring exchanges in the colonial period involved the acquisition of coin (especially silver pesos) and flour from Mexico and the delivery of French textiles, wine, and brandy, as well as Louisiana pitch and tar used in shipbuilding and repair. In the eighteenth century, the greater Veracruz region was second only to Saint-Domingue as one of the most developed plantation economies in the greater Caribbean, with sugar and coffee the main exports, and African and Afro-Mexican slaves providing the primary labor. Louisiana's own fledgling plantation economy became dependent on its colonial trade partners for the supply of slaves after the 1730s.[8] Between 1735 and 1763 (the late French period), of trackable ship routes mentioned in colonial documents, 40 percent were illicit voyages to the Spanish colonies, and the plurality of these were to points in Mexico (35 percent), followed by Florida (25 percent) and Cuba (20 percent).[9] Despite the fact that Cuba has become one of the celebrated roots of the Creole heritage narrative in Louisiana, Mexico was a more significant point of economic contact in both the eighteenth and nineteenth centuries.

While many of these relations were primarily business affairs, over time the larger merchant families of Louisiana extended their branches into Mexico. The off-kilter gender ratio in colonial New Orleans also encouraged men in the trade to look for Mexican brides. Some came to New Orleans to settle before the colony was turned over to the Spanish in the 1760s, and this flow, among the military and economic elites in particular, grew more significant. Unfortunately, the census sources for the colonial periods (both French and Spanish) do not allow us to track the birthplace of settlers, although Spanish surnames were quite common, particularly among sailors and tavern keepers, indicating that men as well as women may have immigrated to the city, and their numbers were not restricted to the elites.

The pattern of New Orleans merchant families having personal ties to Mexico begins in the French period and runs up through the peak of the city's port business in the early twentieth century. The Rasteau family of La

Rochelle, France, sent a son, Paul Rasteau, to New Orleans in the 1740s. In a letter of instructions, elder family members advised Paul to consider the destinations of Veracruz and the coast of Campeche. The company's ship, the *Lion d'Or*, made constant trips between France, Louisiana, Pensacola, and Veracruz, with the captain instructed to give gifts to the harbormaster at Veracruz as needed. The Rasteaus received gold and silver coin in exchange for luxury items such as gilt mirrors and beaver hats.[10]

In the Spanish colonial period (ca. 1766–1804), the Crown formalized trade relations between Louisiana and Mexico, but only under Spain's mercantilist restrictions that specified a short list of goods that could be exchanged between specific colonies. This resulted, however, in a new policy intended to stimulate Louisiana tobacco production and allow it to be sold specifically to Mexico in the 1770s and 1780s. Traffic between New Orleans and the official port of Veracruz grew in these years. The Spanish government also encouraged the importation of slaves, helping to stimulate the plantation economy that had struggled under the French. Many of these slaves came from Mexico, where experiments with the plantation economy in all but the Veracruz region were beginning to wane. One ship, *Nuestra Senora del Carmen*, plied a regular trade of slaves and logwood from Campeche to New Orleans for the last twenty years of the Spanish regime.[11]

The number of residents with Spanish surnames living in the city grew. However, officials in the Spanish government and military were almost entirely European born. The only officially sponsored immigration of Spanish speakers was of Canary Islanders who arrived in the 1770s and 1780s. Still, high-ranking Spanish officials often married into Louisiana families, and their careers then helped create dynasties that spanned across New Orleans, Mexico, and the Atlantic. One example is the St. Maxent sisters, daughters of a prominent New Orleans merchant. Victoire married Juan Antonio de Riaño, intendant of Guanajuato, and Antoinette Marie married Manuel de Flon, intendant of Puebla. Félicité's second marriage was to Bernardo de Gálvez, governor of Louisiana. She followed her husband to Mexico City in 1785, where she gave birth to a daughter named Guadalupe (after the patron saint of Mexico).[12]

Some of the strongest evidence for the strength of contacts between Mexico and New Orleans in the Spanish colonial period comes from the archive related to the Baratarians, the loose confederation of smugglers and privateers associated with Jean and Pierre Laffite. Below the official surface of things, the Laffite brothers inserted themselves into the by-now regular traffic between New Orleans and the Gulf Coast of Mexico. By 1809, they had established the smuggling base camp on Grand Terre at the outlet of Barataria Bay and made regular trips to both Mexico and New Orleans. Their cargo was primarily human, with prices for foreign slaves soaring after the ban of 1808. In early French colonial documents, writers noted that traders who could not be sure of bribing officials in Veracruz could dock at one of the smaller towns up the coast, which were never named. By the Laffite period, these are familiar locations—Nautla and Boquilla de Piedras. Regular shipments flowed between these two towns and Barataria in the 1810s, often bearing arms to stoke the fire of revolution. Flow went both ways. Mexico also had its smugglers and privateers. Mexican ships frequently moored at the mouth of the Mississippi during the Mexican War of Independence. After losing favor with the US government due to his transition from slave smuggling to questionable privateering for both insurgent Mexico and Cartagena during the revolutionary Bolívar period, Jean Laffite was driven out of Louisiana. For a while he established a new independent republic of his own on Matagorda Island (now in Texas, but Mexican territory at the time, which Laffite rather confusingly decided to dub Campeachy). The Baratarians often picked up not only goods from Mexican shores, but crew members, such as when Pierre Laffite completed his crew out of the real Campeche in southern Mexico in 1815. Pierre died in Campeche, where he had collaborated with several Mexican associates (sailors, farmers, and fishermen) in his smuggling and filibustering schemes. Today a monument to the Laffite brothers stands in the Mayan town of Dzilam. This particular Louisiana connection has not been forgotten by Mexico.[13]

Other New Orleanians such as Emile La Sere used their multilingual abilities to build a more legitimate economic and political career based on their expertise in Mexico. La Sere served as a clerk for the merchant house McClannahan and Bogart. They assigned him to Mexico in 1825, where he remained for fifteen years. Returning to New Orleans, he became active in politics and eventually ascended to the US Congress. After the Civil War, his Mexico connections drew him back to build up a lucrative business, and he eventually became president of the Tehuantepec Railroad Company, a politically significant ploy to shorten the route to the Pacific and give New Orleans an even more dominant role in trans-American trade. Toward the end of his career, La Sere returned to New Orleans and the Louisiana-Mexico mercantile trade.[14]

The political landscape of Mexico was tumultuous in the nineteenth century, from the first revolt against the Spanish in 1811 on through independence (1821), the Texas Revolution (1835–36), the Pastry War (1838–39), the Mexican-American War (1846–48), and the invasion of Maximilian (1861–67). While dealing with all these conflicts (the later ones being foreign attacks on Mexican sovereignty), liberal and conservative forces fought one another for control over the new Mexican state, sometimes flipping sides in the process. The active role of smugglers, privateers, mercenaries, spies, and filibusters emanating from New Orleans made events even more complex. One can cite the colorful careers of John Sibley, Daniel Clark Jr., Abner Duncan, Augustus Magee, James Wilkinson, and none other than Aaron Burr, who each had at least one foot in New Orleans. New Orleans merchants such as Daniel Clark were key in providing intelligence on conditions and contacts in Mexico in various political intrigues. New Orleans newspapers avidly covered events across the Gulf throughout these years, not infrequently carrying stories in every issue for weeks on end.

During the Mexican War of Independence, New Orleans provided an important source of support for the Mexican insurgency. Prominent New Orleanians established the Mexican Association a few years before the declaration of revolution, with the express purpose of encouraging an independent Mexico. Louisianans supplied arms and materiel to Mexican rebels and went themselves to fight. Mexican-born revolutionaries such as Francisco Xavier Mina and José Gutiérrez de Lara found New Orleans a convenient base of operations and source of allies in the 1810s. Mina was executed by firing squad upon his return to Mexico, but Gutiérrez eventually succeeded and was appointed governor of Tamaulipas in the new republic in 1825.[15]

The entanglement of commerce, political conflict, and personal relationships continued to characterize traceable contacts between New Orleans and Mexico throughout the nineteenth century. Although they were soon swamped by the much greater influx of immigrants to New Orleans from the United States, Saint-Domingue, Ireland, and Germany, free Spanish speakers continued to come to New Orleans to settle in the antebellum period. Of those identified by origin, the majority come from Mexico. Although they were likely riding the by now well-worn commercial route, many seem to have been political refugees, caught on the wrong side of the many-sided conflicts of the early republic. At one point in the 1830s, their presence in the city was so noticeable that Jean Boze (himself a transplant) reported that although some were of noble origins, others were scoundrels, adding a new danger to the streets of New Orleans.[16]

Mexican independence overall meant a period of free trade between New Orleans and Mexico, and there is strong evidence in the shipping news and personal correspondence out of New Orleans from the 1820s through the

1840s of daily departures and arrivals from Mexico. Like their counterparts, some Mexican merchants such as Francisco Sentmanat y Zayas relocated to New Orleans to conduct their side of the business. A pattern of immigration to Mexico or using New Orleans as a way station between Europe and Mexico also emerges in this period. While Tampico rose to an importance it did not have in the eighteenth century, Veracruz remained the main port for the larger commission merchants, such as the James W. Zacharie Company, which owned five ships it kept busy between New Orleans and its Mexican sister.[17]

One other important effect of Mexican independence was the outlawing of slavery. As in many parts of Latin America, abolition was gradual, instituted through several legal acts between 1810 and 1829. The supply of illegal slaves from Mexico that had profited the Laffites slowed to a stop. Mexico's new state of freedom did not go unnoticed by enslaved people in the territories. One woman named Isabella (last name unknown) attempted to sue for her freedom in 1847 based on the fact that her Anglo owners in Mexican Texas had illegally denied her emancipation and that her entry into Louisiana was as a contraband foreign slave.[18]

The circulation of Mexican and Louisianan political figures between the two coasts of the Gulf were perhaps never so significant as in the middle of the nineteenth century. Two of the most important Mexican presidents of the century had periods of midcareer exile in New Orleans. The onetime ally of Santa Anna and furious liberal reformer Valentín Gómez Farías ended up in New Orleans in 1835 after falling out of favor with the general. Documents suggest that he colluded with freemasons belonging to the mysterious New Orleans Amphietyonic Council that had elite members with Mexican family and commercial ties. As a matter of political convenience, they made a deal with the Anglo-Texans to defeat Santa Anna. Later, a figure no less than Benito Juárez, the future multiterm president and legend of Republican Mexico, ended up in exile in New Orleans in 1853–54 after himself falling out with the long-lived Santa Anna. Ousted from his post as governor of Oaxaca, he spent a year "lodging in a boardinghouse and supporting himself by rolling cigars." But he soon returned to Mexico to end Santa Anna's career and was elected to the presidency in 1861.[19]

New Orleans also served as a convenient base of operations for Anglo-Texans in the Texas Revolution (1836), but as James Denham's careful research has shown, the city was divided over support for the Texans.[20] Before long, the merchant and shipping insurance elites in the city had turned against them, as the newborn Texas navy was effectively blockading the city from its third-largest trading partner. Debates over the Texas question in the New Orleans press bring out how extensive the shipping connection had become in the age of steam and free trade, and how many New Orleanians had family agents located in Tampico, Veracruz, and Matagorda. This family-commercial network had become so thick and profitable (Mexican silver was still the most important import) that New Orleanians no longer tolerated illegal trade, moving them to make what the Texans called "a false imputation of piracy, brought against them by the secret Mexican influence of this city."[21] As was to happen time and again, New Orleans served both sides. During Mexico's losing battle to prevent Texas from seceding, the city also served as a convenient base of operations for Mexican military leaders. Late in the war, rumors flew that a Mexican team in New Orleans was working to recruit Creek and Cherokee mercenaries.

The subsequent Mexican-American War once again interrupted legal trade, and the city's newspapers followed the events nervously, though New Orleans also enjoyed wartime profiteering. In addition to emergency measures that lifted trade regulations and liberalized the agricultural transshipment business, a great number of US military deployments were outfitted in, and sent out from, the city. While much of the official discourse supported the effort, scattered references in family papers, New Orleans newspapers, and biographies suggest that a significant number of Louisianans fought on the Mexican side of the war. Some may have been loyal to their Mexican families, but others were simply loyal to themselves, such as the New Orleans lawyer and career adventurer Chatham Roberdeau Wheat. Wheat eventually rose to the rank of brigadier general under Governor Juan Alvarez of Guerrero state, participating in a successful revolt against President Santa Anna before joining filibuster William Walker in Nicaragua.[22]

The archive shows that Mexican revolutionaries and military leaders flowing in and out of New Orleans were welcomed and supported by a vibrant Mexican immigrant community. The city was home to the first Spanish-language newspaper to be published in the United States. Operating under the names *La Patria* and then *La Union* between 1845 and 1851, the newspaper had a circulation of eight hundred, which, though much smaller than the major English-language newspapers, still suggests a sizeable population of eight hundred literate households. How many more Spanish-speaking households of unlettered laborers and tradesmen may have made New Orleans home is unknown, but circumstantially, these numbers suggest a population of between two and four thousand. The editorial bent of the Spanish paper makes it clear the population was primarily Mexican and pro-Republic. The paper specialized in rapid-fire translation of Mexican newspapers (another indication that ships were arriving from that coast almost daily) and publishing reports from correspondents in Veracruz, Tampico, Mexico City, and Havana. The editors "also conducted interviews with Spanish-speaking merchants and diplomats passing through New Orleans, and printed biographical sketches about leading Mexican military and political leaders who generally were unknown to the American public."[23] *La Patria* built up a wide circulation across the country among English-language editors, who used it as a source for news about Latin America. The contemporary editor of the *Mobile Register* reported that the New Orleans paper was "generally well informed of events in Mexico and appear[ed] to have accurate sources of intelligence among the Mexicans." Although little biographical information is available about the three editors (all with Spanish names), they make their Mexican roots clear in a cranky exchange with the editor of the *New Orleans Evening Mercury*, whom the writer for *La Patria* called "an ass" for continually confusing Mexicans and Spaniards. This ignorant Anglo confusion may have been widespread and a good reason not to look to census records as a reliable source for estimates of the Mexican population.[24]

The late antebellum and Civil War era was particularly rich with exchanges. In the last two decades before the outbreak of the war, the political climate and legal conditions for free people of color in the American South had deteriorated, even in New Orleans with its many educated professionals and skilled members of the middle class. As a result, free people began to form plans to emigrate to other countries. The self-liberated nation of Haiti ranked high on the list, but so did Mexico. One fourteen-year-old New Orleanian wrote a dreamlike letter for his teacher in 1862, saying to his imagined correspondent, "we will go and visit Mexico, the finest country after Paris."[25] As Mary Mitchell's research has uncovered, these dreams became a scheme:

> Free black people from Louisiana had begun migrating to Mexico in 1855, but it was not until two years later that an official agreement was signed . . . to establish a colony named Eureka outside of Tampico. The Mexican Republic may have attracted free blacks from Louisiana, in large part, because of the racial equality that Mexico's leaders promised its colonists. But the lucrative commercial traffic between Veracruz and New Orleans must have also been of interest to free black merchants, grocers, and dry-goods men.[26]

The colony, which appears to have been the brainchild of prominent Louisianans of color such as Nelson Fouché and Armand Lanusse, ultimately failed, although its settlers may have dispersed to other Mexican towns. The New Orleans letters, many addressed to family and friends who had relocated, reflect a reasonably informed view of conditions in Mexico. They also reveal that some free people were attempting to establish themselves as farmers and planters. These correspondents may have been related to another small agricultural colony of ex-Louisianans located in the Tecolutla River basin north of Veracruz (the settlement was called Cazonera, a few miles from Papantla). As Rebecca Scott and Jean Hébrard recount, members of the Tinchant and Gonzales families briefly joined this community after leaving the hostile environment of Union-occupied New Orleans. In their efforts to establish a family business in tobacco with family branch offices in New Orleans, Veracruz, and Belgium, the Mexico offshoot moved inland to Tlapacoyan, at the time gaining a reputation as a region producing high-quality tobacco.[27] Notably, the point of export for this tobacco was Nautla, the same small town that had long been friendly to Louisiana traders. The call for immigration to Mexico continued after the Civil War when elite Creoles of color became frustrated in their efforts to maintain a place of privilege.[28]

Mexico as a refuge and an immigration possibility attracted elite white New Orleanians as well, particularly those sympathetic to the Confederacy. Writer Eliza Ripley fled with her planter husband, giving birth to her daughter in Mexico City. The Grima family of merchants already had one branch of the family settled in Matamoros in northern Mexico when the war broke out. After federal forces occupied New Orleans, several brothers and cousins joined them. Correspondence from letter writers in New Orleans makes it clear that at least four Grima men were living there and carrying on their business affairs in Matamoros. Some writers appealed to them to help friends arriving in Mexico from New Orleans find work. Wartime did not seem to impede the delivery of letters, as thirteen letters made it to Adolphe Grima in Matamoros from New Orleans in 1864. Also safely delivered was a cache of silver, whether to safeguard from federal seizure or to finance the family business is unclear.[29]

Cut off from the Atlantic coast, Confederate governor of Louisiana Henry Watkins Allen strengthened a trade route with Mexico, exporting Louisiana cotton in exchange for medicine, clothing, and food. After federal occupation began, many Confederate leaders exiled themselves to Mexico. Allen was prominent among them and went on to establish an English-language paper in Mexico City called *Mexican Times*. Among other things, the paper promoted the new colony of Carlota, named after the consort of the temporary Emperor Maximilian, who had recently invaded Mexico on behalf of France and who saw a useful ally in the Confederates. After crossing the Rio Grande and eventually making their way from Monterrey to San Luis Potosí to Mexico City, these Southern exiles formalized a colony scheme to sell shares and settle a site located seventy miles west of Veracruz and nine miles southeast of Córdoba, near the present town of Paraje Nuevo, known for its rich mango groves. With a Louisianan as leader of Carlota (which at its peak hosted at least four hundred individuals and, by some counts, a thousand), perhaps it is not surprising that they ended up near Veracruz. Allen died there of yellow fever on April 22, 1866. But when Mexican liberals rid themselves of Maximilian, the Confederates found that even Allen's corpse was not welcome, and it was sent back to New Orleans for interment.[30]

After the Civil War, the 1884 World's Industrial and Cotton Centennial Exposition explicitly promoted the long-standing ties between Mexico and New Orleans. Backers intended this variation on the World's Fair to commemorate the one hundredth anniversary of the first export of US cotton and to stimulate a New South of industrial and commercial possibilities. The lower Mississippi River had recently been revetted and the levees significantly raised, allowing larger ocean-bound steamships to reach the city. New Orleanians harbored hopes for a reinvigorated trade with Latin America. Mexico acted as the dominant, enterprising partner, reaching a hand out to its little sister city, which had begun to slip into dependency and decay in the hard economic years following the Civil War. Enjoying a new period of political peace and prosperity (albeit with growing class disparities), the Mexican government made a significant symbolic investment in the exposition. Mexico was easily the largest foreign participant in the event, sending an extravagant display of 2.5 tons of silver (worth $100,000 at the time), with gardens and buildings (one Moorish, one a fake hacienda) that extended over seventy-six acres, and sending what may have been one of the most lasting contributions to New Orleans culture—a Mexican brass military band that became a surprise hit among locals.[31] In addition, "one observer at New Orleans remarked that 'no event of the exposition attracted more attention than Mexico Day, which was celebrated on May 29th in royal style.' The festivities included a 'monster parade' and an oration by the Mexican commissioner which attracted an audience of fifteen thousand."[32] The Cotton Centennial also featured a performance of the waltz "Sobre las Olas" composed by Juventino Rosas, an Otomi Indian violinist from Guanajuato that became a mainstay of the New Orleans Carnival ball.

The Mexican Revolution of 1910–20 created another wave of crisis immigration that reinforced the New Orleans–Mexico connection. Census rolls of 1910 and 1920 show a significant surge in residents born in Mexico (over two thousand), making it the largest immigrant group from any Latin American country at the time. In a pattern that repeated history, New Orleans became a base of operations and/or a place of refuge for both conservative and socialist leaders in the war, as well as American filibusters. Julie M. Weise tracked this community of immigrants into the Crescent City and argues that "middle-class Mexican immigrants of the 1920s successfully engaged Mexico and shaped the image of 'Mexicans' in ways that secured their place among European-style white immigrants."[33] The wealth and cultural sophistication that the Mexican government had put on display at the Cotton Centennial a generation earlier may have helped lay the ground for a relatively easy assimilation. Weise argues that by using the signs of culture, Mexican immigrants successfully navigated the fraught streets of Jim Crow. Many were entrepreneurial in their business affairs and also quite willing to marry into local Catholic communities. New Orleans was like Mexico in another very important regard. Within a certain range of phenotypic ambiguity, class signs could trump racial ones. Those adept at the manipulation of manners and clothing could glide from stratum to stratum. La Catrina's hat is a symbol of precisely this sort of social mobility that obscures history.

Collective Amnesia

Against the backdrop of this lively, long-term exchange between New Orleans and Mexico, the question remains, why hasn't there been a significant place for Mexico in the historical New Orleans narrative? Why, despite the solid archive of an intimate relationship that I have tried to bring back to the surface here, does it remain largely forgotten in popular thought and, until recently, in so much scholarship? My answers are twofold. First, for immigrants, forgetting Mexico has been part of a process of new identity formation accented by shifting conditions of exclusion. And second, to remember Mexico is to remember Louisiana's long, and perhaps embarrassing, period of little sisterhood. Up through the Civil War, in many ways New Orleans functioned like a dependent colony of Mexico, a political-economic reality in conflict with the rise of American-style racism from the mid-nineteenth through early twentieth centuries, which gradually came to view Mexico and Mexicans as brown and inferior. And in both cases, the tempo of the relationship up through the Mexican Revolution was continuous, if episodic. Even when Louisiana came under Spanish rule in the late eighteenth century, its relationship with Mexico did not so much change as become briefly legitimized.

Connerton shares an example of assimilation in Southeast Asia that could be applied, with some modification, to the immigrant part of the Mexico–New Orleans story.

> Newcomers to islands are transformed into kin through hospitality, through marriage and through having children. The details of their past diversity, in the islands they have now left, cease to be part of their mental furniture. Forgetting them is unacknowledged, it is probably only gradual and implicit, and no particular attention is drawn to it; but it is necessary nonetheless. Forgetting is here part of an active process of a new and shared identity in a new setting.[34]

Patterns of immigration and assimilation for the different contributing populations to New Orleans were distinct and affected the degree to which they are remembered, with race and class being no small factors in facilitating or blocking authenticity claims (as opposed to the more benign forgetting that Connerton describes). From the French colonial period down to the present, Mexicans who immigrated to New Orleans came as a trickle of families and individuals rather than the sudden diasporas of other groups (such as the first French settlers, Africans, the Canary Islanders, Saint-Dominguans, Irish, and Sicilians). There was no mass migration to which to attach an origin story (or, in the case of Saint-Domingue, one to revive through scholarship). And, unlike these other groups, Mexicans have never been stranded in Louisiana for long—they could almost always return if they so desired, so their presence may have been viewed as temporary. Further, because the type of Mexicans who tended to migrate to the city in the eighteenth and nineteenth centuries were either already connected to New Orleans through family-merchant connections or came from the class of political elites, they could quickly pass into Creole society (which was, by definition, composed of the middle and landed classes, regardless of color). Mexicans may have recognized and used the Gulf's long-standing commercial relations to blend in as distant cousins who might, or might not, have access to wealthy markets across the water. If they played it right, Criollos and Mestizos could become Creoles. And in a city that had not fully recovered from the Anglo versus Creole culture wars of the antebellum period, the addition of Spanish surnames to the family tree may have added an air of autochthony, not difference.[35] Given the prideful insistence on mexicanidad by the editors of *La Patria* and the attraction of Mexico as a destination for Louisiana emigrants (including those seeking freedom from the oppressions of a slave state), Mexico did not bear the racialized stigma it would later acquire in the twentieth century. Although anti-Mexican sentiment emerged around the Mexican-American War, as recounted above, New Orleans had enough ties of loyalty to mute that particular racist strain. In other words, Mexican immigrants prior to the 1920s may have been perceived not so much as new arrivals as an index to older structures of power and wealth in the city. What Julie Weise observed about the apparently easy assimilation of middle-class Mexicans into the white-ish Creole elites of the city in the 1920s was even truer for the earlier periods of influx in the eighteenth and nineteenth centuries. In other words, class could overwrite origin. However, as Mae Ngai documents, anti-Mexican racism became virulent in the 1920s–30s in Texas and the Southwest. This wave of hatred involved lynchings, deportations, and vigilante border patrols. Under these conditions, there was clearly no advantage to celebrating Mexican roots, so the motivation for disappearing into the Creole fold in New Orleans accelerated during this period.[36]

The closest parallel to the Mexican immigrant pattern in New Orleans was the Cuban one, although those numbers were comparatively small until the 1959 revolution, when a distinctly white, upper- and middle-class group of Cubans fled socialism. That influx, which followed on the heels of a vibrant New Orleans–Cuba tourism trade in the mid-twentieth century, probably did much to reinvent the "cubanidad" of New Orleans. No similar boost came from Mexico until the labor shortage following Hurricane Katrina, and the race-class nexus of that population was quite distinct from traceable patterns in the city's earlier history.[37]

The intersection of race and class in a climate of nativism would also explain why the largest present-day Hispanic population of New Orleans, immigrants from Honduras, have not really been narrated as a part of the city's identity. They contribute to the economy and its demographics, but they are still perceived as a largely unassimilated group. They do not fit into the "real New Orleans" story except in rarefied contexts such as the folklife pavilions at the New Orleans Jazz and Heritage Festival, which are, if anything, a forced effort to construct memory and identity.[38]

But immigration is in some ways an overly literal and genealogical way to understand cultural formation in which people are imagined to arrive somewhere, settle down, and contribute their cultural genes to the pool. Another way to understand a place-time, and especially that of a port city, is as a node of flows with people and goods flowing in and out. In this creolization model, we can think of influences not so much in terms of kinship lineage as marketplace exchange. Looked at in this way, we can see that the flows between Mexico and Louisiana that I have documented went both ways and that the most salient feature was the porosity of the border between Louisiana and Mexico, not so much a crossing from one distinct region into another. In the colonial period, New Orleans was dependent upon silver specie coming from the Spanish colonies, especially Mexico, and overall it gained more from business with Mexico than with any other trading partner. As the Cotton Centennial emphasized, Mexico had long been a source of wealth and patronage—it was a more lasting metropole than France or Spain for New Orleans and was not overshadowed by Washington, DC, until the early twentieth century.

The second, more political, form of forgetting that the Catrina-Katrina specter has taken is what Connerton calls "repressive erasure." Whether done explicitly by a state or more covertly by elites controlling historical narratives, the omission of embarrassing facts or those that do not fit into a national narrative is consistent with the erasure of Mexico from the New Orleans story. Connerton cites the example of the English conveniently forgetting the Norman conquest: "This is how the English have come to think of themselves as having been a colonizing people, but not as having been a colonized people."[39] As I have written elsewhere, New Orleans's authenticity narrative is heavily dependent upon its construction of Frenchness that invokes a totemic relationship to a distant, and numerically negligible, French immigrant past. For a very long time, the dominant narrative of New Orleans has been how a French city was never quite conquered by Anglo-Americans. And even efforts to stress the city's African-descendent population have veered toward Frenchifying Afro-Creoles as a means to legitimize their claims upon the city, regardless of faith, language, or origin. The fact that colonial Louisiana's political and economic relationship with Mexico examined over two centuries was far more significant than France's ever was does not fit into this story of French resistance to American dominion. Remembering Mexico would disrupt the political origin story that is the root of New Orleans's exceptionalism. This storyline also dubs New Orleans the most northern Caribbean city and lends it a veneer of island-like autonomy that can be a point of political pride. The structural reality that New Orleans in many ways was an outpost of Mexico has no political currency.

The links between Mexico and New Orleans become most active in moments of political crisis and economic shortage, as they have after Katrina. Over time, the Mexico connection has been sporadic but never broken. New

Orleans's mexicanidad belongs to the continuous present. Unlike the diasporic communities, no sudden rupture has occurred to create a retrospective exoticism. Relations with Mexico have crisscrossed constantly across the Gulf. There is no vertical line of descent, just overlapping, horizontal lines of exchange. In New Orleans's habit of auto-orientalism, perhaps the Other it incorporates and represents needs to be distant in time. It needs to be older—like a parent or an ancestor, rather than like the sister cities that Sierra Méndez saw. And the deepest wounds of class and race need to be scarred over, not active, to allow for kinship to be unforgotten.

Notes

Epigraph: Justo Sierra Méndez quoted in Gruesz 2006, 489.

1 It doesn't take much to show that this is no straw man argument. Refer, for example, to the extensive online research guide and bibliography by the Western European Studies section of the Association of College and Research Libraries, "Immigration, Ethnicities and Historical Research in New Orleans," http://wessweb.info/index.php /Immigration,_Ethnicities_and_Historical_Research_in_New_Orleans. Not one reference is available for the history of Mexico and Mexicans in New Orleans. Further, in the J-Stor index for the last fifty years of the journal *Louisiana History*, only twelve references appear with Mexico in the title, three of which are for New Mexico and all of which are book reviews primarily concerning more general US-Mexico wartime relations.

2 Benjamin and Tiedemann 1999, 462.

3 Connerton 2008, 62, 64.

4 In the first eighteen months after the storm, approximately fifty thousand new Latino immigrants arrived in the New Orleans area. Some claim that the taco trucks were unfairly competing with local businesses, but this ignores the rather salient fact that in the neighborhoods where they concentrated, there were no restaurants yet open (due to lack of utilities or slowness of their own rebuilding). John Moreno Gonzales, "Hispanics Add New Flavor to New Orleans as Numbers Rise," *Sun News*, 2007, D3. See also Pavelle 2011; Naughton and Wallace 2006; Trujillo-Pagán 2012. I am not the first to note the intersection of ignorance and racism that the reaction to Latino workers arriving to the city after Katrina revealed; see the introduction to Sluyter et al. 2015.

5 I knew this from my own research (in which I argue for the framing of a Mississippi-Caribbean sphere), but subsequent scholars have done more legwork to flesh out the connections between Latin America and New Orleans. I will not here repeat my arguments against the Atlantic World framing, which I have made elsewhere, except to say that it is representative of a Eurocentric perspective in the historiography that tends to devalue the significant relationships between New Orleans and parts of Latin America, including Mexico (see Dawdy 2007, 2008; and contributions to Sluyter et al. 2015).

6 For want of space and expertise, I am not extending this account far into the twentieth

century, although I know it could be through an examination of the history of the port of New Orleans as a gateway to the Americas, the Gulf oil industry, narco trafficking, and NAFTA.

7   Projet pour la Royalle Compagnie des Indes au Sujet de commerce de Mexique, n.d. (between 1718 and 1728), Archive National de France, AC, C13C 4, ff. 167–75v.

8   Dawdy 2008, chapter 3.

9   Dawdy 2008, 120.

10 Cargo of *Lion d'Or*, September 22, 1743; Fernando de Bustillo to Elie Rasteau, September 23, 1743, Super Council Abstracts, *Louisiana Historical Quarterly* 12 (1) (1929): 154.

11 W. Davis 2006, 20; J. Clark 1970, 189–90; Woodward 2003.

12 "Bernardo de Galvez," in *Dictionary of Louisiana Biography*, accessed September 1, 2018, https://www.lahistory.org/resources/dictionary-louisiana-biography/dictionary -louisiana-biography-g/.

13 W. Davis 2006, 221, 260, 298; Mirabeau Buonoparte Lamar papers, Texas State Library and Archive Commission; Mañé 1984.

14 Gruesz 2006; *Dictionary of Louisiana Biography*.

15 Arthur 1933; Warren 1943; Watson 1970; Blaufarb 2005, 35–39, 63; W. Davis 2006; Narrett 2012.

16 Dessens 2015; Letters of Jean Boze to Ste-Geme Family, MSS 100, f. 143, 13, Historic New Orleans Collection. The US Census did not begin tracking place of birth until 1850, so it is impossible to come up with an accurate estimate of foreign origins prior to that time. The exhaustive work of going through the returns for the city from 1850 to 1970 (when Hispanic origin began to be noted) has yet to be done.

17 Dessens 2015, 42–43, 47; two letters from August 1838, James W. Zacharie and Company Letters, MSS 481, Historic New Orleans Collection.

18 *Dictionary of Louisiana Biography*.

19 Hutchinson 1956; Scott and Hébrard 2012, 104.

20 Denham 1994.

21 William Bryan, cited in Denham 1994, 524.

22 Boyette 1976; *Dictionary of Louisiana Biography*.

23 Reilly 1982, 329.

24 Reilly 1982, 329, 330.

25 Mitchell 2000, 123.

26 Mitchell 2000, 129.

27 Scott and Hébrard 2012, 118–19, 144–49, 223n67.

28 Significant connections may have also existed between elite free people of color and Mexican urban culture. Edmond Dede, for example, a violinist and composer, was sent to Mexico to study in the 1840s before going on to Paris. Another paper could be written on the intellectual and artistic exchanges between Mexico and New Orleans through education, immigration, and travel over the years. See, for example, the biographies of Rudolph Matas, Mary Ashley Townsend, Miguel Bernal-Jimenez, Benjamin Weinstein, Francisco Vargas, and John Gibson in the *Dictionary of Louisiana Biography,* as well as the mid-twentieth-century exchange among artists described in the exhibition catalog *Mexico in New Orleans* (Pfolh 2015).

29 Ripley 1889; letter of March 29, 1864, Grima Family Papers, MS 99, Historic New Orleans Collection.

30 Chiapas and Yucatan had also been considered. See Rister 1945. See also entries for Quintero Allen and Conrad Perkins in *Dictionary of Louisiana Biography*.

31 Yeager 1977; Shepherd 1985.

32 Yaeger 1977, 238.

33 Weise 2015, 29; for census summary see 34.

34 Connerton 2008, 63 (citing Carsten).

35 Domínguez 1986; Hirsch and Logsdon 1992.

36 Gómez 2007; Ngai 2004.

37 Sluyter et al. 2015.

38 Regis and Walton 2008.

39 Connerton 2008, 60.

Charles Gayarré and the Imagining of an Exceptional City

The Literary Roots of the Creole City

RIEN FERTEL

In the autumn of 1827, two New Orleanians waged a war of the printed word. Though both men were cultivated, politically powerful French Louisianans, Bernard de Marigny and Étienne Mazureau exercised their American rights to free speech and suffrage by supporting opposing presidential candidates. Born in 1785, Bernard Xavier Philippe de Marigny de Mandeville had a lifestyle that mirrored his aristocratic French name. In 1822, as president of the state senate, Marigny, in a move on what he called "one of the happiest days of my life," overturned a Louisiana Supreme Court decision to make "null and void" any minutes of meetings not written in English. He was thus deemed "the Defender of the French language."[1] In addition to his status as a Francophone paladin, he was an infamous libertine and an even more notorious gambler. Within six years of inheriting his father's immense plantation landholdings, one block downriver from the city, Marigny was forced, owing to his dice habit, to subdivide the property. He became an Andrew Jackson supporter in 1824, and would forever remain one, primarily because Old Hickory's presidential opponent, John Quincy Adams, had been averse to the Louisiana Purchase two decades prior.[2]

Étienne Mazureau, conversely, was an adamant Adams man. A state attorney general for three terms and Louisiana secretary of state, in 1827 he ranked as one of the city's most accomplished and fiery lawyers and orators. Mazureau "possesses a most extensive and profound knowledge of the civil law, . . . but on certain occasions his eloquence becomes tempestuous," one historian of the period noted. "He is a perfect specimen of the Southern type."[3] When selecting juries, Mazureau often challenged every single potential Anglo-American juror, his goal being to place as many French-speaking citizens on the panel as the judge would allow.[4] In 1831, Alexis de Tocqueville visited the home of the learned Louisiana advocate, whom he called "the eagle of the New Orleans bar," to consult on a series of local issues.[5] "They say that in New Orleans is to be found a mixture of all the nations?" Tocqueville queried. "That's true; you see here a mingling of all races. . . . New Orleans is a patch-work of people," answered the eagle. Tocqueville inquired further, "But in the midst of this confusion what race dominates and gives direction to all the rest?" "The French race, up to now," answered Mazureau. "It's they who set the tone and shape the moeurs [mores]."[6]

Marigny's and Mazureau's opinions on French Louisiana's identity deviated as fiercely as their presidential politics. In a series of late 1827 newspaper editorials and pamphlets, the pair of Francophile New Orleanians attacked each other's candidates, while questioning each other's allegiance to the state and the nation. Additionally, the two men published under pseudonyms befitting their places of birth. Mazureau labeled himself the Citoyen Naturalisé because, though born in France in 1777, he proudly considered himself to have been a naturalized citizen of the United States for at least the past two decades.

Marigny, on the other hand, adopted the sobriquet Un Créole. No less proud of his American citizenship than his adversary, he could make one claim that Mazureau could not: his birthplace was colonial Louisiana. Born to two New Orleanians of French ethnicity in 1785, Marigny before even his eighteenth birthday lived under the flags of the Spanish, French, and nascent US empires. He made sure that Mazureau and any readers knew the difference this birth made. In the last lines of his final riposte, Marigny signed off with the words "Que né créole, je veux vivre et mourir créole" (Born Creole, I want to live and die Creole).[7] Mazureau might be a French Louisianan and a French American, but he would never be a Creole Louisianan or Creole American. In nineteenth-century New Orleans, the designation Creole operated as a birthright, a symbol of exceptionality, and an identity marker. There was power embedded in the word "Creole."

Certainly unbeknownst to him at the time, Bernard de Marigny was at the forefront of a white Creole literary and intellectual culture that thrived during the long nineteenth century. Supported by a democratic right to

expression, the eruption of the modern print culture, and a burgeoning Francophone readership, an elite circle of cultured Creole French Americans produced a Creole New Orleans literature. This Creole body of letters lasted
roughly one hundred years, from the 1820s through the 1920s. During this
era, these Creole French Americans used Creole as a marker of status and
power.

The first French-language publications appeared in Louisiana during the
Spanish colonial era of Marigny's birth. In the late 1770s, the French-born
poet Julien Poydras penned a trio of odes honoring the Spanish Louisiana
governor and military hero Bernardo de Gálvez. By the time Marigny had
sold off his landholdings piecemeal to create what would become the faubourg named in his honor, the stage drama *La Fête du Petit-Blé; ou L'Héroisme
de Poucha-Houmma*, written by the Frenchman Paul Louis Le Blanc de Ville-
neufve, was being performed in New Orleans. In the same late 1827 season
that Marigny and Mazureau battled in print, the Saint-Domingue refugee
François Delaup began publishing the city's first serious semiweekly newspaper. Taking advantage of the nearly twenty thousand Saint-Domingue exiles
who had relocated to New Orleans (along with a not unsubstantial, contemporary French immigration), *L'Abeille de la Nouvelle-Orléans* (at times
published in English as the *Bee*) provided a Francophone forum for real jour-
nalism, political editorials, and art and literary criticism.[8]

In the 1830s and 1840s, the Creole intellectual circle would become fully
formed. By the time Marigny published his brief memoirs in 1853—in both
French and English—readers on both sides of the Atlantic Ocean were de-
vouring the works of Creole authors such as the historian Charles Étienne
Arthur Gayarré and the poet-priest Adrien Rouquette. The print work of
these men and other Creoles came late in the American republic's golden
age of print, a flourishing of print media in the early nineteenth century.
Gayarré, the first great Creole of letters, believed that his homeland exuded
exceptionality, that Louisiana's place, past, and people were special. In the
1830s and early 1840s he started publishing French-language chronicles of
Louisiana history based on real research and containing objective insight. But
beginning with his *Romance of the History of Louisiana* (1848) and continuing well into the 1890s, Gayarré published English-language popular histories that romanticized and embellished episodes in the city's and the state's
past. These later histories precipitated the white Creole print culture, making Gayarré the primary architect of a New Orleans mythos that centered
the history and culture of the city in the realm of Gallic-centric whiteness.

One has only to open any one of the countless popular histories of New Orleans printed over the last century. Lyle Saxon, an immensely prominent Crescent City chronicler from the 1920s to the 1940s and Louisiana's Federal Writers' Project director for Roosevelt's WPA initiative, described his adopted city as "not in any sense an American city," but rather "a strange city, a city that had been first French, then Spanish, and which was now Creole, a blending of both."[9] Saxon's literary contemporaries and apostles agreed. In his novel *Paramours of the Creoles* (1944), Pierre Paul Ebeyer wrote, "No matter where you go, you will never find the customs of this community duplicated anywhere on this planet."[10] Robert Tallant went even further, going galactic to describe the city. "New Orleans is a world," he wrote in 1950. "If Boston is the hub of the solar system. New Orleans is a planet of quite another system."[11]

Back on Earth, in the year of Marigny's death, 1868, the Creole literary circle found itself falling apart. During and following the Civil War, the occupational government and the Republican state legislature fought to enact a series of constitutional acts that would curb the use of the French language, first in all governmental proceedings and finally in every public school. Near the one hundredth anniversary of Marigny's birth, a new generation of Creole writers led by the medical doctor and amateur linguist Alfred Mercier sprung up to continue the work of the defender of the French language. These writers started Francophile clubs, as well as journals that promoted a purely Franco-Louisianan platform, and celebrated official Creole days. They sought to revive a floundering Francophone New Orleans community by defending and preserving the French language. These Creole Francophone defenders worked alongside members of a transnational Pan-Latin movement that sought to combat the creeping influence of Great Britain and the English language.

But it was too little, too late. By the turn of the twentieth century the French language had largely disappeared as a working language in New Orleans. French was forbidden as a language of instruction in public schools; laws were no longer published bilingually; and French presses and periodicals evaporated. The Creoles charged a non-Creole New Orleanian, George Washington Cable, with being disrespectful toward their culture and their bloodlines. The remnants of the Creole literary circle executed a vicious barrage—another, fiercer literary battle—in newspaper columns, published pamphlets, and speeches. This battle over blood, race, and identity occurred at a time when white Southerners were reconciling nationally with their Northern brothers and sisters, while strengthening bonds steeped in the language and theory of white power. During this period, the Creoles, like other ethnic American communities, became white by redefining the word "Creole" to indicate a purely white, Latinate Louisianan.

By the end of the 1890s, the core founders of this white Creole myth were marginalized or dead. As the first generation of Creole writers passed away, they were replaced by a second wave, many of whom, like their leader, Grace King, could not claim a Creole birthright. King became the Creoles' champion par excellence through her short stories, novels, short and long histories and biographies, memoirs, and literary and social criticism, which for the most part glorified the city's and the state's founding families. In her landmark nonfiction work *Creole Families of New Orleans* (1921), King detailed the family trees of the most august Creole lineages, while whitewashing their bloodlines. She too operated within not only the whiteness paradigm but also a cross-national movement that regendered and feminized history and genealogy. King, following the lead of Charles Gayarré and others, cemented the idea of white Creole racial purity, while solidifying the redefinition of New Orleans as a Creole city, built by Creoles and dominated by Creole history, culture, and thought.[12] "Each sphere of life," the cultural philosopher Walter Benjamin wrote, "produced its own tribe of storytellers."[13] And for New Orleans and Louisiana, this storytelling tribe was the Creole circle of writers, a cohort that privileged its own literature over that of other storytellers: black Creoles, Anglo-Americans, and any of the ethnic groups that settled in the city and state during this period.

This essay documents the rise of a white Creole print culture in New Orleans.[14] Bernard de Marigny was among the first of hundreds of Creole Louisianans—mostly men—who composed countless histories, novels, poetic verses, plays, operas, and songs. Along with the numerous newspapers, journals, cultural organizations, and benevolent societies, this print culture enabled New Orleans's white Creole population to imagine itself as a unified community of readers. These Creole intellectuals attended the same salons and clubs. They called one another friend, traveled abroad together, and often wrote one another letters. They positively reviewed one another's books and prepared one another's obituaries. Readers of Louisiana literature today rarely dip into the Creole canon; only a handful of the authors and books even remain in print. But their ideologies, arguably, have filtered through most subsequent literary representations of Louisiana and New Orleans, fiction and nonfiction alike.

As this circle of white Creole intellectuals created their Creole personas in print, they changed the way Americans think of the geographical space that is Louisiana, but especially urban New Orleans, in three ways. First, the

Creoles promoted the idea that their city and state were exceptional. From the state's soil and its river to the city's and the Creoles' history, almost everything about New Orleans, Louisiana, and the Creoles was singular. Second, the Creoles not only claimed an intimate connection to their motherland, France, but, relying on memories of the past, maintained that they were the true inheritors of Francophone blood, language, and culture. Third, they petitioned for the right to be citizens of the United States, while at the same time advocating the idea that they were uncommon Americans. For the white Creoles, biculturalism begat a wholly mythologized exceptionalism.

Occasioned by postcolonial thought, the spread and popularization of new print media forms, and an influx of Francophones from Saint-Domingue and France, this Louisiana Creole print culture had a nationalizing effect. Creoles, through writing and reading, created a bifurcated identity, that of Louisiana Creoles of French and/or Spanish blood and American citizens of the United States. They endeavored to build a vital French-language print community at home, yet they still wished to be incorporated into the nation. In many aspects, their lives bridged two worlds. Many had been educated in France, especially Paris, and in the northern United States. Cultured and bilingual, they spoke and wrote in French and English (and occasionally Spanish, Italian, and/or German). They worshipped at the altar of both Napoleon Bonaparte, who had authorized the sale of their city to the United States in 1803, and President Andrew Jackson, who had masterminded the city's salvation during the Battle of New Orleans a dozen years later. I argue that as the Creoles created Creole and American identities simultaneously, they became more cultural and socially creolized.[15]

This print-based community mirrored other postcolonial creolized peoples in its causes and effects. Marigny's adoption of the sobriquet Un Créole exhibited the first stirrings of a bifurcated Old World–New World sensibility, an identity shift historians working in colonial Latin America today have termed a Creole consciousness.[16] Combating Old World inhabitants' pretensions that individuals born across the ocean were lesser than themselves, elite Creoles, both white and black, throughout the Americas eventually declared their locales to be "the center of human civilization and the highest peak of New World religiosity."[17] Creole nationalist movements sprang up throughout the postcolonial Atlantic world, and New Orleans was no exception. Like Marigny, postcolonial Creoles across the Americas appropriated the identity signifier "Creole," a word that before had implied a "Eurocentric disdain."[18] "Lettered creoles . . . responded time and again to [their] marginalization," the literary scholars Ralph Bauer and José Antonio Mazzotti aptly suggest, "producing numerous pages of their own dedicated to exalting the character and appearance of the distinguished descendants of the conquerors." That is, Creoles performed new identities.[19] Bauer and Mazzotti continue, "These creole intellectuals carried out the immense task of creating a discursive corpus to articulate their own conception" of a communal Creole identity.[20] Creole literatures became the "watchword of nationalistic movements."[21]

The white Creoles of New Orleans and Louisiana were no different. They were an intermediary people, simultaneously American and French, who defined themselves culturally, racially, and socially in contrast to Anglo-Americans and Creoles of color. The white Creole print culture additionally sought to redefine and broaden the word "Creole" from its original use as an identity descriptor. Throughout the nineteenth century, this Creole community endeavored to define Creole in the abstract. Creole became an idea to shape Louisiana's past, a conception indicating social and cultural exceptionality in the present, and a birthright conferring dominion over New Orleans's future. These white Creoles wrote themselves to shape Creole identities, while rewriting New Orleans to fashion the Creole city.

The roots of the Creole city began and ended with Charles Gayarré, who launched his career as the godfather of New Orleans and Louisiana history on an early spring evening in 1847, with a speech that would define the white Creoles' literary project for the next century, while, arguably, laying the cornerstone for the city and state's mythos of exceptionality.

His speech could be boiled down to a single phrase embedded within it: "The history of Louisiana is eminently poetical."[22] As those words reverberated within the brick walls of the Methodist church, the members in the audience undoubtedly nodded in agreement and satisfaction. In New Orleans, history at times must have seemed quite poetic. Anyone over the age of forty-five would have remembered living under the flag of three empires, a seemingly impossible victory battle in Chalmette just outside the city's perimeter, breathtaking population growth, a municipality split in three due to political and ethnic squabbles, and the decennial ebb and flow of yellow fever wasting the city's populace. Life in antebellum Louisiana might certainly have contained a romantic poeticism for many of its most privileged citizens, while the extraordinariness of New Orleans in the late Jacksonian era was unquestionable. Though Charles Gayarré's speech that evening involved a histrionic retelling of history, his portrayal of his city and state rang true.

New Orleans, so the myth goes, is a place that infamously works despite itself, but the city of the 1840s especially could be described as a study in contradiction and cooperation. This was harmonious chaos. That evening's elocutionist could claim impeccable credentials as one of the crème de la crème of Creole society; his maternal and paternal grandfathers had been among, respectively, the French and Spanish founding fathers of colonial Louisiana. Gayarré's life was a study in contrasts. Always flaunting his Latinate roots, at different times he identified as a Creole, a Southerner, and an American. And though an elegant, if bathetic, composer of French prose, on this night he lectured in English.

The New Methodist Church, perched on the uptown-river corner of Poydras and Carondelet, sat in the center of the American sector, just one block behind Lafayette Square, the Americans' public park and political and commercial center.[23] Largely because of European immigration, the city's population had more than doubled in the past decade. In 1836 the competing Creole and American factions that struggled to control the city acquiesced to the seemingly uncontrollable "pattern[s] of segregation," due to the population explosion, and divided the city into three self-governing municipalities.[24] The trio comprised the French quarter, the American sector, and the downriver neighborhoods—basically the Faubourg Marigny—which harbored many of the tens of thousands of Germans and Irish that poured into antebellum New Orleans, along with many white Creoles and Afro-Creoles.

A simultaneous economic boom produced dollar amounts that one historian perspicaciously described as "mind-boggling."[25] These dollars would be generated by the Crescent City's river port, one of the first New World global markets; its outlying cotton- and sugar-plantation system; and North America's largest slave market.[26] One Alabama visitor speculated in 1847 that within a century the city would "reach out her arms and encompass within her limits every town and hamlet for miles around. It will then all be New Orleans, the largest city on the continent of America, and perhaps in the world."[27]

New Orleans deserved an exceptional history, and the Creole Charles Gayarré sought to write those pages. He dismissed this first of four lectures titled "The Poetry, or the Romance of the History of Louisiana," as a "trifling production, the offspring of an hour's thought."[28] But his first speech at the Methodist church, a free event held on March 26, 1847, proved so popular that the People's Lyceum, that night's sponsors, invited Gayarré to deliver three future lectures. His mythic telling of Louisiana's history, this weaving together of "the legendary, the romantic, the traditional, and the strictly historical elements," struck a chord not just with New Orleanians but, because of the eventual publication of his lectures, with a vast Southern and national audience.[29] Firmly influenced by the Scottish author Sir Walter Scott, whose romanticized historical novels he praised as "fascinating" and "immortal," Gayarré considered himself both a historian and a romanticist.[30] In his preface to the four lectures, first collected under the title *Romance of the History of Louisiana*, he admitted to "embellish[ing]" and making "attractive" historical events.[31] By mixing historical objectivity with the subjectivity of the poetic storyteller's pen, he set Louisiana's history, in his words, "in a glittering frame."[32] Gayarré was not the first to frame Louisiana with an ornamental gilding. Years before the settlement of New Orleans, promoters had sold the French Louisiana province to prospective settlers as "the Paradise of America" and "one of the finest Countries in the World."[33] And more than a century later, antebellum commentators painted New Orleans as the "stately Southern Queen."[34]

Gayarré believed that Louisiana's past oozed exceptionality. Literally. "There is poetry in the very foundation of this extraordinary land!" he roared in the opening minutes of his first lecture.[35] This intangible poetic property pervaded everything—the place, the past, and the people—to make Louisiana special. In a trilogy of histories, Gayarré mined the soil of Louisiana's past to cultivate a local literary landscape, a true Creole terroir.[36]

Gayarré's literary project developed at the tail end of the age of print, an early republic and antebellum era when Americans "fashioned a distinctive literature and culture" through numerous print media.[37] The ascent of a Louisiana literature mirrored the rise of similar, fragmented local print-culture communities throughout the United States, each fostered with the right combination of readers, authors, and printers.[38] In his influential study *The Order of Books*, the French historian of the book Roger Chartier characterizes this triangular relationship between writers, their audience, and the technology needed to produce books as the "three poles" necessary to construct "a history of reading."[39] One such community was located in Richmond, Virginia, where the *Southern Literary Messenger*'s first issue, released in 1834, encouraged the South to "build ... up a character of our own, and provid[e] the means of embodying and concentrating the neglected genius of our country" through the spilling of ink on paper.[40] Gayarré likewise urged the cultivation of a homegrown republic of letters, a culture he likened to immortality. "Literature," he wrote, "is the manifestation of how much soul there is in a social body; and those nations which have been without a literature, whatever of power and material wealth they may have obtained, have been nothing but corpses floating like dead logs on the stream of history."[41]

Though he was hardly the first Louisianan to publish, Charles Gayarré should be considered the founding father of the state's literature. By peering into the past and breathing life into local memory and myth, Gayarré birthed a New Orleans–based print-culture community. He was the first to chronicle the history of his people. Issued in French and printed locally, the *Essai historique sur la Louisiane* (1830–31) and the two-volume *Histoire de la Louisiane* (1846–47) provided Francophone Louisianans with a shared written history. His *Romance of the History of Louisiana*, later included in his magisterial, four-volume *History of Louisiana* (1854–66), romanticized and mythologized the place's and the people's past.[42] Written in English and published in New York City, this second round of histories not only found local and national success but changed the way Creoles and Americans, citizens of Louisiana and the world, thought about New Orleans.

Gayarré's *Romance* lectures chronicled the history of Louisiana before the settlement of New Orleans, from the pre-European "primitive state of the country" to De Soto's 1539 expedition to the financier Antoine Crozat's investment in the failing French colony (1713–17).[43] He focused solely on the lives of the great men who founded New Orleans—kings, explorers, soldiers, and priests. Covering nearly two centuries of history, Gayarré often spent pages dramatizing the most insignificant events in Louisiana's development, while occasionally glossing over more meaningful developments. The historian also played fast and loose with historical facts. In his defense, he acknowledged his saccharine writing style, the fabulist tales, and excessive subjectivity. In a preface to the collected lectures, Gayarré denied that he had disfigured history through "inappropriate invention," while admitting that his "artful preparation honies the cup of useful knowledge, and makes it acceptable to the lips of the multitude."[44] Written in English, printed by major New York publishing houses (D. Appleton and Company in 1848 and Harper and Brothers in 1851), and riding the wave of popular history, the Creole historian's lectures brought embellished scenes from Louisiana's past to the widest audience possible.[45]

Gayarré's popular histories, like those of his contemporaries George Bancroft and Evert Duyckinck, were written "in the shadow of eighteenth-century tastes."[46] The literary precursors who influenced European romanticists like Walter Scott continued to sway his ideals and shape his prose, as they did those of so many American readers and writers of the era. The United States remained under the spell of what Mark Twain, traveling in New Orleans, deemed the "Sir Walter disease." This epidemic craze for the Scotsman's romanticized historical novels generated a chivalric cult that "had so large a hand in making southern character," according to Twain, that it was "in great measure responsible for the [Civil War]." Twain exaggerated, as he so often did, calling his diagnosis a "wild proposition."[47] But literary critics have since blamed Scott for stoking the fires of a Southern visionary embrace of "a world that never was: a world of a White southern gentility and aristocracy, built on the backs of a vile and brutish institution that they would wish into the margins."[48]

Pre-Enlightenment masters such as Homer, Dante, the Bard, Cervantes, and Spenser also filled Gayarré's Louisiana chronicle, which he compared to "an Odyssey of woes" and "a Shaksperian [sic] mixture."[49] But he did not just look across the Atlantic and deep into antiquity for inspiration. The stories contained in the lectures could "grace the pages" of James Fenimore Cooper's *Leatherstocking Tales*. Moreover, according to Gayarré, the authentic characters and real incidents from Louisiana history superseded the creations of Washington Irving's imagination.[50] The Creole historian endeavored to situate his birthplace on the same literary plane as Scott's Scotland, Cooper's early American frontier, and Shakespeare's world. Louisiana's past and place, like those of these more famous authors, provided "what materials for romance!"[51]

And what romantic materials Louisiana bestowed upon Gayarré for his first lecture! Her annals constituted "a rich mine, where lies in profusion the purest ore of poetry ... forming an uninterrupted vein through the whole history."[52] Poetry permeated all. There was poetry in "the forests" and poetry in the "landscape," poetry in the "barbaric manners, laws, and wars" of the first American peoples and poetry in the "mysterious migrations ... of human transformations." A future rhapsodist might write "heroic poems" because who, according to the author, "could sit under yonder gigantic oak, the growth of a thousand years" and not have his or her "whole soul glowing with poetical emotions." (It should be noted that these examples are all found on a single page.)[53] From its soil, its climate, and its environment to the people who trod its ground, Louisiana radiated distinctiveness. Early European discoverers found themselves in paradise, "the most magnificent country in the world," Eden at the end of the Mississippi valley, the landscape for a Creole terroir.[54]

Placed on a pedestal and distinguished from the wider world, Gayarré's Louisiana was exceptional, but it still had a place within the United States.

Louisiana might outshine all the other states in the American firmament, but it could rightly call itself one of them. Gayarré's native state assumed the form of the "star which has sprung from her forehead to enrich the American constellation."[55] Gayarré further traced Louisiana's ties with the United States to before the 1803 transfer, deeper into an imagined past. He fantasized that despite their French origins, the first New Orleanians might have looked high into the sky in 1718 and observed "the American eagle . . . towering with repeated gyrations, and uttering loud shrieks which sounded like tones of command."[56] Louisiana and the United States shared a common destiny: the former inevitably would "fall into the motherly lap" of the latter, and the future unraveled to ensure that this destiny would hold true.[57]

Louisiana under France and the United States embodied two temporal poles. In one poignant passage, Gayarré wrote of visiting a crumbling fort near Biloxi, one of the original, pre–New Orleans, French Mississippi River valley settlements. Through a clearing in the overgrowth, just to the right of this primordial site, Gayarré spied "a beautiful villa, occupied by an Anglo American family, . . . replete with all the comforts and resources of modern civilization." On the opposite side of the fort stood a remnant of the French era, "a rude hut, where still reside descendants from the first settlers, living in primitive ignorance and irreclaimable poverty." Close enough to walk over and shake hands, the French and American families were separated by the "immense distance" of history, the gulf of time that both connected and cleaved the past and the present.[58]

As works of history, Gayarré's lectures were suspect. He filled his speeches with "legend and fancy designed to amuse his readers," according to one historian.[59] His second address began with a nautical showdown between the French and English navies, an event that, if read literally, he himself witnessed. Gayarré described watching Iberville, the French Canadian explorer, proudly standing on deck, staring down the enemy forces: "What a noble face! I see the peculiar expression which has settled in that man's eye, in front of such dangers thickening upon him! . . . By heaven! a tear! I saw it."[60]

Gayarré not only romanticized history and placed himself in the narrative as a witness but also distorted facts, knowingly and admittedly misrepresenting reality. Concerning one particularly embellished passage detailing the countenance of the future Louisiana governor Antoine de La Mothe-Cadillac ("His ponderous wig, the curls of which spread like a peacock's tail," "His eyes . . . possessed with a stare of astonishment," etc.), Gayarré confessed to another historian decades later that he had "somewhat fancifully sketched his personal appearance," of which he had known "nothing historical."[61]

But the Cadillac episode cannot compare in artistic enhancement to Gayarré's treatment of the life and career of Antoine Crozat (ca. 1655–1738), a story that ends the fourth and final People's Lyceum lecture. Gayarré repeated the ludicrous legend that Crozat, the proprietary owner of French Louisiana, invested in the French experiment to enable his daughter to marry a duke. After canceling his charter for the floundering colony, Crozat watched as his daughter, Andrea, in anguish because of her unfulfilled love, perished in the most melodramatic fashion. Then he dropped dead from grief. Certainly the historian desired to end his lecture series in dramatic style, privileging fancy over fact. It makes for a distressing but hardly disastrous inclusion, until one reads the only footnote contained in the volume of lectures. Included by Gayarré, the addendum explains that Andrea Crozat's real name was Marie Anne and that she in fact wed her love, the Comte D'Evreux. Gayarré apologizes for "having slightly deviated from historical truth" and blames the name switch on a "capricious whim" and "some spell in the name of Andrea."[62]

Contemporary readers would have been used to this melodramatic illumination of history, but Gayarré's theatrical flights stretched critics' patience to the breaking point. One reviewer, a close friend, cautiously called *Romance of the History of Louisiana* "a very poetic, graphic and attractive production" but hardly a "legitimate history."[63] A critic for the *Southern Literary Messenger* was less kind, writing, "The work of Mr. Gayarré is a pleasing romance of history, which will always find readers. Its pages glow with a poet's imagination . . . but it is not history. It may therefore be doubted whether this volume, so ambitious in style, so redolent in invention, will create the same interest that was accorded to his first work in French."[64]

Throughout his writings, Gayarré scattered encouragements to other Louisiana artists to follow his lead: one missionary's forest sanctuary, where the Tunica tribe gathered for Mass, would make "a beautiful subject for painting!" "An American audience" would clamor to see the adventure-filled life of Louis Juchereau de St. Denis, an early explorer of Louisiana, presented "on the stage." A bizarre love triangle involving Bienville, Cadillac, and the latter's daughter should be captured by "a novel-writer" because "what fact or transaction, commonplace as it would appear anywhere else . . . , does not, when connected with Louisiana, assume a romantic form and shape?"[65]

Gayarré continued to write histories large and small into his ninetieth year. Borrowing from the works of the Creole godfather of Louisiana history and literature became commonplace, expected even. Nearly every Louisiana writer, not just French Creoles, acknowledged their debt to Gayarré. For more than a century and a half, historians have continued to read and reference Gayarré's *History of Louisiana*. One historiographer laureled Gayarré with a weighty and contestable title, calling him "the greatest historian of the Old South."[66] Professional and amateur scholars alike still find his works "useful and entertaining," to quote the most recent historian of New Orleans.[67] The Creole historian also inspired writers of fiction. Just a year after the publication of Gayarré's *Romance of the History of Louisiana*, the French émigré turned Louisianan Charles Testut planned a series of drama-laced novels that traced the region's past. The series was designated simply *Les Veillées Louisianaises, série de romans historiques sur la Louisiane* (Louisiana evenings: A series of historical novels about Louisiana). The first of two volumes in the series (both issued in 1849) collected four tales of Louisiana historical fiction, including Louis-Armand Garreau's Louisiana and Testut's own Saint-Denis.[68] Both novelists borrowed heavily from Gayarré, at times copying whole pages from his histories.[69]

In 1836 Thomas Wharton Collens published one of the first dramatizations of Louisiana history. His five-act tragedy, *The Martyr Patriots; or, Louisiana in 1769*, romanticized the French Creole and German rebellion against the territorial handover to the Spanish government and the state-sponsored execution of the conspirators that followed.[70] Staged at the St. Charles Theatre, Collens's play likely prompted three later French-language portrayals of the same historical episode.[71] In April 1836 the budding playwright, just twenty-three years old, penned Gayarré a fan letter to profess the influence the historian's first effort had had on him. For Collens, Gayarré's life and work exhibited a dualistic quality: an essence of locality imbued and matched with a patriotic allegiance to the nation:

> You have by the publication of your Historical Essay [*Essai historique sur la Louisiane*] done more than any other man to inspire a love of Country, and an attachment to our free institutions to the youth of Louisiana. You have shown that even the infant state to which they belong has heroes and glorious deeds to boast of; and that the union of Louisiana with a republican nation was one of the greatest blessings that could befall her and her children. . . . The enclosed dramatic composition is the result of the vivid impressions left upon my mind by your historical essay. To whom can I dedicate my work rather than to you?[72]

Gayarré had fulfilled his promise to procure the higher branches of literature for his state and its people by laying the foundations of a Creole print terroir. By promoting and popularizing the poetry allegedly inherent in New

Orleans, Louisiana, and their Creole peoples, Gayarré influenced how the city, the state, and the people have been written and read ever since.

Notes

1 Marigny 1853, 3, emphasis in original.
2 For biographical information on Marigny, I consulted the following: Marigny 1853; Tinker 1932, 299–327; Tinker 1933.
3 Gayarré 1888, 890.
4 Gayarré 1888, 891. On Mazureau, see also Tinker 1932, 344–50.
5 Pierson (1938) 1996, 625.
6 Pierson (1938) 1996, 627–28.
7 Marigny 1827, 22, translation mine.
8 Dessens 2007, 19.
9 Saxon 1988, 169, 188.
10 Ebeyer 1944, 153.
11 Tallant 1950, 12.
12 In contrast to other scholars, I trace the foundations of the creation, or mythologizing, of New Orleans to an earlier era and give credit to another group of ideological pioneers. For contrasting views, see Starr 2001; Souther 2006; Stanonis 2006.
13 Benjamin, Arendt, and Zohn 1968, 85.
14 For a fuller account of the rise, crest, and fall of this Creole print culture, see Fertel 2014. This essay draws upon the introduction and first chapter of that book.
15 Nick Spitzer defines cultural creolization as the formation and development of "new traditions, aesthetics, and group identities out of combinations of formerly separate peoples and cultures," but not without an embedded and intrinsic "tension between traditional and transformed," between the old and the new (2003, 58–59.)
16 Brading 1991, 343–61; Bauer and Mazzotti 2009, 25–32.
17 Bauer and Mazzotti 2009, 26.
18 Bauer and Mazzotti 2009, 27.
19 Bauer and Mazzotti 2009, 27.
20 Bauer and Mazzotti 2009, 27.
21 Allen 2002, 52.
22 Gayarré (1854) 1974, 11.
23 Wilson, Christovich, and Toledano 1971, 27–28.
24 The urban historian Mary Ryan (1997, 35) describes New Orleans as "the most obvious, distinct, and actually de jure" city in a period of urban American social segmentation.
25 Kelman 2006, 62.
26 W. Johnson 1999, 1–2; Kelman 2006, 62–63.
27 Pickett 1847, 18.
28 Gayarré 1848, 11.
29 Gayarré (1854) 1974, 8
30 Gayarré (1854) 1974, 7.
31 Gayarré (1854) 1974, 9–186.

32 Gayarré (1854) 1974, 16.

33 Gomez 2006, 55, 58.

34 Barber and Barber 1850, 178.

35 Gayarré (1854) 1974, 14.

36 Gayarré expressed a similar idea in the following line: "The fertility of the brain should correspond with that of the soil" (1890, 342).

37 Gross and Kelley 2010, 4.

38 Loughran 2007.

39 Chartier (1994, 1–23) classifies the three poles as the "technological, formal, and cultural."

40 Heath 1834, 2; Gross and Kelley 2010, 13.

41 Gayarré 1890, 338.

42 One biographer characterized Gayarré's switch as being from "dry scholarship . . . to the other extreme—popularization" (Uzée 1943, 123).

43 Gayarré (1854) 1974, 9.

44 Gayarré (1854) 1974, 7.

45 Also, the English language had since gained ground over French. Gayarré much later acknowledged that "nobody in Louisiana who has mastered the language of Shakespeare and Milton, of Prescott and Longfellow, will henceforth resort to any other in writing a book." Gayarré 1890, 335.

46 O'Brien 2004, 593.

47 Twain 1883, 468–69.

48 Horton 2007.

49 Gayarré (1854) 1974, 20, 86.

50 Gayarré (1854) 1974, quotation on 26, comment about Irving on 128.

51 Gayarré (1854) 1974, 15.

52 Gayarré (1854) 1974, 29.

53 Gayarré (1854) 1974, 13.

54 Gayarré (1854) 1974, 39.

55 Gayarré (1854) 1974, 11.

56 Gayarré (1854) 1974, 235.

57 Gayarré (1854) 1974, 496.

58 Gayarré (1854) 1974, 77–78.

59 Tregle 1999, 46.

60 Gayarré (1854) 1974, 33.

61 Gayarré (1854) 1974, 119.

62 Gayarré (1854) 1974, 107–13, 184–86.

63 De Bow 1852, 383, emphasis in original.

64 S. T. G. 1852, 312.

65 Gayarré (1854) 1974, 60, 173, 134.

66 Eaton 1969.

67 Powell 2012, 401.

68 Testut 1849.

69 Fortier 1915, 15; Caulfield 1998, 25–28, 36, 134.

representational project, presenting the spectator with impossible political options: "You belong, but only in order to not belong," it tells its watcher; "feel both implicated and invited." While clever, such an operation risks using the city's suffering the way that Susan Sontag describes the photographs of war victims—as a "species of rhetoric."[2] Through its rhetorical turns, *Treme* narrates the city's recovery though the alternating tones of a sublime, elegiac ode: measuring funeral dirges as they rise into the celebrations of the second-line parades and then disperse back to desolation.[3] Such sublime narratives of exceptionalism always depend on a material opposition circulating within their own rhetorical routines. Like a wheel within a wheel, the show spins New Orleans's sublime exceptionalism out of the straw of its cultural authenticity—and the maintenance of the entire machine requires the ethnographic hierarchy of insider and outsider that *Treme* perfects.

Cultural authenticity is the unacknowledged and dangerous ally of all the things *Treme* professes to detest.[4] To deflect the dagger of authenticity lurking under the show's cloak, this essay elucidates a politics of inauthenticity out of an unlikely encounter between Lionel Trilling and the Frankfurt School. For Trilling, routine assumptions about culture always contain unconscious and therefore unopposed modes of thought that work to arrange or derange the very values supposed by those assumptions. For instance, Joseph Conrad's *Heart of Darkness* may be "the paradigmatic literary expression of the modern concern with authenticity," but with Conrad's Kurtz as exemplar, modernity makes alienation, destruction, and violence the invisible underpinnings of that authenticity.[5] Swap "literary" for "geographic," novel for city, and what Trilling says of Conrad's Africa could be said today of New Orleans. New Orleans's cultures of authenticity, its exceptionalist myths, too often mask "the reality . . . that post-Katrina New Orleans, as disaster zones go, is thoroughly routine."[6] Even more so, New Orleans's disasters, whether caused by climate or designed by economics, are what authenticate its culture. To interrupt this collusion between authenticity and violence, this essay elaborates the phony politics of New Orleans, exposing how key bearers of the city's mythology have self-consciously positioned their own exceptionalist claims as foreign and fraudulent.

According to Lloyd Pratt, New Orleans has become a crucial site for intellectual realignment. No more can critics counter the rhetoric of the city's exceptionalism by exchanging it with that of the exemplary. The storm of 2005 requires scholars to elaborate a third term of analysis, beyond the poles of exception and example.[7] Pratt forms this polemic in terms of European philosophers of the event, most directly Alain Badiou but also, more distantly,

Martin Heidegger, for whom events elicit new possibilities for subjective and social processes. My wager is this: Katrina's aftermath demands we revitalize a politics of the inauthentic. Following the Frankfurt School, such a politics ends up circling back on the very category of the event that elicited it. Theodor Adorno's attack on the jargon of Heidegger's existentialism displayed how its key terms—event, encounter, originality—directly abetted the marketing logic of industrial culture. My project of inauthenticating New Orleans demands we recognize the identity between destruction and authenticity posited by Trilling, while articulating it through the social critique of Adorno and Benjamin, for whom the culture industry put the mask of authenticity and uniqueness over the routine devastations of everyday life under capitalism. Just as Walter Benjamin saw that authenticity is a property created by the copy (and is therefore not native to the original), the insider, the native, and the original are always concepts complicit in forgery and ironic self-effacement. The ultimate effect of recognizing New Orleans's phony politics is to disrupt the binary between authentic insider and interloping outsider, which have too often defined the logic of its cultural historiography.

To support a renewed politics of inauthenticity, this essay plots several scenes in the literary history of New Orleans. In the main, it considers a modernist set—Jelly Roll Morton and Alan Lomax, Lafcadio Hearn, and Kate Chopin—sketched through the years 1878–1950. These readings bring me into conversation with the literary histories of New Orleans defined by Barbara Eckstein and Violet Bryan. In considering the claims for New Orleans's exceptionalism, Eckstein asks us to consider whose interests those claims serve. She notes that efforts to preserve the unique culture of the city have made it the "model for the commodified US city."[8] For Eckstein, the stories people tell about the city's exceptionalism are always interventions into the city's relationship with industrial capital and the "media of modern (national) society" that surround and pervade it.[9] Likewise, Violet Bryan accounts for the ways in which authors tampered with the mythology of New Orleans, and how their horizon for doing so was delimited by the historical conditions of race and gender. My thesis of the city's self-creation bends these latter categories around one central question of technological modernity: the ontological impact of mechanical reproduction. To consider the impact of reproduction on a human's authentic relationship to place, the essay finally returns to *Treme*, a TV show that cites its own cultural history of the city. Bracketing these two moments in the city's self-narrative— one modernist, one contemporary—allows me to test the historical and contemporary grounds for the following hypothesis: that the city's most important contribution to intellectual life is not as example (of authentic folkway or model city), nor as exception (to national culture), but as an event for thinking the inauthentic.

Let us begin with the primary problem of copying and recording. In his famous essay on photography, Benjamin writes that the creation of the copy and the subsequent "presence of the original is the prerequisite to the concept of authenticity." The split between the original and copy, in other words, produces authenticity ex post facto, thereafter allowing for its "differentiating and grading."[10] Though Benjamin's essay describes the effects of photographic reproduction, much of what he says applies, mutatis mutandis, to phonographic reproduction, something central to the inauthenticity of New Orleans's modernist inception.

In 1938 Alan Lomax interviewed and recorded the jazz composer Jelly Roll Morton at the Library of Congress. It is difficult to characterize the recordings. They are part collaboration, part interrogation. John Szwed calls them a "performed biography."[11] More complicated still is *Mister Jelly Roll*, a 1950 book that cuts up Lomax's reminiscences with the transcripts of Morton's testimonies and assorted interviews Lomax recorded after Morton's in order to mythologize him as the New Orleans Creole who invented jazz. When Lomax began that 1938 recording, he could not help but unleash a world of prejudice. Alexander Weheliye has argued that the entirety of Western modernity depended on the creation, arrangement, and recording of "sonic blackness."[12] In Morton, Lomax found a flat contradiction to what he supposed was authentic sonic blackness. With his "expensive summer straw" hat, flash diamond studs, and smooth Lincoln town car, Morton did not look earthy or real.[13] An openhearted pacifist, he served no cocktail of prison callousness and legitness that Alan Lomax and his father John had savored in rural blues of Son House or the bad-man ballads of Huddie Ledbetter. In John Lomax's account of ballad hunting with his son, he admitted to looking for "genuine Negro" songs, sung by incarcerated black men who were able to "slough off the white idiom," showing their true sonic colors. The son of a slave owner, John Lomax confessed to listening for the "tom-toms of savage blacks" in the American South.[14]

Alan betrays a similar prejudice in his recording of Morton, whose urbanity, wit, and style make him a dubious source of genuine American folklore. Lomax's interview repeatedly turns to race and sexuality to authenticate Morton's past. He leans hard on the questions, "Was he colored?" and "Was he a sissy?" Morton repeatedly resists Lomax's attempts at excavating sexual curiosities, at placing realness in the shallows of identity. At one point, when asked if Tony Jackson was a "fairy," Morton shoots back, "He was either a steamboat or a ferry"—either way it was five cents for a ride. When asked if musicians at the Frenchman's, where Morton says jazz was born, were "white and colored both," Morton pulls Lomax's black-white dichotomy apart, answering that there were all "classes" present: "millionaires and hustlers, Spanish, colored, white, Frenchmen and Americans."[15] Lomax's racializing interrogation operates according to the logic Weheliye describes, where "the white subject's vocal apparatus merely serves to repeat and solidify racial difference... calling attention to how whiteness [needs] blackness in order to appear... much in the same way 'the original' is framed in the phonographic."[16]

The Greek *authenteo* means "to have full power over." The noun form, *authentes,* describes "not only a master and doer, but also a perpetrator, a murderer."[17] As it copied the voice of jazz's inventor, Lomax's device literarily cut a historical record, but figuratively it carved the concept of authenticity into a subject of sonic blackness it sought to invent. As I have argued elsewhere, media modernity lays bare race as an aesthetic technology, misused everywhere it is used.[18] The ability to arrange blackness and whiteness, original and copy, into a cluster of related concerns sets them under the general rubric of "authenticity," a word for colonizing. The Lomaxes' obsession with authenticity reanimates the connotations of power, mastery, and violence that lurk in the word's unconscious. The resisting Morton replies with confabulation, saying, "all my folks came directly from the shores... not the shores, I mean from France, that is across the world, in another world, and they landed in the new world years ago." Unsatisfied, Lomax asks of Morton's grandparents, "Were they all slaves?" Morton pushes back again, parrying Lomax's authenticity probe: "I don't think they had no slaves back then in Louisiana."[19] As part of what John Szwed calls "the first ethnography of community aesthetics," Lomax's vision of New Orleans's aesthetic project—jazz—relies on creolization's racial, geographic, linguistic, and class complexity, but it also depends on the reinvention of race as a central technology of the mechanical record.[20] The more Morton evades the line of questioning, the more Lomax insists on the racial authenticity of his native informant.

Morton is clearly more fascinated by his family's lineage outside "American or English," a heritage that mythically bridges the "new world" to the "other world" that is "across the world." Employing an ahistorical politics of inauthentic myth, Morton poses an alternate history of migration to redeem a history that is "way out of line," as he puts it.[21] This resistance to Lomax's authenticating violence signals what I'm calling the inauthentic politics of a phony city. Not to be confused with the aestheticization of politics, which Benjamin considers fascism, rather it constitutes an aspect of that revolutionary socialist practice that brings politics to art, whereby artists resist the authenticating mastery of the society that tries to contain them. In other words, phony politics shape Morton's art of storytelling wherever he blocks the intrusion of Lomax's quest for authenticity, prevents it from stealing the momentum of his narrative act.

A complete example of this phony strategy appears in the extended conversation he and Lomax have about Robert Charles. Charles was a police-shooting resistance figure; a victim of Southern racism and white mob violence, he became the subject of the kind of black folk songs Morton professed the desire to forget.[22] Lomax's excitement about the "bad men" Aaron Harris and Robert Charles is obvious, and Morton humors him. But Morton's performance also destabilizes Lomax's cultural assumptions. Minor chords dwell below the narrative as it builds to the capture of Charles. He ends by saying, "After the riot, there has never been anything of authenticity." Since the tale is punctuated by chords rather than typographical marks, it is hard to say whether a full stop should appear after "authenticity." It is tempting to hear the sentence spill over: "There never has been anything of authenticity . . . where Robert Charles had been captured."[23] This would imply that the death of Robert Charles brought forth a new stage of inauthenticity for the city, inaugurated about the day jazz was born.

At the very moment he implies all authenticity died with Charles, Morton explodes into a rollicking version of "Game Kid Blues." The emergence of this stomp from the preceding narrative repositions the meaning of the former's violence. The album's song title—"The 1900 New Orleans Riot Pt. 2 & the Game Kid Blues Pt. 1"—speaks to the rupture. "Game Kid," we are told by Morton, was a favorite in the Garden District where white supremacists terrorized the city's cosmopolitan streetcars. In many of the editorial rearrangements that Lomax's book makes, the arrival of "Game Kid" is totally shorn from the context of the riot. In the recording, minor chords underlie Charles's story, making "Game Kid" a major resolution. Meanwhile, the lyrics offer escape through quiet contemplation:

> I could sit right here, and think a thousand miles away
> Yes, I could sit right here and think a thousand miles away,
> I got the blues so bad I cannot remember the day . . .

Once "Game Kid" appears, Morton escapes into another self, a thousand miles away. The striving of musical memory releases him from the site of authenticity's demise, the site of Robert Charles's murder, but also transports him to a place where depression wipes the calendar of history clean.

According to the *Oxford English Dictionary*, "phony," the slang term for fake, comes not from the root *phon-*, related to sound, but from the process of making "fawney" rings. Made of common metals, like brass, fawnies were coated in gold and passed off as the real McCoy. A "fawney-dropper" would pretend to find the ring in front of a mark who would pay less than the ring's gold value but far more than its brass. Even though the word "phony" actually derives from this scam, the spelling normalized around "phon-" in 1893, precisely the time phonographs became more affordable and ubiquitous in America and England. Just as "fawney" became "phony," it also became generalized—in Clarence Cullen's American "hard-luck stories" of 1903—as a word for a fake.[24] Not much later, people too became phonies. In his existential brooding, Holden Caulfield would make the notion laughably common, but George Ade's "Fable of the Cruel Insult" is one of the first stories to suggest that the whole of social relations, including speech and emotion, could be phony. This new sense of phony, and the "phonetic" spelling of the word, emerge amid the common, turn-of-the-century obsession—shared by Ade, Cullen, the Lomaxes—with recording colloquial dialect. Unlike Ade, the Lomaxes make the mistake *Treme* does: of lauding sincerity at the expense of the fake. The tensions between a true original and false copy implied by mimetic machines shed light on the "way literary texts have taken up" the "circulating claims" of New Orleans exceptionalism. As Barbara Eckstein indicates, narratives of exceptionalism are best judged according to what work they do, what truths they purport, whose interests they serve. Similarly, Violet Bryan has described New Orleans culture in terms of various overlapping ideological programs, where the language of its mythology can be appropriated to represent poetic truths.[25]

Authenticity is one such ideological program, and a clear example of its mythic repurposing comes through a story about Lafcadio Hearn. In the months after Katrina, tourist shops in the Quarter began selling jewelry engraved with his remark that it was better to live "in sackcloth and ashes" in New Orleans than to own all of Ohio.[26] Following Eckstein, one must ask what this repackaging of New Orleans mythology does. Clearly it allows tourist shoppers the chance to valorize the city's want—while serving the city's merchants—but to what degree does it actually capture the purported truth of Hearn's vision of New Orleans commercial life? Just as the preservation of New Orleans's architecture made it a model commercial city, it also makes it an example of the commercial circuits where the old is sold as the new, the false as the real, the copy and remix as one and the same.

Hearn came to New Orleans around the same time Edison demonstrated the first phonographic recording, and his stories privilege the ambiguity of sonic and visual reproduction, the literary indistinctness between copy and original. One of his first stories—"The City of the South"—instigates a disagreement between the grammar of exceptionalism and the grammar of representation. Is New Orleans representative—"*the* city of the South," standing for the entire "fair paradise" of "Sugar Country"; or is it the *city* of the South, an urbanized exception within the agrarian subtropics? He leaves both options open, admitting the fact that the city "resembles no other" yet "recalls" a hundred others. Its "peculiar characteristic" of familiarity charms the visitor as much as the city's "tropical beauty."[27] Leading to an obsession with the city's ghosts and esoterica, Hearn takes New Orleans as Freud's *unheimlich* before the fact, an uncanny place associated with dream, premonition, and deja vu. What haunts him is its commercial habits and aesthetic repetitions, not its strangeness.

Elsewhere Hearn draws the city as if it were a well-kept flower of the late Renaissance. The modern dress of the "comely Creole" woman is imagined as worn by the love goddess Cythera, a romantic island lover favored by Venus and painted beguilingly by Jean-Antoine Watteau. The "opaline skin" and graceful figures of New Orleans women conjure "the flushed bronze" of statuary. In passing they leave "the breath of orange flowers." One is reminded of Pater's *History of the Renaissance* as the sense-struck Hearn "dreams of Titian and Veronese and Tintoretto" (15). Hearn's sense of New Orleans is peculiar not for its exceptionalism but for its conviction that Louisiana is the culmination of something, a visual and sensual figure preceded by hundreds of other figures of pre-Raphaelite sensuality.

Hearn consistently fashions the city according to the "secular cult of beauty" that Benjamin sees being eroded by mechanical reproduction.[28] Art history helps familiarize New Orleans, turning it from a site of originality to a field of citation. Nodding to Homer, he calls its carnivalesque nights "wine-colored." Like Thomas Cole's depiction of *Desolation* in his *Course of Empire*, Hearn finds the "moldering" decay of New Orleans to be "luxuriantly romantic" as it reminds him of the "warm pictures of the *Decameron*." The streets don masks in "artificial picturesqueness." He even invents the unlikely descriptor "Rembrandtesqueness" to judge the city's inauthentic Renaissance aesthetics (42–49). As Benjamin writes, "A medieval picture of the Madonna could not yet be said to be 'authentic.' It became 'authentic' only during the succeeding centuries and probably most strikingly so during the last one."[29] The logic of the phonographic age helped Hearn produce New Orleans as a fake, a late-Renaissance copy erupting within the historical cult of the picturesque.

This image of New Orleans as artificial copy cuts against the common view, espoused by Frederick Starr, that Hearn—as a journalist ethnographer attentive to native informants—mythologized as an authentic New Orleans "in the moments before its demise."[30] This version of Hearn's reputation has everything to do with him as a cultist of creolization, a perspective well presented by Valérie Loichot's essay "*Créolité* Nineteenth Century Style: Lafcadio Hearn's Vision" as well as Bill Hardwig's account of his "wooing the Muse of the Odd," a phrase taken from Hearn's correspondence. In Loichot's view, the celebration of cultural mixing central to the doctrine of créolité reinforces a bioracial logic. The problem forecasts the more proximate one of contemporary multiculturalism, where an exaggerated "praise of diversity" unleashes "a new form of exclusive essentialism" that betrays its own premise.[31] Loichot traces the emergence of this problematic back to Hearn's trip to Martinique, the social dynamics of which prompted his denigration of the pure categories white and black and lionization of mixture. For Hardwig, too, Martinique, not New Orleans, provides the space upon which Hearn's racial fantasy of the Creole is projected.

While both Loichot and Hardwig dwell on Hearn's vision—he was blind in one eye and almost blind in the other—neither of them say much about his ear. Capturing New Orleans in the first year of the phonograph, his sketches become obsessed with the sounds of the city and the growing presence of electric machines in its midst. His piece "The Man with the Electric Machine" opens with a cold sound effect: "Br-r-r-r-r-r-r-r-r-r-r-r-r-r-!!" According to Hearn's impression, the man with the machine is a complete charlatan, taxing the energy of passersby and exploiting the desire to see the body's power gauged scientifically (106). Meanwhile, the electric lights cropping up on the city's West End collect "swarms of flies [like] that [which] afflicted the land of Egypt," as well as a "human crowd" whose likeness to the insect swarm is a "most curious one" (107).

Intrusive telegraph wires cast anxious shadows over his writing, appearing to him as the web of an electric spider. Kites stick to it like "gaudy flies" (136). Whereas the old town callers, among the most beleaguered of the city's workers, deserve public blessing and understanding, the new electrified currents of the city earn Hearn's reproach. To his mind they reduce humans to bugs, unconsciously drawn in swarms to the weblike wonders. The man with the automated piano organ and mechanical puppets mocks the crowd he attracts, "unconscious that they are themselves after all but puppets . . . [beholding] a satire upon themselves" (145–46).

If the circulation of spectators mixes light and dark, the power of the labor market meets Hearn's phonographic ear instead of artistic eye. In "Voices of Dawn," he records how the "first liquid gold of sunrise" carries the "sonorous voices" of peddlers. Vocal advertisements merge into musical announcements, where the "trilling tenor" of the vendors confirms "the active circulation of money." The marketplace becomes a chorus singing the "encouraging sign of prosperity" out loud. In his quest to document the sound of New Orleans's commercial life, Hearn modifies English orthography into a sonographic fidelity. In punctuation and capitalization, he brings the graphemes of English closer to the enunciated patois of the city. The fowl vendor advertises "Chick-EN!" The lemon seller, "Lem-ONS." Apples are "Ap-PULLS." Some sell "Straw-BARE-eries," and the Italian purveyor of oddities lets forth a "thunder clap" offer of "la gniap-PA." Hearn makes use of the wordplay of catachresis, where phonetic soundalikes result in linguistic misuse or misapprehension. An advertisement for "Cheap fans" comes across as "chapped hands." The call of "Tom-ate-toes" leaves the listener wondering: who is Tom? And why did he eat toes? (99).

Playfulness aside, Hearn's representative figure of New Orleans's noise is the Clothespole Man. He tenderly records his forlorn and soulful cry, forecasting the elegiac impulses on display in *Treme*. In "Voices of Dawn," which takes its epigraph from the book of Job ("A dreadful sound is in his ears"), the voice of the Clothespole Man is heard from miles off, quavering, as if breaking through waves: "Clo-ho-ho-ho-ho-ho-ho-ho-se-poles!" (99). He later becomes the subject of his own portrait, the only one of the dawn vendors to be so privileged. His stand-alone story is rendered with biblical importance. The man "goeth out beyond the limits of the city into lonesome and swampy places where copperheads and rattlesnakes abound. And there he cutteth him clothes-poles." The "weird" music of the man's call is a "long and lamentable sobbing cry." So "sorrowful in sooth that the sorrow of the city drowneth the sound and sense of the words" chanted in ancient patois. "And we, listening . . . [dream] of the cries of anguish that arise when a clothesline, heavily burdened with snowy freight, falleth upon the mud" (105). The man's sorrow song is a prompt to empathize with the women whose plight it is to hang the "snowy freight" of linen upon it. Those washerwomen are profiled in another of Hearn's sketches, the most lowly of laborers who struggle to clean the clothes of their masters only to have the clothespoles collapse into the mud.

These sketches juxtapose the images of miserable labor and encouraging prosperity that mingle in the wake of the 1877 cotton crash. Scanning for authenticity, Hearn's ear is drawn to dreadful sounds of human pain, recalling the trajectory of authenticity—from realness to violence—that Trilling traces. Hearn wants to record what suffering bodies sound like rather than what they look like. Loichot, Hardwig, and others who would connect Hearn's name to creolization and color repress the auditory fascination defining his record of New Orleans. Such an omission is, of course, necessary. As Derrida explains, writing is "unthinkable without repression." Any selection, of word or topic, implies the "vigilance of censorship" that erases yet implies any other competing word or topic that might have been selected but was not.[32] Such a principle explains why, in Derrida's reading of Freud, writing, like dream language, becomes an apparatus through which the unconscious functions even while absent. Returning repressed content, Hearn's uncanny New Orleans disgorges familiar images from art history that any exceptionalist account would sideline. To extend Eckstein's insight, the way exceptionalism circulates depends on the strategic repression of countertropes that might turn it against itself. Reading New Orleans's inauthenticity means articulating the repressive apparatus that literature harbors, the violent kinds of unconscious habits, thoughts, and styles that Trilling equates with culture. Authentic culture, in other words, risks becoming a repressive apparatus, narrating the city by essentialization and exclusion—positing the ethnographic informant whom the likes of Hearn and Lomax protect by authenticating.

One of the most important artifacts of New Orleans's mythology must be Kate Chopin's *The Awakening* from 1899. The novel is often read as an expression of existential humanism, and although Sartre and Chopin's names are not typically present in the same sentence, they should be. By grounding existentialism in a feminist humanism, *The Awakening* achieves what *Search for a Method* attempts. Violet Bryan notes that the novel's "textual density" is won through the complex layering of its social codes. The dialectical tensions between white Creole society and the dispossessed classes that serve them surround the book's protagonist and eventually engulf her completely. Increasing the existentialist factor, Edna Pontellier dramatizes Kierkegaard's doctrine of radical inwardness, a Protestant mainstay redesigned to escape the perfidy of commodity relations in late modernity. Edna's extreme inwardness means that the social codes of New Orleans matter only insofar as they illuminate "the growth of her interior, personal voice and vision."[33] Unlike

Hearn and Morton, Chopin presents us with the angst-ridden drama of the modern self, where, as Adorno puts it in his excoriation of existential language, the individual "puffs" itself into "selfness, in the way that the futility of selfness sets itself up as what is authentic, as Being."[34] This complaint is angled at Heidegger, whose concept of being-toward-death makes the encounter with nothingness the grounds upon which the ego positions itself. Of course, Edna's annihilation, in the romantic existentialist reading, equally certifies the value of her being; suicide is a bitterly ironic notary of her emancipation. The concussions of successive awakenings she experiences, which paradoxically put her deeper and deeper to sleep in her self, perfectly underscore the critique Adorno aims at Heidegger, where the inward turn to self demonstrates the futility of self in the face of death.

But like those of Hearn, Morton, and Lomax, Chopin's quest to authenticate literary representation occurs in a media ecology where mechanical reproduction has altered the concept of human value. As much as any denizen of the phony city, she encloses the problem of the self within the relationship between authenticity and technical artifice. "Madame Lebrun was busily engaged at the sewing-machine. A little black girl sat on the floor, and with her hands worked the treadle of the machine. The Creole woman does not take any chances which may be avoided of imperiling her health." Madame Lebrun, the matriarch of Grand Isle, appears here before Edna's subtle judgment. The grammatical shift (from "was" and "sat" to "does") indicates her inwardness as the site for sorting social codes. The "Creole woman" does not chance it with the work the "little black girl" does. Politics slips into form as the racially conscious prose slips toward the stream-of-consciousness narration that would define the modernism of Virginia Woolf. The encounter with implicit social dialogue illuminates Edna's interior, through which any social problem reappears as an aspect of self-identity, that choice variety from the existential garden.

However, as in Hearn's sketches of the cityscape, Chopin's staged encounter between Edna and the Lebruns is drowned in a sound that muffles the would-be dialogue of the encounter: "The sewing-machine made a resounding clatter in the room; it was of a ponderous, by-gone make. In the lulls, Robert and his mother exchanged bits of desultory conversation." In describing the women's typing colleges initiated in the mid-nineteenth century, the media historian Friedrich Kittler compares the sewing machine and typewriter as two gendered technologies defining the transition from nineteenth- to twentieth-century discourse production. At this junction, Chopin's attention to textile production cannot help but raise the issue of textual production, and so the character Robert Lebrun conspicuously "took a book from his pocket and began energetically to read it" next to the sewing machine. He reads with "precision and frequency" amid the clatter of the antiquated equipment. And his conversation with his mother resounds among the resounding clatter of the machinery: "'He says to tell you he will be in Vera Cruz the beginning of next month,'—clatter, clatter!—'and if you still have the intention of joining him'—bang! clatter, clatter, bang!"[35] With phonographic attention, Chopin considered not just the sounds pervading her novelistic spaces but also the impact of the machines that made them. Here the machine's clatter disrupts the "small talk" or "chatter" that Heidegger brilliantly describes in *Being and Time*, while at the same time Robert's reading practices mimic the celerity and regularity of those mechanics.

The Remington rifle company patented the first typing machines in the early nineteenth century, and to Kittler's mind they deserve comparison to a number of contemporaneous innovations in discrete figuration including ragtime, jazz, and automatic weapons. Besting the pen, the typewriter can knock out two or three letters in the time it takes a scribe to dot an *i*. It possesses mechanical celerity that operates not just like jazz but "also like rapid-fire weapons." As Kittler puts it, its "basic action not coincidently consists of strikes and triggers [that proceed] in automated and discrete steps, as does ammunitions transport in a revolver and a machine-gun."[36] It is not unthinkable that the clatter disrupting Edna's social environment is the clatter of a miniature and muted gunfire, foreshadowing the violence of her death (the last hallucination she has while drowning is a barking dog) as well as enforcing the violence of authenticity that technical reproduction advances on the beauty cult of art objects.

Describing how technology is "entrenched in our history," Heidegger supposes that mechanical typing machines made "a handwritten letter . . . an antiquated and undesired thing" since "[orthography] disturbs speed reading."[37] In Chopin's scene, some four decades before Heidegger's essay, Robert reads at the mechanical pace of type, a speed enforced by the clattering machinery of textile production. Not only the girl working the treadles is caught up in the web of machinery, but so too Edna, Robert, and Madame Lebrun appear like Hearn's gaudy flies, trapped by the spider of modernity.

On this landscape of nothingness Edna's self is positioned, primarily as a sleeping heroine. In an important article on the novel as a prototype of the genre of awakenings, Susan Rosowski has described how Chopin's novel remediates fables of femininity like *Sleeping Beauty*. As opposed to the male coming-of-age genre, the bildungsroman, stories of awakening feature women who irrupt into maturity, as if awakening from a dream they had no part in making.[38] Edna wakes from a "delicious, grotesque, impossible dream" (ch. 11) only to turn impossibly inward and "discover many a sunny, sleepy corner, fashioned to dream in. And she found it good to dream and to be alone and unmolested" (chapter 19). The sound of the scene, the sound of the self, the sound of the machine: all resolve into the sound of a spurious dream that stills her life in sleep.

In his extended consideration of the impact of machines on human authenticity, Trilling reads the notebooks of a young Marx and finds the astonishing statement: "Let us assume man to be man, and his relation to the world a human one." Trilling claims that once humans confronted the "anxiety of the machine" it became "necessary to make [Marx's] assumption explicit."[39] The categorization of Marx's humanist and posthumanist phase seems less important than the fact that in the face of industrialization the category of the human requires willful positing. According to Gayatri Spivak, the rise of the bourgeois novel, in which Chopin plays an anomalous part, posits in narrative what Marx did through dialectical reasoning. For Spivak, European novels enforce humanization as individuation. Edna's self-destruction at the close of the novel renounces the individuation project by pushing it to its limit. It signals a strategy of noncontainment that Spivak lauds in Shelley's *Frankenstein*. At the end of that text the monster floats on a block of ice out to sea, "lost in darkness and distance." Not even his self-immolation is contained by the text.[40] At the end of *The Awakening* Edna feels the "terror" of "distance" swimming to her death, but that death is contained in her consciousness, in the auditory hallucination of the barking dog, her parents' voices, the rider's spurs on the porch.[41] Even in self-destruction, the ultimate renunciation of the bourgeois project of individuation, Edna completes a radically inward gesture, the final "puff" of selfness that puffs the self into nothingness, as Adorno might put it, skeptically.

The astonishing gesture of Marx, who says, for the sake of argument, that humanity can be seen as human, returns us to the intellectual impasse of New Orleans. After the event of the storm, Pratt predicted that that "vexed category of apprehension"—the sublime—would vie to become the needed third term of analysis. Indeed, Jennie Lightweis-Goff gives almost textbook enunciation to Edmund Burke's definition of the sublime in her remark on "violence that has always been proximate to the city's pleasures."[42] Vincanne Adams has linked the sublime to charitable economies of affect that "fuel structural relations of inequality in the city."[43] In her postcolonial critique of modern literature, Spivak characterizes Kant's influential doctrine of the sublime as a trope for establishing the category of the rational man over the savage man, the woman, the child, and the illiterate. Setting out to answer the question of why it is pleasurable to think, Kant distinguishes between the natural sublime and the dynamic sublime. Sublime events in nature, such as tremendous storms, produce a secondary experience of dynamic sublimity in those who have exerted the power of reason over the raw sensibility of the event. Such domination of nature allows man to feel the terror of the storm while simultaneously enjoying the pleasure of protection from it. Kant writes, "Without development of moral ideas, that which we, prepared by culture, call sublime presents itself to man in the raw [*dem rohen Menschen*] merely as terrible."[44] The mixed mode of sublimity, where terror and pleasure are one, is not merely foreclosed to "man in the raw" (of whom Kant's example is aboriginal Australians and Native Americans), but it becomes the very line that separates the human (free European men) from the subhuman, since the German word for "raw" also translates into "uneducated"; this term, in Kant's usage, also encompasses women, the poor, and children. A vexed category indeed.[45]

But the event of New Orleans after the storm should no more enchant the concept of the authentic than that of the sublime. In one of Adorno's responses to Benjamin on the concept of the origin and aura, he concurred that originality was a concept that emerged historically, along with the techniques of reproduction, but also stressed that it was by consequence "enmeshed in historical injustice." "Originality," Adorno states, serves the "predominance of bourgeois commodities that must touch up the ever-same as the ever-new in order to win customers." Like Edna's last moment, where she slips into death to defy the individuating powers of the white Creole bourgeoisie, originality remains a vexed category "touched by the historical fate of the category of individualism from which it was derived." Cautioning against converting the exceptional into the typical, Adorno saw in the 1960s that "originality was in the process of being transformed into type, a transformation in which originality is changed qualitatively without however, disappearing in the process."[46] Ten years earlier Alan Lomax had discussed an "original man" as character type. Describing the jazz musician Alphonse Picou, he marked "the naïve and dignified self-absorption that often marks an original man."[47] The same radical inwardness or self-absorption that allows the individual to escape from commodity relations becomes the ultimate exemplification of the commodity's logic. Edna's death defeats the demands of bourgeois individuation by satisfying it through the ultimate inwardness of being-toward-death; the process of becoming an original person obeys the logic of commodities, touching up old violence as new truth and passing it to market as innovation.

The politics of the inauthentic are nothing less than the exposure of this ruse. With Morton and Adorno as militant leaders, the thinkers of the inauthentic refuse to let alienation parade as authenticity. Ignorant of Adorno's insights, some thinkers hope that the category of the authentic can provide a bulwark against commodity relations. They are content to let the city parade itself through the naive and dignified self-absorption of jazz originality. HBO's *Treme* is the greatest testimony to the paradoxes and inevitable failures of such an approach. Attempting to document a culture under threat reveals the show's kinship with the Lomaxes and Starr's version of Hearn. Yet the impulse to protect locals from a tour bus of cameras indulges in the contrast between a raw culture and the sublime distance of ethnographic observation. At their most desperate, the show's creators and proponents burnish its political worth by referring to local consultation and sourcing of story and script.[48] Thus they exhume the thoroughly debunked category of the native informant and double down on the ethnographic fascination the show pours over itself like special sauce. Only by admitting the inherent violence contained in the phrase "authentic culture" can we begin to elucidate a repressed soundtrack of a phony city. In this mix, the alternative dimensions of the inauthentic emerge not as a mere critical reflex within the jargon of existentialism that Adorno attacked; instead, phony politics surface as a compelling and ongoing political process washed clean and borne clear by Katrina. It is up to us to carry this process onward from the event.

Notes

1 *Treme*, season 1, episode 3, "Right Place, Wrong Time," dir. Ernest Dickerson, HBO, April 25, 2010.

2 Sontag 2013, 5.

3 Organized as an extended burial procession for the city, *Treme* is fascinated with the sublime moment of the jazz funeral's interruption, as when, later in the season, a gunshot disperses a second line. Sakakeeny (2011b, 305) defines the jazz funeral as "a burial procession that begins with slow dirges performed on the way to the grave site and ends with up-tempo music and dance after the body is laid to rest."

4 See introduction, this volume.

5 Trilling 1972, 125.

6 Sakakeeny 2011a.

7 Pratt (2007) follows Badiou's notion, put forth most basically in his *Ethics*, that events produce radically new truths and require a militant fidelity to the evental site of the truth. Badiou derives the sense of the event as inaugurating a truth from Heidegger.

8 Eckstein 2005, 9.

9 Eckstein 2005, 3.

10 Benjamin, Arendt, and Zohn 1968, 243n2.

11 See John Szwed's liner notes in Morton 2005, page 1.

12 Weheliye 2005, 45.

13 Lomax 1950, 239.

14 As quoted in Barker and Taylor 2007.

15 Morton 2005, disc 1.

16 Weheliye 2005, 42.

17 Trilling 1972, 131.

18 Nyerges 2014.

19 Morton 2005, disc 1, track 5.

20 Szwed 2010, 182.

21 Morton, 2005, disc 1, track 5.

22 Hair 1976, 178–79.

23 Morton, 2005, disc 2, track 4.

24 Cullen 1900, 190.

25 Bryan 1993, 2.

26 For more on this, see Gipson 2014.

27 Hearn (1877) 2001, 13–18. Subsequent citations appear as page numbers in the text.

28 Benjamin, Arendt, and Zohn 1968, 224.

29 Benjamin, Arendt, and Zohn 1968, 243n2.

30 Starr 2001, xxiv.

31 Loichot 2011, 64.

32 Derrida 2008, 285.

33 Bryan 1993, 58.

34 Adorno 1973, 163–64.

35 Chopin (1899) 1984, chapter 8. Robert's business venture in "Vera Cruz" reminds us of the city's overlooked affinity with New Orleans, accounted for in Shannon Dawdy's essay in this volume (chapter 1), as well as Veracruz's lasting strategic importance for world empires. A decade after Chopin's novel was published, Woodrow Wilson would deploy US Marines to Veracruz to protect American business interests in revolutionary Mexico.

36 Kittler 1999, 191–92.

37 Heidegger, quoted in Kittler 1999, 198–200.

38 Rosowski 1979.

39 Trilling 1972, 124–26.

40 Spivak 1999, 139.

41 Chopin (1899) 1984, chapter 39.

42 Lightweis-Goff 2014, 164.

43 V. Adams 2013, 10.

44 Note that this is Spivak's translation. She restores "man in the raw" as the literal translation of *dem rohen Menschen*. J. H. Bernard's text of 1951 reads, "In fact, without development of moral Ideas, that which we, prepared by culture, call sublime, presents

itself to the uneducated man merely as terrible." The 2001 translation by Paul Guyer and Eric Matthews renders it, "In fact, without development of moral ideas, that which we, prepared by culture, call sublime will appear merely repellent to the unrefined person" (148). See Kant 2001.

45 Spivak 1999, 12–13.

46 Adorno 1997, 235.

47 Lomax 1950, 71.

48 In an NPR interview, show creator David Simon claimed he didn't care what anyone outside New Orleans thought of the show. "'After 'The Wire,' Taking On New Orleans in 'Treme,'" *Fresh Air*, NPR Radio, April 5, 2010.

PART TWO

*Producing
Authentic
New Orleans*

4

"Things You'd Imagine Zulu Tribes to Do"

The Zulu Parade in New Orleans Carnival

FELIPE SMITH

From the famed Congo Square of New Orleans's colonial past to the Zulu Social Aid and Pleasure Club parades in modern Carnival celebrations, evocations of Africa have had a prominent but complicated history within black New Orleans festival culture. Gwendolyn Midlo Hall documents that from the earliest days, the city's character was greatly impacted by colonists directly importing relatively homogeneous groups of enslaved Africans largely from the Senegambian region of West Africa in the early eighteenth century. According to Hall, "The fragmentation of language and culture communities associated with the African slave trade and slavery in the Americas was limited among the slaves in Louisiana," where the geography of the colony also facilitated the regrouping of language and social communities.[1] As a result of the early and continuous importance of African technical skills and cultural acumen, according to Hall, "New Orleans remains, in spirit, the most African city in the United States" and "the most significant source of Africanization of the entire [American] culture."[2] New Orleans's Congo Square, located in the historical Faubourg Tremé district that was home to many free people of color, served for more than a century as a meeting place where black citizens, slave and free, preserved and evolved an Afro-Caribbean-inspired culture on the US mainland often free from white supervision.[3]

The African cultural imprint continues most profoundly today in the city's year-round religious, musical, and festive observances, for which the famed Congo Square served as incubator.[4] Comparatively few New Orleans events since the mid-nineteenth century, however, have referenced Africa directly, making the Zulu Social Aid and Pleasure Club parade the city's most visible but also, ironically, its most ambivalent homage to its African heritage. This ambivalence, due in part to the Zulu organization's satirical portrait of Africa and the metropolitan racial context in which the performance unfolds, is a factor in the club's turbulent parading history and, until the 1970s, a long-standing source of public controversy.

Black New Orleans festival style generally has evolved sacred and secular variants preserving forms and grounding concepts, if not the precise content, of their African cultural inspirations. Scholars point to the persistence of African-derived burial rituals in the traditions of funerals with music (jazz funerals), reflecting Kongo influence.[5] After the closure of Congo Square in the nineteenth century, public processions for fraternal organization anniversaries and religious feast days, enlivened by the syncopated music of marching bands, extended the festive and musical traditions nurtured in Congo Square throughout the city, contributing to the evolution of early jazz culture. These ubiquitous processions included a parading style—the second line—traceable to Yoruba and Kongo traditions, according to Robert Farris Thompson, with "rolling" waves of dancers that ritually "cooled" the city "with circling gestures of felicity and good faith."[6] Jason Berry describes the New Orleans second line as a secular, mobile ring shout: a snakelike procession winding through the streets of New Orleans, turning entire neighborhoods into a Conga line.[7] By the early twentieth century, voodoo ceremonies had gone almost entirely underground, and bands of black working-class groups masking as Indian tribal warriors had shifted much of the performance of ancestral veneration away from African to Native American heritage. Absent the specific motive of celebrating African cultural retentions, the festival and musical culture of New Orleans that became globally recognizable through jazz and rhythm and blues evolved with few explicit references to Africa.

Despite its African cultural influences (or, more likely, because of them), New Orleans is perhaps equally well known for its historical ambivalence about Africa. By the late 1800s, a rise in antiblack rhetoric in popular, scientific, and political discourse in America had begun to drive many remnants of African heritage underground or into disguise. Derogatory political, media, academic, and folk attitudes toward Africa that permeated all Western culture in the late nineteenth and early twentieth centuries ensured that there were New Orleanians who felt, as did the American populace at large, that any hint of Africanness was a social liability, especially among the mixed-race Creoles of color in south Louisiana who enjoyed a marginally higher social status, even after the promulgation of the so-called one drop rules of racial classification eliminated mixed-race identity as an officially recognized category of citizenship. Segments of the Creole community of color embraced any claims to European ancestry in attempting to escape the social stigma of African origins.[8] Tales also abound of New Orleans Creoles of color excluding fellow citizens from social events based on dark skin color alone.[9] Prominent Creole jazz musician Jelly Roll Morton paid homage to the Afro-Creole culture of New Orleans but distanced himself from any even remote suspicion of African ancestry, insisting "all my folks came directly from the shores of France."[10] As musician Danny Barker noted, generic references to Africa were used colloquially as terms of derision against dark-skinned New Orleanians, who were referred to as "Zulus, . . . Africans, monkeys, [and] gorillas."[11] Even New Orleans jazz traditionalist Louis Armstrong, the 1949 celebrity Zulu parade king and a future goodwill ambassador to West Africa, negatively invoked the name Zulu as a slur against bebop musicians like Charlie Parker and Dizzy Gillespie who began to change jazz music radically in the 1940s: "They're all trying to take everybody to Africa, that's what they're doing . . . advertising Africa! I've got a book I can show you where they prove that all this bebop is nothing but African and Zulus talk."[12] By contrast, jazz clarinetist Sidney Bechet's autobiography *Treat It Gentle* began with a long (though quite fictional) anecdote about a grandfather Omar who learned to drum in Congo Square and experienced a mystical connection to Africa through his drumming.[13] Though the tale of the one-armed renegade grandfather seems a brazen plagiarism of the story of the legendary maroon and pre–Civil War scourge of slave-holding New Orleans, Bras Coupé, it is significant that Bechet, a man of French Creole ancestry, foregrounded his biography with a fictive genealogy back to Africa through Congo Square, and later curiously explained his decision to live in France on the grounds that "it's closer to Africa. . . . My grandfather, he was Africa. It was like getting back, and I wanted to get as far back as I could."[14]

Blackface Carnival

As Congo Square was coming under assault in the nineteenth century for perpetuating African cultural practices, white New Orleans parading groups were redefining the city's festival culture by staging street performances in blackface to express their contempt for black social and political assertiveness during Reconstruction.[15] Later, some members of the Boston and Pickwick Clubs, the premier whites-only social clubs whose members sponsored the Rex and Comus parades, launched two armed coups against the biracial New Orleans government in the 1870s, actually succeeding in establishing temporary military control over the city in September 1874, before federal troops restored order.[16] Largely drawn from the Anglo-American population that had swept into New Orleans after the Louisiana Purchase in 1803 made the city American territory, the newcomers had begun to change the city's social and political identity during the period when the city became the key port servicing the nation's heartland. Most were from the emerging mercantile, professional, and landowning citizenry that had begun by midcentury to displace the founding French Creoles as the city's governing and social elite. The Anglo-Americans seized control over festival style in the 1850s, mounting ever more spectacular street processions in a manner that would ritually certify their newfound social and economic preeminence. In the process, they irrevocably changed the character of civic celebration, shifting much of Carnival's most prestigious activity from the French Creole downtown area to the Anglo uptown, and challenging the open participatory nature of New Orleans festivity. Uptown Carnival reduced the citizenry at large to onlookers at private organizational pageants played out on public streets.[17] The Anglo-American style of Carnival parading, typified by mock formal processions on moving floats from which the club members towered over the populace below, became the dominant Carnival processional mode in the late nineteenth century, and remains so today. These panoptic spectacles of social mastery gradually altered the social dynamics of Carnival, inaugurating trends that institutionalized a paranoid style in modern New Orleans Carnival, featuring (1) the intensification of the civic prestige of economic, social, and racial elites and their imitators through public, yet exclusive, street performances on elevated platforms; (2) the installation and veneration of a ritually consecrated Anglo-American social hierarchy, as a corrective to the leveling tendencies of the heterogeneous, creolized non-English-speaking Carnival masses; (3) the incorporation of symbols of white supremacy into a postslavery public sphere struggling through an ill-fated egalitarian political realignment; and (4) the fetishizing of a military processional style, projecting an instantly identifiable form of privileged public anonymity and social distancing—a signature mask—constituting an organizational brand and ensuring the exclusivity of their private/public festivities on city streets previously open to promiscuous masking and other improvisational forms of merrymaking.

As the sole organizational representative of African heritage in official New Orleans Carnival, the Zulu parade became distinctive by adapting its satire of life in Africa to this Anglo-American Carnival template, comically reinforcing and mocking the exclusivity of the uptown white Carnival. Some scholars read the Zulu performance as incorporating the leisurely meandering of the black second lines with the corny self-importance of white Carnival's faux-militaristic processions as a burlesque of the overseriousness of Anglo–New Orleans festival culture.[18] Despite its origins among the working-class black population, over the past century the parade has acquired official civic recognition. In its evolution from festival outsider to heavily promoted feature attraction, the Zulu parade has adopted white Carnival's emphasis on spectacle, has maintained an obsessive attachment to a masking tradition historically congruent with white supremacist fantasy, and, regardless of its aura of carefree merrymaking, has over the years adapted many features of white Carnival's paranoid organizational and performance style.

Despite the Zulu name, the organization does not claim a direct line of descent from extant African influences in New Orleans culture, which, in any case, have no known Zulu tribal influences.[19] Rather, the group openly acknowledges its origins in American blackface minstrelsy, a theatrical tradition with a complex history of racial signification. According to a centennial history of the Zulu organization, "The group took its inspiration from a vaudeville troupe known as the Smart Set, which performed a skit featuring a Zulu theme at the Temple Theater. . . . The early Zulu costume was inspired by the skit 'There Never Was and Never Will Be a King Like Me,' in which the characters wore grass skirts and dressed in blackface, a common practice in vaudeville theater, both black and white."[20] Zulu's public presentation of Africa was heavily influenced by nineteenth-century fantasies of Africa as the Dark Continent, popularized by works such as H. Rider Haggard's *King Solomon's Mines*, and Henry Morgan Stanley's 1890 narrative of his mission to aid the Emin Pasha in Sudan, *In Darkest Africa*. The Darkest Africa motif no doubt had also been influenced by generations of social scientists and popular historians who had depicted Africans as a people without history.[21]

Zulu traces its blackface masking tradition back to one of a series of Darkest Africa–themed musical theater productions of the early twentieth century, a genre popularized by black performers Bert Williams and George Walker in productions such as *Jes Lak White F'lks* (1900) and *The Cannibal King* (1901). It took gifted black performers, able simultaneously to enact and yet also subtly to challenge the racist underpinnings of both blackface minstrelsy as a performance genre and the Darkest Africa theme, to avoid perpetuating the racist assumptions that restricted their own professional opportunities. According to David Krasner, the shows' performers were in a structurally ambivalent position vis-à-vis the contradictory demands of their racially divided audiences: whites (who generally required blacks to embody Jim Crow social inferiority, onstage and off) and metropolitan African Americans (who expected from their creative artists occasional validation of African American social achievement).[22] By the time the Smart Set troupe performed their inaugural Zulu skit at the Pythian Temple in New Orleans, the genre typically represented African Americans as comically maladjusted to Western civilization and Africans as incapable of forming civilizations of their own. Black characters aspiring to become businessmen or political leaders would inevitably fail due to "racial traits" of ineptitude, chicanery, and chronic disunity. The Zulu parade came into existence at a historical moment when African American performers had begun to claim ownership over blackface minstrel characterizations and plots, seeing blackface satire as the only way they could earn a living as stage performers. Ultimately, these black performers came to dominate the blackface genre, gradually combining the contrived nineteenth-century minstrel theatrics with performances of the authentic music and dance of modern African American popular culture, and eventually discarding the blackface masking when industry pressures relaxed.[23] Williams and Walker had gained popularity performing under the name "Two Real Coons," which they adopted for tactical reasons similar to Zulu's: "As white men were billing themselves 'coons,' Williams and Walker [decided they] would do well to bill themselves as the 'Two Real Coons,' and so we did. Our bills attracted the attention of managers and gradually we made our way in [show business]."[24] They understood that they were entering a field of racial caricature created and defined by whites, and also that in large part, white audience response would determine their degree of popular success.

On the other hand, Zulu's story of origins omits the decades of New Orleans blackface Carnival masking before their founding. The Krewe (New Orleans Carnival faux-antique spelling of "crew") of Comus had adopted its organizational identity from the 1634 John Milton *The Masque of Comus*, in which the son of Bacchus, god of wine, was attended by "monstrous" figures between men and animals, holding torches aloft in their procession. Similarly, the Krewe of Comus's premiere New Orleans parade in 1857, preceded by a group of rowdy slaves carrying flambeaux (torches), set the template for what one observer described as a "grand and comprehensive system and plan for the enjoyment of the people."[25] By 1859, the black presence in Comus's retinue had swelled to a thousand flambeaux, inaugurating a racial division of labor for night parades constitutive to the club's social and political agendas.[26] In effect, as the opening salvo of the Anglo-American reinvention of Carnival, Comus's "comprehensive system and plan" established the performative niche that Zulu later adapted to its own agenda, one that represented the riotous, debased (Creole) old order through the bodies of comically grotesque, mongrelized black others. Comus color coded the noble white elite and the drunken black mob for ease of audience identification. By contrasting aristocratic whiteness to undisciplined black bodies, they scripted their organizational founding into an enduring Carnival allegory in which the courtly English tradition ritually supplants the old heterogeneous Creole festival style.[27]

Comus's early performances (augmented by those of Rex, Twelfth Night, and others) established a template that subsequent white maskers in blackface adopted for social satires and political commentary on contemporary life. In 1861, a group of Comus paraders in blackface carried an effigy of Abraham Lincoln riding a split rail, weeks before the state's vote to secede from the Union.[28] The inaugural Rex parade in 1872 included a blackfaced group, including one parader wearing a sign that identified him as "Our Future Governor," a mocking reference to the state's Reconstruction-era biracial government. The 1873 parade of the Krewe of Twelfth Night Revelers presented "The Crows in Council" to spoof the biracial state legislature. Twelfth Night Revelers was followed that year by Comus's infamous satire on Reconstruction, the tableau "Missing Links to Darwin's Origins of the Species" that featured a simian black figure wearing a crown, depicting Darwin's missing link as a Reconstruction-era tyrant.[29] The krewes perhaps did not initiate blackface masking in Carnival, given the long Carnival tradition of promiscuous masking by Carnival-goers, but they certainly harnessed its political potential, establishing blackface as a traditional element in furtherance of their white supremacist agenda—to register contempt for antislavery sentiment, to incorporate the concepts of black racial regression and the evolving social Darwinist discourse on racial difference, and to vilify black participation in governance as a crime against civilized virtues—coalescing the symbolic economy of festival blackface masking into which Zulu later emerged.

Though one scholar of Carnival professed himself unable to find any recorded instances of white promiscuous masking in blackface for Carnival before the Civil War, the *Louisiana Tribune* in 1869 remarked on the striking number of people unaffiliated with krewes who masked as "Negro characters."[30] In 1872 the *Louisiana Republican* estimated that fully three-quarters of the whites at Carnival were masking as "irrepressible plantation hands."[31] The same newspaper had remarked only two years earlier that the lack of imagination in Carnival could be deduced from the "astonishing numbers of Ethiopian minstrel" maskers, indicating that blackface very quickly became popular among promiscuous white maskers during the postwar period of violent conflict over the full inclusion of blacks as citizens.[32] Thirty years later (in 1901, the year that Zulu claims for its organizational founding) the *New Orleans Picayune* was still complaining that whites seemed never to get tired of masking in blackface, and concluded that whites "were under the impression that they could enjoy more license disguised as negroes."[33] Nor did blackface masking as a white tradition disappear with the advent of Zulu. The white participants in the racially segregated New Orleans Romance children's parades of the 1930s used stocking masks to create a blackface effect to "represent Negro life" in Louisiana (though, interestingly, not in the 1939 Peoples of New Orleans–themed parade, in which Siamese and Persians, but not Negroes, were celebrated as honored citizens).[34] The city's oldest continuous white marching group, the Jefferson City Buzzards, masked in blackface for nearly seventy years until, in 1958 in the midst of the city's school and public accommodations desegregation battles, they dropped the blackface masking for their "black bird" attire after "realizing" that blackface carried "other associations."[35]

Thus the Zulu Club did not adopt and perpetuate blackface masking in a vacuum, nor did they directly challenge its meaning or change its ritual functions as scripted by white Carnival. They adopted blackface while it was still a white Carnival masking tradition that they, like Williams and Walker, believed they could perform in a style that would improve upon the white imitators, and in the process they partly made their way, through craft and determination, into a festival performance genre that had been evolving for half a century. The zany cast of Zulu characters presented the black urban jungle as a community internally riven by self-aggrandizement and petty one-upmanship, one in which the putative ruler was constantly undermined by his supposed minions, as a result of which their chaotic zigzag through the metropolis all too often deteriorated into scenes of public intoxication and mechanical breakdowns of their barely functional equipment. The local press ritually reported each organizational mishap, whether intentionally comical or accidentally so, less as satire than racial self-revelation. The persistent description of the Zulu parade as a veiled critique of the Rex parade that follows it on Shrove Tuesday (an interpretation that the Zulu Club strenuously denies) reflexively recognizes the two events as linked, but symbolically oppositional expressions of racially inflected cultural paradigms. Despite official denials on both sides, it is a symbiotic relationship that has become more and more formalized in recent years as Zulu has become more openly embraced as a part of the official New Orleans Carnival pantheon, perhaps in

Figure 4.1

King Zulu and his court, 1940, Zulu King-Queen souvenir booklet,
1941. PHOTO COURTESY OF THE HOGAN JAZZ ARCHIVE, TULANE
UNIVERSITY.

recognition of the social, political, and economic value of their visual representation of two racially distinct metropolitan bodies politic.[36]

The adoption of blackface as its signature mask eventually secured a space for the Zulu organization in the Carnival calendar. But the tension between Zulu's status as the black community's only parading group with a reserved date in the official New Orleans Carnival calendar and the cultural significance of the blackface mask that secures that civic presence is the major source of its ambivalent performance of African identity. Bert Williams and George Walker, black pioneers of the original real-coon strategy, understood the danger inherent in trying to hold onto their audience by perpetuating the blackface mask. In 1906, the year white audiences rejected the Williams and Walker musical *Abyssinia* for its attempts to transcend blackface theatrical stereotypes, George Walker declared, "the colored performer would have to get away from the ragtime limitations of the 'darky,' and Williams and Walker decided to make the break, so as to save ourselves and others."[37] Thus, years before the Tramps adopted the Zulu name and blackface masking, two pioneer blacks in blackface, Williams and Walker, had already revolted against becoming forever locked into "coon" and "darky" blackface masking. As Eric Lott observes, even gifted, trained black performers were battling enormous odds in trying to shift the inherent meanings of blackface masking from within the performance genre: "far from providing an immediate corrective to minstrel types, they actually reinforced them, lent them credibility, no doubt, because the newcomers had to fit the ideological forms the minstrel show had helped to generate."[38] Zulu adopted blackface during an era when the practice was widespread among white Carnival maskers, but it continues as one that only Zulu now sponsors, ironically because African American protests against blackface as a demeaning racist caricature have rendered it socially inappropriate for white Mardi Gras maskers. Significantly, Zulu has prospered by maintaining blackface masking as an organizational legacy for which no white parading group can now compete. The very censure that whites risk by performing in blackface in New Orleans ultimately ensures Zulu a profitable monopoly, one that can never fully be reappropriated.

Zulu created a unique space for itself bridging black and white Carnivals, continuing its role among the city's benevolent aid societies with their year-round calendar of street-level parades, but also executing key departures from core black festival traditions in its Mardi Gras day performance. By 1914, four years after its founding, Zulu's Carnival paraders were riding in buggies,[39] and by 1915, Zulu's parade was elevated on flatbed wagons decorated as floats. Had Zulu remained at street level, it would likely have continued to be a niche performance with a modest cult following, such as the similarly black working-class masking Indian groups were for decades. By elevating its performance on moving floats, Zulu was able to expand its territorial reach and visual appeal, and quickly realized that with increased mobility and visibility, its parade was attracting large white as well as black audiences. David Krasner has noted of the pioneers of black musical theater that the task of performing in blackface for different racial audiences with asymmetrical social and economic power produced the vertigo of "double consciousness" that characterizes the Zulu parade's ambivalent politics of racial representation.[40]

Zulu's home base at the time of its founding was on South Rampart Street in an uptown neighborhood that served as an African American shopping and sporting district called Black Storyville to distinguish it from the whites-only Storyville district of high-end legal brothels and inexpensive "cribs" on the downtown side of Canal Street.[41] The neighborhood was made up of largely non-Creole African Americans, in a city whose neighborhood rivalries Zulu incorporated into its portrayal of the Zulu king as beset by the treachery, backbiting, and one-upmanship of his royal court. Uptowners embraced not just the idea of African ancestry but also nationalist causes some downtown Creoles of color considered politically and stylistically retrograde—Ethiopianism and back-to-Africa movements. Zulu's path to Carnival notoriety similarly began with broad black community support, despite pockets of middle-class resistance, but when its popularity began to outstrip its financial resources, Zulu increasingly relied on white sponsors to supplement its base of support in uptown black New Orleans. Zulu appeared on the radar of the New Orleans press shortly after World War I and quickly earned media recommendations as an indispensible Carnival event.[42] In the semiotic cannibalism of New Orleans Carnival, wherein fantasy often reinforces bedrock social arrangements and prevailing stereotypes, Zulu became indispensable to that which it had presumably intended to mock—white Carnival's satire of blackness—and simultaneously emerged as the official civic representative of that which it had adapted as the foundation of its racial caricature: black New Orleans festival style. When, in 1946, Zulu erected racially segregated reviewing stands on South Rampart Street, advertising in the mainstream media that whites would not to have to stand elbow to elbow with black onlookers to enjoy the club in its neighborhood setting, the club was reaffirming its conviction that its future success depended more on accommodating the fantasies of its Jim Crow–era white audience than on risking offense to its black one.[43]

Blackface and Boycott

The official Zulu history references one consequence of Zulu's divided allegiances between black and white community interests, when the black civic mobilization against racial segregation in the 1950s and '60s pitted Zulu against the leaders of the local civil rights movement: "In the 1960's during the height of Black awareness, it was unpopular to be a Zulu. Dressing in a grass skirt and donning a black face were seen as being demeaning. . . . Large numbers of black organizations protested against the Zulu organization, and its membership dwindled to approximately 16 men."[44] Zulu's framing of this history proclaims its survival of this organizational crisis as a triumph of the group's fidelity to its tradition. Noting that "the organization [held] together and slowly [came] back to the forefront" after the black community protests, the statement goes on to claim the episode as a civil rights victory "in that an African American carnival organization became part of the city's official Mardi Gras festivities, and paraded in a public space historically reserved for white parades." The actual circumstances and consequences of the conflict are muted in this history because they show the organization's relationship to the city's white segregationist power structure in a terrible light.

In the 1960s, a series of boycotts of Carnival by local chapters of the major civil rights organizations NAACP and CORE ultimately targeted the Zulu parade as part of the problem. At stake was the united social and economic resistance of black New Orleans to the violent suppression by the police force at the behest of the white business community that had refused to voluntarily desegregate public accommodations. Mardi Gras became one of the local civil rights organizations' targets as New Orleans experienced a hostile and protracted school and public accommodations desegregation struggle. After attempts to reform the Zulu parade evolved into a campaign to put economic pressure on the city through a boycott of Mardi Gras itself, black organizations, including social aid and pleasure clubs, were enlisted in the effort, and asked to pledge to honor the boycott. Zulu voted to join the boycott of Carnival. But after a visit from Mayor Chep Morrison and police chief Joseph Giarusso to the club's headquarters, Zulu changed its decision and voted to parade instead.[45] So in 1961, Zulu paraded in defiance of the civil rights coalition under the protection of armed white policemen, accompanied by police dogs trained to attack black citizens and break up civil rights demonstrations.

The ensuing acrimony between Zulu and the black community resulted in nearly a decade of open conflict over the meaning of its blackface performance. A petition signed by 27,000 black residents condemned Zulu, for its lack of racial solidarity as well as its representation of blackness: "Therefore we resent and repudiate the Zulu parade, in which Negroes are paid by white merchants to wander through the city drinking to excess, dressed as uncivilized savages and throwing coconuts like monkeys. This caricature does not represent us," the petition asserted. "Rather it represents a warped picture of the Negro painted by segregationists and used by them to discriminate against us."[46] The ad in the *Times-Picayune* announcing a black boycott of Zulu as well as Mardi Gras under the banner "Zulu Does Not Represent the Negro" goes on to note, "Therefore we petition all citizens of New Orleans to avoid the Zulu parade. If we want respect from others, we must first demand it of ourselves." The petition carried the endorsement of many black businesses, including some that had been longtime sponsors of the Zulu parade, but Zulu officials' response to this rejection was, amazingly, to deny any responsibility toward black community interests and reaffirm their allegiance to their white patrons. "It's our civic duty to parade," said a Zulu official. "You see, the merchants want the parade on the street," agreed another. "We don't depend on the Negro public," the first spokesman summarized. "We depend on the merchants."[47]

The open admission by Zulu's members that their loyalty was to the city's white economic power brokers that had financially supported them, and not to the black community and its struggle for equality, led club members to further disclaimers, including a denial that their parade even had any connection to African identity: "There is no time that the Zulu Club ever said that its parade represented Negroes. We created a character which had some features from Africa, grass skirts from Hawaii, moss from Louisiana, and coconuts from South America. We created him years ago, named him 'Zulu' and don't say he's anybody in particular. . . . So there's no reason for Negroes to beat their chests and say, 'That's me.'"[48] Eventually, community pressure on the Zulu members forced a temporary capitulation, and in the mid-1960s, Zulu briefly abandoned blackface masking. In response to the stinging criticism that Zulu's "disgraceful, disorderly and despicable [parade] . . . just for a few dollars and laughs from the white folks" was an affront to the "twenty-six African nations that [had] gained their freedom in the past few years," the "New Look" Zulu procession was designed to be "a dignified parade" that "every Negro [would] be able to take pride in," one that would "depict the culture of an African tribe," with the theme "The Watusi, Children of the Lion."[49]

But in 1967, the Zulus returned to their blackface performance, claiming that "nobody" liked them as a sober, dignified procession: "No more of that dignity stuff. We're going back to the old traditions—African face image, grass skirts and earrings in the nose," as perennial King Zulu Milton Bienamee put it.[50] The *New Orleans States-Item* article announcing Zulu's reversal of course quoted the Zulus as wanting to recapture the "real African flavor" because outside "pressure groups" had forced them into "imitating everything but a real African parade."[51] By putting "dignity" and "real African flavor" into irreconcilable opposition, Zulu signaled its belief that a "real African parade" had no room for both. Bienamee complained of outside interference that had caused Zulu to lose track of its "old traditions," noting, "Some other groups want to fancy us up."[52] However, the fact that Zulu's own second-line community parades were "fancy dress" processions consistent with prevailing black festival performance standards meant that it was not a violation of festival practices nor black audience hostility that factored most into their decision to jettison dignity.

With its return to blackface satire, Zulu drew the ire of community activists again, although the major civil rights organizations decided to sit out the renewed conflict over Zulu's satire of Africa. In a move perhaps designed to intervene on the side of Zulu in its struggle against community activists, white New Orleans welcomed Zulu into its official Mardi Gras parade lineup in 1969, awarding Zulu a parade route nearly identical to Rex's later in the day (an event that the organization today refers to as its "Civil Rights victory"). The 1969 parade, with its theme "Black Is Beautiful," drew protesters in vehicles, including former Garveyite Queen Mother Moore of the Universal Association of Ethiopian Women, who followed the parade and decried Zulu's "slandering the image of black people."[53] Internal Zulu organizational strife nearly derailed the city's attempt to rescue Zulu from black New Orleans and its own conflicts, but by 1973 the organization had found sufficient stability that it could begin to translate its Carnival visibility into a sustained growth in public prestige. Characteristically, Zulu's ambivalence about Africa in the post–New Look era created dissonance with a presentational style that local alternative newspaper the *Vieux-Carré Courier* referred to as "the Uncle-Tomism of mock-Africa."[54] On the one hand, Zulu had reverted to the blackface minstrel guise that the group ironically referred to as its "traditional attire." But on the other hand, Zulu began to import its parade souvenir items from apartheid South Africa, so as to acquire for its African impersonation "the stamp of authenticity."[55] Further complicating the organization's representational politics, official Zulu Club spokesmen began yet again to deny any intended reference to Africa in their parade theme. A *States-Item* headline in 1971 declared that Zulu had "No Connection with Africans." "We don't claim to be any part of the Zulus of Africa," the paper quoted Alex Raphael. "We never intended to represent anybody. . . . All we ever wanted to do was have fun."[56] Long forgotten, perhaps, were the quite contradictory attempts to claim the Zulu nation's warrior history as inspiration, such as the article "A Brief History of Zululand," in the 1941 souvenir booklet.[57]

Real Zulus

Appealing yet again to white patrons, Zulu had secured significant assistance in the late 1960s from the Junior Chamber of Commerce and the New Orleans Jazz Club, which had designated Zulu as an organization so unique and representative of New Orleans Carnival that they raised money to underwrite the group's Carnival activities during its renewed struggles with black activists in order to keep Zulu from folding.[58] But with the tensions of the civil rights era waning, both activists and the Zulu hard-liners (reduced in the contentious mid-1960s to an all-time low of sixteen members) began a process of de-emphasizing the struggle over Zulu's blackface minstrelsy, and the organization's membership began a slow transformation through the inclusion of many new professional members whose objective seems to have been to change the organization's profile from within. The old guard grudgingly gave way to a more formally educated, bourgeois, and politically connected leadership in the 1970s, so long as the newcomers agreed to retain the signature blackface mask. With New Orleans soul and funk music helping to propel black music into the American mainstream, it was possible for even the increasingly bourgeois membership and a multiracial extended community that saw Zulu's Carnival events as a space for social reconciliation in racially fragmented greater New Orleans to celebrate openly Zulu's earthy origins and fidelity to its urban cultural roots.

The rapprochement also allowed Zulu to align its politics tenuously within black urban post–civil rights progressivism. As a result of 1960s and '70s white flight to the suburbs, New Orleans became a majority black city by the early 1980s. By the early 1970s, Zulu's foothold in official Carnival had begun to translate into larger social events, allowing Zulu's Carnival ball eventually to become one of the largest and most influential meeting places for the various black neighborhood political groups and a magnet for politicians on the prowl for black votes.[59] In 1969, a white mayor, Moon Landrieu, had been elected with more black than white votes, providing black citizens with an example of how their organized, united political power would soon transform the city.[60] In 1978, the first self-identified mayor of color in New Orleans was elected, Ernest N. "Dutch" Morial, who ironically had been the local NAACP leader during the 1963 Carnival boycott of Zulu. In his successful run for mayor, Morial needed every black vote in his contest against an experienced and well-financed white opponent. Black community arguments over what, if anything, Zulu's parade represented were increasingly muted in the pursuit of a united African American political front (all the more because Morial's own political base in the Creole of color Seventh Ward was itself split by professional and personal rivalries).[61] Brokering a united black political front also helped Morial to weather a crisis one year into his first term, when the New Orleans Police Department went on strike and shut down Mardi Gras civic events. Morial triumphed against the largely white police union, emerging as a symbol of a unified, ascendant black New Orleans, and as mayor went on to pen an annual salute in the Zulu ball souvenir program, describing himself as a "proud and active member of the Zulu Social and Pleasure Club."[62]

Folding the successes of post–civil rights black New Orleans into its own history, Zulu positions its prominence in official Carnival today as an index of that civic progress, according to the organizational history posted on its website: "The Zulu Social Aid & Pleasure Club Inc., is the everyman club. The membership is composed of men from all walks of life—from laborers, City Mayor, City Councilmen, and State Legislators, to United States Congressman, educators, and men of other professions. Zulu's history is illustrious and at times colorful, and could fill volumes. It is also continual, with chapters being written constantly." Zulu's celebration of its transformation from social outsider to a consensus insider organization is justified, and thus calls into question interpretations of the parade since the 1990s as a subversive performance with a "hidden transcript" critiquing white racism in official New Orleans Carnival. As Zulu's official history explains, there's no need to mute its criticism of anyone, given its incorporation of many political power brokers in the city into its ranks.[63]

In the mid-1980s, club leader (and future city councilman) Roy Glapion, one of the professional men who joined Zulu in the 1970s, thought it would be a good idea to have African Zulu people march in the parade. His plan, however, "was met by a storm of protest" by the club, which voted to forbid him to make the trip along with float builder Blaine Kern, who wanted "to recruit Chief Mangosuthu G. Buthelezi of Africa's Zulus and fifty of his warriors."[64] The Zulu old guard's reluctance was not due to an absolute organizational prohibition on invoking the real Africa, though, since the year before, Melvin Simms's celebration as Big Shot was celebrated in Afrocentric garb, as depicted in that year's souvenir program.[65] By 1993, when Simms's wife, Ellenese Simms, was Zulu Queen, most nonparade events again involved stylized Afrocentric designs, and again in 1998, during the celebration of Lundi Gras (the festival day before Mardi Gras, which had been revived by the city in the early 1990s, culminating in a waterfront landing and second-line parade by Zulu royalty into the city) Zulu King Wallace Broussard and his entourage were decked out in caftans, dashikis, kufis, and kente. Subsequent Zulu royalty enjoyed an expanded range of design options at the multiple seasonal events, allowing for the exploration of the Zulu Club's variety of civic identities.

This design shift gave evidence of a desire by some within the Zulu organization to reconceptualize the old standard clownish application of blackface makeup for social events, and of a willingness to experiment with costuming

Figure 4.2

King and queen of Zulu, Sheila and Tyrone A. Mathieu, 2009. PHOTO © JEFFREY EHRENREICH.

styles that have begun in recent years to predominate. The King Zulu poster by Iam Bennu (Benford Davis) for the breakthrough year 1998 projected the king as a visionary entrusted by the city with its classic virtues. Bennu's Harlequin-inspired use of black-white contrast for reimagining the old theatrical blackface points to a Zulu Club emancipated from its self-deprecating mask of clownish futility. Testifying to the fact that not everyone in the organization was ready to enter a new millennium with a new identity, the 1998 Zulu Carnival ball was marked by controversy, as numerous invitees were denied entrance because the Zulu Club rules officially banned African attire for the formal affair. Considering it a distraction from the procession of Carnival royalty, the club enforced its mainstream formal-wear-only policy "at a time when savvy dressers and fashion designers the world over [were] learning to admire the African aesthetic."[66] *Times-Picayune* columnist Lolis Elie noted that so absolute was this policy that Zulu's sartorial gatekeepers even refused admission to the choreographer of the evening's dance program, who was told by the Zulu Club president to leave and change her African-style outfit to something more appropriate. She did not return.

Zulu has been able to shrug off this sort of negative publicity in part because of its many charitable activities (related to its role as a traditional social aid and benevolent association) and its prominence with businessmen and politicians. But with its elevation into the select group of organizations considered indispensable to New Orleans Carnival has come a sense of entitlement. When members of over thirty other social aid and pleasure clubs wanted to stage a unified second line on Lundi Gras in 2008, their parading permit was revoked, and their future permits for parades were threatened when they complained. At a time when tensions between the police force and second-line parading groups were at a high due to aggressive policing and the city's creation of more bureaucratic and economic hurdles for second-line parade sponsors, organizers were stunned to learn that Zulu was opposed to the parade involving other social aid and pleasure clubs and was using its clout with the city to preserve the Lundi Gras celebration as a Zulu-only franchise.[67] Given the many overlapping affiliations that social aid and pleasure club members maintain, throughout its history there is a disturbing consistency in the Zulu Club's willingness to advance its own organizational interests at the expense of black community solidarity.

Still unresolved is the controversy over Zulu's determination to maintain the blackface mask as its organizational brand. The practice has motivated critics to question Zulu's insistence on blackface while whites risk social sanctions for doing so. The New Orleans City Council denied a permit for a Delta Kappa Epsilon (DKE) fraternity house after the organization had been booted off Tulane University's campus for repeated instances of blackface masking, and the 2003 blackface Halloween masquerade by Judge Timothy Ellender of Terrebonne Parish drew a judicial rebuke for "how deeply such an act resonates throughout the African-American community as a harsh reminder of a not-too-distant-past."[68] More troubling is the economic angle. Costs of hosting a massive Carnival parade have driven Zulu to an expedient—paraders who are not club members, but who pay to ride in the parade—that, although not unique to Zulu, resonates differently given the post–civil rights sanction on whites in blackface. The recent expansion of this practice has produced a curious experience for black onlookers faced with float after float of whites dressed in blackface under the aegis of Zulu, putting Zulu de facto in the business of franchising blackface minstrel masking for a hefty rider's fee. Though this has not yet become an issue of official public concern (anecdotal evidence indicates that in the past few years, Zulu has tried to mute public reaction by incorporating white nonmember maskers onto floats with black riders, rather than what had for a number of years been a series of floats with all white riders in blackface), it ironically reflects back on circumstances a century ago when Zulu appropriated the blackface franchise from white New Orleanians. Those maskers' descendants now have the opportunity to relive that experience for a fee. If, for example, Judge Ellender had worn the same blackface costume in the Zulu parade, rather than to a Halloween party, he would likely have avoided a suspension from the bench.[69]

Coda

Fifteen years after the late-1990s cosmopolitanism urged a new public image for the Zulu parade, the organization has quietly moved toward a gradual transition in its public presentation. Spike Lee (post-*Bamboozled*) has ridden in and attended Zulu events, serving as grand marshall in 2003. The commemoration in 2009 of the club's centennial at the Zulu parade was certainly a time for historical reflection, and a presidential acknowledgment engineered by a former queen of Zulu then serving in the Obama White House was

Figure 4.3

Zulu witch doctor, Lundi Gras, 2009. PHOTO © JEFFREY EHRENREICH.

Figure 4.4

Zulu skeleton masker,
Lundi Gras, 2009. PHOTO
© JEFFREY EHRENREICH.

another moment of validation.[70] Maintaining blackface, but stylizing it in
ways predicted by artist Iam Bennu, Zulu audiences have recently seen fewer
hokey, improvised outfits, and more that employ imaginative variations in
face paint and costume design. The Lundi Gras celebration has continued
to provide Zulu royalty with different public personas, as evidenced by the
formally accented Africana among the royalty and designs paying homage
to other local African American masking traditions, such as the Mardi Gras
Indians and the Skeleton maskers. And more recent ball outfits for Zulu
royalty illustrate both the retrospective and revisionist impulses.

Only a few years earlier, Hurricane Katrina's devastation of the city had
left Mardi Gras, and Zulu's participation in it, in doubt. The Ernest N. Morial
Convention Center, which houses the Zulu coronation ball, made news in
the storm's aftermath when federal officials admitted that they were not even
aware that the place was crammed with evacuees surviving on minimal food,
water, and sanitation. Critics of the city's misplaced priorities criticized the
very idea of money being spent on revelry in the midst of a massive disaster
cleanup. But legendary Mardi Gras float builder Blaine Kern decided he had

the perfect gimmick to commemorate Zulu's official return to the streets, and with it the fruition of his twenty-year-old dream: "20 authentic Zulu warriors" from South Africa, in full ethnic regalia, marching at the head of the Zulu Mardi Gras parade, "doing," as Kern breathlessly enthused, "things you'd imagine Zulu tribes to do"![71]

Notes

1. Hall 1992a, 159, 161.
2. Hall 1992b, 590; 1992a, 275–315, 157.
3. Johnson 1991, 124.
4. Donaldson 1984, 64–65.
5. Roach 1996, 10; Sublette 2008, 109.
6. Thompson 1988, 20.
7. Berry 1995, 102.
8. Schafer 2009, 31–32.
9. Mitchell 1995, 184.
10. Lomax 1950, 3.
11. Quoted in Kinser 1990, 235.
12. Brothers 1999, appendix 14, 214.
13. Bechet 1960, 6.
14. Bechet 1960, 45. On Bras-Coupé, see Saxon, Dreyer, and Tallant (1945) 1988, 253–54.
15. Gill 1997, 77–108.
16. Gill 1997, 106–22.
17. So intoxicating was their newfound mastery of the city's festival calendar that the Carnival parades of these organizations had virtually served as public dress rehearsals for the 1870s armed insurrections, with parade floats and marchers viciously ridiculing the same metropolitan police force that they would later murderously attack. After Southern white Redemption returned the black population to a largely servile status, Comus maintained militarism and race nationalism as defining elements with symbolic gestures such as honoring the daughters of Confederate generals at their 1883 court ball (Schindler 1997, 79). See Gill (1997, 77–108) for the connection between the Carnival krewes and the rise of the Klan and the Knights of the White Camellia during Reconstruction. See also Gill (1997, 137) for Confederacy themes in postwar Comus parades. See also Sublette 2009, 267–81.
18. Kinser 1990, 232–40; Mitchell 1995, 151; Roach 1996, 20–24.
19. It is tempting, though, to compare Zulu's blackface with Caribbean masking performances such as Jouvay in Trinidad (see Alleyne-Detmers 2002, 250–52). However, see also Catherine Cole on the Ghanaian "concert party" adaptation of blackface masking as an area of contention over whether white inspirations of the formal practice are more resonant for its practitioners within concert party blackface masking than are Ghanaian folkloric traditions that contributed to the performance (Cole 1996, 183–84).
20. Chamberlain 2009, 1–2.

21 Hegel 1899, 91; Hickey and Wylie 1993, 243.

22 Krasner 1997, 54.

23 Two publications by Lynn Abbott and Doug Seroff re-create the world of black musical shows in the late nineteenth and early twentieth centuries: *Out of Sight: The Rise of African American Popular Music, 1889–1895* (2002) and *Ragged but Right: Black Traveling Shows, "Coon Songs," and the Dark Pathway to Blues and Jazz* (2007). Abbott and Seroff painstakingly document the personalities and performances that crisscrossed the South (and beyond) popularizing the unfolding black musical revolution of blues and jazz. An invaluable resource, based in large part on extensive coverage by black newspapers and periodicals, these volumes document that Zulu's maskers were part of a larger network of performers who sustained minstrelsy, in and out of blackface, into the middle of the twentieth century.

24 Krasner 1997, 26.

25 Gill 1997, 45.

26 Schindler 1997, 35–36; Hardy 2007, 45, 86.

27 The antics of the black slaves as barbarous forerunners to the stately court conforms to Stephen Orgel's description of the sequencing of the English court antimasque and masque as the "central action" in the courtly presentations of Ben Jonson, establishing the generic distinction between the antimasque and the masque as types of performances. In the words of Orgel, "the . . . 'antimasque' . . . represented everything that threatened the ideal world" of the court (Orgel 1981, 35), an idealism that the masque often served to exemplify. Technically, Comus, the son of Bacchus, god of wine, and Circe, the witch who turned men into beasts in mythology, was the representative of those barbaric, unruly forces of nature that threatened social order (Gill 1997, 45–47). However, the Comus organization's adaptation of the Comus myth followed closely Milton's depiction of the god as a transitional figure of the chaotic old order driven from the stage by forces of temperance and reason, and the krewe's enduring legacy very quickly coalesced around an organizational style noted for its wit, erudition, and secrecy, in the service of nobility, order, prestige, decorum, and other courtly virtues (Schindler 1997, 67).

28 Gill 1997, 58; Kinser 1990, 97.

29 Mitchell 1995, 52, 65, 70.

30 Schindler 1997, 143.

31 Kinser 1990, 70; Mitchell 1995, 51.

32 Mitchell 1995, 61.

33 Hair 1976, 86.

34 Mitchell 1995, 165–66.

35 Loda 2010, 13.

36 Consider the seeming equivocation on this point in Zulu's Centennial Exhibition of 2009. While one installation proclaimed that the wording of the organizational charter was "evidence" that Zulu was not established as a "parody of Rex," a narrative attached to a different tableau exclaimed that the parade "ridiculed white pomposity." Presumably, the observer is left to make whatever associations she or he chooses between the old-line Mardi Gras parades and "white pomposity."

37 Krasner 1997, 7.

38 Lott 1993, 103.

39 Gill 1997, 172.

40 See Krasner 1997, 50–54.

41 Rose 1974, 38–39.

42 The press had always played a crucial role in the evolving lore of Anglo-American Carnival, having served as documentarian, public mouthpiece, and mythologist in chief for Comus and Rex since their inceptions (Schindler 1997, 67). In contrast to the near-reverential treatment afforded to the white Carnival royalty, press notices portrayed Zulu as disorganized and obstructive, and worse, spiced articles with anecdotes of white patrons' high-handedness with Zulu's beggar kings, who were often identified as menial employees of prominent New Orleans businessmen. See "Bootblack to Be Zulu King," *Times-Picayune*, February 21, 1941; *New Orleans Item*, February 25, 1938; *Times-Picayune*, February 2, 1940; and *Times-Picayune*, February 19, 1947.

43 *Times-Picayune*, March 3, 1946.

44 Zulu Social Aid and Pleasure Club, *Official 1985 Souvenir Booklet*, 1985.

45 *Times-Picayune*, February 2, 1961.

46 Trillin 1964, 42; *Times-Picayune*, February 13, 1961.

47 Trillin 1964, 53, 73. Evidence that Zulu's spokesman was not referring to black merchants is the fact that longtime Zulu black commercial sponsors such as the black funeral directors and embalmers associations, as well as the black Tavern Owners of Greater New Orleans Association, had endorsed the boycott and joined forces against Zulu (Trillin 1964, 42).

48 Trillin 1964, 50.

49 Trillin 1964, 42; *Louisiana Weekly*, February 20, 1965; *Louisiana Weekly*, February 27, 1965.

50 Mitchell 1995, 189. The notion that the New Look parades were unpopular is not supported by the accounts of the *Louisiana Weekly*, which declared that the 1965 parade "was accepted and highly regarded by the Negro general public" (February 27, 1965).

51 *Times-Picayune*, February 4, 1967; *New Orleans States-Item*, February 3, 1967.

52 *New Orleans States-Item*, January 26, 1967.

53 *Times-Picayune*, February 19, 1969.

54 *Vieux-Carré Courier*, February 16, 1968.

55 *Times-Picayune*, February 4, 1967.

56 *New Orleans States-Item*, February 2, 1971.

57 Zulu Social Aid and Pleasure Club, *Zulu King-Queen Souvenir Booklet*, 1941, 5–6.

58 See *New Orleans States-Item*, February 11, 1967, on the foundation created by the New Orleans Jazz Club to ensure the perpetuation of the "Zulu carnival feature forever." See also *Times-Picayune*, February 12, 1969, for the Junior Chamber of Commerce fundraiser and its certificate of appreciation awarded to Zulu in the midst of its battle with protesters.

59 *Vieux-Carré Courier*, March 9–15, 1973; *New Orleans States-Item*, February 8, 1973.

60 Hirsch 1992, 295.

61 Hirsch 1992, 304–10.

62 Zulu Social Aid and Pleasure Club, *Official 1985 Souvenir Booklet*, 1985, 2.

63 Some scholars have interpreted Zulu's performance largely as a subversive critique of the Anglo–New Orleans Carnival tradition. Samuel Kinser, for example, explains Zulu's Carnival function in terms that emphasize its equivocal satirical intent: "[Zulu] cuts against black people's internalized image of themselves as too low but also too high, too savage and too noble. At the same time it plays with the whites' aristocratic image of themselves as royal and with their idea of blacks as primitive" (1990, 236). After a storm of controversy over a City Council initiative to withhold parade permits from racially segregated Carnival organizations in the early 1990s spawned more interest in Zulu, other observers hailed Zulu as an indictment of New Orleans Carnival's racist subculture (Vennman 1993, 77; Roach 1996, 20–24). (Arguing against this interpretation, though, is the testimony of Zulu traditionalist Alex Rapheal Jr., who insisted in the midst of 1960s civil rights controversies that Zulu's performance was "completely original" and that any suggestion that Zulu references Rex in its design and performance was "completely out of harmony with the original idea" [Trillin 1964, 111–12]). The 1991 showdown over race and New Orleans Carnival traditions resulted in the withdrawal of Comus as a parading group (see Vennman 1993). See also Gill (1997, 221–58) for a different perspective on the controversy. Given Zulu's current relationship to the city's political elite, and to sponsors with real economic clout, it is doubtful in any event that Zulu's continued appeal lies in what James C. Scott refers to as a "hidden transcript," a camouflaged "weapon of the weak" used by those who dare not speak truth to power. See Scott 1990, xii: "Every subordinate group creates, out of its ordeal, a 'hidden transcript' that represents a critique of power spoken behind the back of the dominant."

64 Mitchell 1995, 191.

65 Zulu Social Aid and Pleasure Club, *Zulu Souvenir Program*, 1985, 32.

66 *Times-Picayune*, March 18, 1998.

67 *Times-Picayune*, February 1, 2008.

68 *Times-Picayune*, June 3, 1988; *Times-Picayune*, December 14, 2004.

69 In full disclosure, I was called as an expert witness at the judicial hearing for Judge Ellender (*Times-Picayune*, October 18, 2004). I have also been a float rider in a Zulu parade, as a parent of a member of the royal court. Neither my daughter nor I wore blackface makeup, nor have I ever been a member of the Zulu organization.

70 *Times-Picayune*, March 2, 2009.

71 *Times-Picayune*, February 9, 2006.

5

The Saga of the Junkyard Dog

BRYAN WAGNER

The historical irony of Louis Armstrong Park is frequently noted. The park stands on nine square blocks demolished during the 1960s on the pretext of urban redevelopment. Dedicated not only to Armstrong, one of the area's most celebrated native sons, but also to the entire tradition of jazz in New Orleans, the city established the park as a monument to the culture created in buildings that it had only just destroyed. Writing in *New Orleans* magazine in 1974, Monroe Labouisse puts the point succinctly. "We bulldozed the city's oldest seat of black culture," he complains, "and wound up dedicating the ruins to Satchmo." Labouisse dates this destruction to 1956, the year that Mayor DeLesseps "Chep" Morrison proposed clearing the blocks around the Municipal Auditorium to make way for an enlarged compound of cultural institutions, including an arena and a concert hall, but the truth is that the process dates at least to the 1920s, when the Municipal Auditorium was originally built on land commonly known since the late eighteenth century as Congo Square.[1]

Armstrong Park was designed to capitalize on its historical location. Promoters made sure that nobody would forget that the park literally encompassed Congo Square, the grassy plain where slaves had assembled weekly to drum and dance, blending the musical styles that they had brought from their African homelands into a creole amalgam that would eventually be expressed in jazz. This was the place where musical traditions otherwise repressed under slavery were projected into the future, where they persisted both on the bandstand and in the streets. The park was also right on the border of Faubourg Tremé, next to Storyville, the former red-light district where local musicians including Louis Armstrong had their start. Honoring the origins of the jazz tradition in musical practices retained from West

Africa, the park encouraged visitors to understand black music as "cultural survival," a catchall term introduced by E. B. Tylor in 1871 to refer to customs that were carried into "a new state of society different from that in which they had their original home."[2]

Writers from George Washington Cable to Herbert Asbury, from Rudi Blesh to Sidney Bechet, have imagined this tract as holy ground. City planners, however, had other ideas about the site. Already in the 1920s, various proposals were being floated for the construction of the Municipal Auditorium, a building originally conceived as a memorial to troops who died in World War I, following a trend common at the time in US cities, which led to the public construction of stadiums like Soldier Field in Chicago. Prompted by the perceived need to replace the French Opera House, a landmark at Bourbon and Toulouse that had burned to the ground in 1919, the Municipal Auditorium Commission lobbied for the renovation of the supposed tenement district adjacent to the former Basin and Carondelet Canal, arguing that it should be turned into a state-of-the-art multiplex dedicated to the performing arts. The commission meditated on the site's history only to suggest a change in its purpose. One survey even goes so far as to imagine the "last dance . . . in Congo Square" with the performers stamping their feet and shouting "farewell" as they are "overtaken" by the "march of time." The survey continues, announcing the "new vision" that was being "imposed" on this fading background, a vision of the "new municipal auditorium, the plans for which have been completed." "Soon," we are told, the square would "re-echo" not with the sounds of the "the calinda, the bamboula, [and] the counjaille" but with the "refined harmonies of Debussy, Beethoven, Bach, Schubert, Chopin, and a host of others."[3]

With a total capacity of ten thousand, divided into two halls, an auditorium side on St. Ann Street and a concert side on St. Peter Street, the Municipal Auditorium was lauded as one of the largest and most modern structures of its kind when it opened to the public in 1930. The plan to overhaul the surrounding blocks was stalled by the Great Depression, but the idea never went away. It was a recurring topic for discussion in the meetings of the Municipal Auditorium Commission in the 1940s when members like Pierce Walmsley implored the city to "condemn all those negro shacks" to clear space for a small theater, museum, and concert hall. As Labouisse notes, this concept was adopted by Chep Morrison and expanded by planners in Vic Schiro's administration inspired by the model of New York's Lincoln Center. The city began the demolition process to make space for the Culture Center in the mid-1960s at the same time as the black business corridor, located a few

Figure 5.1

Gouache drawing of New Orleans Cultural Center, Mathes, Bergman, Favrot, and Associates, architects, 1963. Scheffer Studios. COURTESY OF THE SOUTHEASTERN ARCHITECTURAL ARCHIVE, SPECIAL COLLECTIONS DIVISION, TULANE UNIVERSITY LIBRARIES.

blocks away along Claiborne Avenue, was being demolished to make way for the Interstate 10 overpass. The city razed the blocks between Rampart and Villere, Basin and St. Philip, only to abandon the plan for the Culture Center a few years later when funding for the project failed to materialize. Some of these blocks were turned into parking lots to relieve congestion in the winter months when the auditorium hosted a series of white-only Carnival balls, but most of them stood vacant until it was finally decided in the early 1970s to transform them into a public park.[4]

The planning for Armstrong Park was no less fraught than for the abandoned Culture Center, but the debate was framed differently. The century-old Creole cottages that Walmsley had disparaged as "negro shacks" were eulogized by historical preservationists like Labouisse for their gabled roofs and brick-between-post construction. Advocates even managed to rescue a few buildings, including Perseverance Hall, which was added to the National Register of Historic Places in 1973, and the Reimann and Rabassa–de Pouilly houses, which were moved from their original locations into Armstrong Park to save them from the bulldozers. If these vernacular structures had previously seemed like they were destined to be superseded by a make-believe complex of modern cultural institutions anticipated by the Municipal

Auditorium, this impression had changed by the time they were assimilated into Armstrong Park. Along with the remaining acres from Congo Square, they became the touchstones that linked the park to the vernacular heritage that had been decimated by ill-conceived and unfinished projects intended to modernize the city's cultural infrastructure.[5]

This history begs some questions, including whether there are ways other than irony to conceive the relationship between urban redevelopment and cultural conservation. In this essay, however, I am less interested in the particular methods of commemoration that were put into practice at Armstrong Park than in something else that was happening inside the park during the years when it was first opened to the public. On Monday nights between 1979 and 1984, the Municipal Auditorium rocked to the weekly show put on by Mid-South Wrestling, an organization whose featured player, the Junkyard Dog (JYD), was the first black headliner in the history of the sport. While some venues, including the St. Bernard Civic Center, drew a primarily white crowd, and others, including the Superdome and the Irish McNeil's Boys Club in Shreveport, were notable for their mixed patronage, the Municipal Auditorium was where the first black headliner in the history of professional wrestling played to a predominantly black audience. At the heart of Armstrong Park, on acreage that once belonged to Congo Square, the Municipal Auditorium (or the Dog's Yard as it became known) was the Junkyard Dog's home court. No matter how much his enemies cheated and schemed, the Dog never lost there until a fateful match in 1984 that augured his hasty departure for New York.[6]

There is so much to say about the Junkyard Dog, but what matters most to my argument in this essay is his magnetism and specifically his ability to attract five to eight thousand spectators to the Monday night shows at the Municipal Auditorium. On these nights, the auditorium was reinhabited by the people who had been cast out—literally and symbolically—by the redevelopment of the surrounding neighborhood. Obviously, the individuals whose homes were bought or expropriated by the city had not disappeared for good. Many of them were moved across the river to the Fischer Projects, a site that was distant from the urban core for many practical purposes but not far enough to prevent a regular return over the Greater New Orleans Bridge to pay homage to the Junkyard Dog. Many who attended the matches would have had to pass under the I-10 overpass a few blocks from the auditorium, or arrive via the nearby I-10 exit, a thoroughfare constructed at the same time as the blocks near the auditorium were being razed, little more than a decade before the weekly Mid-South matches began, providing another

Figure 5.2

The Junkyard Dog.
COURTESY OF GEORGE
NAPOLITANO.

immediate and unmistakable reminder of the neighborhood destruction wrought by urban renewal. All of this was happening below the radar of politicians and preservationists who were busy planting trees, installing plaques, and putting up statues outside the auditorium.[7]

I am interested in what we can learn about the tract of land now known as Armstrong Park when we anchor its history not in some receding past but instead at the point in time when it was home to the Junkyard Dog and his fans. This tract has been imbued with the cultural capacity to authenticate contemporary social and especially musical practices by establishing their association with Armstrong and by extension Congo Square, but that is not its whole story. Taking the long view, the area looks less like a place where cultural authenticity is secured and more like a place where the meaning of culture has been continually called into question, not least in terms of its relation to commerce and the state. This is a question, I argue, that is also asked with deliberate awareness in the course of the Junkyard Dog's career in Mid-South, from his early feuds to the decisive angle in 1982–83 in which JYD was double-crossed by Ted DiBiase and banned for ninety days, only to return the next week in a mask and red-and-green bodysuit working under the pseudonym Stagger Lee.

The Junkyard Dog arrives in Armstrong Park bearing a peculiar burden of racial representation. Cast as a hero to the city's black population, he lays claim to a building (the Municipal Auditorium) and a landscape (Armstrong Park) that were committed in their design to competing concepts of culture—the elevated high culture of the building and the authentic low culture of the surrounding park—that had no place for him. The auditorium was pictured as a temple for high artistic achievements, a civic institution whose mission was to bring culture not only to the elites who could afford a symphony subscription but also to the masses of the city. Viewed in light of this mission, the surrounding neighborhood seemed like it was lacking in culture, indeed like it was characterized by an absence of culture, its traditions worth no more than its blighted shacks. At best, its residents were untutored natives awaiting enlightenment. The rationale for Armstrong Park was different. The park valued neighborhood traditions in retrospect. It treated vernacular culture as something that was always disappearing, something that had to be preserved before it was too late. From this standpoint, professional wrestling is not an example of culture but a threat to culture. It was cheap entertainment that drew people away from their vernacular practices of music and dance, heralding the inevitable demise of the vernacular tradition in an age of mass culture.[8]

Renting out the Municipal Auditorium on Monday nights, Mid-South Wrestling ridiculed the culture concepts that were installed on-site. Grating against the sensibilities of symphony goers and opera buffs, Mid-South flaunted its total lack of refinement, taking delight in caricature, bawdy melodrama, and outlandish feats of strength and agility. At the same time, Mid-South went out of its way to offend the self-appointed guardians of cultural authenticity, reveling in its insincerity. This was a culture industry that was literally engaged in mass deception, a spectacular hoax that was represented to its audience as something real. Making no apologies, begging the question of its own inauthenticity, Mid-South was self-aware lowbrow entertainment enlivened by the disdain of others, a spectacle performed for patrons who saw themselves as the noisy neighbors.[9]

Whatever else they were doing, the Mid-South shows were participating in an argument over the meaning of culture that had been happening at the

Municipal Auditorium since the beginning. It seems incongruous: a shrine to high culture, a replacement for the venerable French Opera House, built to order for Carnival balls, with a dedication to "Music, Poetry, Art, Drama, Athletics" emblazoned on its facade, turned into the regional headquarters for gaudy entertainment not only suited but specifically designed for consumption by commoners. This was not the original plan for the auditorium, but, especially after it was incorporated as a semiautonomous auxiliary after the adoption of its home rule charter in 1954, the building had to be self-supporting. Coming close to bankruptcy on several occasions, the auditorium's advisory committee had no choice but to compromise its cultural elitism in pursuit of revenue. The auditorium retained its social ties to old-line Carnival organizations and its political commitment to racial segregation (at least until 1963), but once it became obvious that these traditional associations were compromising profits, change became inevitable.[10]

Increasingly in the 1960s, booking at the Municipal Auditorium was defined by its eclecticism. The building hosted not only *Tosca* and *La Traviata*, Bach and Schubert, Proteus and Comus, but also roller derby, talent shows, ice capades, circuses, high school dances, and competitions organized by the New Orleans Cat Fanciers. It rented not only to the Philharmonic Society and Opera House Association but to Larry McKinley's Supersonic Attractions (which brought Jackie Wilson, James Brown, and Sam Cooke). Boxing and wrestling became indispensable sources of revenue, so much so that promoters like Lou Messina were able to force the auditorium to lower its rental fee, knowing that its budget depended on the concessions sold at their events. As its programming became more varied, the auditorium came to rely increasingly on black patronage. Messina's New Orleans Boxing Club brought local black fighters like Joe Dorsey (who was born and trained in the Seventh Ward) and Percy Pugh (who hailed from the Lower Ninth Ward) into the recently desegregated auditorium, drawing sellout crowds. Incorporating a civil rights agenda into his marketing, Messina booked the Eddie Perkins versus Kenny Lane bout in 1965, an event advertised, in Buddy Diliberto's words, as the "first modern mixed match" in the city's history.[11]

In these years, the auditorium was a place where people who were supposed to have nothing to do with one another came into contact. Events were booked back to back, and sometimes they were literally happening simultaneously, as the auditorium's dividing wall made it possible to run more than one event at once. This was a source of irritation in particular to symphony patrons who complained about the noise bleeding from pop concerts ("Chopin Thrown by Rock 'n' Roll" was one headline in the

Times-Picayune) and sporting events ("Victor Borge Wins Out over Wrestling" was another). Another concern was the alleged menace posed by down-market patrons outside in the parking lots when events let out simultaneously. Even worse was the threat that attendees ostensibly faced when the lots were full and they had to park their cars on nearby streets. The governing board tried to address these concerns by strengthening the partition, installing soundproofing, hiring new patrols, and turning demolished residential blocks into new parking lots. Plans for the Culture Center even included a skyway, an elevated corridor that would permit patrons to walk to and from their cars without descending into the surrounding neighborhood. When the Culture Center plan was scrapped, the debate over the site's relation to the neighborhood continued as planners and activists argued over the shape of the new perimeter fence that was to include some buildings but not others inside Armstrong Park.[12]

Despite these efforts to reinforce the cultural distinctions through architectural and landscape design, the Municipal Auditorium remained a place where cultures thought to be a world apart came into close and sometimes uncomfortable proximity. When Mid-South began its weekly show at the auditorium in 1979, it was following the commercial precedents established in the previous decade. Mid-South was formed after Cowboy Bill Watts broke away from Leroy McGuirk's Tri-State promotion. Watts was given the rights to Louisiana and Mississippi, territory that was considered a backwater in contrast to the Oklahoma circuit where Tri-State was based. New Orleans was by far the largest market in the Mid-South territory, and Watts understood that he needed to maximize gate receipts there if his fledgling organization were to have any chance at success. While the seasonal shows at the Superdome remained make-or-break enterprises for Mid-South, the regular bookings at the Municipal Auditorium were the key to the organization's efforts to cultivate a local fan base.[13]

Coming from Oklahoma, Watts believed that New Orleans posed a demographic challenge. In contrast to the rural circuits where Tri-State and other promotions in the National Wrestling Alliance made the majority of their money, New Orleans was a city with an emerging black majority that had just elected its first black mayor. Accordingly, Watts crafted characters and storylines that he imagined would captivate an urban multiracial audience. In the short term, these efforts were successful, as evidenced not only by the sell-out crowds at the Municipal Auditorium but also in the local ratings for the Mid-South television show broadcast on UHF Channel 26 as the lead-in to the syndicated music programs *Solid Gold* and *Soul Train*.[14]

Watts is recalled as a genius among wrestling promoters due to the intricacy of his storylines (which elaborated on angles that had worked in other territories), his innovations in television (which involved broadcasting matches between lead wrestlers rather than pitting them against feckless jobbers), and his advocacy for realism (which put a premium on so-called scientific wrestling and represented Mid-South as a rule-bound and even legalistic institution). It was thought, however, that the key to Mid-South's rapid success was the outsized charisma of its headliner, the Junkyard Dog, a character created in collaboration between Watts (who wrote the scripts) and Sylvester Ritter (who acted the part) to appeal to a city with a history of racial conflict. The Junkyard Dog was promoted, in Greg Klein's words, as a "black superhero," a "champion of good in a land of racial hatred" whose popularity was predicated on his ability to beat back "every challenge the white heels threw at him." With an eye to current circumstances in the city, Watts even tried to capitalize on the politics of the situation, claiming for example that the Junkyard Dog's tag-team partnership with Dick Murdoch was a "civil rights victory," echoing Messina's boxing promotion a decade earlier. Before the Junkyard Dog, there were ethnic babyfaces (the term of art for protagonists) on the East Coast especially, and there were black wrestlers, like Thunderbolt Patterson and Bobo Brazil, who were booked at best as midcard features, but Mid-South was the first promotion to turn a black wrestler into its featured attraction.[15]

After he formed Mid-South, Watts started looking for a protégé to push as his star. He found what he wanted in Sylvester Ritter. Born in North Carolina, Ritter had a stint in professional football before going to work for Stampede Wrestling, a long-running promotion based in Calgary. The Dog never had strong technical skills in the ring. His matches were kept short, relying on his opponents to carry the action. "The Junkyard Dog doesn't get paid by the hour," Watts was fond of saying. The Junkyard Dog's celebrity was therefore based less on his wrestling than on the other aspects of his performance, particularly his skills on the microphone and his capacity to sell his role in the fables of retribution that Watts scripted for him.[16]

Within a year of his introduction, the Junkyard Dog had become not only the best-known wrestler in Mid-South but also a figurehead for the organization with substantial crossover appeal to white fans. The first time the Junkyard Dog headlined at the Superdome in 1980, the event set the record for ticket revenue in the building's history, at the same time breaking the national record for attendance at an indoor wrestling show. When students in the New Orleans public schools were polled in 1982–83 about the professional athlete they would most like to meet, their choice was neither Archie Manning (the quarterback for the Saints) nor "Pistol" Pete Maravich (a point guard who played for both LSU and the Jazz) but instead the Junkyard Dog.[17]

Mid-South was canny in promoting the Junkyard Dog, developing his character, for example, by using music to establish the terms for audience identification. Watts took JYD's name from Jim Croce's "Bad, Bad Leroy Brown," a folk-rock anthem loosely based on vernacular sources that topped the Billboard Hot 100 for two weeks in 1973. Even more important to the Junkyard Dog's characterization, however, was the entrance music that was used to heighten audience anticipation when he approached the ring. The Dog was not the first wrestler to use entrance music, which was employed as early as the 1950s by wrestlers like Gorgeous George, but he is credited with popularizing the practice in the early 1980s before it was adopted and expanded by the World Wrestling Federation through its cross-promotion with MTV. Watts was subtle in using music to address the demographic challenge of marketing wrestling in New Orleans. The Junkyard Dog continued entering to Queen's ubiquitous pop number-one "Another One Bites the Dust" (1980) on television and at venues like the St. Bernard Civic Center even after he abandoned the song for George Clinton's "Atomic Dog" (1982) when he was booked at the Municipal Auditorium. "Atomic Dog" was a telling choice, not least because it went to number one as an R&B single without ever even making it onto the pop charts. As an entrance song, its significance was determined in part by the fact that it was not the song that the Dog used when he appeared on Channel 26. It was an insider's song, demonstrating a special identification between the Dog and a subset of his fans.[18]

When Watts hired Ritter, he was looking specifically for someone who would appeal to a black fan base, but when JYD turned out to be an overnight sensation, Watts adjusted the script accordingly, making him into a figurehead for the entire Mid-South organization. Despite his limited skills in the ring, the Dog was turned into an advocate for clean wrestling dedicated to protecting the legitimacy of the organization he represented. "Fans ultimately loved JYD," Greg Klein explains, "because he faced down and defeated any heel that tried to run roughshod over Mid-South Wrestling." From the start, Mid-South was characterized by its legalism, and so by implication was the Junkyard Dog. Watts worked hard to present Mid-South as a rule-bound organization, something he believed was indispensable to its realism. Obviously, this was a ruse. The rules in wrestling are literally there to be broken, as the drama turns on the moment when the referee is distracted and the sneak attack is launched or the foreign object is introduced. Like the other wrestling organizations that followed his formula, Watts cultivated Mid-South's legitimacy by staging the constraints on its capacity to regulate events happening inside and outside the ring. Mid-South was an entity that could not guarantee justice precisely because it was bound by law. This put the Dog in an interesting position. His ongoing efforts to bolster the legitimacy of Mid-South were made all the more exhilarating by the fact that the law was constantly under threat. At the same time, his own commitment to the law was challenged in storylines where the law provided no remedy for injustices he had suffered at the hands of his enemies.[19]

Watts made the most of this situation by crafting storylines for the Junkyard Dog that were about revenge. Feuds began when the Dog was double-teamed or double-crossed without provocation, and they escalated until the tension reached its climax at a seasonal event at the Superdome. The first significant feud in the Dog's career was with the Fabulous Freebirds. The feud was ignited by a match in which the loser was to have his hair removed. Michael Hayes, one of the Freebirds, took the hair-removal cream that was kept ringside and splashed it into the Dog's eyes, blinding him. True to his formula, Watts was careful to leave open some question as to whether Hayes intended to get the hair cream into the Dog's eyes. Watts believed that this plausible deniability protected the organization's legitimacy, which would have been called into doubt had Hayes acted purposefully and been permitted to get away with his crime. Appearing on television wearing dark glasses and a cane, the Dog swore revenge, but it was alleged he would never wrestle again. Watts even reported that JYD was unable to witness the birth of his first child as a result of his blindness. A month later, when the Dog revealed that his sight had miraculously returned, he took off his sunglasses and began pummeling an astonished Michael Hayes. Weeks later the feud peaked when JYD beat Hayes in a steel-cage match in the Superdome.[20]

The Junkyard Dog's most heated feud was with Ted DiBiase—his former best friend, tag-team partner, and the best man at his wedding. The circumstances leading to DiBiase's heel turn were established over several weeks. At the Municipal Auditorium in June 1982, DiBiase rushed to help when JYD was ambushed by Killer Khan, and was injured in the process. DiBiase was scheduled to face Bob Roop later that night for the North American title, with the stipulation that DiBiase would have to leave Mid-South if he lost. As DiBiase was unable to wrestle, JYD took his place and won the title for himself. Watts explained on television the following week that Mid-South bylaws stipulated that the Dog had to honor the bookings that were made for Roop, which meant defending his title against his best friend in a match that could force DiBiase to leave wrestling.[21]

In interviews leading up to the event, both wrestlers expressed ambivalence about fighting a friend but agreed the match had to happen. "The Junkyard Dog," DiBiase said, "doesn't pay my bills, and he doesn't put a roof over my family's head." The Dog agreed that putting food on the table for his own family had to be his priority. The week before the match, DiBiase hurt his hand and explained that he needed to wear a glove for protection. A few tentative minutes into the match, when both JYD and the referee were distracted, DiBiase took a foreign object from his trunks and placed it in the glove. He knocked the Dog out cold and stole the title, effecting one of the most dramatic heel turns in wrestling history. To make matters worse, months later JYD and Mr. Olympia lost the Mid-South Tag-Team title to DiBiase and Matt Borne when Hacksaw Jim Duggan, disguised in a gorilla suit, interfered in the match. It was stipulated that, as the loser of the fall, JYD had to leave Mid-South for ninety days.[22]

The precarious legalism that characterized so many Mid-South storylines is once again apparent in the run-up to the title matches between DiBiase and the Junkyard Dog. This storyline was determined by the technicalities concerning the scheduling of title defenses, as they also proved decisive in the matches themselves, in which DiBiase was able to get away with stealing the North American title by using a loaded glove and stealing the tag-team title through interference. This sequence seems preposterous, but its melodrama is put to serious purpose. We know, for instance, that DiBiase is a scoundrel for betraying his friend, but even this betrayal is cast as a difficult problem where he must choose between loyalty and self-preservation, as the title match comes with the stipulation that he will have to leave wrestling if he loses. Both DiBiase and JYD agree before the match that their livelihood, the necessity of sheltering and feeding their families, supersedes their friendship, an exigency that has frequently been understood in many contexts to absolve lawbreaking.[23]

On television the week after he double-crossed the Dog, DiBiase was scheduled to face an unknown opponent, likely some second-rate jobber, whose name was given as "S. Lee." DiBiase was in the ring first, taunting the crowd and confirming his complete change in personality. A thin man of indeterminate ethnicity (announced at a measly 150 pounds) then entered the ring, asking the referee to hold one end of a banner that when unfurled read, "S. Lee is Stagger Lee." DiBiase was not impressed: "Big deal. Who is Stagger Lee?" On cue, Lloyd Price's "Stagger Lee" (from 1958; the R&B version) began playing over the sound system. This was a canny choice. Not only did the song evoke a black vernacular tradition concerning Stagger Lee, a badman who brooks no insult and gives no quarter, it gave this tradition a familiar local inflection, as Lloyd Price was a native of the New Orleans area, having been born and raised in nearly Kenner. Locals, in other words, would have immediately understood the important link that DiBiase did not. Soon after the song started, a masked wrestler charged the ring, throttling DiBiase with a series of uppercuts followed by a power slam and a quick three-count. Not done yet, Stagger Lee put a foreign object in his mask and knocked DiBiase from the ring with a head butt. From there, the feud caught fire. The stakes were high, as Watts confirmed that JYD would be banned for life if it were shown that he was wrestling in disguise during his ninety-day suspension. At the 1982 Thanksgiving Extravaganza in the Superdome, Stagger Lee won the title from DiBiase, though he narrowly avoided a lifetime ban when the referee, temporarily knocked cold, failed to witness DiBiase unmasking Stagger Lee to reveal the Junkyard Dog. Stagger Lee would defend the North American title until JYD's suspension was over. At that point, he disappeared, and a round-robin tournament to fill the vacant title was held at the Municipal Auditorium the next month.[24]

If DiBiase's betrayal is cast as a choice between loyalty and self-preservation, JYD's own turn away from the law is cast in similarly conventional and even classical terms as the problem of how to react when the law shows no interest in the injury you have suffered. Mid-South does not go so far as to declare that when it is wrong to load the glove, it is right to return in a mask, but it does admit the irrelevance of its own procedures to the Junkyard Dog's pursuit of justice. At the very least, we know that Stagger Lee is no more criminal than Ted DiBiase even as DiBiase is acknowledged by Mid-South as its legitimate champion. Mid-South engages this seeming paradox by splitting its hero into two characters. If the Junkyard Dog faces his enemies as the representative for an organization defined by its fragile devotion to positive law, Stagger Lee encounters DiBiase in something like a state of nature, where the only norms with any bearing are those concerning ethics in warfare.[25]

When the Junkyard Dog becomes Stagger Lee, his feud with DiBiase is recast in relation to precedents from black vernacular tradition. Stagger Lee was one of several so-called badmen who assumed starring roles in vernacular music at the turn of the twentieth century. Howard Odum writes in 1928 that "Stagger Lee" was especially popular in "Mississippi, Louisiana and Tennessee" though it was known to "Negro vagrants all over the country" who reveled in the outlaw's exploits, hailing him as a "hero of the tribe." More recently, critics such as John W. Roberts and Cecil Brown have placed Stagger Lee at a particular stage in the evolution of the black vernacular tradition, seeing him both as the transformation of an ancient trickster figure as well as an objective model for the first-person address in the blues.[26]

We know that the legend of Stagger Lee is grounded in events that took place in St. Louis in 1895 when Lee Shelton (alias Stagger Lee, or Stack-a-Lee, or Stagolee) murdered William Lyons for taking, or maybe touching, his Stetson hat, but we also know that this tradition has proven extremely flexible over time, with many versions, including some of the earliest ones, failing to mention either Billy Lyons or a fight over a hat. In some cases, Billy Lyons is a police officer. In others, he is a lothario. In still others, Shelton and Lyons are gamblers, bank robbers, sworn enemies, or friendly rivals. There are also many songs in which Stagger Lee is a badman more or less indistinguishable in word and deed from legendary bullies like Railroad Bill and Aaron Harris, and it is in this broad and traditional sense, rather than in its details, that the legend informs the Junkyard Dog's transformation into a fugitive from law.[27]

In Mid-South, the legend of Stagger Lee is invoked to extend themes already expressed in the feud between JYD and DiBiase, raising new questions about the relations between law and justice, betrayal and injury, grievance and obligation. When Stagger Lee is introduced as the Junkyard Dog's alter ego, these matters are recast in terms that reconnect the storyline to the fixed concepts according to which culture was being defined at the Municipal Auditorium. According to the planners who razed the neighborhood to build the Culture Center, Stagger Lee would have seemed like an uncultured brute, fitting the profile of the shysters selling fake parking passes at the auditorium entrance, not to mention the muggers waiting a few blocks away. For the impresarios who built Armstrong Park, Stagger Lee would recall a version of the folk tradition to which the site was dedicated, a tradition that was already thought to be vanishing when the earliest versions of "Stagger Lee" were transcribed by collectors like Odum.

Both of these culture concepts seem insufficient when they are considered in connection with the legend's adaptation in Mid-South. Whether intent on excluding "Stagger Lee" from the domain of culture, on marking it as the kind of thing that you sing when you have no culture, or else on venerating the song as a cultural vestige that has been saved from the bulldozers, thus predicating its value on its attenuated or at best indirect relevance to contemporary politics, these concepts are conspicuous in their failure to account for the problems raised by the Junkyard Dog's transformation into Stagger Lee.

These problems have nothing to do with cultural authenticity. Their meaning is keyed to the contemporary political situation in New Orleans, not only to the struggle over the land around the auditorium but also to the administrative changes that were sweeping the city in the early 1980s. A melancholic attachment to problems without legal remedy or to betrayals where the damage could not be undone was inescapable in places like Armstrong Park where the ghosts of the recent past were not easily dispelled. Seated in the auditorium, the trauma of historical injury and the yearning for revenge would have felt like present concerns to many people in the audience. Moreover, in a city where a generation of civil rights activists had entered the political establishment, many longtime residents were discovering the inescapable practical constraints that inhibited the pursuit of justice in government institutions. This was an experience that would have conditioned how audiences understood Mid-South's legalism just as it also would have shaped their response to the breakdown of the interracial alliance with DiBiase that led to JYD's turn from law. The connections between this storyline and the state of the city were no coincidence: it had been Watts's plan from the start to foster audience identification through plots attuned to local circumstance.[28]

It is also important to note that audience identification with Stagger Lee, like his alter ego the Junkyard Dog, is structured by a musical introduction. In his first match with DiBiase, Lloyd Price's "Stagger Lee" serves a purpose for the masked wrestler similar to the purpose that George Clinton's "Atomic Dog" had served for the Junkyard Dog. "Stagger Lee" is an insider's song that prepares some people, and not others, for what is about to happen in the ring, marking the graduated difference between those who were able to name that tune in one, two, three, or four notes and those who needed the ring announcers, Watts and Boyd Pierce, to tell them what was happening. This demarcation of insider status is furthered by the choice to play the uncensored version of "Stagger Lee" in rotation on black-format radio and not the version sanitized for mass consumption on *American Bandstand*, which went to number one on the pop chart.[29]

When the mystery of "S. Lee" is solved, however, and everyone is invited to root for the masked avenger in the ring, the song's function changes. Rather than identifying with the wrestler through the song, we identify with the song through the wrestler, and not only with Lloyd Price's version of the song but with its precedents in vernacular tradition. The song, in other words, turns out to mark not a difference in the audience but instead a difference between this audience and other people in the world, like Ted DiBiase, who do not know Stagger Lee. "Who," DiBiase asks, "is Stagger Lee?"[30]

Our identification with Stagger Lee the wrestler takes us backward through New Orleanian Lloyd Price's glossy renditions of "Stagger Lee," recorded in Los Angeles for ABC-Paramount, to the self-accompanied barrelhouse jump blues that was cut in two parts in 1950 by Leon T. Gross (under the pseudonym Archibald) in Cosimo Matassa's legendary J&M Recording Studio, where artists like Fats Domino and Little Richard invented rock 'n' roll a few hundred yards from the Municipal Auditorium. It takes us backward through Archibald, backward through commercial records by Ma Rainey, Lovie Austin, Sidney Bechet, and John Hurt; backward to the ballads transcribed by folklore collectors like Howard Odum, John Lomax, and Mary Wheeler, who understood "Stagger Lee" as a remnant of oral tradition.[31]

If folklore collectors interested in the autochthonous origins of jazz and the vernacular roots of blues ballads like "Stagger Lee" complained a lot about corrupting influences, from Tin Pan Alley to the phonograph, that were supposedly compromising the authenticity of black vernacular traditions, their alarm seems both wrongheaded and beside the point when we consider "Stagger Lee" from the standpoint of its adaptation in Mid-South. What matters about Lloyd Price's "Stagger Lee" in this context is not the threat to authenticity posed by its horn section and backing vocals. Rather, it is the song's ability to connect its audience through their identification with the Junkyard Dog to a tradition that already proven time and again its capacity to absorb musical figures and turns of phrase from the most degraded and mass-produced sources, including blackface numbers like May Irwin's "Bully Song" (1895). Something, in other words, we can learn from Mid-South's adaptation of Lloyd Price is that the tradition that existed at Congo Square has turned out to be more resilient than we have sometimes assumed. It is a tradition with a proven capacity to persist in the strangest of places, including the Municipal Auditorium, where it was able to speak back to the culture snobs across the hallway, not to mention the historical preservationists in their new offices in the park, who would have been more than happy to ignore the Junkyard Dog were it not for the fact that his fans were making so much damn noise.[32]

Ironically, it turns out that the best way to take "Stagger Lee" seriously is to refuse the high seriousness that has accompanied the sacralization of culture on this tract of land. The same holds true for the Junkyard Dog. It seems more than a little incongruous to suggest that the Dog should be taken seriously as a vehicle for self-reflection. Entering the ring wearing a collar and steel chain, howling at the crowd, the Dog is hard to claim as a protagonist in the struggle for recognition, not least because his schtick is anathema to the politics of respectability, recalling as it does the bestialization associated with slavery. In promoting other wrestlers, furthermore, Mid-South was more than willing to indulge in racist caricature, notably in the case of heels like Kamala the Ugandan Giant (a character played in grass skirt and war paint by James Harris, a native of Senatobia, Mississippi). But again, before we accept this racism as disqualifying, we need to remember that songs like "Stagger Lee" belonged to a tradition, no less than Mid-South, that traded in stereotypes and cheap tricks. This affinity is one reason why a song like "Stagger Lee" can cross from turpentine forests to professional wrestling without losing its way.

Mid-South Wrestling is a limit case for cultural authenticity in New Orleans. In this context, there is no point in asking whether Lloyd Price's song is a knockoff, or whether Stagger Lee really is the Junkyard Dog, or whether the action in the ring is real or fake, given that in all of these cases, culture's ability to engage with immediate matters of common concern is not only preserved but predicated by its inauthenticity, which forestalls claims made by would-be entrepreneurs eager to bend the city's traditions to their own purposes. One reason the Junkyard Dog remains an important point of reference is that he provides a perspective on the city from which it is impossible to ask about authenticity. There is something about his celebrity, in other words, that resists monumentalization. Some fans have called in recent years for the city to put a statue of the Junkyard Dog in Armstrong Park to commemorate his adventures in Municipal Auditorium, even invoking the statue of Louis Armstrong as a precedent. This strikes me as a weird idea, and what I love about its weirdness is how it reveals the impossibility of transforming the Dog into a symbol whose significance is knowable only in retrospect. Unlike Louis Armstrong, unlike the anonymous musicians and dancers in Congo Square, whose massive genius has proven susceptible to questionable modes of memorialization, it is difficult to credit the Junkyard Dog as anything other than meaningless distraction, a fact that paradoxically preserves the immediate significance of his exploits by making it difficult if not impossible to repackage them as lingering examples of cultural heritage.[33]

When it began its five-year run at the Municipal Auditorium in 1979, Mid-South entered an urban environment in which the boundary between civilization (the symphony) and barbarism (the parking lot) no less than the divide between tradition (Congo Square) and modernity (rock 'n' roll) was being challenged. Culture had served for generations as a way to deny proximity and thus to obscure the questions of public access that had been raised continually over the history of this parcel of land by community organizations including the United Clubs and the Tremé Neighborhood Association. Using the feud as the structuring device for its storylines, Mid-South brought the melodrama of professional wrestling, with its sensationalism and its polarization of good and evil characters, to the Municipal Auditorium, a building whose history was susceptible to explanation in these terms. Originally constructed on the remains of a neighborhood playground for a constituency that frequented the symphony and Carnival balls, the auditorium's history raised questions about retribution, resentment, and even repatriation that were also pertinent to the city at large. How to respond when you are wronged and left without legal redress; how to live in the wake of the double cross; how to conceive obligation in the absence of formal legitimation—Mid-South offers not answers but instead an imaginary orientation to these questions, an orientation that was made tangible on the nights when the Dog took over, albeit temporarily, the ground that had been taken away by lawful means over the preceding decades.[34]

Notes

1   Labouisse 1974, 74–75; Toledano and Christovich 1980, 66; Armstrong Park Corporation, *Master Plan of Armstrong Park* (New Orleans, 1983); Crutcher 2010, 66–81. For the political context of early efforts at urban redevelopment, see Haas 1974. The Municipal Auditorium has remained locked and unused since Hurricane Katrina struck New Orleans in 2005.

2   Tylor 1871, 16; Kmen 1972, 5–17; J. Johnson 1991, 117–57; Roach 1996, 63–68; Souther 2003b; Wagner 2009, 58–115; Raeburn 2009a, 67; Evans 2011, 1–23; Sakakeeny 2011b, 295–304. For an example of Armstrong playing a mythical role in linking Congo Square to the history of jazz, see Brothers 2006, 4–5.

3   Cable 1886, 517–32; Asbury 1936, 180–92; Blesh 1946, 157–58; Bechet 1960, 6–44. For the futuristic auditorium superimposed on the past, see James Wobbe, "N.O. Auditorium Site in Old Days," *Item-Tribune*, October 14, 1928, 1–2; "Auditorium Site Near Beauregard Square Is Assured," *Times-Picayune*, September 12, 1928; "The Auditorium Site," *Times-Picayune*, March 11, 1927; "Why the $2,500,000 Municipal City Auditorium Should Be Built on the Old Beauregard Square Site," *Times-Picayune*, March 19, 1927. See also Crutcher 2010, 37–49.

4   For specifications announced at the time of the opening, see "New Orleans' New $2,500,000 Municipal Auditorium," *Times-Picayune*, May 30, 1930. For Walmsley's comments about "Negro shacks," see Minutes of the Municipal Auditorium Commission and

the Municipal Auditorium Advisory Committee, 1927–1963, Records of the Municipal Auditorium, City Archives, New Orleans Public Library, vol. 1, 25; Labouisse 1974, 75; "Cleared Square to Ease Parking," *Times-Picayune*, January 26, 1967; "U. S. Agency Okays Grant for N.O. Cultural Center," *Times-Picayune*, December 4, 1965; Victor H. Schiro, "Year End Report to the Citizens of New Orleans for 1965," City Archives, New Orleans Public Library; "Grant Okayed for Cultural Center Land," *States-Item*, August 26, 1965; Richard R. Dixon, "Culture Center," *Times-Picayune*, December 19, 1965; "Plan Cultural Building, Plea," *Times-Picayune*, February 23, 1967; Toledano and Christovich 1980, 16–17, 66–71; Campanella and Campanella 1999, 147; Crutcher 2010, 37–41, 67–75. On Schiro's advocacy for the Culture Center, see Haas 2014.

5 Philippe Soule, "Monument to Louie," *Times-Picayune*, July 10, 1971; Emile Lafourcade, "Storm of Protests Brewing over Armstrong Park Plans," *Times-Picayune*, August 12, 1973; "Armstrong Park: Yes and Maybe," *Times-Picayune*, September 14, 1973; "Go-Ahead for Armstrong Park," *Times-Picayune*, October 19, 1973; Paul Atkinson, "Jazz Event to Dedicate Park," *Times-Picayune*, March 8, 1980; Kelly Tucker, "A Memorial to Satchmo," *Times-Picayune*, April 11, 1980; Toledano and Christovich 1980, 68; Crutcher 2010, 66–81.

6 Watts and Williams 2006, 144–45, 158–60; G. Klein 2012, 47–62. Across this essay, I rely on the excellent documentation of regional wrestling territories provided by fans on the Kayfabe Memories website and message board. Kayfabe Memories, "Mid-South," n.d., http://www.kayfabememories.com/Regions/midsouth/msw.htm.

7 Toledano and Christovich 1980, 66–71; Campanella and Campanella 1999, 147; Crutcher 2010, 50–65.

8 This sense of cultural mission is anticipated and best expressed in the famous passage from the original preface to Matthew Arnold's *Culture and Anarchy*. "The whole scope of the essay," Arnold writes, "is to recommend culture as the great help out of our present difficulties; culture being a pursuit of our total perfection by means of getting to know, on all the matters which most concern us, the best which has been thought and said in the world, and, through this knowledge, turning a stream of fresh and free thought upon our stock notions and habits ([1869] 1909, viii). From this perspective, Mid-South stands for "anarchy" and for the "stock notions" and unexamined prejudices associated with popular culture and everyday life. On this tradition of thought, see also Williams 1958. On the sacralization of vernacular culture, see Lears 1981 and Stewart 1984.

9 The allusion here is to Horkheimer and Adorno (1972, 120–67).

10 On Carnival and cultural pretension, especially its appeals to literary tradition, see Roach (1996, 239–60). On the financial problems at the auditorium in the 1960s, see "Auditorium Fund Crisis Outlined," *States-Item*, May 7, 1962; "Orleans Symphony Crisis," *Times-Picayune*, April 14, 1965; "Wider Base for Culture," *Times-Picayune*, June 1, 1965. Through protests and repeated appeals, African Americans won the right to use the auditorium in 1953 and 1954. The auditorium would remain segregated, however, until 1963 ("Three Judges Sign Segregation Bar," *Times-Picayune*, August 6, 1963). On the efforts first to gain access and then to desegregate the auditorium, see Rogers 1993, 26, 37–38.

11 For this pattern of diversification in auditorium bookings, see Rental Calendar 1930–1965, Records of the Municipal Auditorium. The music schedule in the early 1960s included concerts by Jackie Wilson, James Brown, Elvis Presley, and Herman's Hermits.

On the auditorium, pop music, and youth culture, see Paul Atkinson, "Herman and the Hermits Greeted by Girl Brigade," *Times-Picayune*, August 2, 1965. On the controversy over the boxing and wrestling subsidies, see Minutes, vol. 2, 114–15; "Auditorium Costs High—Messina: Seeks Low Rent for Fights," *Times-Picayune*, May 19, 1965; "Fights—None Too Many?," *Times-Picayune*, May 24, 1965. On the Perkins versus Lane event, see "Lane-Perkins Fight to Make La. History," *Washington Afro-American*, October 12, 1965; "Eddie Perkins Battles 'Lefty' Lane at Auditorium Tonight," *Times-Picayune*, October 25, 1965; Buddy Diliberto, "Floors Vet Twice in Early Rounds: Fight First Modern Mixed Match in New Orleans," *Times-Picayune*, October 26, 1965.

12 Frank Gagnard, "Chopin Thrown by Rock 'n' Roll," *Times-Picayune*, March 19, 1963; Frank Gagnard, "Victor Borge Wins Out over Wrestling," *Times-Picayune*, November 17, 1961; Charles L. DuFour, "Boxing Crowd, Dancers KO Musical Program," *States-Item*, February 26, 1964; Ross Yocky, "Auditorium Great for Pugilists but for Operatic Tunes? Forget It," *States-Item*, October 15, 1966. For the governing board's discussion of soundproofing and the partition structure, see Minutes, vol. 2, 25; "Municipal Auditorium to Have Acoustical Shell," *Times-Picayune*, September 17, 1964; "Concert, Fight Noise Compete," *Times-Picayune*, February 26, 1964; "Auditorium Exec Warns on Parking," *Times-Picayune*, July 28, 1965; "Thug Snatches Fur Stole from Woman after Ball," *Times-Picayune*, January 27, 1967; Paul Atkinson, "Fall to Bring Easy Parking at Auditorium, Arts Center," *Times-Picayune*, May 19, 1979. The *Times-Picayune* reported one source saying that "opera and symphony buffs will buy the park concept including 'their' concert hall only if the park is fenced and with the community center located outside" (David Cuthbert, "High School Arts Center Conflicts with Park Plans," *Times-Picayune*, June 11, 1973); Emile Lafourcade, "Storm of Protests Brewing over Armstrong Park Plans," *Times-Picayune*, August 12, 1973.

13 Watts and Williams 2006, 138–65; G. Klein 2012, 29–62; Kayfabe Memories, "Mid-South." Watts also followed Messina in his weekly Monday night booking, which Messina demanded, and received, in the 1960s. "Fights—None Too Many?" *Times-Picayune*, May 24, 1965.

14 Kayfabe Memories, "Mid-South"; Watts and Williams 2006, 138–65; G. Klein 2012, 29–62.

15 Watts and Williams 2006, 138–51; G. Klein 2012, 6, 68, 84–85; Kayfabe Memories, "Mid-South."

16 Meltzer 2001, 93–105; Watts and Williams 2006, 113, 133, 140–45; G. Klein 2012, 3–5, 15–27, 78. See also Shoemaker 2013, 143–50.

17 Watts and Williams 2006, 144–45, 158–60; G. Klein 2012, 10. According to Kayfabe Memories, JYD "held the North American Heavyweight Title 4 times, the Mid-South Tag Team Title 8 times . . . the Louisiana Heavyweight Title 3 times, and the Mississippi Heavyweight Title 1 time." This was "unparalleled." See Kayfabe Memories, "Mid-South."

18 Meltzer 2001, 93–105; Watts and Williams 2006, 140; G. Klein 2012, 9; Kayfabe Memories, "Mid-South."

19 G. Klein 2012, x–xi, 75–102.

20 Watts and Williams 2006, 144–45; G. Klein 2012, 68–72; Kayfabe Memories, "Mid-South."

21 Watts and Williams 2006, 158–60; G. Klein 2012, 89–96; Kayfabe Memories, "Mid-South."

22 *Mid-South Wrestling* (TV show), June 24, 1982; *Mid-South Wrestling*, October 28, 1982; Watts and Williams 2006, 158–60, 175; DiBiase 2008, 126–32; G. Klein 2012, 89–96.

23 Tuck 2001, 78–96, 140–65; DiBiase 2008, 126–32; G. Klein 2012, 89–96; Kayfabe Memories, "Mid-South."

24 *Mid-South Wrestling*, November 4, 1982; Watts and Williams 2006, 158–60; DiBiase 2008, 126–32; G. Klein 2012, 89–96.

25 On these issues in natural law, Tuck 2001, 1–16.

26 Odum and Johnson 1925, 164–65, 196–206; Roberts 1989, 171–215; Brown 2003.

27 Brown 2003, 1–20, 37–47, 59–69.

28 Piliawsky 1985, 5–23; Hirsch 1990, 461–84; Tate 1993; G. Klein 2012, 47–62.

29 *Mid-South Wrestling*, November 4, 1982.

30 *Mid-South Wrestling*, November 4, 1982.

31 Odum and Johnson 1925, 196–98; Lomax and Lomax 1934, 93–99; Wheeler 1944, 100.

32 On anxiety about contamination endemic to folk song collection, see for example Hamilton (2009).

33 On the proposed JYD statue in the park, Jules Bentley, "Lost Dog: The Search for a Forgotten New Orleans Superhero," *Antigravity*, July 2012, 22, http://www.antigravitymagazine.com/2012/07/junkyard-dog/.

34 For the early controversy over the construction of the Municipal Auditorium, see "Society Protests Auditorium Site," *Times-Picayune*, March 24, 1927; "Tots Plead against Auditorium Site," *Times-Picayune*, April 19, 1928; "Injunction Looms over Beauregard for Auditorium: Council Hears Protests to Using Historic Square for Public Building," *Times-Picayune*, April 25, 1928; "Club Opposes Square as Auditorium Site," *Times-Picayune*, May 8, 1928. On the legal challenge to the city's right to expropriate the land, see "Urge Court Test on Use of Square for Auditorium: Commission Asks O'Keefe to Designate Beauregard Officially," *Times-Picayune*, May 23, 1928. On the Culture Center, "Action to Save Square Urged," *Times-Picayune*, October 25, 1965. On neighborhood activism in the time of Armstrong Park, see Dwight Ott, "Treme Group Demands Half Culture Center Jobs," *Times-Picayune*, March 5, 1972; "Officials Give Treme Pledge: Vow Aid to Area as Culture Center Built," *Times-Picayune*, March 7, 1972; J. E. Bourgoyne, "Treme Area Waiting Its Turn for Something Good to Happen," *Times-Picayune*, June 23, 1974; "NORD Adds New Playgrounds to Serve Community," *Times-Picayune*, January 30, 1977; "Revitalizing Tremé East Is Goal of Organization," *Times-Picayune*, January 7, 1978; Kathleen Frick, "Watchful Neighborhood Surrounds Armstrong Park," *Times-Picayune*, August 18, 1980; "Tremé Leader: Park to Hurt Poor Blacks," *Times-Picayune*, March 11, 1983.

6

Local, Native, Creole, Black

Claiming Belonging, Producing Autochthony

HELEN A. REGIS

The tension between autochthony's apparent self-evidence and its receding qualities in practice comes again sharply to the fore.

—PETER GESCHIERE, *The Perils of Belonging*

We aren't Houma Indian on both sides or full-blooded Tangipahoa. So we really can't go on and rant about how we're Natives, and they're not, you know?

—DAVIS, *Ex Machina*

You get on the boat, you lose your indigeneity.

—SAVANNAH SHANGE, *Gallery of the Streets*

How do you know a local when you see one? Who counts as indigenous in the diasporic spaces of New Orleans?

Here I consider several ethnographic moments in my personal engagement with the public culture of the city, following parading clubs, studying festivals, and working with cultural nonprofits and grassroots organizations. I also draw on experiences shared by friends, neighbors, and other chroniclers of the city to explore how ethnoracial categories, articulated with cultural heritage, are wielded by anthropologists, activists, artists, journalists, festival producers, and others working in the cultural industries of New Orleans. The examples in this chapter explore how New Orleans residents and visitors evaluate each other, drawing lines around what constitutes real belonging and cultural citizenship. They also raise questions about how scholars—as researchers, community organizers, and collaborators—become complicit in enforcing boundaries of belonging, indigeneity, and autochthony. What are the ethical and practical issues faced by cultural workers in these institutional border zones? How does the wielding of categorical identities and the policing of social and cultural borders play into the dialectics of New Orleans exceptionalism?

New Orleanians these days are obsessed with belonging. The issue is widespread, particularly among young professionals who have relocated to the city since 2005, notably those coming to work in the nonprofit sector and cultural industries. These newcomers are simultaneously applauded and criticized for the rise in housing costs, the proliferation of STRs (short-term rentals), and what some are calling the "gentrification of the culture." The discourse of belonging in New Orleans is complex, stratified, and racialized. And yet this is not a uniquely local phenomenon. Many of the local patterns of wielding categorical identities reflect global trends heightened through neoliberal governance.[1] However, the intensity and complexity of this discourse in New Orleans, its ubiquity in city life and its internalized rankings, reflect a distinctive sense of place and peoplehood. Indeed, it may be said that belonging in contemporary New Orleans is exceptionally contested. While there has been a noticeable intensification of racializing practices in the city since the floods of 2005,[2] these are practices with a long history, predating Katrina, levee failures, FEMA, HOPE VI and historic districts, redlining and interstates, suburbanization, white flight, and gentrification. Others have explored the intensification of identity-work and the linkages between these and the struggle for citizenship rights.[3] Through examples drawn from the 1970s to the post-Katrina era, I suggest that we consider these practices as part of a wider (and longer) discourse of autochthony in New Orleans, and as a moment in categorical claims making about ethnoracial identity, cultural heritage, and social belonging. This is a discourse that is still evolving and that reflects (or reacts to) contemporary social and political realities, and thus the examples offered here can only illustrate moments in its unfolding, which are already, as of this writing, history.

Both long-term residents and newcomers to the city wield categorical identities like "local" and "transplant," "gentrifier" and "community" member, "indigenous" and "newcomer," terms that are often implicitly or explicitly racialized in their usage. While indigenous and indigeneity are now part of the New Orleans vernacular, *autochtone* and autochthony are not. In fact, the latter terms are more widely used in francophone contexts to refer to First Nations or aboriginal populations in contrast to settlers, migrants, (post)colonials, or expats. I strategically draw on the literature on autochthony emerging from francophone sub-Saharan Africa to highlight the political and economic dimensions of identity claims making in contemporary New Orleans.

These examples, from sites as diverse as community gardens, bars, festivals, hurricane anniversaries, and theatrical performances, show how residents and visitors interpolate each other, assert their own claims, and assess each other's claims to belong. For heuristic purposes, I've grouped them into four categories, reflecting four of the major ways in which belonging claims are made. These groupings are neither exhaustive nor mutually exclusive. First is the outsider gaze of tourists, journalists, and researchers—exoticizing, orientalizing, or colonizing and inevitably shaped by their agendas, imaginations, and longings to connect across social divides. Our visitors project their desires onto a city and population that have undergone a flood of mass media coverage, tourism (including disaster tourism), faith-based missions, service-learning classes, and community-engaged research.[4] These visitors make determinations about which residents they wish to interact with and how. Over time, these encounters have shaped how area residents understand their own identities, whether through affirming, resisting, or confronting the outsider's gaze. Second, as residents we rank each other's belonging as more or less central to the city's identity through our claims to indigeneity and autochthony, as well as cultural property—all of which often leverage familiar tropes of ethnoracial identity. Third, the deployment of time scales allows for an endlessly evolving ranking as degrees of belonging are asserted based on length of residence in the city. A fourth, performative claim to belonging operates through highly valued activities recognized as socially and culturally salient and as transformative, such as festivals, Carnival, and parades. These distinctive ways of asserting belonging may operate simultaneously and are highly context dependent and temporally evolving. While all of these are widely observable in everyday conversations, they may not all be accepted as valid by any specific individual or collectivity.

Claims to belonging are ubiquitous in the social life of the city, and New Orleans residents are undergoing evaluations of their claims all the time.

One example underlines the quotidian nature of these discussions. Barbara, a white professional woman in her fifties, was in conversation with a Lyft driver who asked her, "Are you from here?" "No, but I've been living here for over thirty years," she answered. "Thirty years! Well, you're from here then," he affirmed. "Now, you know that's not true," she replied. He laughed, "Oh yeah, you mean you can't answer the question about where you went to high school! That's what it's all about in New Orleans." This exemplary exchange involves two people playing with each other and their delight in their shared knowledge of the game, even if it positions them in different locations in the social landscape. The friendly banter between the driver and the passenger can even be read as a marker of conviviality—of pleasure in acknowledging each other's participation in a shared social world. Even as the rider acknowledges her own outsider status (not being from here), she claims a community of practice through her knowledge of the rules of discourse. The driver simultaneously offers belonging ("Thirty years? You're from here") and laughingly acknowledges that such status is ultimately elusive (the high school question). The driver's inclusive gesture is especially generous since, as other writers in this volume observe, many New Orleanians take it for granted that their city is special, if not exceptional. They may well assume that visitors and newer residents often very much want to belong. A startlingly similar scene is enacted by performance artist Dante Anthony Fuoco in his one-man show *Transplant*. In Fuoco's version, the new arrival to the city gushes about his eagerness to participate in his first second line, while an Uber driver, portrayed with a Siri-like computer-generated voice, challenges the young rider with the history of the destruction of the North Claiborne corridor by Interstate 10 as she drives him to his Tremé-area rental. "Wow. I didn't know that," the young rider concedes in a subdued tone. "White privilege," the Siri-like voice replies, "means you don't have to confront uncomfortable histories." Whereas Barbara, in the above example, is a longtime resident who frankly acknowledges that she'll never be a native, the young and earnest Teach for America worker in *Transplant* is caught up in a profound longing to belong and has yet to confront his role in the evolving societal structure of the city. Fuoco's play confronts revanchist capitalism, the crisis in affordable housing accelerated by the influx of young professionals, and white newcomers' longing for acceptance.

But in addition to the evident struggles of the émigré, there is also a fragility to belonging for many people who appear at first glance to belong to the city unequivocally. And this fragility bespeaks a certain vulnerability. Ruth, an African American writer from New Orleans, recently told me that although she is an accomplished cook, she does not make classic New Orleans recipes like gumbos and étouffées, because, while she grew up in the city, she doesn't come from a long line of Creole cooks. Thus, while she is clearly from here in many ways, she lacks both a long line of local ancestors and specifically Creole ones. This example illustrates how belonging and cultural property feed into each other, as she suggests that gumbos and étouffées somehow are not hers—they were not transmitted to her in the hearth, as it were, from one cook to another. And not being Creole, as others have written, brings with it an awareness that some New Orleanians will not claim you as theirs.[5] Not completely.

Part One: The Visitor's Gaze

"Will There Be Hurricane Survivors Here?"
The year is 2006. The location is a community garden in the Seventh Ward. As members of the Porch Seventh Ward Cultural Organization gathered for a workday in the garden, a visitor working on a book about hurricane survivors asked one of the gardeners, "Will there be hurricane survivors here?" The gardener was stunned. Clearly, the visitor assumed that the gardener's whiteness meant he was not a survivor—or at least, not an authentic one. This visitor was later found in a remote area of the garden, tape-recording an interview with an African American child about his traumatic experiences during the storm.

The writer's own whiteness may have informed her understanding of survivors as distinguished from other residents and workers as people whose bodies bore the visible marks of oppression. This understanding was no doubt shaped by weeks and months of totalizing media representations of Katrina victims as both poor and black—images that have been thoroughly critiqued.[6] But it also brings to light two additional dynamics in postdisaster landscapes of the city:

1. White volunteers and activists' desires for contact with black victims and a related search for cathartic experiences in which they might both exorcise white guilt and reach out to people most visibly and brutally affected by neoliberal revanchist capitalism
2. The mediating role for black-led and black-centered nonprofits in providing access to poor black residents for white or middle-class individuals, organizations, or foundations and cultural activists, disaster workers, or volunteers of all stripes

Elsewhere, I've explored how public cultural events like the Jazz Fest mediate black folk cultures for middle/upper-class consumers seeking communion and transcendence,[7] as do a variety of nonprofits laboring in the postdisaster landscapes of uneven development and reconstruction. While this particular nonprofit in no way intended to provide this service, we found ourselves complicit in this process. As an anthropologist who is also a longtime resident of the neighborhood and a Porch member, I found myself facilitating this practice, to my dismay and frustration. While I confronted the journalist about the ethics of interviewing children, I was left with the feeling that our efforts at community building could be exploited in ways that we had not anticipated, as progressive journalists and policy wonks who wanted to meet real people (meaning: not middle class and not white) would come to our events and meetings. In their search for unmediated encounters with black subjects, they subsequently often erased our multiracial organization from their representations.[8]

Some took pains to show the complexity of Katrina. For example, Spike Lee's 2006 film *When the Levees Broke* is notable for showing white victims in various states of abjection alongside black victims. Luisa Dantas's 2011 film *Land of Opportunity* takes an even more expansive view, including architects and planners among her featured characters, alongside middle-class residents of Gentilly, public housing activists, and community organizers in the Lower Ninth Ward. She also portrays migrant workers from Brazil who came to the city to find work, and she tracks their aspirations and disappointments side by side with those of other city residents looking to create a viable future for themselves and their families. Other representations from the mainstream media seemed to focus almost exclusively on black victims and white affluent residents who manage to escape the worst. Adolph Reed has warned of the limits of the race concept for addressing pervasive and growing social inequality in the United States (see chapter 14, this volume).[9] As Cedric Johnson and John Arena have argued, racial identity politics can be self-defeating as a foundational political strategy.[10] Dwelling on blackness feeds into both the poverty industries and the culture industries that commodify blackness as a signifier of both social suffering and redemptive creativity. Black-run, black-centered, and small-scale nonprofits active in the postdisaster landscape had the potential to create meaningful and potentially transformative experiences and initiatives for those involved. But with the systematic dismantling of public institutions (including schools, hospitals, and libraries), these organizations were put in an untenable position.[11] They could not rebuild 100,000 homes or replace public schools or public libraries or after-school programs. They also risked being used as poster children for neoliberal triumphalism. The emphasis on self-help and autonomy in grassroots organizing and nonprofit organizations recalls the pull-yourself-up-by-your-bootstraps capitalism of Booker T. Washington—strategies that resonate with all those disheartened by the failure of public institutions but that are ill-matched to either the depth of long-term structural violence or the geographical scale of an un-natural disaster like a Katrina.[12]

I began by highlighting the usage of the terms "indigenous" and "survivor," which are clearly at play in a discursive field that includes the terms "local," "native," "creole," and "black" (in uppercase and lowercase variations). The meanings of these terms depend, of course on the context in which they are uttered—both social and temporal—and they always imply their others. "Indigenous" has always distinguished those who came before from those who came later. In the Western Hemisphere, indigenous people as a category came into being with the arrival of Columbus and the virulent diseases and genocidal practices that soon followed. The term "Creole," which once distinguished New World Africans and Europeans from those born in Africa or Europe, was repurposed after the Louisiana Purchase to highlight the cultural resis-tance of francophone New Orleanians, including free people of color, to the processes of Americanization.[13] As it became increasingly associated with Creoles of color, the term was later rejected by white Creoles.[14] The Civil War, Reconstruction, and the brutal institutionalization of Jim Crow and disenfranchisement of thousands of African Americans became pivotal mo-ments of crisis and resistance that galvanized a heightened discourse of cul-tural belonging alongside claims to citizenship. The nativism of Louisiana Creoles in the face of American incomers is legendary.[15] With the rise of Jim Crow in the 1890s, Louisiana folklorists used the collecting of folklore—especially African American folklore—as a way to clarify and reinforce their own identity claims as members of a high-status group of intellectu-als who were both white and Southern.[16] In post-Katrina New Orleans, "natives" came to distinguish those who were born there from the newcom-ers who came after the flood as insurance adjusters, contractors, workers, or volunteers to be a part of the rebuilding. The term "local"—a more inclusive term than "native"—was increasingly claimed by pre-Katrina arrivals whose return to the city after the flood concretized their commitment to place.

My argument here is that the local—rather than being apparent or organic—is just as problematic as all the other terms that have come before, like Creole. It was precisely produced by the disaster and by the experts (like the journalist) who came (and continued to come) in its wake with their desperate need to consume or create local knowledge, local perspectives, and local partners.

Community, Neoliberal Capitalism, and Autochthony
In his book, *The Perils of Belonging: Autochthony, Citizenship, and Exclusion in Africa and Europe*, Peter Geschiere examined the resurgence of discourses of autochthony in neoliberalizing contexts—especially in West Africa and Europe—including Cameroon, Ivory Coast, and the Netherlands. In an American Anthropological Association conference panel, he remarked,

> The neoliberal is always the celebration of the market and the celebration of community. And because they never define what they mean by it, this creates a situation where members of local populations have to fight it out to determine who belongs in this community. Despite being told that we now live in a cosmopolitan world, more and more people have begun to assert their identities in ways that are deeply rooted in the local. These claims of autochthony, meaning "born from the soil"—seek to establish an irrefutable, primordial right to belong and are often employed in po-litically charged attempts to exclude outsiders.[17]

While Geschiere's analysis of African identity politics might seem misplaced in an analysis of New Orleans, I would suggest that the mix of economic, political, and cultural crises engendered by the ongoing manmade disaster that followed the 2005 floods are not entirely dissimilar to the crises that have unfolded in post–Cold War African societies, with the advent of po-litical and economic restructuring catalyzed by the Washington Consensus, also known as the "neoliberal vulgate."[18] As Geschiere writes, "the tension between autochthony's apparent self-evidence and its receding qualities in practice comes again sharply to the fore."[19]

Working in a similar vein, Achille Mbembe has discussed the troubling role of funding agencies in the realm of arts and culture in Africa. Mbembe is well positioned to speak about the policies of funders in Africa. He ran a major research institute for several years, in which his primary role was culti-vating relationships with philanthropic agencies and developing projects. He calls attention to several troubling trends, including

> the conflation of African art, culture and aesthetics with ethnicity or community or communalism. The dominant but false idea—shared by many Africans and many donors—is that the act of creativity is neces-sarily a collective act; that African artistic forms are not aesthetic objects

per se but ciphers of a deeper level of the "real" that is fundamentally ethnographic and expressive of Africa's ontological cultural difference or "authenticity." *It is this African "difference" and this African "authenticity" donors are keen to find, support and, if necessary, manufacture.*[20]

This manufacturing of authenticity and difference is also observable in other locations that have been positioned, as Michel-Rolph Trouillot would have it, "in the savage slot."[21]

In a 2009 article, Rachel Breunlin and I analyzed the tendency of funders working in New Orleans to seek to affiliate with the grassroots, the real, and the marginalized, oppressed, and radical constituencies, who are most easily identified by their own discourse of alterity, indigeneity, victimization, and community empowerment. Multiracial alliances and organizations with a less obviously indigenous aesthetic can be sidelined or distorted by these dynamics. Journalists who have worked in New Orleans post-Katrina have displayed similar tendencies, as my first example illustrates. But it is important to recognize that scholars working in New Orleans have been engaged in similar practices—including some academics involved in service learning and other forms of community-engaged teaching and research—practices that intensified and proliferated after the flood. As a city resident, teacher, and researcher, I have participated in these engagements from both sides.

With limited time in the field and a strong desire to craft articles or research agendas that are clearly aligned with social justice imperatives and the authenticity of blackness, scholars tend to reify and reproduce black/white and rich/poor binaries that significantly underestimate the presence of middle-class African Americans, Creoles, Vietnamese, Hondurans, multiethnic workers, and un- (or under)employed anarchist or radical whites. The overrepresentation of the Lower Ninth Ward and the near erasure of adjacent mostly white St. Bernard Parish and more affluent Lakeview in scholarly works reproduces media fixation with blackness as victimhood. The invisibility of black middle-class neighborhoods like Pontchartrain Park and economically diverse and mostly black and Latino New Orleans East in the public transcript heightens social suffering and perpetuates sensationalizing accounts that obscure real structural processes in times of crisis as in ordinary times.[22] Antoinette Jackson, in her 2011 essay "Diversifying the Dialogue Post-Katrina," points to the blatant disregard of those she calls "boring black people," people who did not participate in second-line parades or mask as Indians but were nonetheless city residents.[23] As Jackson demonstrates, many black professionals struggled (and sometimes hesitated) to return in the precarious landscape of post-2005 New Orleans, yet their struggles were often overlooked. As one former public school teacher told me, speaking of her mostly African American colleagues, "The teachers I worked with at a public school—they felt invisible. They're middle class. They had good incomes. They mostly had stable marriages. None of them belonged to Mardi Gras Indian tribes or Social and Pleasure Clubs. I remember talking with one of them about the second-lines and she said 'Our families just didn't do things like that.'"[24] The symbolic violence of this kind of invisibility afflicts communities that have been largely ignored by scholars (including urban sociologists and anthropologists) until recently as well as the mainstream media.[25] They have long been underrepresented in the popular culture's obsession with and commodification of insurgent and creative blackness.[26]

In a series of blog entries, Catherine Michna has written insightfully about the hunger for authentic black culture in postdiluvial New Orleans. She is onto something here. This desire for an idealized and essentialized blackness, which is imagined to be somehow outside of capitalism and outside of history, is a profound motivator for many. And this obsession with authentic black working-class street culture has other consequences in erasing other experiences, other subjectivities. The former teacher reflected, "What the white middle class and the black middle class have in common in New Orleans is our invisibility. Our stories are not told. Or they are marginalized as unimportant." The accompanying fetishization and reification of black vernacular countercultures and the links between this process and the reemergence of forms of ethnic absolutism and fascism has preoccupied Paul Gilroy, who writes,

> We can appreciate the hunger for cultural forms that stand outside the immorality and corruption of the overdeveloped world, but imprisoning the primitive other in a fantasy of innocence can only be catastrophic for all parties involved. This danger is compounded when the interests of the romantic consumers begin to converge with those of people inside minority communities who want to enforce another definition of invariant (and therefore authentic) ethnicity for their own dubious disciplinary reasons.[27]

Under the gaze of outsiders, including tourists, journalists, and anthropologists, certain cultural identities have been made hypervisible and valorized, even as those who create second-line parades and brass-band music and others working to create the highly desirable cultural commodities promoted in tourism brochures continue to struggle with the structural violence of depressed wages, aggressive and uneven policing, and restricted access to good housing, education, health care, and transportation.[28]

Part Two: Cultural Property as Belonging

New Orleans is often proclaimed to be the most African city in America,[29] and the discourse of heritage in institutions like the New Orleans Jazz and Heritage Festival is highly attuned to a diasporic analysis of the city's contemporary cultural and musical productions.[30] When Jazz Fest initiated a series of international pavilions in the early 1990s, the first year was devoted to Haiti, the second year to Mali. Participants in these cross-cultural exchanges were encouraged to consider historic linkages and ancestral connections between their countries and Louisiana—linkages often conceived through a black Atlantic/African diasporic lens.[31] In the 1990s, a member of a Jewish marching krewe was told by a festival producer that his organization would not be invited to parade at Jazz Fest because "Jews are not indigenous." If the festival context could be said to be one where talk of diaspora is hegemonic, why then this usage of the term "indigenous"? The vernacular discourse of New Orleans festival workers and producers reflects American multiculturalism, so it is understandable that the folk whose heritage is on display at the festival primarily come from historically marginalized, excluded, or oppressed groups—and in New Orleans today, the festival worker is clear: that means not Jews.

To unpack this example, we need to look back at the narratives about the origins of New Orleans's distinctive culture, particularly in one place, Congo Square. As one scholar put it, "All that New Orleans *is*—is a result of Congo Square."[32] The mytho-history of Congo Square attributes the distinctiveness of New Orleans's Afro-Creole culture to the social, cultural, and economic exchanges and performances that took place there in the eighteenth and early nineteenth centuries. This place is remembered as a sacred site and a powerful cultural cauldron, from which emerged all of American popular music and dance—from jazz, blues, and eventually rock and roll, to the city's Mardi Gras Indian traditions and iconic second-line parades. Forged from African and Native American traditions, but made into something new, the city's distinctive culture—and indeed American popular culture—came out of the earth in this place. Of course, this myth, like all myths, has a history.[33] This canonical narrative about the square and its generative influence as axis mundi, omphalos, and genealogical fount was produced in specific historical moments, including critical moments in the jazz revival of the 1930s and '40s. Matt Sakakeeny critically examines the process through which the centrality of Congo Square was enshrined by music writers and musicians themselves. Writing about the creation of this narrative, he explains that specific contemporary practices are imagined to link—in a sacralized time-space portal—back to their origins: "More precisely, jazz funerals and second line parades have been reimagined as a conduit that links jazz back to the celebrated slave dances at Congo Square and, by implication, to Africa."[34] Sakakeeny's analysis suggests that Smith and Ramsey, the authors of *Jazzmen*, had a large role in shaping that claim. "In New Orleans," they write, "you could still hear the bamboula on Congo Square when Buddy Bolden cut his first chorus on cornet."[35] Evidence presented by Sakakeeny is suggestive of a long dialogue between writers, musicians, dancers, and other narrators, who both claim and shape the genealogies linking contemporary art forms to the mytho-history of Congo Square.

The centrality of Congo Square in Black Arts poetry and literature out of New Orleans almost seems inevitable. But historically, it was the result of a concerted effort by public intellectuals, notably Tom Dent and Kalamu ya Salaam, whose work as writers, educators, and organizers with the Congo Square Writers Union, sought to place black history at the center of the city's public culture.[36] They were among a group of African American activists who fought to create their own structures of curation and their own standards of belonging in the city and the festival. One of those structures was the Afrikan American Jazz Festival Coalition.

The Afrikan American Jazz Festival Coalition

In 1979, the New Orleans Jazz and Heritage Festival program book announced the creation of Koindu: A Place of Exchange, a new section of the festival making its debut at the fairgrounds:

> KOINDU seeks to correct a legacy of paternalism which had non-Blacks speak for and determine the authenticity and work of African culture. At KOINDU the creators of African and African-American culture will perform, explain and evaluate their own cultural works. Everyone is welcomed to share, and no one is allowed to dominate.

> KOINDU marks the continuation of the conscious affirmation of the importance and quality of African contributions to world culture.[37]

In his oral history, Koindu founder Hajj Khalil remembers the early Koindu marketplace as an immersive experience in which one could sample crafts, food, music, and dance of a continent that was much misunderstood. Cofounder Bilal Sunni-Ali describes the Koindu area as a place for "intensified" experience of black/African culture, in contrast to the rest of the festival where this experience was "dispersed." What's at stake for Khalil and Sunni-Ali is the Koindu area's capacity to educate, to raise consciousness, to politicize, and to activate people through exposure to African and African diaspora culture, art, and music. The fact that Koindu was run by coalition members concretized a specific goal of the Black Arts Movement—control of the means of cultural production. Though others were welcome to visit, Koindu was made by and for black people. The curation, production, performance, and commerce were in the hands of African Americans.

How a Black Arts space came to be created in the middle of a (mostly) white-run festival is a story that is not widely known, and one too rich and complex to fully recount here (see Regis 2013; Regis and Walton 2008). In brief, it came about through struggle. As the festival grew and became more successful in the 1970s, critiques of its production structures circulated among intellectuals and political activists. A number of craftspeople were complaining that they were being rejected from the festival's marketplace, and others objected to what they saw as underrepresentation of African Americans among those profiting from this festival. One of the organizers, Muhammed Yungai, recalled how they understood the problem: "The Jazz Festival is an institution whose reason for being is basically the culture of Black people in America. So it's founded on Black culture, but the Black artists, artisans, and people that were actually making a living selling things that we made, were pretty much being rejected."[38] Building on intersecting citywide networks, with hundreds of residents attending their meetings, the coalition activists were poised to disrupt the festival in 1978. Festival producer George Wein recalled a tense meeting with a group of black activists arguing, "You have been ripping off black culture. The community is not benefiting nearly enough by what's happening."[39] Koindu was an immediate result of these negotiations. It became not only a marketplace but a social and cultural space for music, dance, poetry, and self-representation. The coalition also achieved an increase in community representation on the board of directors and an agreement that a portion of festival proceeds would be reinvested in the African American community through grants and public programs. The physical presence of Koindu in the festival landscape and the coalition's gains on the board provided a platform to push for ongoing structural changes in hiring practices to bring more black professionals on staff, and to work toward a pragmatic model of governance, which Bill Rouselle called power-sharing.[40]

All of these developments grew out of activists' vision of the links to be made between culturalist claims and political and economic goals. The coalition advanced a persuasive claim to jazz and jazz heritage as the cultural property of African Americans. But it was their political capacity to disrupt the festival that brought festival producers to the table. As a result of the agreements that emerged from those meetings, the coalition members' views became a part of the festival's governing structure. Their push to place black people, as well as black music and heritage, at the center of the festival began to shape the processes of curation and production beyond Koindu. Ultimately, the coalition's creation, Koindu, was assimilated into the festival's central production structures and renamed Congo Square in 1989.

From Belonging to Indigeneity

The Afrikan American Jazz Festival Coalition's intervention in the public culture of the city complicates our understanding of indigeneity/autochthony as they simultaneous claim belonging in the city and in any major event going on in the city, and made a claim to ownership of jazz as a collective cultural property. These developments illustrate how claims to belonging in place can work and what's at stake in claims to autochthony and indigeneity. Claiming jazz as cultural property, African American activists effectively made the claim that they belonged at Jazz Fest—not only on the stages as musicians but also as producers, curators, and artists, and also as professional members of the staff, trained technicians, contractors and vendors, decision makers, and members of the festival's board of directors. Ultimately, the coalition claimed the right to curate their own culture. The culture belonged to them and therefore they belonged to any institutional structure that claimed to represent it. Autochthony here works to underwrite a political strategy. And it worked. At least for a time.

The festival producers' long encounter with politicized cultural activists shaped their usage of the term "indigenous." Coalition activists saw the current predicament and potential futures of black New Orleanians as being linked to colonized people everywhere.[41] Indigenous, in addition to its connotations of rootedness in place, underlines the commonalities of black and indigenous peoples through their historical subjection to settler colonialism and enslavement, displacement, violence, and dispossession—including the theft of their culture and the prohibition of their cultural practices and religious practices through colonial lawmaking. So black folks in New Orleans are indigenous in that they were (and perhaps still are) colonized and struggling to create their own social and cultural spaces under the weight of (post)colonial cultural economic and political systems not of their own making. This usage of a term—analogous with subaltern—may function as a decolonizing move. But my observations suggest that when this term is redeployed in the context of festival productions, it is depoliticized and figures as both a euphemism for race and a way to make the festival seem more attuned to cultural nationalist concerns than it actually is. The category indigenous also brings with it all manner of problematic cultural baggage, which is the legacy of early twentieth-century anthropology, including the assumption that cultures are bounded and isolated from each other and that they have a purity and authenticity that can be identified and cataloged. This concept empowers scholars (notably anthropologists themselves), curators of culture, and the most prominent proponents of revitalization while it marginalizes the everyday practitioners of subaltern cultural groups, even as their cultural productions are idealized and praised by the experts.[42]

It would be a mistake to conclude from these examples either that we all want to belong or that drawing boundaries is ridiculous. Claims to belonging are being made in situations of vast power inequality. By juxtaposing them, there is a risk that even making a comparison across them implies a leveling. Because social and cultural claims are made in such profoundly unequal conditions, the stakes may be quite different. This critical engagement with moments of (top-down) curation and festival production are meant to expose the distorting power/knowledge dynamics in play with claims to belonging. Any critical examination of the claims to autochthony that does not clearly demonstrate what's at stake for those making bottom-up claims to belonging and cultural property risks reproducing a strictly culturalist argument that further erases the structural oppression and violence black cultural activists are working against.

Part Three: The Timescales of Autochthonous Citizenship

In the aftermath of the floods of 2005, and the massive forced migration and long-term displacements that resulted from levee failures and local, state, and federal policies that followed, the claims to indigeneity made by (and on behalf of) black folk in New Orleans took on a whole other cast. In the spring of 2006, with the mayoral campaigns in full swing, the question of who belonged in the city and who could or should vote made the political implications of "local" clear. As city maps were being redrawn by expert planners and revanchist fantasies evoked wiping the slate clean and reconstituting a smaller, whiter, and more affluent city, citizens sought to assert their claims to the city in unambiguous categorical terms, as Arnold Hirsh has argued in "Fade to Black."

As Campbell Robertson, writing for the *New York Times*, reflected on the occasion of the tenth anniversary: "As of 2013, there were nearly 100,000 fewer black residents than in 2000, their absences falling equally across income levels. The white population decreased by about 11,000, but it is wealthier."[43] Robertson quotes Michael Hecht of Greater New Orleans Inc., a group concerned with economic development, about the significant brain gain in the city since the floods:

> "New Orleans attracted some of the best and most passionate people in the world after Katrina to help rebuild," Mr. Hecht said. "You just had a talent influx. A lot of people saw New Orleans as the Peace Corps with better food."

Framing New Orleans as a Peace Corps destination underlines the common experience of visitors to the city that they have somehow exited the United States to enter an adjacent Third World country. But as Kristin Koptiuch has argued in a classic article, "Third-Worlding at Home," the profound inequalities and disinvestment in public institutions and infrastructure are in fact integral to contemporary US society rather than exceptions.

An Anniversary in Fragments

The year is 2015. On the occasion of the tenth anniversary of the levee failures, a black feminist collective creates ECOHYBRIDITY: LOVE SONG FOR NOLA, a series of performances and site-specific installations, which they called "a visual [black] opera" staged at sites throughout the city.[44] At this moment, the city was once gain inundated by national media and major players from national nonprofits and funders to reflect on the state of affairs and assess the achievements, failures, and ongoing challenges of the unnatural disasters. The intervention of this intriguing and elusive group of black feminist activists and artists speaks directly to the malaise around place, identity, and belonging that was gripping the city. A short film posted by the collective features cultural anthropologist Savannah Shange, a participating artist, speaking directly to the uses of indigeneity as a trope for thinking through displacement, gentrification, and structural violence in contemporary North America.

You see, to me the idea that everyone is indigenous, by definition does not apply to Black people. So Blackness is made by the lack of indigeneity, otherwise we'd be Igbo, otherwise, we'd be Kikuyu. We ain't, we Black. That's the whole fucking thing. See, Black people . . . you get on the boat, you loose your indigeneity. And any gesture toward erasing that is getting caught up in this story, that we want to be like them.[45]

With this in mind, lead artist Kai Barrow proposes ECOHYBRIDITY "as an art and organizing hybrid, that looks at decolonizing the imagination." She explains, "Ecohybridity is the idea of how we as Black people are constantly hybridizing, going from one location to another location, from the middle passage to the prison industrial complex, to Jim Crow to current-day displacement around spatial inequity." The project considers the importance of Katrina, "looking at one of the most important events that impacted Black Life in the last century," and asking, "what does this mean for us in terms of questions of home, questions of just Black existence period?"[46]

Elsewhere in the city, other events focused on the Latinx role in the rebuilding. Casa Borrega, a Mexican tavern in Central City, hosted an event saying "thank you" to those who rebuilt the city and supported the Right to Remain movement. The Congress of Day Laborers and their allies had called for a moratorium on deportations. Located across the street from the Ashé Cultural Arts Center, Casa Borrega has often hosted black/brown dialogues around human rights issues as well as musical performances. This event circulated an ethical claim—advanced by the labor activists affiliated with the Congress of Day Laborers and the Workers' Center for Racial Justice—that reconstruction workers had earned their place in the city and should be exempt from deportation. Just two years earlier, the congress had a won a significant victory as Sheriff Marlin Gusman, then the lead official in charge of Orleans Parish jail, agreed to cease cooperating with US Immigration and Customs Enforcement officials on August 14, 2013.[47] As *Colorlines* writer Aura Bogado put it, "New Orleans is the first jurisdiction in the South to opt out of Secure Communities [S-Comm], a federal program that critics say tears immigrant communities apart." The project, piloted by the George W. Bush administration and expanded under President Obama, was intended to focus on deporting dangerous criminals but was instead "sweeping up a broad swath of nonviolent offenders and even citizens."[48] One local resident, a member of the Congress of Day Laborers, was "held in a New Orleans prison for six months" for not paying a fine. Cities around the US were refusing to participate in S-Comm, but New Orleans was the first city in the

South to do so. A video released by the Congress of Day Laborers showed the sheriff "listening to harrowing stories" from people who had been unfairly detained. Moved by what he was seeing, the sheriff helped to close out the meeting, donning a Congress T-shirt and chanting, along with the assembled community, "No papers! No fear!" As Bogado concludes, "That a sheriff in the deep South is shouting a slogan coined and used by the immigrant rights movement indicates just how much work has been done to change the way at least some in law enforcement are thinking about immigration."

Conversations throughout the city reflected on expert panels, rituals, plays, and documentary screenings marking ten years of reconstruction. One such conversation happened in my backyard with Antonio Garza and Kayla Andrews, writers and English as a second language teachers who think deeply about culture, race, neighborhoods, and borders of all kinds. Antonio also holds a special place in the parade history of the city as the organizer of the first Latinx Carnival krewe in the city, Los Amigos de los Amigos.[49] Its first annual parade, pointedly held on Cinco de Mayo, was titled A Marching Fiesta, and it moved from Tremé to the French Quarter, with a stop for "debt payment," and into the Iberville area, where a wreath was laid at the feet of revolutionary Benito Juárez, the first indigenous president of Mexico. The parade route self-consciously crossed the social terrain of the city from front of town to back of town, French Quarter to the projects, with pointed references to class, race, struggles for freedom, and ongoing structures of oppression.

When I met with Antonio and Kayla, I had just been to the Theater at St. Claude for a performance titled *Be a New Orleanian: A Swearing-in Ceremony*. Written and performed by Jim Fitzmorris, it was a reflection of the city's obsession with belonging and cultural citizenship.[50] Kayla and Antonio launched themselves into the conversation about place, neighborhood, and belonging with enthusiasm. "I'm so tired of it," Kayla said. "It's like, when people ask you where you're from or they start to quiz you to figure out how long you've lived here or how New Orleanian you are," she said. "I call it measuring our New Orleans dicks. It's like, let's all pull out our dicks and measure them and see who's more of a New Orleanian." We all paused, letting that image sink in a moment. Then Antonio jumped in:

> It's always the pre-Katrina arrivals, who are trying to haze you as a post-Katrina arrival. There was [a] party at Molly's [a bar in the French Quarter] the day after the anniversary and they had an event set up like a quiz show. The whole thing was like a hazing ritual, where the sophomores

were those who arrived pre-Katrina and the freshmen were those who arrived after Katrina. The sophomores were hazing the freshmen on their knowledge of the city.

As Abram Himelstein writes, "Like most of America, there is a current, near-evangelical pride in the hyper-local. But most of this pride is manifest by the *arrivistes* (to disparage in the hyper-local way of 200 years ago)."[51] Thinking along similar lines, Ronald W. Lewis, cross-cultural educator and curator of the House of Dance & Feathers Museum in the Lower Ninth Ward, has observed that many newcomers to the city, full of excitement and enthusiasm for the African American cultural practices of New Orleans, are "Columbusing."[52] Just because you stumbled into it doesn't mean you own it—or have the right to police its borders. As Trey, a devoted second liner, told me years ago, reflecting on the zeal of white second-line converts who seek to immerse themselves in the black culture of the city: "They think they've discovered the second line, but guess what? It was already there."

Part Four: Claiming Belonging through Performance

City residents have long used parades to claim the city as theirs and to assert their right to belong.[53] Parades create an embodied citizenship that is not necessarily indigenous or grounded in claims to autochthony. Parading opens a space for participation. In the book *Coming Out the Door for the Ninth Ward*, members of Nine Times Social Club explain how they came into the parade tradition from a neighborhood, the Upper Ninth, that was not inhabited by parades in the same way as the Sixth Ward, the Seventh Ward, or Central City. In fact, many of the members' families came from the country—the sugar-growing parishes up the river from New Orleans—and moved into the city, where they were assimilated into neighborhood cultures. As Nine Times members trace how they were mentored about parades by friends, neighbors, godparents, and other teachers, they demonstrate that parading is a form of embodied knowledge that can be learned. Troy Materre recalls that when Nine Times began to parade, its members wanted to make their own contributions to the parading traditions in the city: "We wanted to put our feet into the circuit of parades."[54] They're not from here. But they made their claims to the city through parading.

In this sense, members of Nine Times are not entirely unlike other public figures whose identity claims are grounded in their experiences of parading. As I've argued elsewhere, numerous public figures, including musicians and music festival producers who were not necessarily born into the culture of parades, were nonetheless socialized into it.[55] Parading, in part, made them (or dare I say us?) who they (we) are. As an ethnographer working in the city, and in over twenty years of following parades, I've seen how parades have their own pedagogy and ontology—they teach us about the city, and they also theorize the real: This is the city. We are the people.[56] As a transplant to the city with roots in France and Texas, I have personally experienced this citizenship of parading. I also understand its citizenship as provisional, providing a doorway to more enduring friendships and alliances.

My own work comes out of fertile dialogues between musicians, parade makers, photographers, and anthropologists: in doing ethnography over decades, the work of documenting and living with (and participating) in living traditions, you can see that these practices are not timeless, self-contained, or disconnected from history and the larger society. If culture is a house we dwell in, it is not a house without doors and windows. It is porous, and we learn a lot from what (and who) passes in and out of these openings. This work is part of a conversation with parade makers and parade theorists, including musicians, neighbors, filmmakers, songwriters, and anthropologists.

Conclusion

How does the wielding of categorical identities and the policing of social and cultural borders play into the dialectics of New Orleans exceptionalism? The current obsession of New Orleanians with belonging, indigeneity, and autochthony stems from a specific political and social history. From the colonial period to Reconstruction, the boom and bust of the oil industry, the intensification of tourism, the massive displacements engendered by post-Katrina policies, and the current housing crisis accelerated by short-term rentals, each moment has engendered its own claims to autochthony. The shape of these claims continues to shift, along with political circumstances and specific social movements emerging from them. The provisional observations suggest that culturalist and materialist arguments intersect as claims to belonging are used to underwrite vastly different personal and collective agendas. Claims to belonging may advance a moral claim to reside in the city or to participate in social, cultural, economic, and political institutions. The stakes vary widely. The member of the Congress of Day Laborers and the Teach for America transplant both are migrants to the city; both came for work; both claim to belong. But only one risks deportation.

The claims to autochthony made by political organizers in the 1970s sought to break the economic stranglehold of mostly white festival producers over the festival (a de facto monopoly on the profits generated by Jazz and Heritage). When those same logics are wielded by festival producers forty years later, they may be evacuated of their political and economic meanings and carry a strictly culturalist force. Such usage may only empower those few who now hold producer positions and have the decision-making power to decide who gets in, who is excluded, and how. As claims made from the bottom up are taken up by institutions and wielded from the top down, they may have very different consequences. In such conditions, it may come to be that those most invested in identity claims and in policing the boundaries of autochthony are those whose own cultural activism (whether they are working in the public, the for-profit, or the nonprofit sector) or entrepreneurial role requires them to assert their own legitimacy or authenticity as arbiters of taste, as curators of public displays, or as producers of public culture. When do claims to belong strengthen or undermine social movements for human rights or social equality? And when do they reinforce the social and cultural power of established institutions or the social capital of specific individuals or groups?

While artists, musicians, and small nonprofits are rarely in the position to articulate their discontent with the categories and essentialized identities invoked by producers, curators, and philanthropic institutions, surely public anthropologists, folklorists, and others can find a way to include an analysis of these trends as part of a project to "study up" in the contemporary realm of cultural production. All too often, we find ourselves complicit in established practices whether we are working as allies with or participants in organizations that are deeply invested in notions of autochthony and indigeneity.

Notes

This chapter was written in conversation with neighbors, friends, and colleagues, over a period of nearly a decade. Earlier versions were presented at the American Anthropological Association, the Association of American Geographers, and at the New Orleans Workshop, as well as "New Orleans as Subject: Beyond Authenticity and Exceptionalism." Thanks to Matt Sakakeeny, Thomas Adams, and Sue Mobley for inviting me to present at that conference and for encouraging me to deepen and refine the arguments for this volume. The chapter also benefited from insightful discussions with Vincanne Adams, Antoinette Jackson, Rachel Breunlin, David Beriss, Cedric Johnson, Joel Dinerstein, Alecia Long, Vicki Mayer, Yolanda Moses, Rebecca Sheehan, Adolph Reed, Kodi Roberts, Bryan Wagner, Felipe Smith, Sean Mallin, Martha Radice, Daniella Santoro, and Shana

Walton. Participants in the 2017 New Orleans Workshop provided generous, collegial and incisive readings. Over the years, conversations with friends, neighbors, artists, musicians, journalists, scholars, and activists shaped my arguments, especially Kayla Andrews, Ron Bechet, Wendy Billiot, Willie Birch, Rachel Carrico, Lora Ann Chaisson, James A. Charbonnet, Jan Cohen-Cruz, Frank de Caro, Antonio Garza, Cynthia Garza, Jeffrey Ehrenreich, Dan Etheridge, Rick Fifield, Ariana Hall, Gentry Hanks, Abram Himelstein, Joyce Jackson, Rosan Jordan, Tomás Montoya, Ronald Lewis, Rachel Lyons, Angie Mason, Deborah Oppenheim, Jessi Parfait, Miriam Reed, Davis Rogan, Gwen Thompkins, Nikki Thanos, Jose Torres-Tama, Kelli Welch, and Robin White. I am especially grateful to Rachel Breunlin, Antoinette Jackson, John Parker, Matt Sakakeeny, and Shana Walton, who read multiple drafts and provided critiques, edits, and encouragement in helpful portions. If I failed to take your advice, I have only myself to blame. Yaafu! I am forever indebted to those who inspired this chapter and are not named to protect their privacy.

1 See Geschiere 2009.

2 See Hirsch 2007.

3 See Domínguez 1986; Hirsch and Logsdon 1992.

4 See Thomas 2014.

5 See Smith 2003.

6 See Barrios 2011; Breunlin and Regis 2009; Jackson 2011. Victims are alternatively attributed exaggerated agency and blamed for making bad choices (e.g., "they chose to stay") or abject victimhood without capacity to act.

7 See Regis and Walton 2008.

8 Breunlin and Regis 2009. See Jordan and de Caro 1996.

9 Reed 2016.

10 Johnson 2007; Arena 2012.

11 See V. Adams 2013.

12 See V. Adams 2013; Johnson 2011; Arena 2012; and T. Adams 2015. For a comparative perspective, see Gundewardena and Schuller 2008.

13 As previous scholars have demonstrated, the term "Creole"—whose meaning was contested through much of its history—was instrumentalized during the nineteenth century to distinguish Catholic and French/Creole-speaking people of New Orleans, those who were here prior to Americanization, from the English-speaking newcomers. Those who claimed Creole identities were doing so in part as an act of resistance to the growing hegemony of Anglo-American social norms, economic power, and political institutions (see Domínguez 1986; Hirsch and Logsdon 1992). In the early twentieth century, usage of the term "Creole" came under pressure from Jim Crow as racial segregation became the law of the land. The term increasingly became the property of people of color and was abandoned by white Creoles in favor of French identity.

14 Tregle 1992, 132–41.

15 Tregle 1992, 138.

16 Jordan and de Caro 1996, 41.

17 Geschiere 2009. See also Joseph 2002.

18 Geschiere 2009, 68. See also Bourdieu and Wacquant 2001.

19 Geschiere 2009, 69.

20 Mbembe 2009.

21 Trouillot 1991. See Breunlin and Regis 2009, 135.

22 Jackson 2011. See also Patillo-McCoy 1999 and chapter 9, this volume. This is not to suggest that wealth and poverty are not racialized (they clearly are) or to question the value of researching the intersections of multiple oppressions. Rather, research agendas shaped by a culturally overdetermined desire for authenticity at those intersections can enact colonizing moves, reifying racial difference and undermining multiracial organizing.

23 Jackson 2011.

24 Personal communication, March 2016.

25 Duneier 1992.

26 See also Patillo-McCoy 1999; Barnes 2016; Carter 2014.

27 Gilroy 2000, 253.

28 These contradictions are incisively explored and critiqued in Matt Sakakeeny's 2013 ethnography of brass-band musicians.

29 Cf. Hall 1992a; Evans 2011; Becker et al. 2013; Himelstein 2015; Watts and Porter 2013, 5.

30 Himelstein (2015) quotes Kalamu ya Salaam, calling New Orleans "the only African city in North America."

31 Regis 2013.

32 Tommye Myrick, Center for African and African American Studies, Southern University at New Orleans. This phrase was part of a call for papers for a conference reflecting on the cultural history of Congo Square.

33 "Myth" here refers to a foundational narrative that conveys a cultural truth about how things came to be. In this sense, myths are true stories.

34 Sakakeeny 2011b, 292.

35 Ramsey and Smith 1939, 5.

36 Dent 2018.

37 Festival Program Book 1979, 60.

38 Yungai 2015.

39 Yungai 2015.

40 For Rouselle (2009), who joined the board during the coalition's organizing push and went on to become its president, it represented "the most democratic sharing of power that exists in this community" and became a model for other nonprofits in the city and region.

41 See Regis 2013.

42 See Povinelli 2002.

43 Campbell Robertson, "10 Years after Katrina," *New York Times*, August 26, 2015, https://www.nytimes.com/interactive/2015/08/26/us/ten-years-after-katrina.html.

44 The founder and artistic director of Gallery in the Streets is Kai Lumumba Barrow (2015), whose blog details the project.

45 ECOHYBRIDITY Collective 2015.

46 See also *ECOHYBRIDITY: Tiny House, Moving Installation*, which was a participant in the commemorative second line on August 29, 2015. The house façade was inscribed

with the affirmation "housing is a human right." "ECOHYBRIDITY: Site-Specific Performance and Installation at Orleans Parish Prison in New Orleans, LA"; "ECOHYBRIDITY: Direct Action/Performance at the St. Roch Market, New Orleans, LA."

47 "The Sheriff's Office shall decline all voluntary ICE detainer requests except if an individual is charged with first degree murder, second degree murder, aggravated rape, aggravated kidnapping, or armed robbery involving a firearm" ("Sheriff Gusman Revises ICE Policy," Orleans Parish Sheriff's Office, August 14, 2013, www.opcso.org, http://www.opcso.org/index.php?option=com_content&view=article&id=367:sheriff-gusman-revises-ice-policy&catid=1:latest-news.

48 Bogado 2013. See also Quigley 2013.

49 The parade, inspired by Krewe du Jieux and Zulu, uses self-parody as an intervention in Carnival politics, deploying Mexican and Latinx ethnic stereotypes of the sombrero, the piñata, and the Carmen Miranda headdress (and her embodiment of the minstrelized and sexualized Latina entertainer; see Breunlin and Button 2000).

50 Fitzmorris 2015.

51 Himelstein 2015.

52 See Breunlin and Lewis 2009.

53 Boll 2009; de Caro 2010.

54 Nine Times Social Club 2006, 111.

55 Regis 2011, 2013.

56 Regis 2009b.

7

The Contradictions of the Film Welfare Economy, or, For the Love of *Treme*

VICKI MAYER, HEIDI SCHMALBACH, & TOBY MILLER

In the snarky atmosphere of the Twitterscape, the short but public tiff between director David Simon (*The Wire, Treme*), celebrity chef Anthony Bourdain, and Bravo Television's programming executive Andy Cohen looked like it had all the makings of a street game of the dozens. On May 15, 2013, Bourdain began by attacking Cohen's decision to accept recovery funding from British Petroleum in the 2012 production of *Top Chef: New Orleans*, a reality program that spotlights the culinary traditions and culture of the host city. To this, Cohen upbraided Bourdain to read more about the tax credits that all productions in New Orleans have access to, even the ones for shows that he appears on. "Call me abt *Treme*'s tax credits from NOLA," Cohen tweeted, drawing a peeved Simon into the roil. In his expletive-laden blog post, "Why I Don't Tweet," Simon finished the fight over which program had the moral high ground in the postdisaster film economy: "For Mr. Cohen to flippantly imply that because HBO failed somehow to refuse the same tax rates that Louisiana offers to every production, we are in the same boat as *Top Chef* and its extended negotiations for a BP payout is just, well, horseshit."[1] End scene.

Over a brief but very intense period, many fans excitedly entered the fray to defend the great job both these programs were doing for local culture and the economy. But their political-economic underpinnings were never discussed: namely, that all major film and television productions in Louisiana rely on some form of public subsidy regardless of their content. And this silence has extended far beyond the twenty-four-hour spat between TV executives. In most press coverage, the economic impacts of these productions are disaggregated from their public subsidies in terms of both how much taxpayer money goes to production and, ergo, how much money is taken from elsewhere in the public coffer. Producers for *Top Chef* and *Treme* were initially certified to receive nearly $134 million in public funds to "incentivize" their already-localized location shoots.[2] That was hardly exceptional.

This chapter seeks to remedy that absence by exploring the HBO television series *Treme* (2009–13) in terms of regional film policy and the New Orleans creative economy. In 2014, Louisiana outpaced California as the number-one US location for shooting major motion pictures. Dubbed "Hollywood South" in its own aspirational language, Louisiana's achievement was based on a law to offer a generous package of public subsidies for Hollywood filmmaking. The epicenter of the policy's impacts has been New Orleans, where the film industry has been cited as an agent of recovery and renewal post-Katrina, as a self-sustaining creative economy. *Treme* was both special and typical among big-budget dramatic productions. It was special because most production drawn away from Hollywood, to Canada or Australia for example, conceals its actual place of filming rather than making it part of the diegesis. This has been true of Louisiana's share of such runaway productions. *Treme* broke the mold somewhat. In keeping with a minority of other New Orleans productions, it made a textual virtue of its location, borrowing from a discourse of cultural authenticity that nevertheless still borrowed from political-economic duplicity.[3]

Treme transferred public funds to Hollywood and local elites under the guise of boosting cultural value and a creative economy. The policy, enacted in a variety of ways by forty-five US states and over thirty countries and regions across the globe, has obscured an industrial race to the bottom for film labor. In addition, *Treme* navigated the local economy's corporate philanthropy by directing attention and even largesse at the creative workforce that the program celebrates. Yet as our survey research indicates, creative work in the city has been structurally precarious, something that a film-based economic strategy cannot resolve and in fact relies on.

Treme, Creative Economy Policy, and Film Tax Credits

As revealed in the opening Twitter tiff, every major audiovisual production in Louisiana receives tax incentives to attract location shooting—Hollywood's most mobile sector. This incentive reflects a broader entrepreneurial trend in urban governance, referred to by the optimistic euphemism "creative economy." This is a very old-fashioned concept, as venerable as the state of

Louisiana itself. In 1848, Ralph Waldo Emerson wrote that "a creative economy is the fuel of magnificence."[4] And Ronald Reagan's speech that launched
his successful 1966 campaign for the governorship of California began with
these words to counter the Great Society's welfare promises: "I propose . . . 'A
Creative Society' . . . to discover, enlist and mobilize the incredibly rich human
resources of California [through] innumerable people of creative talent."[5] Its
contemporary iteration is built on commercial industries whose profits are
largely based on intellectual property, such as film, publishing, fashion, and
high-tech design. The concept was enshrined in the language of international
development through the United Nations Conference on Trade and Development and the urban planning of the lapsed-Marxist geographer Richard
Florida and a multitude of coin-operated consultants, get-rich-quick schemes,
and credulous mandarins.[6] In bonding the language of creativity and economy,
these sectoral shifts signal an overall redefinition of culture in terms of its expedient instrumentality and "creative work" into a professional class formation
that is supposedly redeveloping cities worldwide.[7]

Over the past two decades, this redefinition has manifested as the flag-
ship economic development policy for many cities in the US and elsewhere.
Although creative-city strategies have been implemented throughout the
UK for the past two decades, the trend made its way to the United States
primarily through Florida's 2002 airport newsstand best seller, *The Rise of the
Creative Class*. Florida has even trademarked the concept: his claim to own
the "creative class®" is asserted with the US Patent and Trademark Office
registration number 3298801.

Creative-class theory followed the entrepreneurial logic dictating that
cities must compete against each other to secure mobile capital investment.
Meanwhile, the investment would attract "free-footed" creatives, new consumers, and tourists, replacing raw materials and labor as the primary drivers
of competitive economic advantage. Cities should therefore strive to attract
members of this new creative class, which, untethered to existing industrial
geographies, would make their locational decisions based on lifestyle factors
including diversity, values, and cultural amenities. What a perfect synergy
with the economic aims of location-based film production industries.

The harsh realities of capital accumulation in postindustrial societies determine the fate of these perfect promises. Much of the world's most developed
countries rely on intellectual property development and trade for economic
growth. In the United States, intellectual property—including trademarks,
patents, and copyrights—accounted for some 35 percent of the national gross
domestic product (GDP) and 19 percent of its total workforce. Correlating

figures are higher in Western Europe.[8] The aggregation of high tech, big pharma, and mass media industries under the term "creative economy" has signaled less an embrace of creativity—even less the support of organic creative production associated with artists, musicians, authors, or performers— and more a global economic realignment toward immaterial goods and their corporate owners. Entertainment industries alone, including film, television, music, and publishing, dominated 6.5 percent of the US GDP in 2012, and while copyrights, royalties, and licensing concentrate most of that wealth among its highest-level executives and shareholders, the sheer volume of this trade translates to a mean salary of about $85,600 per worker, or 33 percent more than other US workers.[9] Seduced by the regenerative promises associated with the creative economy, urban and regional policy makers have thus met minds with film industry lobbyists who have argued that film production is the cornerstone for building a new sustainable economy.[10]

Yet film production does not automatically seed a new or sustainable creative economy. Regional governments wanting a piece of that action have had to scramble for the material production processes associated with intellectual property generation, since these geographic centers, like their corporate owners, tend to be highly concentrated in a few historic areas.[11] In the film and television industry, most of the wealth remains in Los Angeles, while regional governments elsewhere compete to attract location shooting as the necessary realization of the film script's material form.

In terms of labor markets, the clustering of workers associated with film and television production is a byproduct of decades of industrial agglomeration. Through short-term contracted projects, workers within the various trade and occupational designations for film production benefit from their close proximity to one another in order to piece together regular employment.[12] This typically includes work in other creative industries, such as gaming or design firms, as well as service industries, such as restaurants and hotels, and independent creative production. In other words, regional film production may employ creative personnel from the general labor market, such as artists, designers, photographers, and woodworkers, but their employment is only a byproduct of the aims of creative economy policy more generally: to attract the investment to create a creative class associated with high levels of consumption and intellectual property receipts. These aims were firmly embedded in Louisiana's creative economy policies, beginning with a film tax credit.

Established in 2002, Louisiana's Motion Picture Investor Tax Credit policy has enjoyed nearly universal support from both political parties, leading to continual renewal past any sunset clause and expansion into other commercial media and theatrical productions. First proposed by a former lobbyist for a California film payroll company, the policy was touted by then-Governor Mike Foster, a Republican, and then–Lieutenant Governor Mitch Landrieu, a Democrat in charge of the Louisiana Department of Culture, Recreation and Tourism. Landrieu's role, expressed in the hiring of a private consulting firm to make the case on behalf of his department, continued through his role as mayor of New Orleans from 2006. Representing himself as the champion of creative economy measures in New Orleans, Landrieu echoed Florida's blueprint for a future creative class on the eve of the second anniversary of Katrina: "If you build a place where smart, creative people live, you will create an economic engine."[13] The only brake on this engine has been the near bankruptcy of the state, which has set limits to the amount the state could afford to reimburse film production yearly since 2016.

During the peak of film policy boosterism, Louisiana offered funds for any project whose budget exceeded $300,000—a bar low enough to capture most television productions and national advertising, but high enough to exclude most indie or amateur projects. *Treme* fit in the middle of this financial spectrum. Blockbuster films, such as *Dawn of the Planet of the Apes* (2014), dwarf television budgets. But as a recurring high-value dramatic series lasting almost four years, *Treme*'s budget topped any previous television project in the state. These dollars could be topped off with other incentives, such as when *Top Chef* producers negotiated an extra $375,000 of tourism-directed monies generated from the BP oil spill settlement.[14] For every dollar invested in local goods or services, the state awarded the local production team 30 percent of its investment back in the form of a resalable tax credit. Hollywood-based studios do not have a tax burden in Louisiana, so the credits get brokered through a relatively closed market of state-based companies and wealthy residents who buy the credits at a discount to offset their own dues. In purely financial terms, the first local benefactors of film tax credits have been the accountants, insurers, and lawyers who manage these exchanges. From there, wealth was supposed to trickle down: from the hands of energy and oil executives at the top to the caterers, truck drivers, and hotel maids far removed from any direct payout.

Local employment merited an extra 5 percent credit, an incentive that supporters of the policy say creates jobs in a new economy of highly skilled, green, well-paid work. This assertion—strongly rejected by state budget hawks—has been the central political appeal of film tax credit policies since the neoliberal restructuring of the American economy that commenced in the late 1970s. Like other states, Louisiana steadily lost federal funding for basic social services even as its tax base was eroded by industrial flight and closures, a stagnant middle class, and a political climate hostile to raising corporate taxes. Film revenues, say boosters, would be the silver linings on this otherwise gloomy skyline.

Adding together every possible economic multiplier that film might bring, the state claimed that the industry generated over $1.7 billion in revenues between 2010 and 2012. Meanwhile, it slashed spending for higher education, health care, and social services to cover a little over $150 million in budget shortfalls.[15] In other words, government officials and some uninquisitive press touted creative economy growth at the same time ordinary workers in that economy suffered real declines in their living standards and services. *Treme* benefited from both these realities; taking film incentives for a production that centered on life in post-Katrina New Orleans, thereby reaping financial gain for its copyright holders and textual indexicality for its political donors.

Treme as a Good Corporate Citizen in New Orleans

On the surface, *Treme* seemed cut from the same cloth as the region's 2005 cultural economy assessment *Louisiana: Where Culture Means Business*. Released on the eve of Katrina, the report defended the conversion of culture into economic capital and job growth. Subsequent updates for New Orleans have touted film, music, and the culinary arts as exemplary successes. *Treme* touched on these successes as a film production that sought to uplift other creative industries and producers in the city. It focused on the practitioners and educators behind the city's music, restaurants, and entertainment industries. Shot as an ensemble production, the show tracked the post-Katrina lives of three musicians, a disc jockey–turned–recording artist, a chef, the family of a humanities professor, a Mardi Gras Indian and his musician son, and a bar owner who provided the space for Indian practices. Nearly all the characters, and many supporting ones, acted as creative entrepreneurs in the recovering city. They opened new businesses, invested in new products and talent, and assumed the risks of working without a social safety net. The series interwove the storylines to position viewers as both witnesses to the production of authentic local culture and collaborators in its rescue after Katrina.

In historicizing the production of the authentic in *Treme*, Lynnell Thomas writes, the series cultivated a "touristic gaze" toward black expressive cultures, while reconceptualizing a new kind of tourist-viewer. Viewers gained access to the most minute and intimate details of people involved in vernacular working-class black culture. Episodes incorporated didactic lessons on musical, dance, and culinary traditions. Star cameos indexed the real people who survived on the production of this culture. Like its preceding tourism narratives, *Treme* revived tropes associating "real" New Orleans culture with black "rhythm, improvisation, cultural creativity, and spirituality."[16] The newspaper TV critic Dave Walker and other boosters acted as tour guides to the program's oft-arcane cultural references via weekly online blogs. This led national critics to call the show both "boring" and "authentic."[17]

At the same time, *Treme* viewers were hailed to surpass their tourist roles by participating in the virtuous acts the production sponsored. Many of the program's stars became associated with local charities, from schoolbook and musical instrument drives to home restorations in historically black neighborhoods.[18] Charity balls for corporate social ventures, such as Habitat for Humanity, allowed audiences to simultaneously fetishize Hollywood celebrities and local auction goods in the name of a healthy creative economy. These acts of corporate social responsibility were part of the reason HBO gave *Treme* the green light. As Simon explained at a public forum on the program, a program broadly focused on New Orleans's exceptional culture was "a really hard pitch, meeting in LA, where they just want to hear it in two or three sentences." After Katrina, *Treme* suddenly had a functional role, cultivating what Thomas calls the "contradictory impulses of desire and disaster" in supporting the resilience of black culture against the structural displacement of black people.[19] As Simon relayed, "The storm gave it [the program idea] an immediate gravitas, a city that had suffered a near-death experience."[20]

While celebrity philanthropy was certainly not unique to *Treme*, linking each star's image to local and (often) black culture followed the very recipe advocated by the city's creative economy development plans. This odd confluence was especially evident during the 2012 bicentennial celebration of the Tremé neighborhood. Aside from the obvious mutuality between the place and the series, city planners referenced the noir marketing of the TV show by using the same font, lighting, and background in its own campaign to promote the history of the "oldest Black neighborhood in the U.S." Bicentennial banners hung at the entry of the event showed "Uncle" Lionel Batiste, a musician who not only represented brass band musical traditions in the neighborhood, but made two appearances in the series.

By the time shooting wrapped, Simon publicly claimed *Treme* had left more than $500,000 with local charities. The contradictions that surrounded both profiteering from local culture and preserving it were most evident in the enrollment of Louisiana labor for the series. On the one hand, producers knew that local hires accrued cost savings: their payroll earned an extra 5 percent in tax credits, and local hires saved on housing, transportation, and meals. On the other hand, the presence of so many residents in the program underwrote producers' claims about authenticity. Hundreds of local extras, also known as background actors, did not need to do anything but hang around with others to give credence to the idea of New Orleans as a unique place, where black and white people together re-create the tired food trope of the city as a gumbo.

Merging these two agendas, the producers of *Treme* rationalized that hiring locals was economically efficient in gaining more tax credits and the basis for a more moral creative economy. In the words of a hiring director on the series, "It's just the right thing to do."[21] In 2011, *Treme* hired 220 in-state crew compared to only forty from out of state. As stated in the previous section, an in-state hire does not necessarily mean that person has been in the state for a long time. *Treme*, however, made a rare effort to collaborate with the New Orleans Video Access Center (NOVAC), the oldest community media nonprofit in the region. In 2010, they sponsored workforce training workshops, mutually benefiting migrant film workers needing in-state certifications and homegrown aspirant workers. In subsequent seasons, at least ten department heads and managers from the production gave mentoring advice to future classes of production assistants, a low-paid gateway to film opportunities. Of these alumni, NOVAC reported that one rose to be executive assistant to *Treme* executive producer Nina Noble. *Treme* carried through on the meritocratic promise that someone could potentially work their way up the production hierarchy toward a stable industry career. The hiring director talked about this promise in 2011 as a form of loyalty to *Treme*, regardless of its economic outcome: "We're asking people to commit to us, and we will commit to them," he said. "People aren't in our production for the money. . . . You have to want to be here for what *Treme* is about."

Beyond short-term and low-wage contract jobs, *Treme* was about labor volunteerism as civic engagement. Although the wages for *Treme* did not deviate from union scales, one extra on the program punned that Louisiana was a "right-to-exploit state."[22] Local workers said they felt crew members treated them more respectfully than in other productions, remembering their names or, in one case, helping an aspiring actor join the Screen Actors Guild. In turn, they were called upon to volunteer nights and weekends to thank the neighborhood residents who sacrificed their spatial and temporal routines in service to trailers and crews. Those local residents understood

Treme was trying to be better than other productions. Some said the production crews were courteous in notifying them about street closures. Others said they were unique in thanking residents with neighborhood parties, barbecues, and screenings. In sum, the anecdotes told by local workers and residents cast *Treme* as a different kind of film production from the others they had become familiar with in the city.[23] In short, the show made people feel good about the place where they lived and worked even as film productions partook in the restructuring of neighborhoods and labor.

Creative Labor in Tremé and the Precarious Creative Economy

Beyond the screen stories of heroic Indians, proud performers, and other cultural survivors of the storm, the conditions for being a creative worker in New Orleans remain opaque. For all the boosterism around film jobs and creative economy, there has been strikingly little empirical data about who works in creative industry professions and their material conditions for living. Existing empirical data on cultural production is limited by a reliance on national statistics that are biased toward traditional, primary, full-time employment.[24] The most notable example, the Mayor's Office of Cultural Economy's annual *Cultural Economy Snapshot*, primarily references employment statistics from the Census, the American Community Survey, and the Bureau of Labor Statistics, which use the North American Industry Classification System of employment sectors. These categorizations fail to account for the blurred boundaries between the creative and other economies—most notably services—and the boundaries between amateur and professional status in many creative fields. As a result, the most halcyon figures cited in white papers and reproduced through the press maximize the economic impacts of local film economies through multipliers, an estimated calculus based on trade-secret algorithms. While *Treme* was mobilizing the masses to witness, buy, and donate labor for the creative economy, we decided to look more closely at the actual numbers of people affected by creative economy policy in its namesake neighborhood.

The historic neighborhood of Faubourg Tremé lies lakeside, or on the northern border of the French Quarter. For over two centuries, Tremé has been home to countless musicians, performers, and culture bearers, making it "ground zero for the city's identity as an exceptional place."[25] It has also been subject to multiple waves of urban renewal and spatial restructuring that have disrupted and displaced residents, including bifurcation via construction of Interstate 10, and the leveling of numerous blocks of historic homes, mostly belonging to African Americans, to build the controversial Louis Armstrong Park.[26] In recent years, beginning before but accelerated by Katrina, Tremé became popular for transplants and eager first-time home buyers, including many young creative professionals who cite the neighborhood's cultural distinctiveness and racial diversity as primary attractions. Despite the aura of exceptionality, Tremé is thus a harbinger of national trends.

These understandings of the Tremé neighborhood influenced our decision to work with a community partner in developing a pilot survey to see whether the creative economy policies touted in the city had really stimulated an "economic engine" where "creative people" live, in the words of the mayor. Our partner, the Creative Alliance of New Orleans (CANO), wanted a census-style survey to extend their mission of assisting neighborhood artists and cultural producers. In spring 2014, our students and CANO staffers covered the wide swaths of city popularly recognized as Tremé today.[27] Survey questions were organized to record data on the labor roles and practices highlighted as drivers of creative economy growth. To serve CANO, the survey further aimed to gather some empirical insights into these celebrated workers' real professional and social needs, as well as the impacts they were having on the character and feel of their neighborhood. The half-hour, door-to-door assessment promised a nuanced understanding of how the subjects of creative economy policy saw their own labor and framed it in the context of neighborhood life and community membership.

Our pilot survey demonstrated that the average Tremé resident regularly holds more than one position and relies on serial contracts and multiple jobs each year. Of 127 respondents, 44 percent $(N = 57)$ identified themselves as involved in one or more creative professions, including the jobs featured so prominently on *Treme*. While this figure was significantly higher than the percentage of creative workers in the city's 2013 estimate that 13.7 percent of jobs in the overall economy were cultural, the figure only included two of the more than 2,300 local people reported to have been employed by *Treme* in 2013.[28] The participants' candid responses both confirm and complicate the information presented by economic impact reports aimed primarily at celebrating local creative economy policies, including the motion picture tax credit.

The data also reveal the complicated reality of work in the creative industries: a precarious existence marked by inconsistent opportunities, sixty- to seventy-hour work weeks without the benefits of full-time employment, perennially low wages, and rapidly increasing housing costs. The total income of all creative workers ranged from zero dollars annually, for the recently un-employed, to over $100,000 for those with high-paying primary jobs. The majority reported total annual incomes of $25,001–$45,000, a range gen-erally consistent with the city's estimate that the average salary for creative jobs in New Orleans hovered around $34,000, which is around the median income for all workers in the city. The most stable jobs in our sample were in the culinary industry, a sector not included in national creative economy figures, but overrepresented in New Orleans's workforce.[29] In Tremé, chefs, bakers, and workers in craft and specialty foods described their culinary role as their primary profession, earning them between $25,000 and $65,000 an-nually. Two restaurant entrepreneurs reported bringing in over $100,000. Unsurprisingly, however, the music industry was the most heavily represented creative field in the survey; almost half the respondents identified as musi-cians, producers, or sound technicians, though only a few could make this their primary job.

Most creative professionals were working multiple positions, often re-quiring work weeks of sixty hours or more. This is important because the city can inflate the number of creative jobs in the labor market without showing how most individuals in creative sectors have to hold more than one of these jobs to make ends meet. In addition to their primary occupation, those in the music industry spent between three and thirty hours per week on their creative work. These extra hours of work accounted for up to 75 percent of each individual's income, though many respondents admitted that they did not report cash received from gigs on their tax returns. And whether they were employed full or part time, these creatives incurred significant expenses for their outputs—68 percent spent an average of $6,000 a year on creative production, with more than a handful barely breaking even between income and expenses.

Creative producers appeared to cobble together modest incomes by working in multiple roles, requiring them to migrate in and out of creative sectors, without the securities of traditional employment: health insurance, paid leave, and retirement benefits. The majority of musicians maintained positions outside the creative sector, many in health and services, while pursu-ing secondary or even tertiary musical careers at night or on the weekend. A similar profile can be painted for performing artists in the Tremé neighbor-hood. Not one of the twenty dancers, thespians, production managers, or the-ater technicians who participated in the survey held a primary position in the performing arts. The majority were with small local theater companies, as a supplement to their full-time positions or simply for personal enjoyment.

Knocking on doors in the Tremé, one is likely to sit down with a nurse or-derly who makes 75 percent of his income composing music, designing cus-tom furniture, and editing films, or a photographer-chef-woodworker who spends upward of fifty hours per week doing manual labor in the shipyards. Taken together, only 39 percent of the fifty-seven self-identified creative pro-fessionals listed a dedicated creative job as their primary occupation.

The fabled affluent and stable film worker was absent from our sample. There appeared to be little crossover between performing arts and the film industry. Though five working actors were identified in the survey, none worked in television or film. Follow-up conversations with several actors revealed the difficulty in breaking into film, despite the recent ballooning of production in the city. Neither of the two residents who described par-ticipating as extras in the TV series *Treme* regarded this as creative work. The survey suggests that very few of New Orleans's estimated 1,294 film work-ers lived in the neighborhood; just five respondents reported working in the industry, and only one, a lighting technician, full time. As mentioned, although productions filmed in New Orleans are eligible for an additional 5 percent tax incentive if they use local labor, it is difficult to verify whether the individuals working in these positions were truly local, or relocated tem-porarily to work on specific projects. Accounting for local labor has been left in the hands of the production companies themselves, who contracted with payroll firms to capture employment numbers.[30]

Beyond employment, the work of the creative economy accountants could not capture what residents felt was a neighborhood becoming ever more removed from its creative and cultural roots. Over the first decade of the new century, Tremé became 255 percent whiter; the number of resi-dents holding at least a bachelor's degree increased 128 percent, according to 2000–2010 US Census figures. Though nothing can be said conclusively about the causal factors behind the demographic shifts, the majority of our respondents attributed these changes to an influx of mostly white, young, and professional transplants after Katrina. In short, they described key indi-cators of the gentrification process associated with creative economies.

Beyond celebrating the importance of creative workers in New Orleans, *Treme* helped brand the city's neighborhoods as places of elite consump-tion and speculation. Like other cities held in the sway of the Floridian cre-ative economy mantra, New Orleans has embraced an urban redevelopment agenda based on real estate receipts and the "exaltation of representation over function" when cities are reconfigured to prioritize cultural consumption over production.[31] In other words, Tremé may have come to symbolize black creative expression for national audiences, but nary a black creative worker could afford to live there.

Affordable housing near places of business and affordable work spaces ranked as the two most critical needs facing creative workers in our survey. A series of informal follow-up questions with creative professionals who rented in the neighborhood revealed that, although many would have liked to become homeowners, they faced significant barriers, including the ability to prove consistent income from serial gigs and contracts. One chef and restaurant owner warned that the lack of affordable housing convenient to downtown workplaces was even threatening the sustainability of New Orleans culinary culture—ironically, the most significant and stable employment sector in the neighborhood.

Denouement

Treme wrapped with a flourish of local press coverage, social media fanfare, and finale parties. Simon wrote a public farewell to his sweetheart (deal) city. Fee Nah Nay, the LLC created to accrue and then sell the series' film tax credits, ceased to exist, other than to submit audits to the state for final certification. Although the program cast a spotlight on the creative economy of New Orleans and its creative laborers, its most poignant lesson about these industries came when the production disappeared. For all the hubbub about *Treme* building a local film economy, New Orleans was just one more location.

Similarly, the precarity described by creative workers in Tremé was far from a unique predicament.[32] Despite the allure of entrepreneurial, creative economy strategies, economic policy and a general approach to governance that privileges symbolic over material value can have negative impacts for both individuals and urban neighborhoods—masking labor challenges while intensifying spatial stratification based on income. In New Orleans, just as in many other cities across the globe, these injuries often go unnoticed, while creative industry policies disproportionately benefit nonresidents and elites.

In addition to collecting employment and neighborhood data, the survey asked respondents to rank their professional and social needs over the past several years. The former was motivated by CANO's interest in expanding and tailoring services to best meet the needs of local creatives. The responses underscore the need for more critical attention to the risks faced by creative and cultural producers in the community and contextualizing the impacts of an economic strategy that prioritizes the recapitalization of the city over basic needs, particularly affordable housing and health care. If creative economy strategies are to produce sustainable futures for cities, they must simultaneously address these two issues as the real risks that workers assume in becoming impresarios of their own careers. Without this, cities can ironically, and more poignantly, embrace the sad mantra in the title of *Treme*'s first episode: "Dream Your Troubles Away."

Notes

1 David Simon, "Why I Don't Tweet. Example #47," May 15, 2013, http://davidsimon .com/why-i-dont-tweet-example-47.

2 At the time of writing, only the first three seasons of *Treme* had completed the audits for final budget certification. These equal approximately $113,320,000. Data come from the Louisiana Entertainment Office, which certifies tax credit eligibility for in-state film and television productions.

3 Much of the historical context and general arguments made here can be found in extended form in Mayer 2017.

4 Emerson 1909.

5 Ronald Reagan, "The Creative Society," speech at the University of Southern California, April 19, 1966, http://reagan.convio.net/site/DocServer/ReaganMomentsFeb-_3_-The _Creative_Society_-_April_19__19.pdf?docID=583.

6 Florida 2002.

7 Gill and Pratt 2008.

8 This report is no longer available but was at one time found via US Department of Commerce, March 2012 Report. www.uspto.gov.

9 Stephen E. Siwek, "Copyright Industries in the U.S. Economy: The 2013 Report," Intellectual Property Alliance, 2013, https://www.tipo.gov.tw/public/Attachment /3123115424457.pdf.

10 Christopherson and Clark 2009.

11 Storper 2013.

12 Scott 2005.

13 Doug MacCash, "Cashing in on Culture—Forum to Focus on Using Arts to Prime State's Economic Pump," *Times-Picayune*, August 23, 2007.

14 Dave Walker, "State, Local Tourism Offices Paying $375,000 to Underwrite *Top Chef: New Orleans*," *Times-Picayune*, May 13, 2013.

15 These figures are drawn from various sources and cited in Mayer 2017.

16 Thomas 2014.

17 See, for example, Rolf Potts, "*Treme*'s Big Problem: Authenticity," *Atlantic*, November 27, 2013; and Emily Nussbaum, "Roux with a View," *New Yorker*, October 1, 2012.

18 Helen Morgan Parmett, "Disneyomatics: Media, Branding, and Urban Space in Post-Katrina New Orleans," *Mediascape*, Winter 2012, http://www.tft.ucla.edu/mediascape /Winter2012_Disneyomatics.html.

19 Thomas 2014, 167.

20 Quoted in R. Morris, "David Simon of HBO's *Treme*: 'Any Story That's about Everything Is about Nothing,'" *Uptown Messenger*, October 28, 2010, http://uptownmessenger.com /2010/10/treme-symposium-at-tulane-live-coverage/.

21 Phone interview with hiring director, 2011.

22 All names are withheld in accordance with the provisions of an institutional research board approval.

23 Despite this general sentiment, some neighborhoods did complain to the local press. See S. Yerton, "Hollywood on Oak: The Stars Hit Carrollton's Old-Style Retail Strip to Film the Classic Novel *All the King's Men*," *Times-Picayune*, January 24, 2003.

24 Murray and Gollmitzer 2012.

25 Sakakeeny 2013, 26.

26 Crutcher 2010.

27 The geographic scope of the study was broader than the historical neighborhood in order to capture the post-Katrina political economy and the collective memories of its residents (see Campanella 2013). Under the guidance of the coauthors, CANO and Tulane students conducted the survey interviews in Tremé during eight-hour periods over three consecutive weekends.

28 Mayor's Office of Cultural Economy, *2013 New Orleans Cultural Economy Snapshot* (New Orleans, 2013), 8.

29 The *2013 New Orleans Cultural Economy Snapshot* reported the culinary industry accounted for the lion's share of creative jobs in the city (13,627), including servers, many of whom earned less than minimum wage, and lacked either benefits or job security.

30 Gordon Russell, "Giving Away Louisiana: Film Tax Incentives," *The Advocate*, December 2, 2014, https://theadvocate.com/baton_rouge/news/article_7bee81e0-3458-5b75 -883e-3396afce0983.html.

31 Ley 2003, 2528.

32 See, for example, Gill and Pratt 2003; Flew 2011.

PART THREE

What Is New Orleans Identity?

8

"Queers, Fairies, and Ne'er-Do-Wells"

Rethinking the Notion of a Sexually Liberal New Orleans

ALECIA P. LONG

For most of its history, New Orleans has endured and sometimes earned a reputation as an exotic, erotic hot spot. The letters of eighteenth-century clerics and colonizers and the observations of nineteenth-century travelers and writers provide the evidentiary basis for claims that New Orleans served as a sexually liberal oasis within an otherwise deeply conservative state and region. Ample evidence exists to demonstrate that, well into the twentieth century, New Orleans served as a "geographic and metaphoric safety valve . . . where southerners" and other Americans "came to escape, if only temporarily from the racial, religious and behavioral strictures that dominated their home communities."[1] Given that history, and the city's current reputation as a gay-friendly party destination, readers might assume that New Orleans has always been openly welcoming to homosexuals in the same way it has been to tourists and transplants more generally.

That misconception is understandable, especially given the fact that in the early twentieth century the French Quarter became home to a circle of writers, artists, and colorful locals, some of whom were men and women we would recognize today as queer. There, in the mostly run-down, still affordable boundaries of the original eighteenth-century city, a group of people—some of whom would become quite famous—created what the sociologist John Shelton Reed has described as a Dixie Bohemia.[2]

Whether it was sexual liberality, a reputation for it, or some combination of the two that drew tourists and temporary residents to the city, reformers were also a part of the local scene. Yet their attempts to reign in or regulate people whose behavior they deemed disreputable and even a danger to the city are an underappreciated aspect of the city's history. It was William Faulkner, the most famous member of Reed's circle of French Quarter bohemians, who described the city as "a courtesan, not old and yet no longer young, who shuns the sunlight that the illusion of her former glory be preserved."[3] If there is merit to Faulkner's metaphor, that aging courtesan always had disapproving counterparts looking over her perfumed shoulder with concern. In the decade of the 1950s, such self-styled reformers repeatedly initiated cleanup campaigns designed to keep the sexually disreputable portion of the city's reputation under control, especially in its economically important, tourist-friendly, and, by the 1950s, rapidly gentrifying French Quarter. As the neighborhood's historic real estate became more valuable and tourism more deeply integrated into the Quarter's economy, those with conservative social values repeatedly argued for the urgency of monitoring and, if possible, discouraging the presence of visible homosexuals, especially in the French Quarter.

While most historians of sexuality in New Orleans have trained their lenses on heterosexual behavior and sexual commerce, certainly sexual acts between people of the same gender took place from the colony's earliest days. In his history of same-sex desire in the city, for example, Richard D. Clark recounts the scandal that erupted in 1724 when rumors of a sexual relationship between a Captain Beauchamp and a cabin boy on his ship became common knowledge. In response, the French Superior Council ordered the boy moved to another vessel. Undaunted, Beauchamp either rescued or kidnapped the object of his desire, returned to his ship, and sailed downriver posthaste.[4]

Whatever the prevalence of same-sex behavior in the colonial period, it was not until 1805 that sodomy technically became illegal as part of the criminal code adopted for the Territory of Orleans. In that code, often referred to as the Crimes Act of 1805, such behavior was described in imprecise though vivid terms as "the detestable and abominable crime against nature." Those convicted of such behavior could "face imprisonment at hard labor for life." Although the law changed little in the next few decades, in 1896 the state legislature clarified the sanctioned behaviors in question. In the ironically named Act 69, oral sex was added to the criminal definition of crime against nature. The new legislation specified that "Whoever shall be convicted of the detestable and abominable crime against nature committed with mankind or beast with the sectual [*sic*] organs or with the mouth, shall suffer imprisonment at hard labor for not less than two years and not more than ten years."[5] When those convicted of crime against nature fought such charges, their lawyers often claimed that the statute itself lacked specificity or that the penalties imposed were too harsh. Judges tended to disagree with such arguments, and, when persons who challenged the law's validity were found guilty, they were routinely sentenced to terms of incarceration at hard labor.[6]

As was the case in the rest of the United States, only after World War II did concerns about the issue of homosexuality and its increasing visibility in New Orleans receive close and systematic attention from reformers. Those efforts began under Mayor deLesseps Story Morrison, known commonly as "Chep." Morrison was a World War II veteran and long-shot candidate who won his first term as mayor in 1946. Morrison's challenger and predecessor was a Long-era politician named Robert Maestri who spent much of his time and energy distributing political spoils, lining his own pockets, and profiting personally from the city's long tolerance of gambling and prostitution. During his first campaign for the mayoralty, some of Morrison's female supporters staged a parade down Canal Street, in which they carried brooms and swept the streets as they went, symbolizing their belief that Morrison was a reformer who could and would sweep the city clean of vice and corruption. One might say that Morrison was, quite literally, swept into office by reform-minded New Orleanians.[7]

As Morrison's biographer Edward Haas makes clear, the new mayor's commitment to moral reform was less vigorous and thoroughgoing than many of his supporters believed, especially when it came to the issue of gambling. However, an event near the end of his first term forced him to move, at least symbolically, in a more overtly reformist direction. A wealthy tourist named Robert Dunn had come from Nashville to New Orleans to celebrate the New Year. After a night of imbibing, Dunn entered a Bourbon Street bar early on the morning of January 1, 1950. Although the exact chain of events that led to his death remained in dispute, there was no denying the presence of "chloral hydrate—'knockout drops'—in Dunn's body." The publicity surrounding the tourist's death made a cleanup of the French Quarter not only politically unavoidable but also economically critical to retaining the city's ever-growing tourist traffic. In response, Morrison began to assemble members for what would come to be called the mayor's Special Citizens Committee for the Vieux Carre (SCCVC). The thirteen-member committee held its first meeting on March 31, 1950, and appointed local manufacturer and longtime civic activist Richard Foster committee chair.[8]

As with Morrison, what proportion of economic versus moral concerns drove the individual committee members is hard to say, but the issues they raised in their meetings and related correspondence suggest that many of them took the opportunity presented by Dunn's unfortunate demise to address concerns about a variety of people whose behaviors and visibility they deemed problematic. And, if the activities they deemed objectionable were not already illegal, they developed legislation or sought de facto ways to make those people and their activities criminal offenses.

The committee's initial list of concerns focused on finding ways to better control prostitution and improving the image and the tourist appeal of the French Quarter, especially on Bourbon Street. Foster explained the city's appeal, and the problems that arose from it, this way:

> When one considers the background of New Orleans, it is easy to see it is the sort of city where gambling, prostitution and other crimes can flourish. The basic culture of its people; its position as a major port; its attractiveness to the tourist—all contribute to this. Tourists are its second largest source of income and a great many of those who come here want to come in contact with the bizarre, the unusual, to do and see things they wouldn't think of doing at home.[9]

Yet even in the permissive environment Foster described, not all tourists were as welcome as others, and the committee's members were concerned that one group of people in particular found the Quarter too appealing and hospitable. In the committee's first meeting, Foster made clear that one of his concerns was the city's growing—or at least increasingly visible and assertive—population of homosexuals. The meeting minutes record that he "brought up the subject of homosexual persons who are congregating in greater numbers in the Quarter and stated that they are not tolerated in other cities and migrate down here." He concluded that "these persons have crept into the Vieux Carre in increasing number during the last year or two." Foster and other committee members wanted to find ways to limit the presence and visibility of homosexuals in the French Quarter and, if possible, drive them out of the city for good.[10]

Evidence from late in the decade makes clear that the goal of evicting all homosexuals from the city had not been achieved. A 1958 report authored by Jacob Morrison—the mayor's half-brother and a tireless antihomosexual crusader in his own right—virtually repeated Foster's description and concerns from years earlier: "New Orleans has always prided herself on being care-free, broad-minded and easy-going. . . . We recommend nothing here that would change her traditional character. People flock to New Orleans to 'see something different.' We don't believe the word 'different' should include the unnatural and the degenerate which must certainly disgust the great majority of visitors."[11] While reformers like Foster and Morrison wished to maintain the city's traditional character, their decade-long campaign aimed at homosexuals in New Orleans, and statewide events created in its wake, challenge the belief that a laissez-faire sexual morality characterized the Crescent City and particularly its French Quarter. Reformers like Foster and Morrison were aware that the French Quarter held a particular appeal for homosexuals, and they were far from laissez in the face of this recognition. They were, however, always more focused on male homosexuality and cross-dressing in public than they were with the less remarked-upon presence of lesbians in the Quarter. Their desire to address what they saw as an increasingly troubling issue led reformers to seek solutions from like-minded individuals and police agencies in urban areas across the nation. New Orleans reformers sought to learn from other cities and integrate their solutions into revised ordinances. In this case, they were determined to be more like other cities rather than to set themselves apart.

In the balance of this essay I explore how the actions of reformers, preservationists, and police complicate commonly held beliefs about the sexual liberality of the French Quarter and its residents. Second, I explore how the antihomosexual reform drives of the 1950s reflected complicated beliefs about homosexuality. Even for the staunchest reformers, there was no single kind of French Quarter queer. Nor were all gay men deemed equally objectionable. The testimony offered by police, residents, and reformers indicates that there were various gay communities in the French Quarter, each of which exhibited definite class and behavioral dimensions. Finally, I consider how the antihomosexual reform campaigns of the 1950s, which began in the French Quarter, made their way to the state capitol, where legislators introduced and passed laws designed to supplement the state's crime against nature statute and expand the legal regime aimed at reducing the visibility if not the presence of the state's gay population. This section, in particular, challenges the common belief that, historically, sexual conservatism characterized every place in Louisiana except New Orleans. In fact, the city's antihomosexual reform campaigns in the 1950s were the seedbed for creating explicit scrutiny, harassment, and legislation directed toward gay and lesbian people statewide by the early 1960s.

New Orleans had certainly been inhabited and visited by homosexual people throughout its history. Yet historians including George Chauncey, John D'Emilio, and Martin Meeker have suggested that urban populations of gay men and lesbians began to cohere into self-conscious communities with recognizably modern gay identities only in the immediate post–World War II period. The pace and timing of these changes varied across the nation, but, as Allan Bérubé has argued, while military officials sought to exclude gay men and lesbians from the military services, those who served gained new perspectives on their own sexual desires through meeting and interacting with others like themselves in the course of their wartime deployments.[12]

Those interactions would have been multiplied in bustling cities like New Orleans, which drew thousands of civilian workers to the city's burgeoning war industries. The city also served as an army quartermaster supply depot and, by mid-1941, was upgraded to a port of embarkation, "a status at the time shared only with New York, San Francisco, Seattle, and Charleston." According to Richard Campanella, 174,651 troops moved through the city in the process of transfer and deployment to other ports of call. If only a very small percentage of those troops were homosexual, they still numbered in the thousands.

The influx of soldiers on leave was also constant in the city throughout the war "and military officials did little to fight it" while the war raged. In the years following 1945, however, military officials declared several French Quarter bars off-limits to soldiers and sailors because of "conditions that are detrimental or inimical to the welfare of service personnel."[13] Three of the five French Quarter bars declared off limits in 1949 were known as hangouts and pickup spots for homosexuals, or sex deviates as they were often termed in the press at the time. Two of the bars, the Starlet Lounge and Tony Bacino's, also became the targets of French Quarter reformers in the 1950s. In fact, the increasing visibility and public assertiveness of the patrons who frequented and staffed these bars set reformers like Foster and Morrison in motion.

If, as Foster noted in 1950, the city's population of homosexuals had been on the rise since the late 1940s, by early 1951 members of the SCCVC were describing that trend as "an alarming influx." As these men considered what to do, they were forced to acknowledge that unless homosexuals were caught in a sexual act for which they could be charged under the state's crime against nature statute, there was not much police or judges could do beyond charging suspected homosexuals with vagrancy or other misdemeanors.[14]

According to Major Albert Blancher of the New Orleans Police Department, these "people can't be arrested because they are homosexuals, but they are picked up whenever noticed, and charged with loitering." Chairman Foster asked Blancher if he had "suggestions as to a means of making these people leave New Orleans." Blancher suggested passing the word to precinct captains "that we are trying to rid the city of them, and if they are found to be from out of town, the police could make it tough for them." If judges would then levy the heaviest penalties possible "or give a suspended sentence with instructions to leave town, this would remove many of them from the city [since] few stay any length of time without being handled by the police."[15]

The committee also queried several municipal judges about their opinions and suggestions. Municipal court judge Harold Moore expressed concern that in most crime against nature cases, "testimony is so weak that you cannot convict and brand a man a homosexual." But, he told the committee, even in cases of lesser offenses "he was not in favor of suspended sentences." Instead, "he was in favor of a jail sentence with a lengthier one upon conviction of a second offense. The judge also advocated the creation of a probation department so as to keep track of continual violators or first offenders as well as second offenders."[16]

Some members suggested using tactics that went beyond the law per se. Committee member Leonard Huber weighed in with a rather blunt suggestion in 1951. Referring "to a comment contained in an American Social Hygiene Report—he said therein it was indicated that about the only thing one could do about homosexuals was to club them out of town."[17] Whatever committee members thought about the merits or practicality of Huber's suggestion, their subsequent actions suggest they likely agreed with Methodist minister and frequent guest at SCCVC meetings Robert T. Jamieson, who opined that at present, "the police [did] not have 'the tool in their hands' to do anything about it." Thus, the committee also sought to amend existing city ordinances and to develop new legislation designed to be introduced "at the next session of the State Legislat[ure]."[18]

The committee was particularly focused on developing ways to discourage gay men from congregating in public or from behaving in ways that marked them as overtly homosexual, particularly by dressing or behaving in gender nonconforming ways. The committee was, for example, successful in making it illegal for those defined as "sexual perverts" to join a laundry list of other types of people—including those described as "lewd, immoral, or dissolute"—barred from employment in establishments that had liquor licenses. The amended ordinance also barred the same long list of people from congregating in or frequenting bars.[19]

Like most city ordinances aimed at vice interests, enforcement was uneven, intermittent, and tended to focus on establishments that individual
reformers found particularly troublesome. For example, when committee
chairman Foster wrote police superintendent Joseph Scheuering in June 1951
with a laundry list of concerns, he noted the following under the heading
"Homosexuals":

> Although the list of suspected places is considerably larger, the seven
> establishments listed below openly cater to homosexuals of both sexes:
>
>> Dixie's Bar of Music
>> The Chez When
>> Starlet Lounge
>> Tony Bacino
>> Lafitte's Blacksmith Shop
>> Mimi's Bar
>> Cinderella Club[20]

Foster expressed the committee's belief "that every effort should be made to
clean up these places or put them out of business." He closed the letter with a
dramatic reminder to Scheuering that leading "criminologists and psycholo-
gists in America state that every sexual deviate is a potential murderer and
the more of this type we can drive out of New Orleans, the better [the city]
will be."[21]

Despite the hyperbole, not everyone agreed that the matter was so dire,
or that all establishments where homosexuals congregated were problematic per se. In an SCCVC meeting in 1950, veteran police captain Joseph
Sonnenberg noted that "a man wearing women's clothing" in the street
would be "immediately arrested on sight." However, he also admitted that
"there are two places known at the time which features [sic] homosexuals
as entertainers. Nobody sees them but themselves, yet everybody knows
they are there . . . but as long as they behave themselves, the police does
not interfere."[22]

The following year, Sonnenberg reiterated that bars against which there
were no complaints ought to be left alone by law enforcement. Speaking specifically about Dixie's Bar of Music and the Chez When, both of which Foster had singled out, Sonnenberg "said that no complaint had been registered
against either." He added that Thomas Griffin, who had a daily column in
the *States-Item*, reported "that the class of people who go there behave themselves" and added that "he had issued strict instructions to his force that these

places be left alone." The committee report quoted his observation that the patrons in these spots "behave themselves like children in a Sunday school."[23]

Apparently, the neighbors surrounding the well-known Dixie's Bar of Music also supported the bar's existence, even though it was a place known to welcome "discreet" homosexuals into its midst. When the bar was closed temporarily in early 1951, many residents in the immediate vicinity signed a petition in support of the bar and asking for it to reopen. Jacob Morrison explained what, to him, was a puzzling outcome by suggesting that "through some political pull" the bar's owners were "able to get the deputy assessors to exert pressure on property owners in that section, thereby compelling them to some extent to sign the petition in favor of this establishment." Not satisfied with the attitude of the bar's neighbors or apparently legal outcome in this particular case, Morrison insisted, "something should be done about this type of practice as well."[24]

Whether it was political pull, neighborhood support, or the discreet behavior and gender-normative dress and deportment of its homosexual clientele that kept Dixie's in business, there were other establishments that both police and reformers would, over time, focus on more intensely and successfully. Even after the SCCVC ceased to exist in late 1952, Morrison continued his antihomosexual reform efforts. For example, in 1953, he and others led a drive to shut down the Starlet Lounge, located at the corner of Chartres and St. Peter streets. Morrison's focus on that particular establishment was likely driven, at least in part, by its proximity to his residence. In court testimony offered years later, Morrison recalled that he had been concerned about the place since 1950, when he had visited and had been waited on by a bartender named Louise. "I thought Louise was a woman and it was only later that I found out she was not a woman but a man." Certainly the cross-dressing scandalized Morrison, but he also abhorred the clientele generally. In 1953, Morrison described the Starlet Lounge as a hangout for "queers, fairies, and ne'er-do-wells" and described it as a "congregating point of homosexuals of every age imaginable."[25]

Even its critics had to admit the lounge was popular among a varied homosexual clientele, but pressure from angry and influential neighbors forced the police to act. For much of September 1953, the newspapers were filled with headlines describing a crackdown on French Quarter vice bars. Still, some police officers seemed less than enthusiastic about the crusade. Captain Thomas Kelly, the daytime commanding officer in the French Quarter's main police station, was quoted as saying "he would not arrest homosexuals unless he had complaints or disturbances." Morrison and like-minded neighborhood residents obliged, both with individual complaints and in a more organized fashion when the members of the French Quarter Residents Association called "for the suspension of city police officers who feel that male degenerates are object[s] of sympathy and should not be arrested."[26]

Morrison and his supporters succeeded in having the Starlet Lounge shuttered temporarily in 1953 and closed permanently by order of the City Council in mid-1954. After the closure, two of the Starlet's popular bartenders, including Louise, quickly found work elsewhere. Louise, whose given name was Louis Robichaux, became a bartender at Tony Bacino's later the same year. He was joined by another Starlet Lounge alum named Amos McFarlane, who used the performance name Candy Lee.

Part of the SCCVC's legacy was amending alcoholic beverage outlet ordinances so that they specifically barred "sexual perverts" from working in or even frequenting bars. Their actions literally helped to construct the closet within which many homosexuals existed, since their mere presence together in public became a misdemeanor offense. Using this tool, the arrest and harassment of homosexuals continued after the 1953 crackdown abated, but arrests occurred on an ad hoc basis. Aside from the men and the small number of women who were arrested for or charged with violating the crime against nature statue (or were entrapped into doing so), others who were arrested or became the focus of police attention were those who made themselves visible by dressing or behaving in ways that marked them as "queer."

Minutely detailed descriptions of the myriad offenses allegedly committed by Robichaux and Macfarlane while working at Tony Bacino's suggest some of the behavior or activities that could and did generate complaints from reformers and, when pressed, arrests by law enforcement. The city's answer to Macfarlane and Robichaux's complaint about their repeated arrests in 1958 described not only their lewd conduct but also argued that they were identifiable as homosexual

> by their use of feminine cosmetics, by their use of semi-feminine or completely feminine garments, by their use of feminine hair dressings and hair style, by the lewd loud and vulgar exchange of pleasantries with customers ... and while off duty [from the bar] ... meeting, consorting, dancing, romancing, and socializing with all sexual perverts in or about the City of New Orleans.[27]

If the above descriptions of Louise and Candy Lee's behavior and appearance were accurate, they were certainly presenting in ways that marked them as homosexual. Yet not all homosexuals behaved in ways or gathered in places that attracted criticism from reformers. The very high-profile business executive Clay Lavergne Shaw, for example, appeared in the press constantly in his role as managing director of the city's International Trade Mart. Shaw was so well regarded that he was tapped to organize the city's 1953 Sesquicentennial Celebrations. He was a large, strikingly handsome man who, publicly at least, dressed conservatively and comported himself in a conventionally masculine fashion. Though he was understood to be a bachelor—a polite term often used to describe upper-class male homosexuals—Shaw was also a respected resident and active preservationist in the French Quarter.

In fact, Shaw was responsible for buying and rehabilitating numerous properties, many of which he resold for a handsome profit. The installation of graceful swimming pools was a trademark of Shaw's renovations, and he is credited with installing the first swimming pool in the French Quarter. This fact was so well recognized that at least two times in the second half of the 1950s, his pools were featured as part of glossy photo spreads in the Sunday supplement to the *Times-Picayune*. In pictures from 1956 and 1958, photos of his pools and patios prominently featured Shaw's friend and then-lover William Henry Formyduval. The photo from 1958 captioned "Fountains cool Clay Shaw pool, 927 Burgundy, as William Formyduval, dog relax" suggests something more than a casual connection between the two men. In another image from October 1958, Shaw was featured in a story about New Orleanians and their pets. In a striking photograph, Shaw, conservatively dressed in a light-colored suit, stared sideways at the camera while holding his pet macaw Dorian on one shoulder. Shaw must have liked the picture, since he clipped it and saved it among his personal papers. And, just as surely, the macaw's name paid homage to iconic gay author Oscar Wilde's short story "The Picture of Dorian Gray." If so, Shaw's public profile, though entirely respectable, demonstrated the subtle but unmistakably self-assertive ways a person of privilege could push back against the strictures of homosexual invisibility pursued by reformers like Morrison.

One can only wonder if these slyly provocative photos raised eyebrows among Shaw's French Quarter neighbors, including Jacob Morrison. If they did, men like Shaw were beyond the reach and seemed to be outside the concerns of most reformers. Though he certainly frequented bars like Dixie's and Lafitte's Blacksmith Shop, Shaw, like other well-heeled homosexuals of his social class, also had the option of organizing private gatherings or attending parties with male escorts or lovers in the homes of those who shared or accepted their sexual choices and identities. The writer and social critic Gore Vidal knew Shaw and described attending parties at his home "a number of times in the 1950s." Even decades later, Vidal stressed that they were "highly correct parties" thrown for visiting celebrities or literati like himself.[28]

Wealthy, property-owning homosexuals like Shaw were not entirely im-
mune from arrest or prosecution, but, unless one was caught in flagrante de-
licto, or cross-dressing in public any day other than Mardi Gras, class privilege
offered men like Shaw advantages that were even recognized by some law enforcement officials. To put it in the words of a police captain named Dwyer,
it was difficult to arrest people he described as "high type" persons.[29]

Fewer difficulties were involved in arresting homosexuals who gathered
in public places, particularly if they behaved in ways reformers found repug-
nant. As a court record from 1958 makes clear, the bartenders Louise and
Candy Lee at Tony Bacino's bar could be very easily arrested, since "Louis
Robichaux and Amos McFarlane were and are notorious, well known and
well advertised homosexuals and sex perverts." The two men "advertised" their
homosexuality in their roles as bartenders and entertainers at Bacino's, which
even the bar's manager, Roy Maggio, admitted was "the queer shop" of New
Orleans. Part of the bar's visibility was related to its location on Toulouse
Street, near the corner and within eyeshot of Bourbon Street.[30]

The specific events that precipitated the lawsuit *Roy Maggio et al. v. City
of New Orleans* began with the arrests of Robichaux and McFarlane on the
evening of July 22, 1958. The men were charged with violating 828 M.C.S.
Section 5-66, which barred "sexual perverts" from working in establishments
that held liquor licenses. Had things gone as they often did in these kinds of
cases, the two men would likely have pled guilty to a lesser charge, paid a
fine, and—after the heat was off—gone back to business behind the bar at
Bacino's. In the summer of 1958, however, police showed more determination than usual. Officers returned to the bar the following evening, and for
six more nights in a row, resulting in eight arrests each for Robichaux and
McFarlane. Maggio, the bar's manager, was arrested at least four times in that
same period. Rather than leave town for a while, as Robichaux had done
when the Starlet Lounge closed in 1954, the three men decided to take legal
action.[31]

They filed a complaint specifying that they had been arrested multiple
times "without a warrant and without probable" cause. They claimed their
rights had been violated and requested a judge issue a restraining order to
prevent additional arrests. Their request was granted, and the restraining
order was issued on August 6, 1958. Rather than settling the matter, the order
seemed to inflame the situation—and reformers like Morrison—who were
furious that a judge had made such a decision. The case went to court quickly
and testimony was taken before Judge Frank J. Stitch on August 13 and 14.[32]

In its answer to the complaint filed by Maggio and the two bartenders, the city attorneys offered the court an extensive list of reasons why the restraining order should be withdrawn. The principal point in all of the objections was that both Robichaux and Macfarlane were admitted homosexuals, which made them, by definition, sex perverts, and therefore employing them at Bacino's was prohibited by 828 M.C.S. Section 5-66.[33]

Forty-nine people were subpoenaed or called to testify in the case, and interested onlookers filled the courtroom to capacity both days. City attorneys presented extensive and explicit evidence that, they argued, provided definitive proof that both men were sex perverts. Both had extensive arrest records, Macfarlane's dating all the way back to 1943. The city also claimed it could produce witnesses who would confirm that "on or about the 8th day of November, 1954," Robichaux "confessed in the presence of three persons . . . that he was a sexual pervert and that he had been a sexual pervert all his life."[34]

The city also procured and produced a statement McFarlane had signed in 1957, which confirmed his homosexuality. More than one witness provided testimony that suggested McFarlane had a particular penchant for men in uniform (and some of them for him), which had led to a run-in with officials at Fort Polk, near Shreveport, in 1957. During questioning by military police, McFarlane described sexual activities between himself and a soldier who "placed his penis in my rectum on several occasions, but never did commit oral sodomy." City officials were able to obtain this classified record from Fort Polk via the intervention of Louisiana congressman F. Edward Hebért.[35]

In addition to presenting specific evidence that incriminated the two men, the city attorneys also called witnesses who offered testimony about the more general law enforcement problems associated with homosexuality. Aaron Kohn was a former FBI agent who had come to New Orleans in the early 1950s and was named the first managing director of the Metropolitan Crime Commission at the time of its founding in 1954. In his testimony, Kohn authoritatively described a great many aspects of homosexual culture. As he began, he reiterated the distinction between visible homosexuals and those who were more discreet. Making clear that he was using "terminology which we know is used in this social group," Kohn contended "the quiet persons" in the homosexual subculture were called "sneaky queens" or "sneaky fruit."[36]

In contrast, Kohn explained that men like Robichaux and McFarlane could be characterized as "flaming queens" who "are inclined to lend themselves to simulating, as much as they can, female characteristics." He went on to inform the court that "a great many of the lesbians who frequent flaming queen establishments generally are also prostitutes," and that a boy or man who was not homosexual but who would have sex with a homosexual "in exchange for money" was called a "penus [*sic*] peddler."[37]

On cross-examination, Kohn was forced to admit that on Mardi Gras day 1955 he and a small group of friends had gone into Tony Bacino's Bar. The court transcript indicates that Kohn, who had been downright loquacious up to this point, became more halting and, ultimately, defensive when asked to give the names of his friends and to describe what he had seen on his visit to Bacino's. After being required to identify his friends, Kohn was asked, "Did you see McFarlane or Robichaux . . . on that date?" Kohn responded, "Well, for your information I actually would not or could not at this point identify any persons, other than to say our visit was very brief, and the primary purpose was to get a direct and personal observation of things we had been told about this place, and we found this gathering of very flagrantly dressed males in the simulation of females, with cosmetics and simulated breasts, and we didn't even have a drink during our visit."[38] Kohn also had to admit that "he had never witnessed any perverted or homosexual act on the part of any of" the plaintiffs. When he finished testifying, Kohn was invited to join the city's attorneys at their table, suggesting how close the relationship was between the reformers and the city's lawyers, at least in this instance. Jacob Morrison, who testified right after Kohn, was also extended this privilege.[39]

Despite the eyewitness and documentary evidence presented by the city, neither McFarlane nor Robichaux was willing to admit to being a homosexual. McFarlane's reluctance to do so was likely overshadowed by the facts presented in the statement he had signed at Fort Polk the previous year. Robichaux, on the other hand, stressed that he was married. He acknowledged that he had "admitted homosexual things behind the bar and working, but when I leave that place I go home to my wife." To a contemporary observer, their reluctance to be frank about their sexuality under the circumstances and under oath, especially given the extensive testimony offered to prove it, might seem curious. Yet their reluctance, and the legal conundrum that drove it, also reminds us just how difficult and dangerous life could be— and could be made to be—for admitted homosexuals. If they said they were homosexual, their claim of harassment would lose any legal force, since their homosexuality would legally class them as sexual perverts, putting them in violation of the ordinance in question. At the very least, they would lose their jobs. They would also face the risk that state felony charges could be brought against them using the state's crime against nature statute. A conviction on such charges could result in a term of at least two years at hard labor in the state's notorious penitentiary at Angola. Even without their direct admission of homosexuality, the court sided with the city. The restraining order was rescinded and the plaintiffs' subsequent appeal was unsuccessful. In the aftermath of the case Tony Bacino's closed, though another gay-friendly bar opened in the same location the following year.

Maggio v. City of New Orleans was just a single case, but the fact that the bartenders and bar manager even filed it—in the view of people like Jacob Morrison even had "the brazen temerity to file it"—indicated a much more widespread problem. On July 22, 1958, the City Council had authorized Morrison "to form a committee to study the acute problems caused by sex deviates in New Orleans." That was the same date on which police had begun the serial arrests of Robichaux and McFarlane.[40]

Over the course of several months, Morrison and his committee contacted and received replies from chambers of commerce and similar business-oriented groups in twenty cities. At the same time, the superintendent of police queried his counterparts in forty-two cities. He received twenty-four responses. The responses from law enforcement and business leaders varied. Officials in Louisville, Kentucky, for example, noted that the problem was minor in their community and no action was needed. Authorities in Seattle responded that they dealt "with the problem as it presents itself." Other cities, like Houston, Texas, and Dayton, Ohio, outlined an approach that favored raids on known homosexual hangouts. Dayton's response was recorded as "use of harassment method. Very effective," while Houston authorities noted that they kept records "on all known degenerates." Though the responses varied considerably, many reflected the view that present laws were not sufficient to stem the tide of what most perceived as a growing problem. The response from Tampa noted that their police conducted continuous surveillance on bars that catered to homosexuals. When asked what action they took against such bars, their recorded response was, "All undesirables are arrested and fingerprinted, and released with strict orders to leave the City." Even if this was unofficial policy, it also suggested that misdemeanor convictions were only one way legal and law enforcement regimes were evolving to deal with the growing visibility of homosexuals in their cities.

Morrison combined the survey data with reports generated by American cities and even by national governing bodies, including the 1957 "Report of the Committee on Homosexual Offenses and Prostitution," which had been compiled by the government of Great Britain for submission to Parliament. Morrison also cited acknowledged experts on sexology including

Alfred Kinsey and Havelock Ellis. This was no parochial, only-in-New-Orleans report. Its breadth and systematic comparisons with other cities put to rest the notion of a sexual exceptionalism in New Orleans, at least when it came to the way in which reformers sought to shape the policing and social sanctioning of known homosexuals or sex deviates, terms the report used interchangeably.

Despite his obvious prejudices, Morrison compiled a thoughtful document in which he acknowledged that ending homosexuality or "curing" homosexuals was unlikely, and he presented council members with a long list of well-known historical figures who were reputed to be homosexual. Yet, with a wry flourish, Morrison reminded his readers that throughout "the ages, sexual perversion, though sterile itself, has bred crime, inspired lust, and been a fruitful source of corruption." He also observed that the "fact of simply *being* a sex deviate, or having homosexual tendencies is not illegal and may not even be sinful or immoral. It's what these unfortunates *do*; not what they *are* that the law is concerned with."[41]

Morrison cautioned that while social tolerance for homosexuality seemed to be on the rise, it was wrongheaded and actually contributed to the problem. Allowing homosexuals to congregate openly could lead to the "awakening or stimulation of otherwise latent tendencies by contact with 'practicing homosexuals.'" Conversely, he opined, "the regulation of the conduct of the sex deviate may well prevent the *spread* of the evils of sex deviation."[42]

Morrison noted that other cities had "been successful in preventing the spread of the activities of such person[s] by constant raids and arrests for such offenses as vagrancy and disorderly conduct. By 'harassment' in general." To make his point, Morrison summarized the "recent case of *Maggio, et al. vs. City of Orleans*" and its significance. "What came out of it," he wrote, "was an expose of the disgusting facts of sexual perversion and its wide-spread affect [*sic*]." He concluded that the case "illustrates the effectiveness of relentless law enforcement—'legal harassment,' if you will."[43]

One of his three concluding recommendations was that police continue such "legal harassment." The second recommendation advised, "persons who don't hesitate to rent their premises to individuals with all the appearances, mannerisms, or repulsive conduct of sex deviates, should take a new look at the sordid consequences that stem from the acts of such persons. Don't rent or lease to sex deviates."[44] Finally, he offered a list of "practical and enforceable amendments to the City Code," most of them aimed at further tightening restrictions on alcoholic beverage outlets and classing "agents who rent or lease property as congregation points for known sex deviates" in the same ordinances that controlled houses of prostitution, assignation, and ill fame.[45]

The author conceded that even if all of his recommendations were followed, "the same percentage of homosexuals would remain as estimated by Dr. Kinsey and other authorities." However, "their lewd activities would not have an easy outlet, their lascivious conduct would be far less offensive and would not become a stench in the nostrils of the public." In short, they would be less visible.[46]

Despite his obvious enthusiasm and thoroughness, Morrison reminded council members that "the City's power to legislate for the punishment of illegal acts extends only to misdemeanors; whereas, the great majority of sex offenses are felonies, falling within the jurisdiction of the State." He also noted that "a municipality can exercise only such control as the State grants it." The implication of this section was that efforts would have to be undertaken in the legislature for reforms to be effective. Morrison made this clear, writing, "It is significant that as our report is being written, a Joint Legislative Committee of the State Legislature is beginning to hold meetings to study the entire problem of sex deviation."[47]

F. Edward LeBreton, a member of the Louisiana House of Representatives from New Orleans, chaired the committee that came to be known as the Legislative Sex Crimes Study Committee. Only a few months after Morrison presented his report to the New Orleans City Council, LeBreton's committee appointed a fifteen-member advisory group to study the problem and "hold hearings in key parts of the state on sexual deviation problems." The committee planned to write a report and make recommendations "to the governor and the Legislature at the 1960 regular session." Advisory group member and Baton Rouge district attorney J. St. Clair Favrot was quoted as saying, "We have a terrific problem on sex crimes . . . particularly in the large cities. Only a very small percentage of it ever comes to public attention."[48]

Actually, a great deal about sexual deviation and homosexuality had come to public attention in New Orleans between 1950 and 1960. And the antihomosexual activism was generated within and by New Orleanians, spreading to the other parts of the state from within the supposedly liberal, laissez-faire confines of the French Quarter. In fact, the reform drive led by Jacob Morrison in 1958 and 1959 called for and actually led to the adoption of three new laws during the 1960 legislative session, including one that reflected his suggestion that knowingly renting or leasing premises to homosexuals be made an offense against the law.[49]

These events and the chain of causality that led to them run counter to what most contemporary observers and many scholars would expect about the history of sexuality in New Orleans. Yet a close look at the history of antihomosexual reform efforts between 1950 and 1960 helps us reconsider or at least provide nuance to claims that New Orleans had an exceptional or even singular culture of sexuality regionally and nationally. Jacob Morrison wanted to know what officials and leaders in other cities were doing, and he wanted New Orleans to show municipal leadership regarding a problem that he believed "had become so acute in all of its phases that we could not avoid exploring certain of its aspects that are not, strictly speaking, our concern." The activism of men like Richard Foster and Jacob Morrison reminds us that even as gay and lesbian people continued to be drawn to New Orleans, they were not universally welcomed. In fact, in some quarters, they were viewed as specters of a serious municipal problem that required state-level legislative attention.[50]

Notes

1 Long 2004, 203, 7. My own approach to these questions has led me to conclude that scholars who are willing to acknowledge "the city's complex combination of similarity and difference" are likely to draw balanced historical conclusions.

2 Reed 2012.

3 Faulkner 1958, 13.

4 R. Clark 2009, 227.

5 R. Clark 2009, 228–31.

6 R. Clark 2009, 228–31.

7 Morrison would go on to be elected to the mayor's office four times. He also ran twice for Louisiana governor, both times unsuccessfully (see Haas 1974).

8 Haas 1974, 181–89. See also Richard R. Foster Civic and Community Papers, MSS 553, Williams Research Center, Historic New Orleans Collection (hereafter cited as Foster MSS). The records of the SCCVC are concentrated in box 5, folder 46.

9 Copy of speech delivered to the Presbyterian Laymen's Association, April 30, 1954, Foster MSS, box 4, folder 38.

10 Meeting minutes, March 30, 1950, Foster MSS, box 5, folder 46.

11 Jacob Morrison, "Report of Committee on the Problem of Sex Deviates in New Orleans," 1958, box 102, MSS 553, 14, in Mary Meeks Morrison and Jacob Morrison Papers, Williams Research Center, Historic New Orleans Collection (hereafter cited as Morrison MSS).

12 See Chauncey 1994; D'Emilio 1998; Meeker 2006; Bérubé 1990.

13 "Ban Is Put on 28 Places by Navy; Five French Quarter Spots Out-of-Bounds," *Times-Picayune*, March 11, 1949, 5; "June Off-Limits List Is Announced," *Times-Picayune*, June 18, 1949, 5.

14 Foster MSS, box 5, folder 46.

15 Meeting minutes, August 23, 1950, Foster MSS.

16 Meeting minutes, September 6, 1950, Foster MSS.

17 Meeting minutes, June 13, 1951, Foster MSS.

18 Meeting minutes, April 19, 1951, Foster MSS.

19 See 828 M.C.S. Section 5-66, which reads as follows: "No person of lewd, immoral or dissolute character, sexual pervert, inmate of a brothel or house of prostitution or as-signation, B drinker, person who gambles illegally, as defined by law, lottery operator, lottery collector, lottery vendor or seller or user of narcotics, either paid or unpaid, shall be employed in such a place of business as a singer, dancer, beer carrier, waiter, bartender, waitress, girl bartender or barmaid. Nor shall such persons be allowed to congregate or frequent such place of business" (CCS Ord. No. 18,537, sec. 6). See also *Maggio et al. v. City of New Orleans* 364–219, Civil District Court, Division F Docket F, August 6, 1958.

20 Letter from Foster to Police Superintendent Joseph Scheuering, June 5, 1961, Foster MSS, box 2, folder 15.

21 Foster MSS.

22 Meeting minutes, August 23, 1950, Foster MSS, box 5, folder 46.

23 Undated meeting minutes, probably April 1951, Foster MSS, box 5, folder 46.

24 Meeting minutes, April 19, 1951, Foster MSS, box 5, folder 46.

25 Testimony given in *Maggio et al. v. City of New Orleans* (1958). The crusade against the Starlet Lounge was also chronicled in the *New Orleans States-Item*. Morrison retained many clipping in his personal records. See, for example, "Starlet Lounge Loses Licenses for 6 Months," *States-Item*, September 15, 1953, Morrison MSS, box 102, folder 11.

26 *New Orleans States-Item*, September 18, 1953, Morrison MSS, box 102, folder 11.

27 *Maggio et al. v. City of New Orleans* (1958).

28 See Carpenter 2014, loc. 5869, citations 1030–32. The quotations are drawn from cor-respondence between Carpenter and Vidal.

29 Meeting minutes, June 13, 1951, Foster MSS.

30 *Maggio et al. v. City of New Orleans* (1958).

31 *Maggio et al. v. City of New Orleans* (1958).

32 *Maggio et al. v. City of New Orleans* (1958).

33 *Maggio et al. v. City of New Orleans* (1958).

34 *Maggio et al. v. City of New Orleans* (1958).

35 *Maggio et al. v. City of New Orleans* (1958).

36 *Maggio et al. v. City of New Orleans* (1958).

37 *Maggio et al. v. City of New Orleans* (1958).

38 *Maggio et al. v. City of New Orleans* (1958).

39 *Maggio et al. v. City of New Orleans* (1958).

40 Morrison, "Report of Committee on the Problem," Morrison MSS.

41 Morrison, "Report of Committee on the Problem," 7, Morrison MSS, emphasis in original.

42 Morrison, "Report of Committee on the Problem," 8, Morrison MSS, emphasis in original.

43 Morrison, "Report of Committee on the Problem," 12, Morrison MSS.

44 Morrison, "Report of Committee on the Problem," 14, Morrison MSS.

45 Morrison, "Report of Committee on the Problem," 14–15, Morrison MSS.

46 Morrison, "Report of Committee on the Problem," 11, Morrison MSS.

47 Morrison, "Report of Committee on the Problem," 14, Morrison MSS.

48 *Times-Picayune*, February 17, 1959.

49 "LA House Votes Obscenity Bills," *Times-Picayune*, June 14, 1960, 33; "Obscenity Law Bills Approved; Senate Gives Final Okay to 3 Measures," *Times-Picayune*, June 22, 1960, 47.

50 Morrison, "Report of Committee on the Problem," 2, Morrison MSS.

9

Building Black Suburbs in New Orleans

VERN BAXTER & MARIA CASATI

Pontchartrain Park is a historic middle-class suburb carved out of the swamps of eastern New Orleans in the waning years of segregation for aspiring black homeowners. Canals and dead-end streets wall off black suburbia from surrounding white neighborhoods to create what resident Cheryl Hayes calls a "Leave it to Beaverland." Her childhood recalled "three kids from television who had a jump rope or a ball and walked down the block and knocked on someone's door when they wanted to play." For Hayes and many other African Americans, Pontchartrain Park represented the 1950s American dream of home ownership and full membership in an affluent society. A representative of the Federal Housing Administration (FHA) proclaimed at its opening that Pontchartrain Park was an effort to "guide builders in the market of housing for the wealthier Negro families." Featuring a golf course, curvilinear streets, and California ranch-style homes, Pontchartrain Park promised black residents "a whole new way of life—in clean, fresh, open surroundings just off the lakefront."[1] Pontchartrain Park was also separate but equal housing and recreational facilities for black people, constructed at the same moment the US Supreme Court formally struck down the separate-but-equal doctrine in *Brown vs. Board of Education*.

How did one of the first suburban subdivisions for African Americans sprout in eastern New Orleans on land coveted and largely governed by whites? This chapter is an inquiry into the racial and class politics of urban development in the cauldron of post–World War II housing shortages and struggles over civil rights. It is the story of an entrenched but fractured segregationist regime in New Orleans that met stiff resistance from an increasingly mobilized yet also fractured black politics that demanded access to housing and leisure resources and the advance of civil rights. Local struggles over affordable housing for middle-class black people formed a layer within a contested national housing politics that favored private over public solutions to housing shortages and, in the process, extended racial exclusion and residential segregation.

A formidable coalition of real estate interests and segregationists in New Orleans sought private extraction of rents from land whose value increased by racial exclusion. Demands of civil rights activists for racial integration of Pontchartrain Park challenged a tradition of black elite accommodation to white direction of segregated development. Black elites in New Orleans and other cities brokered deals with local growth coalitions to construct segregated housing in the context of latent threats of white violence and a dim possibility of integration within the existing racial order. Federal involvement in urban policy further dimmed prospects for integration by extending racial residential segregation between 1940 and 1960.[2] New Orleans was no exception to this contested and racialized process. As happened in other cities at this time, grassroots action, legal initiatives, and informal struggles for integration and full procedural equality ramped up to challenge the politics of accommodation.[3]

The chapter challenges the exceptionalist conception of New Orleans as a city defined by its urban black poor when, like other cities, New Orleans nurtured a fractured but vibrant black middle class. Despite the uniqueness of New Orleans politics, the development of Pontchartrain Park aligns with literature that documents race- and class-driven struggles and accommodations over urban development in cities like Atlanta, Dallas, Cleveland, Detroit, Philadelphia, and Kansas City.[4] The findings establish an exemplary case of the power of racial exclusion and class politics that invite pragmatic accommodation by middle-class blacks.

Pontchartrain Park is also an instance of mid-twentieth-century advance of both civil rights and racial residential segregation. Construction of Pontchartrain Park for middle-class blacks, and federally funded public housing projects built for low-income blacks, extended racial homogeneity and isolation beyond levels previously seen in New Orleans. The exclusionary influence of national coalitions of housing capital on federal and local urban development policy was evident in many other cities, which makes New Orleans exemplary rather than exceptional.[5] Suburban migration and urban development extended residential segregation patterns in New Orleans that more closely mirrored those found in other American cities.[6]

Postwar Urban Policy

Severe housing shortages and blighted housing conditions of low-income citizens, particularly low-income black citizens, stimulated postwar debates over slum clearance and public housing. The balance of political forces nationwide included conservative business interests like the National Association of Real Estate Brokers (NAREB), National Association of Home Builders (NAHB), US Savings and Loan League, and the US Chamber of Commerce. These organizations generally favored racial exclusion and mobilized antigovernment and anticommunist ideology to build support for private financing of suburban housing. They also opposed funding for public housing.[7] Proponents of public housing and federal involvement in slum clearance included President Harry Truman, organized labor, and liberal organizations like the National Association of Social Workers, the National Public Housing Conference, and the National Conference of Mayors.[8] Liberal arguments in favor of slum clearance and public housing emphasized health concerns and an improved moral climate for urban residents.

The liberal-minded urban coalition in place since the New Deal was successful in securing federal funding for public housing in the federal Housing Act of 1949. The development stage of Pontchartrain Park occurred within this model of public housing and government subsidy of suburban development, but construction of Pontchartrain Park proceeded later under the more conservative market model governed by private initiative that gained the upper hand in the Housing Act of 1954. Whether enthusiastic or reluctant, advocates of both models advanced racial projects that increased racial residential segregation despite court-ordered mandates to end segregation and restrictive racial covenants that institutionalized racial exclusion from white neighborhoods.

Federal housing legislation passed by Congress in the decade after World War II favored construction of new suburban housing over slum clearance and the construction of public housing.[9] Federal land appraisals and loan policies institutionalized racial exclusion while they preserved and enhanced land values. Arnold Hirsch shows that, despite fierce resistance from black activists in the Racial Relations Service of the Housing and Home Finance Agency (HHFA), early slum clearance plans in cities like Baltimore displaced mostly minority residents and then used gentlemen's agreements to ban them from living in redeveloped neighborhoods. Similar links existed between slum clearance and exclusion of blacks from suburban expansion in Philadelphia, Dallas, and other cities.[10]

The FHA's mortgage underwriting standards and practices undervalued property in predominantly black and mixed-race neighborhoods, and discouraged lending in areas populated by lower-status residents. Its mortgage underwriting handbooks stated, "if a neighborhood is to retain stability, it is necessary that properties shall continue to be occupied by the same social and racial classes."[11] The FHA's underwriting practices also encouraged racially restrictive covenants that prohibited sale of properties in white neighborhoods to black buyers. The US Supreme Court ruled in the 1948 *Shelley v. Kramer* decision that racial covenants were unconstitutional, but this did not alter local or FHA underwriting guidelines. Executive Director John M. Ducey of the FHA wrote the following to local agency members in December 1949: "The recent announcement of a revised policy of the Federal Housing Administration on restrictive covenants, coupled with a newspaper story about an FHA disapproval of a project in Charlotte, NC on grounds of racial policy, will almost surely result in widespread misunderstanding and unnecessary commotion. FHA's racial policy does not forbid segregation; neither does the FHA."[12] Urban scholar Kenneth Jackson concludes that the federal government after World War II continued to embrace racially discriminatory attitudes and markets with policies designed to maintain economic stability.[13]

Race and Urban Politics in Postwar New Orleans

Factions active in postwar New Orleans politics lined up with those active in national urban politics. The deeply segregationist and conservative Old Regulars coalition faced serious challenges after 1946 from reform-minded whites led by newly elected Mayor deLesseps "Chep" Morrison. Mayor Morrison hired black city workers but still upheld residential segregation. A persistent duality prevailed in local black politics between better-educated descendants of free people of color (Creole Catholics) whose quasi-citizenship status eroded after abolition, and American blacks (largely Protestant) descended from slaves.[14]

The National Association for the Advancement of Colored People (NAACP) carried forward a commitment to equality and racial integration into the grassroots civil rights struggle in the second half of the twentieth century. The New Orleans Urban League devoted itself to equal-opportunity assimilation of all ethnic groups and relied on a board of directors populated by elite blacks and reform-minded whites that brokered deals to advance equality.[15] Members of the New Orleans Urban League included land developer Edgar Stern and his aide Lester Kabacoff, both of whom were close advisors of Mayor Morrison. Stern was president of Pontchartrain Park Homes, formed in 1954 to develop Pontchartrain Park.[16] Charles Keller and his wife, Rosa Freeman Keller, were also active white members of the Urban League; Mrs. Keller served as Urban League president in 1953 and her husband, codeveloper of Pontchartrain Park, was a member of President Eisenhower's National Committee on Negro Housing.[17]

African Americans were nearly 30 percent of the 495,000 residents of New Orleans in 1940, but only four hundred black people registered to vote.[18] Black people often accessed the political system through black civic and church leaders (e.g., A. L. Davis of Inter-denominational Ministerial Alliance) that informed white ward bosses of important issues in the black community and sought patronage. Most black people turned inward for assistance to self-help organizations like Carnival krewes, the Second Ward Voters League, and the Seventh Ward Civic Club, formed in 1927 to improve education and voting rights.[19] The winds of electoral change blew hard after 1950 as the black middle class expanded and voter registration drives proliferated, increasing black voter registration to thirteen thousand in 1948 and thirty thousand in 1958 (see table 9.1).

Extensive subaltern resistance to segregation was evident in the New Orleans black community during the Jim Crow era. An all-white police department used force to keep parks segregated and the racial order intact. Civic groups mobilized against police brutality and segregation at public meetings, and many working-class African Americans risked arrest and police beatings when they dared use all-white playgrounds, beaches, and whites-only Audubon and City Parks.[20]

Housing Shortages in New Orleans

Housing shortages, particularly for people of color with little money, are a persistent problem in a capitalist economy. The problem is exacerbated in New Orleans by a shortage of dry land and the enormous expense required to drain land and protect it from flooding in the alluvial floodplain on which most of the city is built.[21] Expensive land and high land preparation costs (e.g., levees, drainage canals) require extraordinary public investment to construct housing in New Orleans.

A 1953 study of housing conditions fielded by the Urban League identified 47,000 dilapidated housing units in New Orleans and a black vacancy rate of less than 1 percent.[22] The same report stated that less than 1,000 of 48,000

Table 9.1 | BLACK MIDDLE CLASS IN NEW ORLEANS URBAN AREA, 1950–1970

VARIABLE	1950[a] TOTAL	%	1960[a] TOTAL	%	1970 TOTAL	%
Total population, 14 years and older	433,280	100	596,938	100	748,333	100
White population, 14 years and older	303,195	70	427,744	71.6	533,241	71.3
Black population, 14 years and older	129,520	29.8	167,858	28.1	212,867	28.7
White median income	$2,061		$3,348		$4,747	
Black median income	$986		$1,565		$2,386	
White annual income, $1–4,999	169,795	66.8	205,572	64.5	201,754	63.2
Black annual income, $1–4,999	83,775	33.0	112,271	35.2	116,065	36.4
White annual income, $5,000–9,999	12,585	98.0	72,697	92.4	115,082	79.7
Black annual income, $5,000–9,999	240	1.8	5,767	7.3	28,887	20.0
White annual income, over $10,000	4,550	98.9	17,827	99.0	71,963	95.4
Black annual income, over $10,000	35	.008	166	.009	3,364	.044
Black professional, technical, kindred workers compared to all black workers	2,332	.018	3,717	.022	6,616	.031
Black, 1–3 years college education, compared to total black population	2,080	.016	3,220	.019	6,226	.029
Black, 4 or more years college education, compared to total black population	1,605	.012	3,336	.020	5,608	.026

a. Percentage totals for 1950 and 1960 do not add up to 100 because census category "other race" is omitted.

Source: US Census, "Census of Population and Housing," 1950, 1960, 1970, www.census.gov./production/decennial.html.

new homes built in the city since 1945 were for blacks. A subsequent study funded by the National Commission on Race and Housing concluded that 80 percent of housing occupied by black people in New Orleans in 1956 was either dilapidated or lacked essential sanitary facilities like indoor toilets.[23]

Disputes over Integration of Public Parks Influence Land Use

Development of Pontchartrain Park would not have happened without involvement of black civic and civil rights organizations and the resistance of many local black residents who illegally used segregated parks and stood up to local police harassment. Local swimming pools, parks, and golf courses were all segregated, and there was no large park or golf course available for black people. Mayor Morrison believed in the importance of public parks, recreation facilities, and public housing on the outskirts of the city. Members of the Seventh Ward Civic Improvement Association and the local chapter of the NAACP put pressure on the mayor to build a park for black people, while use of local parks by blacks riled segregationist sentiment. The mayor addressed the problem in 1947 by forming an Advisory Committee on Expansion of Negro Recreation Facilities. The committee reported, "the most pressing need is a park with all facilities generally found in well-appointed amusement parks."[24] The City Planning Department asked local realtor Gerald Pratt if the city might purchase 226 acres of his land in the Gentilly area for a black park isolated from white residents (see map 9.1).[25] Integration of existing parks was not on the agenda, and important segments of the white community either did not want blacks passing through their neighborhoods to a black park or did not want to spend scarce land and money on a black park when there were white suburbs and industrial sites to develop. The mayor appointed a Colored City Park Commission in April 1948 in an effort to overcome "strenuous objections from white property owners" who lived near the proposed black park.[26] Leonard Huber, chairman of the Civic Committee of the New Orleans Association of Commerce, told members of the association that the city received numerous applications from Negroes to use white parks, and the NAACP threatened an integration lawsuit that the city would likely lose. Huber identified "a steady encroachment on the facilities of the white population and an element of danger involved through disturbed racial conditions." He reported that local business interests were worried about the potential for a race riot from continued black infiltration of Audubon and City Parks.[27]

NAACP legal counsel A. P. Tureaud filed several lawsuits in the late 1940s over segregation of parks and golf courses, and the deplorable conditions for black children in the New Orleans public school system.[28] One lawsuit arose in a dispute over the right of black people to continue a tradition of swimming at the Seabrook Beach on Lake Pontchartrain.[29] Meanwhile, city officials and the State Board of Levee Commissioners that governed the lakefront spent state money to erect a bathhouse for blacks at Lincoln Beach, six miles up the lakefront from Seabrook. In March 1949, NAACP officials charged that black people had no input into the choice of Lincoln Beach for a black park, that it was too far from where black people lived, and the water at Lincoln Beach was contaminated.[30]

An informal survey fielded by the Association of Commerce revealed extensive resistance to segregated leisure facilities. The survey also found that five thousand blacks bathed at Seabrook Beach on May 18, 1949, while only

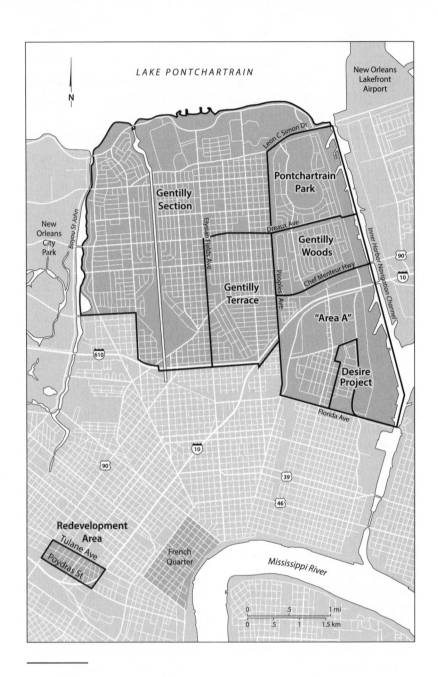

Map 9.1

New Orleans residential development in the 1950s. Map by Bill Nelson.

fifteen bathed at Lincoln Beach.[31] Representatives of the Levee Board met with NAACP leaders in July and agreed that blacks could use Seabrook Beach for the remainder of the season, and a new site near Seabrook would be prepared and made available for blacks in the future.[32]

Mayor Morrison met with black leaders in late May and promised to build a black park funded by the private Wisner Fund. But nothing happened, as money from the fund went instead to buy more land for Audubon Park and to build a bridge in a white neighborhood.[33] Passage of the national Housing Act of 1949 prompted the mayor to send representatives to Washington to negotiate a $10 million grant to pay for the black park and 250 housing units on the Seabrook tract near the lake.[34] The mayor then brokered a tentative solution to both the need for a segregated black park and segregated black housing at a meeting in December with city housing officials and local builders W. H. Crawford and Charles Tessier. He proposed development of the three-hundred-acre Seeger tract (Gentilly Woods) as 1,400 housing units for white people and the adjacent 366-acre Seabrook tract (Pontchartrain Park) as a combination privately developed black subdivision (200 acres) and black park (166 acres) "laid out as close as possible to the Negro beach area at Seabrook" (see map 9.1).[35] The mayor proposed that the local Sewer and Water Board contribute $3.7 million to build three covered drainage canals and install a pumping station, and that the city spend $600,000 for installation of shell streets with open gutters and subsurface drainage. The city would purchase the Seabrook property and, because of the black housing component, finance the entire project with a Title I loan from the HHFA under category 4 (Open Areas) of the Housing Act of 1949.[36]

Reminiscent of concurrent struggles over suburban expansion on the edge of many American cities, white opposition erupted immediately to the plan for suburban black housing and a black park in New Orleans. Several groups of white residents from recently developed suburban neighborhoods in the adjacent Gentilly section circulated petitions against the plan. A segregationist discourse framed around racial fear and declining property values permeated the debate. Participants at a public meeting attended by three hundred residents in April 1950 charged that the proposal seriously injured property values, and would "disrupt our peaceful surroundings by bringing another area of mixed population to our already spotty city planning."[37] Stewart Gast of the local chapter of the NAHB suggested a downtown location for the black subdivision instead of the cloistered suburban one, stating, "we are going to isolate the Negroes in a dead end behind a Chinese Wall, . . .

but there is no way for covenants to protect adjacent white development from invasion."[38] A. D. Mumme, president of Gentilly Gardens Improvement Association, told the local *Gentilly Herald* "no matter what barriers they tell you will separate the Negroes from the adjoining white areas, the bounds will not be effective."[39] Malcolm Mundy of the association said in a more scholarly tone, "I don't think it makes good sociological sense to bring colored people into a white area—when the colored man goes in values go down."[40]

Despite opposition, the New Orleans Commission Council passed two ordinances on April 28, 1950, that empowered the mayor to acquire land, begin construction of the black park, and proceed with both housing developments. Mayor Morrison wrote opponents of the plan in May 1950 that it was best for the city to build both a black and a white housing development. His often-quoted comment in support of the plan: "We have just got to make up our minds that if we are going to preserve traditions and habits of our city (which includes segregation) that we are going to have to provide facilities to meet the demands of the Negro group."[41] J. H. Burton of the New Gentilly Improvement Association agreed with Mayor Morrison: "we must do something now or we will be forced by the courts to allow Negroes into public parks."[42] The nature of white support was further revealed by this quote from city finance commissioner Lionel Ott, who told the *Times-Picayune* that "he had friends in the Gentilly section who would be for it [black housing], particularly since they felt a Negro housing development would help them get domestic help."[43]

The city allocated $25,000 in 1951 to start work on the black park. Work proceeded slowly, and Mayor Morrison had to reassure black leaders in August 1952 that, despite slow progress, the park was a "top priority project."[44] The park was actually not a top priority project. It was rearguarded by more pressing and profitable concern with construction of the whites-only Gentilly Woods subdivision. The *Times-Picayune* reported in January 1951 that construction would begin immediately on the $15 million plan to build 1,423 homes for whites on the Seeger tract in Gentilly Woods, the largest home construction project in city history.[45] The subdivision opened in June 1951, and developers immediately presented site plans for a new shopping center next to the subdivision. Black activism leveraged housing and park reform, but the local growth coalition, segregationist politics, and racist discourse prevented much from happening without federal support, available only if a larger urban redevelopment plan for the city was put in place under provisions of the federal Housing Act of 1949.

Conservative Turn in National Housing Policy

Congress cut funding for slum clearance and public housing programs in 1950, which put in jeopardy federal funding for Pontchartrain Park. NAREB spearheaded a national anti–public housing campaign that resonated strongly with the New Orleans chapter. Congress voted in April 1953 to suspend grants for construction of low-rent public housing projects.[46] Ties were necessary between Pontchartrain Park, slum clearance, and public housing because the city expected a federal urban redevelopment grant of at least $3 million if a redevelopment proposal was approved that specified rights of way, demolition of structures, property sales, expropriation costs, a black park, and new housing units.[47]

The national debate on public housing took another conservative turn when, in 1953, newly elected Republican president Dwight Eisenhower appointed a panel of businessmen and real estate professionals to his Advisory Committee on Government Housing Policies and Programs.[48] The committee opposed public housing and shifted the focus of debate to private-enterprise solutions that protected and rehabilitated sound but threatened neighborhoods.[49] The convergence of antigovernment sentiment and racial politics peeled off support for slum clearance and public housing from the liberal coalition within the US Conference of Mayors. Many mayors were under intense pressure from constituents to embrace Advisory Committee plans for urban renewal that included more subsidies for public works and business.[50] Grassroots white opposition to public housing on racial grounds was another reason for the shift toward urban renewal. The FHA did little to interfere with pressure to submerge any federal commitment to residential desegregation, citing priority of local preferences as their cover.[51] In a victory for racial exclusion and increased rents for real estate and finance capital, the Housing Act of 1954 advanced federal subsidies to exploit private property free of racial constraints and accepted increased residential segregation into the bargain.[52] President Eisenhower offered liberals and civil rights activists his support for inclusion in the act of provisions to improve financing for minority homeowners and, according to Albert Cole, administrator of the HHFA, a commitment to "expand and improve the local housing supplies available to Negroes."[53] The new act implicitly endorsed extension of racially segregated housing markets and increased racial residential segregation in a national political victory for the beleaguered but not beaten segregationist racial order.

End of Urban Redevelopment in New Orleans

Consistent with national policy, local efforts intensified to cancel plans for slum clearance and expansion of public housing. Militant opposition emerged from the business community to the massive public housing program already underway in New Orleans, which included projects to add 774 units for whites and 4,120 for blacks (see map 9.1).[54] The local chapter of the NAHB staged a public meeting in December 1952 where they called for a referendum on any further addition to the all-black Magnolia and Desire projects, the latter sited on vacant land next to the Industrial Canal that home builders thought best zoned for industrial and commercial use.[55]

Opponents branded the purchase of land for public housing and urban redevelopment an unnecessary socialist experiment. City assessor James E. Comiskey, a stalwart of the Old Regulars political faction, formed the Owners-Tenant Association (OTA) to defeat the urban redevelopment proposal for his district (see map 9.1).[56] Many local property owners, the local real estate board, and some black residents who feared homelessness if displaced by slum clearance joined the fight against expropriation and what OTA attorney Albert J. Flettrich called "the dangerous concentration of power in municipal and federal agencies."[57]

The New Orleans Chamber of Commerce issued a report in March 1953 that echoed the president's commission recommendation that rather than urban redevelopment the city should pursue rehabilitation through improved housing law enforcement.[58] The report advised the mayor to prepare a workable minimum housing standards ordinance for the city. The chamber recommended appointments to a new housing committee, and the mayor closely followed that advice. Committee members included real estate executives and building contractors like F. Poche Waguespack and Clifford Favrot; Fred Loucks, president of the local home builders association; banker C. E. Whitmore; Omer Keubel of the Real Estate Board; and William W. F. Riggs, executive vice president of the Chamber of Commerce. The committee also included black leaders like Urban League president J. Westbrook McPherson and Albert Dent, president of historically black Dillard University; white Urban League stalwarts Edgar Stern and Charles Keller; and liberal slumlord Abel Katz.[59]

Chep Morrison was among those in the US Conference of Mayors that publicly reversed course and embraced the conservative turn against urban redevelopment and slum clearance. Moved by threats to his electoral ambitions evident in formation of the OTA and reflected in a 7–0 vote by the New Orleans Commission Council against the redevelopment plan, he embraced private enterprise solutions and enforcement of minimum housing standards.[60] He wrote the FHA on May 7, 1953, that 80 percent of slums in New Orleans could be corrected by rehabilitation through neighborhood and individual action in accordance with minimum standards, and that the city was "calling a halt" to its redevelopment program for slum clearance.[61] The city of New Orleans embraced policies advocated by the NAHB and already implemented in Baltimore that favored private initiatives to construct housing and eradicate slums. The move cost the city $2.9 million in federal funds reserved under Title I of the Housing Act of 1949 and additional funds for Pontchartrain Park that were contingent on continued participation in the slum clearance program.[62]

The Commission Council passed the improved minimum housing standards ordinance in July 1953 and established a new city agency to deal with housing improvement and slum prevention.[63] Mayor Morrison appointed E. Yates Cook, architect of the Baltimore redevelopment plan and national housing rehabilitation director of the NAHB, as acting director of the new agency. When J. Westbrook McPherson of the Urban League requested use of the new agency's housing rehabilitation program to increase the supply of available housing and demolish some undesirable properties, executive committee chair Clifford Favrot responded that he "felt this was an assignment outside the scope of this group."[64]

The OTA further undermined urban redevelopment in New Orleans when it successfully pressed a state law in 1954 that prohibited use of eminent domain powers for property sales to private interests and limited eminent domain to direct public uses. The law effectively killed urban redevelopment and left Louisiana the only state without an urban redevelopment program.[65] The arch-segregationist Old Regulars prevailed upon allies in Baton Rouge to preserve a racial project dominated by large and small real estate capital and segregationists.

End Game in the Struggle over Urban Renewal and Pontchartrain Park

The pro-business climate that surrounded national and local housing policy implied that segregated housing was an acceptable approach to urban development and the black housing crisis. The black community split on acceptance of continued segregation as a practical reality that informed increases in the supply of housing. An anti-redlining editorial in the *Louisiana Weekly* published in October 1953 pointed out that 98 percent of private home financing in New Orleans was for whites, which left blacks to purchase homes abandoned by whites.[66] The editorial called for a progressive mortgage broker to take on the proposed subdivision at Pontchartrain Park and make a tidy sum in the process because, it said, "the market is here for several Negro housing subdivisions. It is just waiting to be discovered."[67] The Urban League chimed in with a report on black housing that reminded officials of earlier efforts to allocate 350 acres in Area A near the Industrial Canal for development of private residential housing to alleviate the black housing shortage (see map 9.1).[68]

In a clear act of accommodation to perceptions of political inevitability, Urban League members on the mayor's housing committee supported the housing rehabilitation plan and minimum standards ordinances passed by the Commission Council.[69] By this time only 110 acres remained in the Area A tract near the Industrial Canal, and the mayor wanted them zoned light industrial in a land exchange designed to "provide an even better chance for the [black] housing in a much more desirable section."[70]

The more desirable section was Pontchartrain Park. Mayor Morrison backed off slum clearance and urban redevelopment and distanced himself from any black residential development near the Desire Project and Industrial Canal. He knew the new railroad terminal and City Hall construction projects underway downtown would displace black residents and further intensify the housing shortage for those who did not qualify for public housing.[71] He met with white Urban League champions the Sterns and Kellers and encouraged them to develop Pontchartrain Park. Charles Keller recruited W. H. Crawford as builder and set out to demonstrate that blacks could afford to own and would keep up their property.[72] Lester Kabacoff and Edgar Stern, along with developers Morgan Earnest and Charles Keller, formed Pontchartrain Park Homes to develop the subdivision in concert with the city's construction of the black park and golf course.

A major remaining sticking point was how to wall off the subdivision from adjacent white neighborhoods. Members of the Gentilly Woods Improvement Association made a last stand against Pontchartrain Park in November 1953 when they held public meetings and submitted a petition with one thousand signatures in opposition to "any such planned Negro development." The usual segregationist discourse prevailed as Ralph Lichtlus, president of the association, lamented that "owners of Gentilly Woods homes are faced with the devaluation of our properties and are faced with the loss of an equity which constitutes their only savings." Richard Hatfield, president of the Bay Civic Club, described the project as "trying to mix oil with water," adding that "development of the park there would increase traffic, probably undesirable traffic in and through Gentilly Woods."[73]

A ceremony at the site in November 1954 announced with great fanfare development of the Pontchartrain Park subdivision. Plans were unveiled for a 222-acre subdivision of one thousand prefabricated Crawford Homes with financing provided by local Hibernia National Bank and First National Bank of Chicago. George Snowden, director of the race relations staff of the FHA, and Neal Hardy, director of the National Housing Center, an affiliate of the NAHB, both attended the ceremony.[74] The subdivision was constructed in a curvilinear street design that offered no real passage out of the neighborhood save the route from Press Drive to Gentilly Boulevard. Lakefront access was limited to a narrow drawbridge off Hayne Boulevard. The Dwyer Canal provided drainage and segregated the subdivision from Gentilly Woods, while the Industrial Canal secured the eastern boundary.

The New Orleans NAACP was not part of the celebration at Pontchartrain Park. The organization opposed Urban League support of resolutions for segregated housing developments either near the Industrial Canal or at Pontchartrain Park, calling them a discriminatory way to ease the black housing shortage. A. J. Chapital, president of the New Orleans chapter of the NAACP, wrote Mrs. Moises Cahn, chair of the Urban League Housing Committee, on April 4, 1953, to clarify that the NAACP opposed all forms of segregation based on race. He encouraged the Urban League to do the same: "It is our belief that any effort to establish a residential area should be done without a direct or implied reference to race."[75] Chapital also wrote the New Orleans Commission Council to inform them that the NAACP knew the New Orleans Housing Authority, FHA, and local builders made decisions based on race, so the NAACP opposed Commission Council proposals based on recommendations of the mayor's housing committee.[76]

Chapters of the NAACP mobilized nationally against segregated housing projects and subdivisions. The organization opposed racial quotas advanced by the NAHB and advocated for removal of race from conditions for extending federal aid or assistance for slum clearance, urban renewal, or housing.[77] Local NAACP president Chapital wrote NAACP administrator Roy Wilkins in January 1955 that Morgan Earnest, executive vice president of Pontchartrain Park Homes, was making speeches nationally that celebrated Pontchartrain Park as a model copied by builders in other cities, making New

Orleans "a bright spot in America's attempt to provide new and better housing for Negroes."[78] The NAACP filed lawsuits against segregated housing in
Levittown, New York, and Olney Gardens, Pennsylvania, to resist the tide of
segregated urban and suburban development that rose above court decisions
to end segregation.[79]

Eager buyers flocked to the subdivision, and 115 homes sold within forty-
five days of the initial announcement. Pontchartrain Park officially opened
in June 1955 amid much fanfare about how public and private cooperation
could create high-quality housing for blacks.[80] A middle-class black community grew and thrived in this bounded patch of suburbia that, by the end of
the 1950s, featured Bethany Methodist Church, Coghill elementary school,
and historically black Southern University of New Orleans. Pontchartrain
Park residents worked in the school system, as lawyers, pastors, postal workers, and musicians, and served as politicians, like Ernest "Dutch" Morial
who, in 1978, became the first African American mayor of New Orleans.
Alana Miller's parents moved to Pontchartrain Park from the housing projects, while others moved over from Hollygrove, from uptown, all striving for
a better life, striving for the same things for their families as everyone else.

Conclusion

Development of a segregated suburban subdivision and park for African
Americans in New Orleans in the mid-1950s engaged political alliances and
policies that crossed racial and social class lines. Racial discourse that demonized black bodies as dangerous and called black homeowners unreliable
drainers of equity reveals the veneer of liberalism and legal equality grafted
onto deep traditions of racial exclusion and exploitation. Federal support
of overwhelmingly white suburbanization and opposition to public housing
for low-income citizens prevailed. A more business-friendly consensus that
reinforced segregationist policies eclipsed the liberal New Deal urban coalition. The new consensus promoted a racial discourse couched in property
values that most liberals grudgingly accepted, including black elites in the
New Orleans chapter of the Urban League. Accommodation of continued
segregation by some black elites in exchange for "access to the fruits of suburban space" came with increased residential segregation, uneven urban development, and a host of social problems associated with the concentration of
poverty experienced in dilapidated central cities across the country.[81]

A combination of integrationist black politics spearheaded by the NAACP
and subaltern resistance against segregated leisure facilities put integrated

parks and housing on the civic agenda in New Orleans. A brokered accommodation helped tip the balance toward construction of Pontchartrain Park after defeat of a racially integrated solution by an alliance of business and white segregationists at the local, state, and federal levels. The segregationist compromise at Pontchartrain Park was no exception; it was a model, a national example of enlightened paternalism in business and race relations that acknowledged profit was available from African Americans hungry for home ownership and access to the postwar American Dream.

The experience of the 1950s illustrates that race discrimination and segregationist discourse is embedded in the landscape of New Orleans and provides a spatial reminder of white power and class power inscribed in the built environment of cities across the country. Race and class politics allied in a search for ground rent gained support for segregated solutions to housing shortages from elements of the black middle class in many cities, including New Orleans. The subsequent convergence of racial residential segregation patterns in New Orleans with those in other cities illustrates convergence of urban form in mid-twentieth-century cities that belies the status of New Orleans as an exception.

Notes

The authors acknowledge financial support from the Bill and Melinda Gates Foundation. Pamela Jenkins, Steve Kroll-Smith, and Rachel Luft provided helpful comments that strengthened the chapter. The authors especially acknowledge Arnold Hirsch's work on urban renewal in New Orleans. The authors alone are responsible for the final product.

1 "Formal Dedication of $15 Million Pontchartrain Park Homes Sunday," *Louisiana Weekly*, June 25, 1955, 1.
2 Consider here the theory of racialized space and racial formations developed by Omi and Winant (1994). Racialized space refers to historical processes that produce particular racial configurations in the city. Racialized space is an aspect of a particular racial formation, defined as a "socio-historical process by which racial categories are created, inhabited, transformed, and destroyed" (55). The meanings ascribed to race inform the organization of space, but those meanings change as the racial organization of space shifts over time (see also Gotham 2002; Lipsitz 2001). Freund (2007) illustrates historical shifts in white racial thought from overt racial hierarchies and exclusion of blacks from white neighborhoods on grounds of biological inferiority in the 1920s to market-driven efforts of whites in the 1960s to protect property values by excluding blacks from predominantly white neighborhoods. The social construction of black bodies as dangerous and black homeowners as destructive of real estate equity provides essential cover for the construction of segregated housing markets.
3 Kelley 1993; Reed 1999, 18.

4   Countryman 2006; Freund 2007; Gotham 2002; Wiese 2004, 189–207; Wolfinger 2012.

5   Hirsch 2000a, 2000b; Weise 2004.

6   Campanella 2007; Spain 1979.

7   Flanagan 1997; Von Hoffman 2000.

8   Flanagan 1997; Von Hoffman 2000.

9   Checkoway 1980; Von Hoffman 2000.

10 Countryman 2006; Hirsch 2000b; Wiese 2004.

11 K. Jackson 1985, 196–204, 208.

12 John M. Ducey to Public Housing Administration, Re: Racial Policy of Public Housing Administration, Letter #70, December 1949, in Morrison Papers, Collection 270, box 86, "Housing Papers," Tulane University Library.

13 K. Jackson 1985.

14 Hirsch 2007; Logsdon and Bell 1992.

15 Hirsch 1992; Betsy Petersen, "The Urban League: A Selling Story," *Dixie Magazine*, November 23, 1954, 7.

16 Hirsch 2000a; "1000 Home Negro Progect Slated to Cost $15 million," *Times-Picayune*, November 23, 1954, 1, 15.

17 Rosa Freeman Keller, "Loving Cup Announcement," 1985, in Rosa Freeman Keller Papers, box 5, folder 7, Amistad Research Center, Tulane University.

18 Moore 2010, 19.

19 Hirsch 1992.

20 Moore 2010, 37.

21 Colten 2005, 3–5.

22 J. Miller McPherson, *The Problem of Housing for Negroes in New Orleans*, 1953, NAACP Papers, MSS 28, box 51, "NAACP Housing Committee," Louisiana and Special Collections, Earl Long Library, University of New Orleans (hereafter cited as NAACP Papers).

23 LaViolette 1960.

24 Thomas Primm, "Minutes of the Mayor's Advisory Committee on Expansion of Negro Recreational Facilities in New Orleans, September 22, 1947," in NAACP Papers, MSS 28, box 67.

25 New Orleans City Planner William Wiedorn to Gerald Pratt, August 2, 1947, in Morrison Papers, Collection 270, box S56-25, "Negro Park folder," New Orleans Public Library; Hirsch 2000a.

26 DeLesseps Morrison, "Establishment of Colored City Park Commission, April 15, 1948," in Morrison Papers, Collection 270, box S56-25, "Negro Park folder," New Orleans Public Library.

27 New Orleans [N.O.] Association of Commerce, "Minutes Civic Affairs Committee, October 24, 1949," in Minutes of New Orleans Association of Commerce, Dec. 1948–Dec. 1949, vol. 1, Louisiana and Special Collections, Earl Long Library, University of New Orleans; N.O. Association of Commerce, "Minutes of Civic Affairs Committee, May 18, 1949," in Minutes of New Orleans Association of Commerce, Dec. 1948–Dec. 1949, vol. 2, Louisiana and Special Collections, Earl Long Library, University of New Orleans.

28 Hirsch 1992, 2000a.

29 Daniel Byrd, Assistant Field Secretary, NAACP to Mayor deLesseps Morrison, March 17, 1949, in NAACP Papers, MSS 28, box 67.

30 National Association for the Advancement of Colored People, "Contamination at Lincoln Beach," April 14, 1949, in NAACP Papers, MSS 28, box 67.

31 N.O. Association of Commerce, "Minutes of Civic Affairs Committee, November 16, 1949 p. 13."

32 National Association for the Advancement of Colored People, "Press Release," July 16, 1949, in NAACP Papers, MSS 28, box 67.

33 N.O. Association of Commerce, "Minutes of Civic Affairs Committee, November 16, 1949 p. 13."

34 N.O. Association of Commerce, "Minutes of Civic Affairs Committee, November 16, 1949 p. 13."

35 DeLesseps Morrison, "Minutes of Conference in Mayor's Office on Development of Seeger Tract and Seabrook Realty Tract, December 14, 1949," in Morrison Papers, Collection 270, box 86, "Housing, 1949," Tulane University Library.

36 Morrison, "Minutes of Conference in Mayor's Office on Development of Seeger Tract and Seabrook Realty Tract, December 14, 1949."

37 "Gentilly Civic Group Circulate Petitions against Seabrook Site for Negro Park," *Louisiana Weekly*, April 15, 1950, 1.

38 "Ordinances Adopted for Housing Project," *Times-Picayune*, April 29, 1950, 1, 3.

39 "Reasons for and against Negro Park Are Aired," *Gentilly Herald*, February 10, 1950, 1.

40 "Ordinances Adopted for Housing Project," 1, 3.

41 Mayor deLesseps Morrison to J. Andre Couturie, April 30, 1950, in Morrison Papers, Collection 270, box S56-25, New Orleans Public Library.

42 "Reasons for and against Negro Park Are Aired," 1.

43 "Ordinances Adopted for Housing Project," 1, 3.

44 "Mayor to Brief Leaders on Park, Housing Sites in Seabrook Area," *Louisiana Weekly*, August 30, 1952.

45 "Work Set on 1423 Gentilly Homes," *Times-Picayune*, January 14, 1951, 1.

46 "Linn Says Action Won't Halt Plan," *Times-Picayune*, April 24, 1953, 8.

47 "W. Ray Scheuring to Mayor Morrison, February 28, 1953," in Morrison Papers, Collection 270, box S56-25, New Orleans Public Library.

48 Flanagan 1997, 265–86.

49 Hirsch 2000b, 419.

50 Checkoway 1980.

51 Hirsch 2000b.

52 Hirsch 2000b.

53 Hirsch 2000b, 425.

54 "Linn Says Action Won't Halt Plan," 8.

55 Elias A. McCollister, "Public Housing Referendum Sought by President of Home Builders Association," *New Orleans Item*, December 7, 1952, 1.

56 Hirsch 2000a.

57 Quoted in Hirsch 2000a, 228.

58 Chamber of Commerce of the New Orleans Area to Mayor deLesseps Morrison, Re: Improvement of Substandard Housing, March 1953, in Morrison Papers, Collection 270, box 86, "Housing, 1953," Tulane University Library.

59 DeLesseps Morrison, "Mayor's Citizens Committee to Study Housing Rehabilitation, October 5, 1953," in Morrison Papers, Collection 270, box 86, "Housing, 1953," Tulane University Library.

60 "Federal Agency Told of Letter," *Times-Picayune*, May 8, 1953, 6.

61 "Linn Says Action Won't Halt Plan," 6.

62 "Federal Agency Told of Letter," 6.

63 "Council Moves to End Slums," *New Orleans Item*, July 19, 1953, 1, 3.

64 New Orleans Committee on Housing Improvement and Slum Clearance, "Minutes of Executive Committee on Housing Improvement and Slum Clearance, September 29, 1953," in Morrison Papers, Collection 270, box 86, "Housing, 1953," Tulane University Library.

65 Hirsch 2000a.

66 "Number 1 Housing Need: Homes for Negroes," *Louisiana Weekly*, October 24, 1953.

67 "Number 1 Housing Need: Homes for Negroes."

68 McPherson, *The Problem of Housing for Negroes in New Orleans*.

69 "Negro Housing Steps Planned," *Times-Picayune*, April 2, 1953, 26.

70 "Negro Housing Steps Planned."

71 Keller, "Loving Cup Announcement."

72 Keller, "Loving Cup Announcement."

73 "Gentilly Group Hits Park Plan," *Times-Picayune*, November 25, 1953, 19.

74 "1000 Home Negro Project Slated to Cost $15 Million," *Times-Picayune*, November 23, 1954, 1, 15.

75 Arthur Chapital Jr. to Mrs. Moises Cahn, April 4, 1953, in NAACP Papers, MSS 28, box 68.

76 Arthur Chapital Jr. to New Orleans Commission Council, April 9, 1953, in NAACP Papers, MSS 28, box 68.

77 National Association for the Advancement of Colored People, "Outline of Basic NAACP Housing Policy and Program," February 25, 1955, in NAACP Papers, MSS 28, box 51.

78 Arthur Chapital, Jr. to Roy Wilkins, Administrator, NAACP, September 23, 1955, in NAACP Papers, MSS 28, box 68.

79 Motley 1955.

80 "Negro Housing Project Opens," *Times-Picayune*, June 27, 1955, 19.

81 Wiese 2004, 196.

10

Refugee Pastoralism

Vietnamese American Self-Representation in New Orleans

MARGUERITE NGUYEN

In the genre of autobiography, or life narrative, authenticity constitutes part of the contract that exists between an author or speaker and the audience.[1] The violation of this contract is considered to be a violation of what Philippe Lejeune calls the "autobiographical pact."[2] However, within a broader sphere of social and cultural production, multiple autobiographies circulate and shift in relation to changing historical circumstances, potentially resulting in new autobiographical pacts and altered norms of identity and belonging.

By some of their own accounts, the dense population of Vietnamese Americans in New Orleans lived quietly before Hurricane Katrina. As Father Vien Nguyen, former pastor of Mary Queen of Vietnam church (MQVN)—a social and spiritual anchor for many in the area—states, "We lived below the radar." The community lacked the powers of cultural and political self-representation or, to put it another way, a strong autobiographical voice.[3] But this changed dramatically after Hurricane Katrina. With one of the highest rates of return and rebuilding in the area, Vietnamese Americans found themselves thrust into the limelight of local, national, and international media attention. This essay examines how local racial logics and refugee geopolitics illuminate the norms within which Vietnamese American self-representation has emerged in the Crescent City. I suggest that refugee pastoralism has been an effective yet precarious mode through which Vietnamese Americans have gained recognition as life narrators and political subjects in New Orleans.

Literary Authenticity

Authenticity is a concept that runs throughout discussions of autobio-graphical representation. Sidonie Smith and Julia Watson note that with life narrative, "we expect particular kinds of stories to be told by those who have a direct and personal knowledge of that experience," reflecting inherent readerly investments in the *"authority* and *authenticity"* of autobiographers.[4] Firsthand experience of events is crucial to a work's perceived authenticity, as is the notion that in autobiographical works, an understanding exists on the part of the reader that the author and protagonist of the story are one and the same. A core question when encountering life narratives is, in other words, how real or truthful does the person's account appear to the audi-ence? When the autobiographical pact is undermined—if a life narrative is exposed as containing lies and fabrications—the authenticity of the tale is, in turn, called into question, and public uproars over such instances demonstrate the stakes that audiences have in the perceived authenticity of autobiographical texts.

Firsthand knowledge thus bestows authority and legitimacy upon the author-protagonist as an autobiographical subject, and the presumed full disclosure involving the autobiographer, reader, and publisher are largely what distinguish autobiography from fictional texts. But there is something else at work within this genre, too. For many critics, the autobiographical subject's authority is nothing without readers' recognition; autobiographers must be able to transmit experience and emotion to an audience. Chantelle Warner notes, "for the work to *feel authentic* to the reader the gap between the act of narrating and the embodied experience of that which is being narrated must somehow be eroded."[5] Unlike realistic literature, where de-scriptive attention to details drawn from the material world gives rise to the real, in autobiographical narrative the effect of authenticity hinges on personal knowledge conveyed with immediacy and feeling that transfers to the audience.[6] This shared basis in affect and experience can serve as grounds for evoking "readers' emotional responses upon which their potential po-litical power is based."[7] Autobiographical authenticity is important for this reason, since immersing others in one's story world can become "a metaphor for literary agency"—a way to elicit the audience's emotions and turn them toward political action.[8]

Autobiographical authenticity is not always perceived as fully enabling, however. Lionel Trilling's *Sincerity and Authenticity*, a well-known examina-tion of "the moral life" in postwar America, critiques authenticity's claims to

cultural genuineness by rereading the concept as a capitalist-driven myth.[9]
For Trilling, authenticity is a perplexing concept, one he distrusts: "That the word has become part of the moral slang of our day points to the peculiar nature of our fallen condition, our anxiety over the credibility of existence and of individual existences."[10] Trilling suggests that typical claims to authenticity exaggerate the self's importance and capabilities while failing to acknowledge how institutions and political systems limit the self; commercial and corporate networks play a large role in defining what is authentic, severely constraining the agency that individuals think they have. Still, although Trilling is skeptical about authenticity, he sees one way in which it holds promise. Noting its roots in Romanticism as a critical mode, Trilling posits that authenticity as a more radical vocation can help locate the self in relation to bourgeois, hegemonic systems and practices. Distanced from dominant matrices, subjects can be more discerning of their surroundings and, rather than reify notions of cultural legitimacy, perhaps realize that what "was once thought to make up the very fabric of culture has come to [be] mere fantasy or ritual, or downright falsification."[11] For Trilling, the authentic position is a self-reflexive, structural one. Approached critically, it enables individuals to identify how they are situated relative to structures of power and to carve out desires and values that are alternatives to normative conditions.

Thus, even though certain hypostatizations of authenticity are overly bound up in the self and fail to represent one's subjection to market demands, it is also impossible to dismiss the significance of the concept. Authenticity's continued prevalence emerges strongly in New Orleans scholarship, where, as Kevin Fox Gotham asserts, the post-Katrina moment is especially marked by "the interlocking nature of conflicts over race, culture, and authenticity." As the city presents "conflicting conceptions of itself and its past" to confront an uncertain future, heterogeneous autobiographical pacts emerge.[12] Rather than assume that there is an authentic New Orleans narrative, this essay understands the concept as a structure of narration within an ongoing process of meaning making that involves creating shifting authenticity effects, which can then serve as launch pads for making broader demands. By amplifying moments when authenticity is claimed, we can then observe how those claims are made and to what questions or problems they respond.

Below, I explain that Vietnamese American autobiographical expression in post-Katrina New Orleans has gained recognition by drawing on the pastoral genre to assert local and national belonging and, in turn, authenticate political demands. However, public recognition of these pastoral narratives has come with certain conditions—primarily a downplaying of black struggle after the hurricane and a disconnection of Vietnamese American life in the city from complex histories of refugee experience and US imperialism in Southeast Asia. Autobiographical subjectivity as I understand it in this chapter emerges from a range of nonfictional representations rather than fictional texts, reflecting my expansive view of what constitutes the literary, particularly in a milieu where diverse forms of Southeast Asian American cultural production are still in the process of emergence.

Pastoralism as Vietnamese American Authenticity

Resettled in 1975 through the efforts of New Orleans archbishop Phillip M. Hannan and Associated Catholic Charities, most Vietnamese refugees were from Phat Diem, Bui Chu, and Nghe An in northern Vietnam and had migrated to South Vietnam after the division of the country in 1954 before arriving in the US.[13] As soon as they resettled in the Village de l'Est area of eastern New Orleans, Vietnamese began cultivating farms.[14] These farms began as small plots in front of individual apartments but were eventually relegated to a nearby lake after apartment management feared that the apartment grounds would become "one big garden."[15] In 1978, an agreement between the Archdiocese of New Orleans and the New Orleans East Corporation, a land development corporation, permitted Vietnamese to farm a large piece of land near Lagoon Maxent, which ran behind the levee protecting eastern New Orleans neighborhoods.[16]

The farms remained a point of interest for the public throughout pre-Katrina Vietnamese American history in New Orleans. Yet that they were consistently relegated to undeveloped land relatively outside of public view says something significant about the aesthetic of the eastern New Orleans landscape. Vietnamese and their farms were welcome idiosyncrasies, but they were also seen as foreign and finite. Many questioned the tenability of Vietnamese farming over the long term: "The acculturation process may ultimately lead to the disappearance of the market gardens."[17] Those who saw promise for New Orleans Vietnamese based their predictions on the willingness of the community to assimilate. Martha Ward, a University of New Orleans anthropologist, drolly noted, "in 20 years we'll be into a second generation, they will all speak English, there will be a lot more social mobility and they'll lose their refugee status. . . . New Orleans will be proud of its Asian population and we'll all go to the Tet Festival every year. . . . All will be forgiven if they throw beads and cook good food."[18] Clarence Barney, then executive director of the Urban League of New Orleans, stated in 1985, "The

Vietnamese are productive, creative *contributing citizens*. . . . I think that to the extent we can integrate more of them into the economic life of this city, we will be better off."[19] The implicit autobiographical contract offered to Vietnamese—the understood conditions under which the community could present itself and be accepted as legitimate local subjects—stipulated Vietnamese cultural and economic contributions but did not specify possibilities for political subjectivity engaged in democratic participation.

By now it is well known that a year after Hurricane Katrina, Vietnamese Americans in New Orleans East had one of the highest rates of return of any community in the city—over 90 percent by 2007.[20] (As of the 2010 census, there were 3,010 Vietnamese living in the area.)[21] But public perceptions of the community's apoliticism continued to prevail for a time. The community's efforts at rescue and rebuilding after the storm were initially dismissed, as shown in S. Leo Chiang's documentary *A Village Called Versailles*. Mary Tran, a New Orleans East resident and activist, notes in the film,[22] "They underestimated us, you know. They didn't come to us and ask us, . . . what's your recovery rate, how many people have returned."[23] The city's original Bring New Orleans Back (BNOB) blueprint excluded New Orleans East from redevelopment based on recommendations from the Urban Land Institute, which deemed parts of New Orleans East a flood-prone area unfit for rebuilding and in danger of becoming a post-Katrina "shanty town."[24] In the words of Cynthia Willard-Lewis, New Orleans City Council member, District E, the plan "said to almost 40% of the city's population, 'We don't want you back.'" Father Vien recalls, "I remember looking at, on the screen and asked the people around me, 'Where are we?' The map ended. Right on our border."[25] Adding to this, Mayor Ray Nagin exercised state-of-emergency powers to grant Waste Management a permit to construct and open a one hundred-acre landfill in New Orleans East, a mere half mile from the Vietnamese American neighborhood.

United by their shared position on the wrong side of the BNOB plan's borders, the eastern New Orleans community protested the plan and landfill, with MQVN helping to spearhead a cross-racial challenge to the Urban Land Institute's report. *A Village Called Versailles* includes a striking clip from a BNOB commission meeting that took place just three months after the floods. Father Vien confronts commission members, many of whom are corporate officers and developers, in front of a standing-room crowd of Vietnamese Americans and African Americans: "When we saw this Urban Land Institute Report, I, we were shocked. We were never invited to the table. We have a right to be part of the community-driven process. . . . I'm speaking here not only for just my parish. I believe I speak for the people in New Orleans East as well."[26]

Father Vien's firsthand account communicates residents' anger as he takes the podium as a representative voice—"I believe I speak for the people in New Orleans East." If prior to Katrina, the media and public viewed Vietnamese Americans primarily in cultural and economic terms, here the community makes an explicit first-person claim to civic engagement and political agency. Spatially, Father Vien and the New Orleans residents challenge the commission members who are seated at the front of the room, while thematically, the content of Father Vien's words articulates the severe power differential that distinguishes the two sides. Moreover, while Father Vien roots his comments in the autobiographical "I," the movement to "we" demonstrates the collective, nonmonolithic, and cross-racial impetus of his assertions in the face of figures of power. This scene combines Warner's and Trilling's politicized understandings of authenticity, as Father Vien's claims both are emotionally resonant and act as a critique of the city's profit-seeking agendas. Eventually, younger and older generations worked cross-racially to successfully demand the inclusion of all New Orleans East in rebuilding and, with the help of Willard-Lewis and environmental attorney Joel Waltzer, the closure of the landfill.

The moment of self-representation staged at the BNOB town meeting presaged what eventually became plans for the Viet Village Urban Farm. Viet Village is an ambitious farming project aimed at giving the community some control over land cultivation and food sourcing while providing resources for the wider New Orleans population. I have explored this project in more depth elsewhere as an example of the community's practice of cultural citizenship.[27] But I would like to extend here that it is also a form of Vietnamese diasporic autobiographical narrative that situates the community as authentic and politicized. In its current redesign, Viet Village's aquaponics philosophy avoids dependence on water and soil—both had been contaminated by the hurricane and the Deepwater Horizon oil spill—and helps ameliorate postdisaster unemployment by providing a means of income. Viet Village exemplifies what Yuki Kato, Catarina Passidomo, and Daina Harvey define as the contingency and shifting dynamics of "explicitly political" urban farms of a "broad scope"—those that are concerned first with "food security" but also understand urban farming and food justice issues as ways to address broader inequalities that result from "failing social and political institutions."[28] The farm project constitutes a form of life narrative in the public sphere, directly responding to the the failures of local governance post-Katrina and uneven structures of capital that have put the community's livelihood at risk.

The heightened visibility of the Vietnamese diasporic farm in depictions of eastern New Orleans suggests the prominence of pastoralism as a narrative mode for authentic Vietnamese American self-representation in New Orleans.[29] According to Leo Marx, pastoralism has long "[defined] the meaning of America ever since the age of discovery."[30] Put most simply, it is a genre that explores humans' relationships to land and exemplifies how subjects adapt creatively to existing cultural rites and conventions. Paul Alpers clarifies that pastoralism is not about the mere representation of "landscape or idealized nature" but convenes a space in which "the human centers are herdsmen or their equivalents," and the story of these figures' lives is a "representative anecdote" that narrates humans' "strength relative to the world."[31] For these literary critics, the farm is a material fact, but it is also a cultural mode. As the latter, it tends to take one of two conflicting configurations, both emerging from America's symbolic status as the world's final frontier: (1) America as an unruly and devilish wilderness—a complex, perilous, and unwieldy terrain that needs human action in order to control it; and (2) America as a garden—a space of harmony, pleasure, and freedom, a site where problems find utopic resolution. Over time, writers have tried to reconcile individuals' relationship to an American landscape that is both a challenging wilderness and bucolic ideal.

While the media and scholars often understand the Vietnamese diasporic farm as a site of cultural difference, when interpreted through a literary pastoral frame, it acquires a local and national authenticity by emplotting Vietnamese within the quintessentially American dilemma of how to negotiate the duality of national space as dystopic landscape and utopic imaginary.[32] As a spearheader of the urban farm project and one of the most prominent voices of post-Katrina Vietnamese American life in New Orleans, Father Vien has played a visible role in maximizing the image of the farm in a way that immerses wider audiences into a recognizable Vietnamese American–authored story world of New Orleans. The call for political recognition that Father Vien makes at the BNOB meeting becomes an avenue for materially rooting that politics in local land: "We had to fight, because this is our land. We are connected to this land. New Orleans is home."[33] The expressed devotion to the city's territory accomplishes two things: it reinforces the community's local belonging by affirming a long-standing connection to city space, and it affirms national belonging by affiliating with America's historical commitment to working productively with the country's terrain. This cross-scalar reclamation of belonging then makes a transnational move: "we are very much an agricultural society, . . . we are people who are tied to the land." The trope of land acts as a surface of deictic transference that encourages audiences to reorient themselves in relation to Vietnamese American cultural and economic histories, formerly viewed as distant, foreign milieus.[34] The motif of cultivating plants substantially bolsters the community's claims, metonymically asserting the community's more general growth and productivity: the desire for "growing areas, . . . [where] the people will own the crops they grow" resonates with a vision for them "to be able to grow [their] community systematically, methodically."[35]

Pastoralism materially marks Vietnamese diasporic presence in eastern New Orleans and abstractly validates their political desires. Since it can always be started from scratch and adapted to a given set of contingencies, the Vietnamese American farm exhibits how pastoral life enables humans to make a home in the world time and time again. Diasporic subjects demonstrate an ability to navigate the American pastoral conundrum of cultivating and protecting a landscape that can at once be unruly and beautiful. Furthermore, the enduring issue of struggle in a changing environment has also garnered recognition from the area's majority black population.[36] Black leaders recall Vietnamese diasporic outreach during Katrina, "grateful for the way in which its leaders shared limited resources with black residents."[37] Through pastoralism, Vietnamese Americans "root" themselves as legitimate local and national subjects, evoking the black community's long-standing work of claiming rights for all New Orleanians.[38] Rather than exceptional migrants who exist under the radar, pastoralized Vietnamese Americans become exemplary New Orleans residents and American citizens.

By placing Vietnamese refugees at the center of the eastern New Orleans landscape, pastoralism serves as a "representative anecdote" about humans' "strength relative to the world," mobilizing agrarian themes to anchor a relationship to land and identity in a city undergoing an emotional process of rebuilding. It allows for the affective experience of getting into a story that Warner argues is critical to the effect of authenticity, and it draws attention to the uneven structures of power and capital which Trilling asserts that authenticity, in its most generative and critical forms, identifies. By playing a noticeable role in establishing eastern New Orleans as a relevant city space within the American nation after the storm, Vietnamese Americans have forged a new kind of autobiographical pact in the city, articulating and securing cross-racial recognition for the viability of their political activity and self-representation.[39]

Yet the evolving story of Vietnamese refugees in the city raises the issue of how power frames authenticity effects. What conditions enable the recognition of certain subjects as authentic, and whose authenticity effects count? Recognition only happens as political circumstances allow, requiring understanding of the norms and conditions under which life narratives and their attendant political claims emerge.

Local and Geopolitical Dynamics of Vietnamese American
Self-Representation

In *Giving an Account of Oneself*, Judith Butler states that "the 'I' has no story of its own that is not also the story of a relation—or set of relations—to a set of norms."[40] Telling a story about oneself is always conditional, contingent upon "regimes of truth" that determine which subjects will or will not be recognized. Butler notes, "when the 'I' seeks to give an account of itself," it must maneuver among prevailing models of social relations and insert itself as a legitimate identity therein.[41] For Butler, autobiographical subject formation is like the work of poetry—a subject must adapt to existing conventions, like words set to meter or poetic structure.[42]

In New Orleans, examining how the Vietnamese American "I" has surfaced within "a set of norms" means attending to local and geopolitical frames that shape the poetics of authentic self-representation as achieved through the pastoral form. On the local level, attention to the Vietnamese American community means triangulating black and white models of race to encompass a comparative understanding of social relations in the city.[43] In New Orleans, there is a prevailing tendency to view Vietnamese refugee arrival as a new Asian phase in the area's diverse history. One *Times-Picayune* article characteristically asserts, "Even in New Orleans, with its varied immigration history, the Vietnamese were a new phenomenon because the city had never had a substantial Asian population."[44] Cultural scholarship often further entrenches this logic. Joseph Roach delimits his influential study of circum-Atlantic performance in New Orleans and London by the categories of "Europe, Africa, and the Americas, North and South." He positions an Atlantic-based cartography as "the most visible evidence of an oceanic interculture" that illuminates "what it means to live through memory in cities of the dead."[45] Gotham's study of authenticity in New Orleans highlights how "'whiteness,' 'blackness,' 'creole,' 'diversity,' and 'multiculturalism'" have "long been major signifiers of local identity, as well as sources of division and conflict."[46] In both models, generalized categories, such as "'diversity' and 'multiculturalism,'" stand in for other networks of racial relations in addition to black and white models. The point here is not to critique existing approaches for these omissions, as projects such as Roach's and Gotham's have different points of focus. But it is worth highlighting how a relational approach to race enables examination of what Colleen Lye describes as the "genuine multiplicity of racial logics" that operate in US social life.[47]

In an effort to tease out the historical record, several scholars have foregrounded New Orleans's long-standing Pacific ties. Moon-Ho Jung's *Coolies and Cane* brings into relief the thousands of Chinese laborers who worked alongside blacks in postbellum Louisiana, demonstrating the "coolie" figure's crucial role in discourses of America's transition from slave to immigrant labor and, more broadly, from slavery to ideologies of freedom.[48] Richard Campanella's pivotal work outlines New Orleans's two lost Chinatowns, overturning the idea that a significant population of Asians in New Orleans prior to Vietnam War refugee arrival did not exist.[49] As Campanella notes, a glance at writings by some of New Orleans's major figures, such as Jelly Roll Morton, Louis Armstrong, and Tennessee Williams, reveals how Asian and Asian American things, peoples, and ideas have historically been interwoven into the city's everyday life.[50]

This history provides important context for understanding the racial dynamics of discourses about Vietnamese Americans post-Katrina. Eric Tang unpacks the complexity of these conversations in his analysis of racialized media portrayals of Katrina victims. After the hurricane, he notes, "the corporate media pulled no punches, working feverishly to promulgate all of the core 'underclass' tropes: Poor Blacks, unable to do anything for themselves, laying blame on a government rescue. . . . Armed and dangerous thugs looting and preying on their very own."[51] Tang elaborates that "spinmeisters" began to focus on tales of resilience—those "of the people who did get out—and who did so without the least bit of government assistance." Vietnamese soon emblematized this arc in the media, providing a convenient antidote for those who did not want to confront the "hard truths coming from the regions' hardest hit Black communities."[52] Model minority stereotypes emerged in full swing after the storm to put forth a cultural argument of Vietnamese virtue to explain the community's return in a way that circumvented the sufferings and efforts of blacks by implication, if not by design.

In contrast to a racial logic that places groups in opposition, Tang shows how the media's privileging of Vietnamese American post-Katrina rebuilding efforts overlooked moments of collaboration with blacks before and after the storm. He illustrates that prominent moments of black-Asian tensions, as in the unrest after the 1992 Rodney King verdict, did not erupt in eastern New Orleans because the area was quite heterogeneous in terms of class and, therefore, did not experience deep-seated social antagonism.[53] Furthermore, blacks' own experiences of racism echoed those of the Vietnamese, as blacks had already struggled through prior hurricanes, such as Hurricane Betsy in 1965, and had also faced the racism of the local shrimping industry, as had the Vietnamese.[54] Thus, immediately after the storm, Father Vien led a search-and-rescue effort to aid persons across racial lines, connecting the Vietnamese American "I" to other subjects cross-racially and cross-generationally.[55] "Resonant histories" of economic marginalization and displacement motivated both communities' returns and outreach throughout Katrina, resulting in important moments of affiliation.[56] However, the media's highlighting of Vietnamese resilience, with little to no reference to histories of black-Asian relations that give a fuller picture of experiences of disaster in eastern New Orleans, reveals the conditional nature of Vietnamese diasporic self-representation: public legitimation of Vietnamese American grievances has often been predicated upon highlighting the community's resilience to downplay black dispossession and desires to rebuild.

In addition to local racial dynamics that reveal how recognition of Vietnamese refugee self-representation in New Orleans has gone hand in hand with muting histories of other racial groups that expose ongoing state neglect, the community's perceived authenticity is also related to the elision of geopolitical factors that recall the US's long historical role in Euro-American imperialism, wherein the US features as a cause of, rather than passive setting for and/or savior of, the forcibly displaced. The Vietnamese refugee farm, though depicted as a quaint, traditional Vietnamese practice imported from Southeast Asia, has had a long social and political history. Yet this context tends to remain absent from public accounts. For instance, the northern Vietnamese villages of Phat Diem, Bui Chu, and Nghe An, from which a large number of Vietnamese in eastern New Orleans originally hail, have long been vulnerable to natural disasters. In the pre-French state, a system of aid developed that was based on tax relief, mutual assistance, communal farming systems, and granaries to supply rice and help regulate prices during times of flood and famine. Under the French state, the granary system was dismantled, and officials often attributed famine to natural disaster instead of failed state relief. Colonial reports often noted the damage done to infrastructure and crops but not to Indochinese subjects.[57]

The fluctuating, somewhat improvisational history of the region continued during the First Indochina War (1946–54), when Phat Diem and Bui Chu constituted a Catholic autonomous zone—"the only areas in central and northern Vietnam not under DRV [Viet Minh–led Democratic Republic of Vietnam] or French control."[58] As Charles Keith notes, Catholic leaders here created a separate social, political, economic, and military state.[59] The area "had a standing army, a widespread intelligence network, a service for information and propaganda, and even its own newspapers and radio station."[60] It also became a site for experimenting with social and political reconstruction through programs of "agrarian reform and nationalized industry" and "rural cooperatives and labor unions."[61] When the 1954 Geneva Conference divided Vietnam at the seventeenth parallel after France's defeat at Dien Bien Phu, the US and France provided financial and transportation assistance to Vietnamese Catholic leaders who orchestrated mass migrations of thousands of Catholics and Buddhists to South Vietnam, revealing American involvement in a pre–Vietnam War refugee evacuation stemming from a French conflict that the US largely funded.[62]

This complex, albeit abridged, history reveals what I believe to be an undergirding refusal on the part of the American state and public to acknowledge fully America's long imperial involvement in Southeast Asia—a historical amnesia that makes it easier to suggest that the US helps refugees rebuild rather than creates refugees. As Viet Thanh Nguyen argues, "All wars are fought twice, the first time on the battlefield, the second time in memory."[63] American memory of the conflict excises long and knotty histories that led to the war in Vietnam and its aftermath. The history sketched here reveals Vietnamese agrarian life as a historically contested political site; when recognized not simply as a quaint, innocuous Vietnamese American space but as a Vietnamese refugee space, the farm is always and already bound up in local, national, and international struggles for power that have long involved America. But in more picturesque, utopic renderings of Vietnamese diasporic farming, these geopolitical dimensions are relatively absent or made subsidiary, sidestepping the question of how various levels of Euro-American governance have multiply dispossessed Vietnamese refugees across time and space.

Depictions of Vietnamese refugee farms in New Orleans are thus more complicated than they may appear to be. If, for Vietnamese diasporics, pastoralism enables the community's self-representation as authentic local and national subjects, for mainstream media, the genre smooths the contradictions of belonging that the term "refugee" raises. Evocations of forced displacement remind us that belonging and citizenship are tenuous categories and that refugees are often rescued by those powers that help bring about the conditions that create refugees. These tensions erupted in New Orleans in heated debates over use of the term "refugee" after the storm to describe black evacuees, a discussion primarily divided into two camps. A number of journalists perceived the evacuation attempts, material losses, and uncertain futures of the city's marginalized—punctuated by the presence of "armed men in fatigues"—as analogous to a refugee situation.[64] Others emphasized that Katrina victims were not refugees but US citizens and thus "victims of neglect"—"not refugees wandering somewhere looking for charity," in the words of Reverend Al Sharpton.[65] According to Lisa Marie Cacho, this position rejects "refugee" because it incorrectly categorizes US citizens, risks denying them rights, and is "criminalizing" and "alienating" toward blacks.[66]

These discursive efforts to connect to or distance from the refugee figure reveal how the refugee category raises complex questions regarding the relationship between citizenship and rights. Citing Hannah Arendt, legal and Asian American studies scholar Leti Volpp notes, "citizenship is a necessary grounding for the 'right to have rights.'"[67] At the same time, Volpp asserts, "the liberal universalizing discourse of citizenship . . . does not guarantee equal citizenship in fact."[68] Following Volpp, the heated debate over use of "refugee" in post-Katrina New Orleans testifies to both the importance and limits of relying on formal legal citizenship as the basis for demanding rights. As Cacho argues, to claim rights by disclaiming refugee status "renders less worthy the many refugees who were also Hurricane Katrina victims," such as Vietnamese and Hondurans.[69] I would add that denigrating refugees can also inadvertently devalue heterogeneous black experiences. A refugee from Sierra Leone, though not a resident of New Orleans, noted this about the "refugee" debate: "'They think refugee is a bad word, but it is not.'"[70] There is a pragmatic rationale for turning to the legal definition of citizenship to ensure that citizens do receive their rights. But it is also necessary to recognize that maintaining an aversion to the refugee label can replicate post–Vietnam War racializations of refugees as dirty and helpless subjects of color, consequently disengaging America's culpability for wars and forms of violence that produce stateless persons on a mass scale. Dispossessions of subjects at home and abroad, whether citizens or not, are interlocking and work toward common goals of maintaining hegemony and uneven access to resources "here" and "over there." Thinking broadly and conceptually, impassioned debates over the term "refugee" in post-Katrina New Orleans reveal not the clear distinction between a stateless person and citizen but, rather, the fine line between rightfulness and rightlessness, between citizen and refugee.

Refugee Pastoralism

Complementing an understanding of local dynamics of race with geopolitical factors helps us to understand the different norms that have shaped Vietnamese American self-representation in New Orleans. Specifically, pastoralism has facilitated the emergence of Vietnamese Americans as self-articulating, self-representing autobiographical subjects who are authentic local and national citizens. At the same time, these authenticity claims have been appropriated into state and media narratives for various political agendas that collapse dynamic local and geopolitical histories of imperialism, decolonization, and refugee resettlement. I would like to begin closing this essay by positing refugee pastoralism as a literary aesthetic—and a refugee aesthetic—that embeds possibilities for maintaining a critical position outside premises of local and national belonging and citizenship.[71] As Nguyen writes in his critique of exclusionary, citizenship-based claims, "the blind spot of citizenship [is] where the refugee lives," and claiming rights this way also means bearing "the responsibilities of being a US citizen in an age when the United States willingly wields the power to wage war and create refugees."[72] As a critical tool, refugee positioning affords an ethical stance toward war violence and various levels of state neglect carried out in the name of a nation and its citizens. It can enact a politicized approach to authenticity that strives to locate and interrogate changing configurations of power.

If pastoralism draws attention to human connectedness to land, refugee pastoralism asks us to think about territorial dispossession and pastoral insecurity as opposed to what Alpers[73] describes as pastoral "strength." From this perspective, Vietnamese refugees are not simply inserted into New Orleans's existing norms and cultural practices but actively negotiate a nexus of multiple experiences of migration, loss, and failed state relief as it has evolved transnationally and across the *longue durée*. The agrarian life at the center of refugee pastoralism is of an extended, global story that demonstrates how what is defined as New Orleanian, American, and Vietnamese is not self-evidently authentic but entangled in colonialism, postcolonialism, diaspora, and media desires. It shows how the pastoral changes day by day as refugees maneuver multiple sociopolitical forces and uncertain futures. Refugees are not only products of various local, national, and international agendas, they are also subjects who, in Yen Le Espiritu's words, "possess and enact their *own* politics as they emerge out of the ruins of war and its aftermath."[74]

While Southeast Asian American histories and cultural practices have shaped political discourses of belonging and rights in New Orleans, more recent discussions continue to cast Vietnamese Americans as romantic visionaries at a time of "garden mania"—what Rebecca Solnit describes as a time when "people want to be tillers of the earth, tied to something coherent, calm, tangible, and sensual, to an old slow process whose result is sustenance itself."[75] But as Robert Ku, Anita Mannur, and Martin Manalansan suggest, these discourses risk depoliticizing and dehistoricizing their topics by posing "the pleasures" of food-related activities as solutions to much more complex structural problems.[76] In New Orleans, farms and their cultivators in low-lying and low-income areas are vulnerable to heat and storms during many months of the year, calling into question the long-term sustainability of broad-scope urban farms. Parts of eastern New Orleans continue to be USDA-identified food deserts, and numerous illegal dumpsites still line the area.[77] A properly critical approach to refugee pastoralism attends to these overlapping factors, whereas an overly celebratory narrative of refugee farming risks neglecting sites where a premise for pastoralism—land—is unavailable or communities did not bounce back, as in the case of Vietnamese Americans in Biloxi, Mississippi.

Refugee pastoralism is ultimately a subgenre that acknowledges such instability, since storms and all levels of governance can take away farms and lives. In the New Orleans example, it has afforded narrative and political recognition. But for refugee stories to gain traction, as Gillian Whitlock notes, "the refugee narrative needs 'national history on its side' and must become linked to 'civic virtue and the national good.'" Changing historical circumstances can change this at a moment's notice, altering power dynamics and configurations in unpredictable ways. This "disparity has everything to do with 'whose lives count, and under what circumstances,'" and thus whose and what kinds of self-representations will be recognized as well as the kind of authenticity they will have.[78] Rather than make a definitive statement about whether or not authenticity should be used to explain how New Orleans continues to be remade, this essay aligns with the editors' spirit of engaging with the concept to understand the authentic self as related to power and capital. A literary pastoral approach to this question illustrates the structural conditions within which subjects narrate themselves, make autobiographical pacts, and craft demands. Public recognition of Vietnamese Americans in post-Katrina New Orleans as exemplary rather than exceptional narrators with legitimate political claims has coexisted with a diminishment of black grievances, a severing of Vietnamese diasporic politics from America's long history of dispossessing Southeast Asians, and media co-optation of Vietnamese refugee farms into the city's marketing of racial and cultural diversity; making Vietnamese Americans prominent shows that New Orleans is not only a black city, as the editors of this volume note, but also an Asian one.

Refugee pastoralism cannot exceed these state, media, and corporate forces. But it can draw attention to the contingency of the pastoral farm and farmer because the possibility of refugee status and dispossession always looms large; changing historical conditions necessitate altered authenticity effects and strategies of self-representation, and an exemplary citizen who is of a marginalized group can slide into becoming a perceived or actual refugee. Given current contexts of endless war and environmental degradation, as a literary mode and critical approach, refugee pastoralism invites further consideration of how local, national, and geopolitical dynamics of race, space, and rights define who can be a New Orleanian at a particular point in time.

Notes

I first presented on the politics of Vietnamese American farming and refugee status pre- and post-Katrina (a topic I initially researched in 2008) at the American Cultures workshop at Tulane University in February 2010, where I benefited from conversations with Tulane faculty. I am especially grateful to Thomas Adams, Matt Sakakeeny, and Sue Mobley for organizing the "New Orleans as Subject" workshop, which allowed me to extend this research into the current essay, and for reading the essay with such care.

1   I use "autobiography" and "life narrative" interchangeably, but Sidonie Smith and Julia Watson make the important distinction that autobiography's cultural history is rooted in a "traditional Western mode" while life narrative is "more inclusive of the heterogeneity of self-referential practices." That is, life narrative includes written and nonwritten forms (see Smith and Watson 2010, 4).

2   Lejeune 1989, 3–30.

3   Chiang 2009.

4   Smith and Watson 2010, 74. My treatment of autobiographical works spans various forms, including but not limited to printed texts.

5   Warner 2009, 20.

6   Warner 2009, 11.

7   Warner 2009, 8.

8   Warner 2009, 9.

9   Trilling 1972, 1.

10 Trilling 1972, 93.

11 Trilling 1972, 11.

12 Gotham 2007a, 4–5.

13 Several scholars have examined the influence of Vietnamese Catholic history on the Vietnamese American community in New Orleans, but these analyses tend to focus on cultural rather than geopolitical dynamics (see Bankston 2000; Airriess 2002; and Airriess et al. 2008). This essay has benefited from recent archive-based scholarship in Vietnam studies that outlines a more detailed, historically and politically complex account of the evolution of Vietnamese Catholicism (see especially Keith 2012).

14 Airriess 2002. Hannan secured housing for an initial wave of one thousand Vietnamese refugees in Versailles Arms Apartments in Village de l'Est, with an additional two thousand following in 1976 (Bankston 2000). For an insightful discussion of New Orleans East's history, see Souther 2008. I use "farm" instead of the media's preferred term "garden" because the prominence of "garden" in discussions about Vietnamese Americans in New Orleans risks eliding the long labor, political economies, and transnational dimensions tied to the plots, tilting the discourse toward imperialist tamings of space into purely aesthetic, pleasurable designs.

15 Bankston 2000, 49.

16 John Cummings eventually purchased the land from the New Orleans East Corporation, and in 1994 he worked with MQVN—a spiritual and social heart of the community—to lease the parcel to Vietnamese gardeners at a cost of $1 per month; the rent was instituted to prevent "unrestricted squatting" and ensure clarity of ownership (see Bankston 2000).

17 Airriess and Clawson 1994, 30–31. It is worth noting that in Empire, Plaquemines Parish, Vietnam War refugees were blamed for job competition, disrupting the local lifestyle, and violating regulations. One person noted, "'There once were plenty of shrimp for everybody. People worked from sunrise to sunset, and if you didn't find enough one day, they say, you'd be sure to make it up the next.'" Jack Greenfield, assistant director for National Marine Fisheries Service for the Gulf of Mexico at the time, noted that, by dint of their refugee status, Vietnamese violated federal laws that "'[required] vessels over five net tons to be majority-owned by US citizens, and to have at least one citizen on board while at sea.'" See Gayle Ashton, "Shrimping: A Small Revolution on the Water," *Times-Picayune*, April 22, 1985. I have briefly explored the topic of Vietnamese shrimping around the gulf (M. Nguyen 2013).

18 Gayle Ashton, "Prejudice: Refugees Struggle for Acceptance," *Times-Picayune*, April 21, 1985.

19 "Refugees Showed They Are Survivors," *Times-Picayune*, April 22, 1985, emphasis added.

20 Mark VanLandingham has analyzed the multiple factors that help explain why the return and rebuilding rate for Vietnamese was so high. He argues against a specifically cultural understanding of Vietnamese "resilience" and instead draws on multiple cultural, material, and historical forces (see VanLandingham 2017). My argument is less premised upon the notion of Vietnamese diasporic success in the city after Katrina, focusing more on the rhetorical and narrative strategies that those in the community have used to represent themselves in the public sphere.

21 The 2010 census records the number of "Vietnamese along or in any combination" for census tracts 17.49 and 17.50, which includes the MQVN area, as 3,010. A somewhat

broader area (zip code 70129) totals 3,546. See US Census Bureau, Census 2010. *Population 70129*, generated using *American Factfinder* (October 20, 2015), https://factfinder .census.gov/faces/nav/jsf/pages/community_facts.xhtml. Some note that the number is higher, around six thousand. See Chiang 2009; see also Li et al. 2008.

22 The following quotations are transcribed from the film.

23 Chiang 2009.

24 Leslie Williams, "Under the Radar," *Times-Picayune*, November 27, 2005.

25 Chiang 2009.

26 Chiang 2009.

27 M. Nguyen 2013, 279.

28 Kato, Passidomo, and Harvey 2014, 1837.

29 For a treatment of Vietnamese Buddhist practices in New Orleans as an example of how the community has imagined itself within the broader landscape of the city, see Truitt 2015.

30 Marx 1964, 3.

31 Alpers 1996, 22, 28, 50.

32 Truitt (2012, 323) argues, "the community continually [reasserts] its presence as Vietnamese by structuring development initiatives around those features defined as culturally authentic even as the projects themselves sought to transform those features." My essay's different impetus focuses on pastoralism as a formal narrative frame for Vietnamese diasporic claims to authenticity and on the constraints that local and geopolitical forces impose on those rhetorical tactics.

33 Chiang 2009.

34 Deixis can be thought of as "the ways in which speakers position themselves, one another, and the time and place of interaction" (Warner 2009, 13).

35 Renee Peck, "In New Orleans Vietnamese American Community, Gardening Is a Way of Life," *Times-Picayune*, September 27, 2008; Nguyen and Rowell 2006, 1081.

36 To be sure, Afro-Asian connections have had a long history in the city, spanning the spectrum of antagonism and mutual support, which scholars have discussed elsewhere. Vietnamese American and African American linkages in the city post-Katrina are a continuation of this past (see Tang 2011; M. Nguyen 2013).

37 Tang 2011, 123.

38 It bears noting that I do not think Asian American pastoralisms have inherent progressive value. As the long history of Asian and Asian American labor shows, images of these subjects working the land have legitimated a range of racist agendas, from exploitive Asian labor in Hawaii and the US South to Japanese American internment during World War II.

39 This newly recognized presence seemed to peak in 2009, when New Orleans resident Joseph Cao, a former Independent turned Republican, was elected to the US House of Representatives. Cao was the first Republican to hold the seat of the strongly Democratic Second Congressional District and the first Vietnamese American to serve in the US Congress. The Second Congressional District in Louisiana consists of almost all of New Orleans and some suburbs in neighboring Jefferson Parish; Hamilton D. Coleman was the last Republican to represent it in 1891. Cao defeated nine-term incumbent William Jefferson in 2008 in an election delayed by Hurricane Gustav and amid charges of

Jefferson's corruption. Cao was instrumental in addressing language barrier problems within the Vietnamese diasporic community in the wake of the BP oil spill. However, he ran on a conservative ticket, and his "tightrope act" as a Republican for reform who at times distanced himself from his party has evolved into a hard ideological line. See Suzy Khimm, "Joseph Cao's Tightrope Act," *Mother Jones*, August 10, 2010, http://www.motherjones.com/politics/2010/08/joseph-cao-reelection-louisiana. In his 2016 campaign for the Louisiana Senate, he expressed support for the Second Amendment, the war on terror, and stronger border security. See Joseph Cao for US Senate, http://josephcaoforsenate.com.

40 Butler 2005, 8.

41 Butler 2005, 7–8.

42 Butler 2005, 21.

43 For a treatment of the concept of racial triangulation in relation to Asian Americans, see Kim 1999.

44 Gayle Ashton, "Prejudice: Refugees Struggle for Acceptance," *Times-Picayune*, April 21, 1985, A-14.

45 Roach 1996, xi–xii.

46 Gotham 2007a, 4–5.

47 Lye 2008, 1733.

48 Jung 2006.

49 Richard Campanella, "The Lost History of New Orleans' Two Chinatowns," *Times-Picayune*, March 4, 2015.

50 Richard Campanella, "Chinatown," in *Know Louisiana Encyclopedia of Louisiana*, ed. David Johnson (Louisiana Endowment for the Humanities, 2013), http://www.knowlouisiana.org/entry/chinatown.

51 Tang 2006. Blacks made up 67 percent of the New Orleans population at this time.

52 Tang 2006.

53 Tang 2011, 120–21.

54 Tang 2011, 135, 143.

55 Tang 2011, 123. Such collaborations exemplify the reframing of interracial "conflict into solidarity" that Vijay Prashad (2006, xxi) argues is at the heart of Afro-Asian work seeking to dismantle a comparative racial logic that pits racial groups against each other. However, Jared Sexton (2010) cautions against centering interracial solidarity, a move that can reinforce antiblackness by flattening out structural and historical differences that have enabled Asian Americans to gain higher socioeconomic standing than blacks. It is worth noting that Southeast Asian Americans do not fit the model minority myth in terms of income and education.

56 Tang 2011, 138–44.

57 Nguyen-Marshall 2005, 239–44.

58 Keith 2012.

59 Keith (2012, 223) notes that French Catholic missionaries often criticized French military aggression.

60 Keith 2012.

61 A figure named Father Hoang Quynh of Phat Diem was particularly important, pooling resources for communal support and protecting and promoting these programs. For a

time, Catholic leaders in Phat Diem and Bui Chu attempted to ally with the revolution, but these efforts ultimately failed (Keith 2012, 209). Quynh mobilized his diocese southward but stayed in Saigon after the Vietnam War and was arrested for resistance against the DRV. He died in prison in early 1977, reportedly from "beatings and torture."

62 Keith 2012.

63 V. Nguyen 2016, 4.

64 Mike Pesca, "Are Katrina Victims 'Refugees' or 'Evacuees?,'" *Reporter's Notebook*, National Public Radio, September 5, 2005, http://www.npr.org/templates/story/story .php?storyId=4833613; Masquelier 2006, 737. As Kimberly Rivers Roberts expresses in the documentary *Trouble the Water*, she and other blacks had been rendered "un-American" after the hurricane—"*like* we lost our citizenship" (Lessin and Deal 2008).

65 John M. Broder, "Amid Criticism of Federal Efforts, Charges of Racism Are Lodged," *New York Times*, September 5, 2005.

66 Cacho 2012, 15.

67 Volpp 2005, 21.

68 Volpp 2005, 22.

69 Cacho 2012, 14–15.

70 Nina Bernstein, "Refugee Groups Reaching Out to Victims of Hurricane," *New York Times*, September 18, 2005, http://www.nytimes.com/2005/09/18/nyregion/refugee -groups-reaching-out-to-victims-of-hurricane.html.

71 Elsewhere, I have briefly introduced pastoralism as a genre to consider in analyzing narratives about Vietnamese Americans in New Orleans (see M. Nguyen 2015). The current essay's deeper study of the pastoral form as a pretext for defining refugee pastoralism significantly expands on and specifies my earlier treatment.

72 V. Nguyen 2012, 931, 939.

73 Alpers 1996, 50.

74 Espiritu 2014, 11.

75 Solnit 2009b.

76 Ku, Mannur, and Manalansan 2013, 3.

77 For a longer discussion of the problems that Vietnamese Americans in Versailles face after Katrina, see Seidman 2013.

78 Gillian Whitlock quoted in Espiritu 2014, 19.

PART FOUR

Predictive City?

11

Boosting the Private Sector

Federal Aid and Downtown Development in the 1970s

MEGAN FRENCH-MARCELIN

The proliferation of new scholarship on New Orleans has linked patterns of exclusion to trends in US urban political development that have been occurring since the early 1970s. In the Crescent City, these trends include the removal of low-income people of color to make way for speculative real estate projects (most recently through the destruction of public housing); the reconstruction of public spaces as exclusive sites of consumption (typi-fied by the erection of walls around Louis Armstrong Park); the increased reliance on public-private partnerships for urban economic development (as realized by groups like the Business Council and the Downtown Develop-ment District); a market-first approach to low-income housing (exemplified by federal programs like the HOPE VI "revitalization" of public housing); and the privatization of social service delivery. These processes have reshaped the city through practices that are now commonplace in US municipalities. None are new; none are exceptional. The reorganization of cities throughout the United States as a result of deindustrialization, stagflation, and subse-quent federal disinvestment was shaped by policies that placed a premium on reclaiming a lost middle class. As such courses of action necessitate uneven development, proponents of these urban strategies have become more and more adept at silencing any political opposition attempted by those who do not derive benefits from this growth.[1] Despite the presence of protest move-ments, this brand of urban development has continued relatively unabated throughout the nation.

Since Hurricane Katrina, private developers have taken advantage of disaster to reimagine the city through extreme variations of these trends. When real estate mogul Joseph Canizaro described, with glee, the appalling aftermath of Katrina as a potential "clean sheet," he invoked a narrative that has been reiterated frequently by those who see the forced removal of low-income people of color as an opportunity for profit making.[2] Thus, for future neoliberal modes of urban development, New Orleans has become a laboratory of the Frankenstein sort.[3] With the move toward an all-charter school system—a process that has removed education from the public sphere, initiated the firing of more than seven thousand teachers, circumscribed access for children with special needs, and facilitated a gold rush of education profiteering—it very much appears that New Orleans will be a garrison from which to cultivate and refine mechanisms of privatization. If left unchallenged, these forces will—and have begun already to—overwhelm voices of opposition and eliminate whole sections of the city.[4]

This chapter contributes to the movement away from relying on tropes of exceptionalism by detailing the centrality of the Crescent City's local leadership in the innovation of pro-market governing strategies now central to urban governance. However, whereas studies often situate the genesis of neoliberal urban development practices in the 1980s under the reign of Ronald Reagan, I argue that transformations in federal urban aid policy that occurred during the Nixon administration, and were reinforced under President Carter, facilitated the rise of these methods. As the decimation of antipoverty structures coincided with the federal devolution of urban aid initiatives and concurrent capital flight, cities were charged with balancing the dual crises of urban poverty and fiscal solvency. Because the Nixon administration's rhetoric articulated these crises as necessitating opposing solutions—and because solutions for the former were no longer realizable given the assured decline of federal urban aid—mayors across the nation abandoned redistributive antipoverty projects in order to enable broad private-sector urban revitalization.[5] New mechanisms of federal urban aid—which sanctioned citywide use and local discretion—permitted local governments to dramatically and intentionally reorganize city power and urban economies in ways that precipitated neoliberal approaches to urban development. By the mid-1970s, civic and business leaders alike articulated clearing the way for private-sector enterprise as the primary function of local government.

Such action was necessitated, mayors then argued, by the mismatch of expanding demands on municipal revenue and the inability of low-income residents to contribute to city coffers.[6] If governing officials wanted to revitalize their municipalities, the doctrine went, they must direct resources to reclaiming a fleeing middle class.[7] Accordingly, new political ideologies proffered that cities should ensure the unmitigated autonomy of private development interests now believed better suited than federal agencies to encourage renewal.

In cities across the nation, private-sector sovereignty was organized around consumption-oriented investment and the rapid redevelopment of central business districts, tourist attractions, and waterfronts. New development reimagined downtown districts as urban playgrounds for the rich and white while, in the South, suggesting that touristic growth was a critical function in assuring the New South was an integrated South. Though local governing officials were well acquainted with the limitations of such strategies for the majority of current residents, poor and unskilled, they nevertheless promoted the idea that private-sector-led economic development was essential to remaking the city's landscape. Thus, in New Orleans, as in cities across the country, local officials deployed new federal urban aid in ways that provided private-sector developers with the insularity necessary to conduct development in ways that excluded low-income residents from a share in the city's economic future.

The transformation of federal urban aid was at the center of facilitating this approach. As the centerpiece of the Housing and Community Development Act of 1974, the Community Development Block Grant (CDBG) program exploited the request of mayors for local decision making to refocus federal urban aid activities around citywide physical revitalization and blight prevention.[8] The new program gave mayors autonomy over a broad range of physical development activities, while narrowing redistributive programs and cutting more comprehensive antipoverty programs. As local administrators pursued speculative economic aims, CDBGs had direct influence on this agenda. Officials certainly appropriated funds for activities in low-income neighborhoods, but CDBG funding as it was most commonly deployed—private housing rehabilitation, street-paving programs, playground construction, and day care support—offered few opportunities to expand political or economic inclusion for low-income residents. Additionally, neighborhood-based development eroded links between and among low-income sections of the city, diminishing the capacity of residents to mobilize around broader issues of inclusion, community participation, and access.[9] Residents, while all too cognizant of this potential impact, felt compelled to make demands within the framework of community development so as not to risk neighborhood divestment altogether.[10] While many mayors were frustrated with this limitation, it also ensured that community-level action would not jeopardize the ability of private-sector interests to pattern the city's economic development agenda without opposition.[11]

Thus, as the efforts of local administrators to alleviate conditions through these incremental place-based fixes gave an impression (at least to some degree) that governing officials were doing what they could, the grants reinforced a clear bifurcation between community development as neighborhood maintenance through public money and economic development as revitalization through private investment. While this delineation clearly protected economic development interests from community involvement, it did not prevent developers from laying claim to funding designed to address community issues. By the end of the decade, federal aid—originally enacted to assist low-income community economic development—was being used to leverage private growth.

While President Nixon had long declared the urban crisis over, the economic crisis in cities across the nation was in full force. Federal devolution and disinvestment coincided with global economic transformations that brought about the flight of industry overseas, coupled with growing stagflation, which undermined any sense of security or permanence cities like New Orleans had once touted. Tourism took on new economic importance in New Orleans, as it did in Baltimore, Philadelphia, and New York during the early 1970s.[12] Tourism thus dovetailed with the quick real estate fix approach being pursued in other cities such as Boston and New York.[13] With reports predicting a budget deficit of over $45 million by 1975, the city—under the direction of recently elected Mayor Landrieu—began organizing downtown interests in an effort to grow the Central Business District and foster gentrification in surrounding neighborhoods.[14] Officials envisioned a downtown centered on "office jobs, hotels and tourism," where new development—including a skating rink, bowling alleys, and a riverside fencing club—would attract new human and capital investment.[15] While early internal reports stressed that an overreliance on tourism would have detrimental repercussions on the city's poor residents, detailing the potential that tourism would only create thousands of dead-end jobs, the mayor made clear his intention to provide broad managerial latitude to private developers in the process of initiating downtown projects.[16]

From the outset, Mayor Moon Landrieu, elected on a platform that linked the civil rights agenda with new forms of economic growth, went out of his way to champion development interests. "We are going to be here supporting those projects," he told reporters. They are going to get nothing but support from this administration—they are not going to find obstacles in their way."[17] For those young developers who had backed his campaign in the previous year, Landrieu created new cadres of social capital, appointing the developers to important municipal boards and commissions.[18] In remarkably transparent fashion, the mayor held a 1971 press conference in the unfinished Lykes Center, a twenty-one-story skyscraper financed by the young and bois-terous Biloxi-born developer Joseph Canizaro. Canizaro, a former chair of Landrieu's campaign, had used his new appointments to several major city boards and commissions to become one of the city's most important new businessmen in a matter of just years.

Flexing his mayoral muscle in 1973, Landrieu propelled a land swap through the City Council, thus allowing Canizaro to aggregate land parcels along the city's coveted riverfront for a megamall development project at an appraised cost that had curiously been lowered by some $3.3 million between the city's first assessment and the deal's final estimation of value.[19] Moreover, the city expanded mechanisms to entice further private investment. By 1972, the city had formed an industrial revenue board authorized to issue tax-exempt bonds to developers (importantly, without the public referendum required by municipal bonding) and began a comprehensive zoning evalu-ation designed to facilitate the concentration of growth in the downtown district.

At the suggestion of Wallace, McHarg, Roberts and Todd—a planning firm that had managed redevelopment of Baltimore's Inner Harbor and New York's South Street Seaport—the city pursued the creation of a special tax district downtown to concentrate control of the area's economic strast-egy.[20] The firm would later design the city's application to replace St. Thomas public housing with a HOPE VI project that would signify for many the be-ginning of the end of public housing in New Orleans. Yet, in 1974, though rejecting the city's attempt to enact a progressive municipal income tax, the state legislature authorized the nation's first business improvement district in downtown New Orleans.[21] The board of the new Core Area Development District (CADD) was composed of businessmen appointed jointly by the mayor and Chamber of Commerce. The chamber, which had by the early 1970s been transformed by the introduction of out-of-state financiers and entrepreneurs, appointed by Landrieu, had taken its place as the unofficial economic develop-ment arm of the city. Operating on the principle that private-sector interests could better direct the efficient management of the area, the board imme-diately assumed authority over capital investment decisions and strategic design within its boundaries. With the district's jigsaw-like perimeter conveniently skirting all nearby public housing, local officials explained that growth was best accomplished in areas organized around homogenous interests. Though leadership of the nascent public-private partnership insisted that growth of the area would benefit all residents, the omission of low-income neighborhoods (and the opinions of their residents) from the growth zone ensured that redevelopment and redistribution would not be coterminous.[22] Indeed, if the local state promoted their role as facilitator to a new free market, its method was not a simple deference to business. Rather, the exclusion hinged on boundaries wherein a predominantly black, low-income labor force denied unionization was also criminalized in those spaces when not operating as labor. Therein, growth was maintained by making certain spaces, places, and people subject to the threat of a police state.

Nevertheless, the board's capacity to ensure development at a time of fiscal insecurity gave it powerful leverage to make demands on public resources. By the mid-1970s, the city's participation in antipoverty programs had established a cadre of professionalized planners and analysts who were now equipped to deploy sizable development projects in a city whose elite had undermined touristic growth since the 1920s. Quickly, the Landrieu administration marshaled the resources of several of the former antipoverty agencies to participate in the downtown plan. While agencies like the Community Improvement Agency, the city's urban renewal wing, offered management and planning expertise, the windfall in affiliating the downtown with these government entities was the potential to open state and federal aid to the area.[23] The city promised that as an improvement zone, the CADD could make claims to the new community development funding as well.[24]

Though CDBG was a program conceived to benefit low- and moderate-income areas, the ambiguous language within the legislation actually facilitated the proposed diversion of aid. The legislation's rhetoric, which replaced poverty with blight as the central enemy of cities, was deployed throughout the act without definitional clarity.[25] If seemingly innocuous, the shift in vocabulary reinforced the notion that addressing economic inequality was no longer critical to the survival of cities so much as the restoration of a physical environment reflective of a consumer class. As a result, blight and its attendant symptoms assumed a political malleability: Blight could be anywhere. Thus, city community development plans defined their project scope in language that ranged from environmental and physical to sociopsychological and pathogen-like. In New Orleans, as elsewhere, local officials seized on this "terminological inexactitude" to shepherd resources and manpower into the downtown. New Orleans city officials thus felt justified in advocating for reapportionment, arguing that the imminent fiscal crisis necessitated utilizing funding where programs could generate a "major multiplier effect."[26] Diminished federal aid and shrinking municipal revenue streams required local officials to develop a program whose success would be "gauged in large part by the amount of private sector resources it is able to generate."[27]

Thus, it caused little shock when the Community Improvement Agency reported blighted conditions throughout the downtown area: broken windows marred the retail corridor along Canal Street; sidewalks were deteriorating; a skid row was attracting vagrants of all kinds; and historic buildings were being allowed to waste away in disrepair. Agency planners detailed that symptoms of blight were not only rampant, but "retarding the Central Business District's overall ability" to function in the economic interests of the city's citizens. To formally blight the area, opening it up to federal and state aid, was imperative to the "preservation of the city's tax and economic base." Improvement agency officials suggested that access to community development funding could begin to "induce improvements where market forces alone [were] not sufficient."[28]

Leaders of the CADD invoked this report when, in 1977, they solicited the local government to divert community development funds to the area. Approaching the city government after public hearings on CDBG allocations had concluded, the CADD board of directors requested funding for a range of development projects they wished to complete. Though the group was scheduled to take in more than $1 million from its district tax, members attached a five-year projection budget anticipating subsidies totaling $17 million from city government and $16.2 million in federal aid. Business leaders argued that community development could cover a broad range of beautification activities that included repairing sidewalks, construction of transit shelters, and landscaping, all of which were vital to encouraging the area's successful turnaround.[29]

Core Area Development District director Warren Berault expressed disappointment that the city had not already directed CDBG funds into the commercial area. Clearly, while trying to uphold the "integrity of the act," the city had neglected the "importance, function, dynamics and special needs" of business leaders, CADD members contended. If nothing else, the funds were justified "because they [were] used throughout the country in this fashion"; to disregard their request would put the city at a competitive disadvantage.[30] Reminding city leadership of the Central Business District's centrality in generating employment, CADD made the strong suggestion that it was the responsibility of city officials to sell the downtown as a legitimate community development zone. If Berault's scolding of the mayor was not enough, Canizaro followed suit, imploring the mayor to see that CADD's needs trumped those of low-income neighborhoods throughout the city. Plus, he added, the downtown projects would not only attack blight, but "correct flight" and stabilize the city's tax base.[31] Within days, city officials sent word to CADD that its request for CDBG funds had been approved.[32] Though the funding was minimal, it signified the willingness of local authorities to reallocate urban aid to serve the purposes of development.

Exploiting the CDBG program's undetermined flexibility, local authorities approved projects that did not directly benefit low-income residents. The support of central business districts, rehabilitative middle-income housing, and beautification projects aimed at gentrification became popular CDBG activities nationwide.[33] In Rochester, New York, urban planners recommended the city focus on directing aid into transitional neighborhoods, a program that would exclude the poorest areas of the municipality.[34] An official in Cleveland reported using similar strategies to regenerate neighborhoods that were still considered "salvageable."[35] Far from exceptional, the diversion of federal aid in New Orleans to projects aimed at spawning middle-class growth was commonplace.

As early as 1975, analysts for the National League of Cities (NLC) suggested that the opportunity to repurpose community development funds to expand the resources and amenities available for middle-class residents in central cities demanded consideration from the nation's lawmakers.[36] Cautioning a narrow antipoverty focus for grant delivery, analysts for the NLC argued that while needs of middle- and upper-income residents were not as dire as those of low-income residents, to not meet those needs, cities would "once again lose the sector of society which contributes economic and social stability to the area." Community development aid, the NLC proposed, could—with careful planning and effective management—be utilized to encourage the "return of the more affluent to the city." Since aid intervention would fail to make a significant difference in low-income neighborhoods, according to the NLC's reasoning, such strategies were not only necessary but offered the only means of turning cities around.[37]

As local administrators continued to articulate a vision of the functional city as requiring the middle class to return, it became clear that few municipalities interpreted the new funding system as an extension of antipoverty aid. In fact, low-income residents played little role in this understanding of urban renewal. The urban crisis, mayors said, obligated them to use CDBG funds to stimulate economic growth. The role of city governing officials in this new atmosphere, as Landrieu candidly told reporters, was to "create an environment where business can best function."[38] Yet local officials did not insist that where aid was directed to private-sector growth, it should be precluded by considerations for low-income participation. Instead, they repeatedly claimed that to compel developers to do so would jeopardize investment and, with it, the opportunity to grow the economy and stabilize the tax base.

Of course, the idea that private investment would occur only in areas of unburdened access and control was a cardinal falsehood: there were certainly ways to stipulate inclusive models of development or compel contingencies for low-income communities.[39] Yet local officials, intent on securing a share in the new economy, sanctioned the disaggregation of activities where differing treatments—commercial districts reimagined to cultivate enclaves for luxury consumption separate from activity in low-income neighborhoods—underscored an assumption that the needs of the middle class were dissimilar, unrelated, and necessitated spatial segregation from the needs of poor people. Undoubtedly, this assumption implied that amid revitalization, poor residents were not capable of being active participants in the making of the new economy, nor visible citizens of the future city.

Thus, local officials raised the excuse that private-sector investment would be unwilling to operate in low-income areas where profit margins would be undercut. Accordingly, the flexibility granted to private-sector interests tended to undermine community-led economic development projects as well. Neighborhoods with high levels of poverty frequently lacked the organizational capacity, people, and capital necessary to enable complex projects to get off the ground. In these instances, local administrators suggested that community leadership cede control to developers. Yet the private sector often undermined or disposed of community participation, limited inclusive economic models, and encouraged gentrification. The inability to escape this paradox was further exacerbated when, in the rare cases when city administrators approved neighborhood economic development, they neither supported nor invested resources with the same vigor found in their boosting of downtown.

In New Orleans, this was true in the neighborhood of Central City, where the rates of poverty, overcrowding, and dilapidation made conditions some of the worst in the city. Nearly half the structures in the area were substandard, and unemployment was exponentially higher than in the rest of the city. In response to the expansive need in the area, the outspoken and charismatic director of the Urban League of Greater New Orleans, Clarence Barney, proposed a comprehensive community economic development project to systematically strengthen the neighborhood through job creation, counseling, building rehabilitation, and educational services. The project would propose developing three thousand new manufacturing and service jobs, a community center replete with health and counseling services, commercial support for small business owners, and new housing. Barney argued that where economic activity was inclusive of poor people, the city could counteract development "where terms of trade [were] encrusted with discrimination and the market flow[ed] not freely but unfairly."[40]

Despite the dearth of community economic development projects, the city provided minimal capital and planning resources for Barney's initiative, instead taking what community leaders characterized as a "show me approach."[41] City analysts reasoned that the project could not generate the kind of capital necessary for the aggressive design without relinquishing strategic authority to private developers.[42] Nor was the city capable, rationalized the director of the Community Improvement Agency, of providing the $2.7 million needed for the project to take shape in the way that community leaders hoped would give residents control. As Central City residents and leadership balked at the proposed rearrangement under private direction, the project lost steam, was apportioned into more modest projects, and ultimately abandoned.[43]

The failure of the Central City project, like the dismantling of antipoverty programs, was used as proof of the need to allow private developers to shape future urban development even as such reasoning ignored the asymmetry of funding where downtown interests were championed and community projects were scrutinized. Increasingly, both federal policy and local planning prescribed economic strategies that reinforced an urban vision of private-sector-led development. Although amendments to the Housing and Community Development Act made in 1977 seemed to pivot policy aims toward a more conscientious focus on low-income communities by requiring more extensive citizen participation and new targeting prerequisites, the majority of legislation demonstrated the growing bias toward privatization.[44] Mayors who had once championed antipoverty efforts now were at the forefront of lobbying for the authority to redirect resources to private developers. In fact, the US Conference of Mayors strongly rejected the addition of ratios designed to ensure funds were directed into low-income areas.[45]

Thus, the outcome of the majority of new urban policy expanded mechanisms by which to transfer control and federal aid into projects designed by the private sector. New provisions allowed local officials to use funds for development capable of "induc[ing] higher income persons to remain in, or return to, the community."[46] Loopholes of this nature ensured that funding would continue to be diverted to areas and activities that would have little effect on low-income communities. This practice was crystallized most clearly in the legislation's central innovation—Urban Development Action Grants (UDAGs). The $400 million outlay for the UDAG program was designed to provide gap financing of new projects (that theoretically would not materialize without the addition of such funds) approved by city authorities or, in other words, to create direct federal aid opportunities for private investors.

As one-time awards, UDAGs were promoted as a mechanism to bolster urban economic revitalization through a balanced approach of commercial, downtown, and neighborhood-based economic development projects. In practice, the promotion of downtown districts as "vital" to urban tax bases and "essential" centers for employment sanctioned a clear imbalance.[47] Going so far as to suggest that hotel development had provided some of the best jobs for poor and working people worldwide, the new federal Housing and Urban Development (HUD) secretary, Patricia Harris, clearly supported such use despite other rhetorical claims to focusing on truly redistributive housing policies.[48] Although the Presidential Commission on Neighborhoods argued that the concentration of UDAGs in service sector economies would be unable to provide economic mobility to low- and moderate-income residents, the board nevertheless found that in the first round of grants not only had HUD officials given preference in funding to downtown projects, they had encouraged them.[49] In the first year of the UDAG program, thirty cities sought the grants to build luxury chain hotels in their downtowns; fifteen were given funding.[50] Urban Development Action Grants were, in fact, the loophole in Community Development Block Grants that local officials demanded.

It was a strategy that the Landrieu administration was quick to deploy in order to further aggregate economic development within the city's downtown tourism and convention trade. With the technical assistance of the Community Improvement Agency, the city promoted a spectrum of downtown development projects as eligible for action grants. Reiterating the language of blight, hoteliers and developers stressed that renovations and new development in the Central Business District were paramount to protecting the city from further deterioration. Applications described the potential of a domino effect where blight would spread, crime would rise, and, inevitably, the disaster would begin to diminish the ability to attract tourism.[51] As development interests were given more and more power over the design of urban economic growth, city officials feared that failure to provide funds to developers would undermine the city's economic expansion.

Thus city officials, in New Orleans and elsewhere, allotted significant shares of their UDAG funds to downtown development. By 1979, New Orleans's new mayor, Ernest "Dutch" Morial, announced an initiative to consolidate downtown efforts under a new private-public umbrella. The Megalink project, as it was called, would join a new massive convention center including a Sheraton hotel, new parking lots, and developer Joseph Canizaro's Canal Street development, which had been enabled by the land swap and was renewing the dilapidated retail corridor with new office space, luxury apartments, and a Saks Fifth Avenue. In doing so, the Megalink would complete a passage from the glittering new Superdome to the Mississippi River, thus providing tourists with a New Orleans unencumbered by poverty or decline. In 1979, the city sought more than $25 million in action grants for developers, including nearly $5 million for Canizaro's controversial Canal Place shopping development. The new secretary of HUD, former mayor Landrieu, awarded one of the largest UDAGs to date: some $17 million for the convention and hotel project.[52]

City officials and private developers alike claimed the grants were central to reversing the city's fortunes. At a city-sponsored conference on the UDAG system, now Secretary Landrieu praised the program as the most important innovation in recent urban policy. Urban Development Action Grants, he said, reaffirmed the reality that "the private sector built this country and it is going to continue to be the private sector that builds it and rebuilds it." Panelist after panelist reiterated this idea. Cities, businessman Howard Green stated, were most "efficiently revitalized by the private sector" when public aid was mobilized to "make opportunities within the distressed cities comparable with opportunities developers have in the suburbs."[53] The boom in hotels, office space, and convention goers confirmed the supremacy of private-sector-led economic development, conference participants claimed, and championed the "triangular partnerships" emerging between city halls, federal agencies, and private investors as the hallmark of the future.[54]

Though talks of triangular partnerships heralded the role that public agencies played in subsidizing downtown, boom rhetoric that conflated economic growth with the efficiency and efficacy of private efforts downplayed just how substantial the role of federal aid had become. A national study of the program's first year found that nearly 40 percent of UDAGs were acquired for commercial development and that cities had deployed some $191 million of other federal aid to assist UDAG projects, almost a quarter of which came from CDBG funding. With more and more frequency, city officials bundled UDAG funds with access to CDBGs, tax abatements, building subsidies, and tax-exempt bonding.[55] By the early 1980s, the Industrial Development Board had issued $15 million in bonds alongside UDAGs, and the city had enhanced new construction with an incentivized zoning program, second in the nation only to New York's.[56] While maintaining the inability to channel such funds into low-income neighborhoods and complaining of diminishing federal aid, local administrators had used federal grants to willingly enhance the authority of private development interests.

Local administrators nationwide stressed that growing competition between cities placed a premium on expanding convention centers, tourist attractions, and festival marketplaces over more redistributive forms of economic growth. As a result of this competition and despite the site-specific nature of tourism, these processes developed through projects that were remarkably homogenous and culturally indistinct. In 1983, New Orleans awarded a UDAG to the Rouse Company for development of a festival marketplace along the city's waterfront in preparation for the 1984 World's Fair. The development group—renowned for similar projects in Boston (Faneuil Hall) and New York City (South Street Seaport)—received some $110 million in action grants for twelve projects over the course of the 1980s. In the way that Rouse Company projects popped up in cities from New York to Boston to Baltimore, the conversion of wharfs into cosmopolitan riverfronts and the promotion of destination cities through tourism and convention industries did not make cities appear more unique. It did, however, inherently widen the gap between private-sector development and the needs of low-income city residents.[57]

The autonomy granted to private interests to pursue development for profit without contingencies for low-income people ensured that the benefits of new development were circumscribed: the majority of jobs created through new office space and convention development were white collar. Yet, by 1980, rather than staving off white flight and promoting a return to the city, the city's economy supported 100,000 export workers commuting into town from the increasingly white and more affluent suburbs surrounding the urban core. These benefits were also proven largely speculative in the 1982 oil bust, which drove oil companies out of their Poydras Street offices and back to Houston. White flight continued rapidly throughout the 1970s and early 1980s.[58] By 1990, there was a 25 percent vacancy rate in Class A office space in the city's downtown.

For low-income residents, the economic growth could hardly be described as a boon.[59] Nearly 30 percent of the city's jobs by 1980 were located in the largely seasonal and nonunion tourist industry, and this figure has only continued to rise.[60] Although poverty rates remained unchanging through this time, poverty was, by 1990, more concentrated than ever before. An estimated 10 percent of the city's population resided in public housing.[61] The top quartile of income earners in the metropolis earned more than 44 percent of the city's gross income, while the bottom quartile earned less than 5 percent.[62] A 1978 Urban League report, compiled from surveys with hundreds of low-income city residents, echoed the language of the Kerner Commission's report, issued a decade prior, in suggesting that the tourism boom masked the reality of two economies: one prospering from the deprivation of the other.[63]

The reality was that public officials in New Orleans had done little to encourage economic inclusion as a principle for community development. Even leadership that insisted on diversifying the economy—such as Mayor Morial, whose development strategy emphasized an attempt to build an industrial base—made no effort to curb the public subsidization of downtown development. Instead Morial, like his predecessor, continued to enhance private power at the expense of democratic decision making. Isolated within poverty neighborhoods, community development had little capacity to foster discourse about resource equity, let alone action capable of addressing structural or institutional inequality. Certainly, the nature of CDBGs, rooted as they were in a physical development program, made supporting comprehensive projects more difficult; nevertheless, the presence of federal urban aid as well as an interracial executive office allowed leadership to seem progressive while promoting private-sector development in ways counter to the interests of poor people.[64]

This mirage would end with the 1981 Omnibus Reconciliation Act, which cut nearly 40 percent of federal urban aid. But by promoting economic development that undermined the mobility and inclusion of low-income residents, city leaders had already abandoned their residents. The autonomy granted to private-sector interests to determine the economic agenda has ensured that development remains uneven and strategic decision making undemocratic.

By the mid-1980s, New Orleans leadership no longer felt it necessary to balance the pursuit of speculative economic development practices with a commitment to socially progressive ideals. With the election of Mayor Sidney Barthelemy, the city actively cut public sector employment, undermined public housing where downtown interests saw the opportunity for expansion, and doubled down on the touristic economy by encouraging the gambling industry.[65] As CDBGs were increasingly apportioned to private companies and nonprofit organizations under the belief that their operations would yield more efficient results, the city also began experimenting with mechanisms to privatize the delivery of other public services and aid.[66]

Making use of the perpetual urban fiscal crisis (which privatization has failed to solve), local leaders have continued to utilize transitions in urban aid that on their face appear to offer new opportunities through the open market—Section 8, Clinton-era welfare reform, HOPE VI, Moving to Opportunity—to mask choices that have excluded low-income residents and diminished opportunities for inclusion within the city's political economy. Despite the multitude of evidence that such programs do little to promote equality, the popularity of such strategies continues. The processes that we see being actualized in post-Katrina New Orleans, where low-income residents are being forcefully removed in favor of outrageous modes of gentrification, are the legacy of this era during which city administrators came to imagine the role of privatization as taking precedence over the preservation of the social welfare state.

If New York has not had the political (or environmental) rationale for decimating public housing like the fell swoop of New Orleans, policies that raise the maximum income of housing tenants and link new low-income housing to mixed-income developments will assuredly make those most vulnerable in the city far more so.[67] The same is true for government strategies that have sought to reimagine deindustrialized spaces—Detroit, Baltimore, and yes New Orleans—as creative commons for young tech entrepreneurs, a strategy that may bring new capital but will only exacerbate already precarious conditions for working-class communities of color.[68]

There is nothing exceptional about these shifts; rather, while New Orleans may continue in the post-Katrina era to be an incubator for new forms of revanchist privatization, these patterns define the last forty years of urban development in cities across the nation.

Notes

1 Detroit, Michigan, provides another extreme example, as the takeover of the city by a nonelected emergency manager has precipitated calls for privatization of city services and urban shrinkage.

2 Quoted in Peck 2006, 696.

3 N. Klein 2008.

4 N. Klein 2008; Campbell Robertson, "Louisiana Illegally Fired 7,500 Teachers, Judge Says," *New York Times*, June 21, 2012.

5 The decline of federal urban aid was, of course, not inevitable or final but due to the bipartisan assault on former antipoverty programs.

6 "Mayor Gives Challenge to Business Community," *Times-Picayune*, December 8, 1971, 23.

7 This rhetoric underscored another point that was central to dismantling antipoverty activities. According to the Nixon administration, the failure of the war on poverty to make middle-class citizens out of poor people only demonstrated further the need to encourage the departed (white) residents back to urban cores.

8 Though enacted at a moment when antipoverty programs were being dismantled, CDBGS did not seek to reinvent antipoverty activity. Instead they were offered as broad urban revitalization tools. The grant consolidated several programs previously run through the Department of Housing and Urban Development into one block grant that was controlled with the discretion of the mayor. Congress had minimal oversight initially, but in order to qualify, cities had to submit a plan for activities and how they would ensure community participation, as well as a housing plan for low-income development (though new housing was not an approved activity). While many have imagined CDBGS as the failure of Nixon's attempts to enact federalism, the grants facilitated a radical shift in the way governing officials approached issues of urban poverty. The new grant program successfully allowed the national government to divest itself of responsibility for urban inequality, while the final arrangement minimized links between physical development and social services and evaded provisions that would have confined use to poverty zones. For an overview of the legislation, see Fishman 1975.

9 Planners were actually often suspicious of community-led involvement. Thus, although planners believed it was important to spend time in local communities, they dismissed the opinions and motivations of community leaders in low-income communities as antidemocratic and dictatorial. For a discussion of the effect of this behavior on community-government relations, see French-Marcelin 2014.

10 Dwight Ott, "Community Act Program Is 'Nightmare,'" *Times-Picayune*, January 4, 1975, 5.

11 This is not to say that these neighborhood improvements did not matter, nor is it to say that they were not things that low-income people asked for. I am simply saying that the reorganization of aid around physical development made the exclusion of low-income residents from economic development much easier. Although it was true that resources were insufficient given the needs of low-income residents, the architecture of the grant made comprehensive projects politically undesirable to local officials. The ability to deploy community development activities citywide discouraged comprehensive approaches that would limit action to one or two neighborhoods or curb the opportunity for grants to be used as political patronage.

12 While economic conditions made tourism the central driver of the post-1960s New Orleans economy, civic boosters had been pushing tourism development in earnest since the early twentieth century (see Souther 2006; Stanonis 2006). For more on the 1970s tourism efforts, see Whelan, Young, and Lauria (1994); Mosher, Keim, and Franques (1995).

13 See Gotham and Greenberg 2014.

14 See Matteson Associates 1966.

15 "Report: Central Business District as a Community Improvement Area," 1974, box 108, folder Central Business District as a Community Improvement Area, Moon Landrieu Papers, Loyola University Libraries.

16 As a southern liberal, Landrieu promoted integration as essential to the potential for growth (which was indeed true, as tourism depended on inclusivity where tourists were concerned). While Landrieu frequently conflated integration and growth as part of the same project, his rhetoric regularly ignored that growth of this kind offered only a select few the opportunity and means to realize integration, political or economic. This omission was not unique but a result of the triumph of growth liberalism over leftist critiques that sought redistribution in wealth and access. See "Report: Manpower Needs Assessment," box 15, folder MP-MAPC-GEN, Office of Policy Planning and Analysis Collection, New Orleans Public Library.

17 "Ban on CBD Demolition Is Approved by Council," *Times-Picayune*, April 19, 1974, 1.

18 "Mayor Takes Press for a Ride," *Times-Picayune*, May 22, 1971, 8.

19 Canizaro, a young smooth-talking mogul from Biloxi, represented just one in a cadre of new real estate hopefuls that descended on the city to answer Landrieu's call for new growth. The municipal land, originally valued by the city's assessor at over $5 million, was reassessed at a value of $1.6 million prior to the Canizaro swap, a fact that more than one person found questionable. See "Planning Unit Gives Okay to Swap of Land," *Times-Picayune*, December 27, 1973, 1; "Canizaro Got Good Deal in Land Swap with City," *Times-Picayune*, August 10, 1979, 1; "Beer Asks Specific Data on Why Appraisal Dropped," *Times-Picayune*, January 11, 1974, 5.

20 Wallace, McHarg, Roberts, and Todd 1975. For a discussion of HOPE VI in New Orleans, see also Arena 2013.

21 The supermajority clause of the Louisiana legislature, requiring a two-thirds majority for any change in taxation legislation or millage increases, was the direct consequence of fear of black political power following the passage of the Voting Rights Act in 1966. The Louisiana State Legislature believed that it could limit progressive, integrationist legislation by making it more difficult for black politicians to gain access to a majority. In reality, the clause hindered all tax legislation that could have equalized values between city and suburb. Furthermore, the Louisiana legislature did not just reject the municipal income tax, but embedded a ban on such levies within the state's constitution. In line with nearly a century of punitive state action against progressive economic policy, the legislature's ban prevented any future city government from enacting progressive taxation.

22 "Report: Central Business District as a Community Improvement Area."

23 While the transition from model cities to central business district planning struck some as irresponsible, the improvement agency's leadership had, from the outset, been tied to the speculative real estate community. In spite of protests from antipoverty and civil rights leadership, five of the seven founding members of the agency's board of directors had ties to speculative business practices. As urban renewal activities mobilized new construction and building throughout the city, the improvement agency had developed a planning capacity and management resources to furnish downtown development.

24 Memo: Francis Keevers to the Chamber of Commerce, May 13, 1975, box 134, folder Community Improvement Agency, Moon Landrieu Papers, Loyola University Libraries.

25 For a detailed history of the use of the term "blight" within planning circles and policy measures, see Robick 2011. Robick argues that originally the concept was used almost

exclusively to describe environmentally unsound conditions and unmanaged growth. Yet, as federal renewal programs opened new opportunities to marshal resources toward specific political gain, blight took on a more ambiguous, open-ended meaning. Under renewal, the threat of blight became means to justify the razing of entire neighborhoods to make way for speculative development projects.

26 Notes: Preparation for Citizen Participation Meeting, 1974, box 1: CD-PRGR-74, Office of Policy Planning and Analysis Papers, New Orleans City Archives.

27 Notes: Preparation for Citizen Participation Meeting.

28 "Report: Community Improvement Agency Report on the Central Business District."

29 Memo: Warren Berault to City Hall, April 21, 1977, box 9, folder Core Area Development District, Moon Landrieu Papers, Loyola University Libraries.

30 Memo: Warren L. Berault to Anthony Gagliano, March 22, 1977, box 9, folder Core Area Development District: January–August 1977, Moon Landrieu Papers, Loyola University Libraries.

31 Memo: Joseph Canizaro to Moon Landrieu, April 21, 1977, box 9, folder Core Area Development District: January–August 1977, Moon Landrieu Papers, Loyola University Libraries.

32 This was met with extreme resistance. The Association of Community Organizations for Reform Now (ACORN) was at the forefront of challenging this misuse. Central to exposing the use of CDBGs to build neutral medians and pave streets in higher-income areas, the group challenged the utilization of block grant funding in the Central Business District. While the group's suit brought new attention to the issue, it did not reform the practice. See ACORN, press release, "ACORN Files HUD Protest against N.O. CD Misallocations," June 17, 1977, box 22: RF-7/06-ADP: Incoming Mail, Office of Policy Planning and Analysis Papers, City Archives of New Orleans, New Orleans Public Library.

33 In their study on the use of CDBGs in Southern cities, the Southern Regional Council found that communities had used the aid to build parking lots for downtown shopping centers and baseball diamonds in wealthy neighborhoods, pave streets around convention centers, and fund direct city council patronage. See Senate Committee on Banking, Housing and Urban Affairs, *On Oversight on the Administration of the Housing and Community Development Act of 1974*, 94th Cong., 2nd sess., August 22–24, 1976, 24.

34 Liebschutz 1983.

35 Nathan et al. 1977, 230.

36 Similarly, a 1974 HUD-issued report generated by the Real Estate Research Corporation provided a series of deployment strategies that local governing officials could use to make decisions about where to direct their resources. The inability to address urban poverty directly, the firm argued, was offset by allowing local officials to direct funding and redevelopment resources into areas of marginal, rather than complete, decline. Given the dire crisis facing cities and the federal urban policy climate—where, as the popular discourse of the day concluded, spending reductions were clearly only going to continue—the corporation contended that investing in neighborhoods with the potential to induce private investment capital was imperative. It was a strategy that was not only "*more necessary* than ever ... it [was] probably also *more easily possible* under the Community Development program" (Real Estate Research Corporation 1974, II-16).

37 Report: Policy Issue Paper, 1974, box 123, folder Policy Issue Paper Prepared for the

Meeting of the Community Development Steering Committee of the National League of Cities, Moon Landrieu Papers, Loyola University Libraries.

38 Jason Berry, "The 'Upgrading' of New Orleans," *The Nation*, September 23, 1978, 270.

39 An example of this comes from the successful efforts of the Dudley Street Neighborhood Initiative to compel Boston to build in stipulations of low-income inclusion in private development projects in the Roxbury area of the city.

40 Report: Clarence Barney, "Community Economic Development," box B21, folder Economic Development 1978, Ernest N. Morial Collection, New Orleans Public Library.

41 "150,000 Grant to New Orleans League," *Times-Picayune*, April 11, 1975, 19.

42 Memo: Frank Keevers to Clarence Barney, November 25, 1974, box 8, ED-HSQ-GEN: General Information on Heritage Square, Office of Policy Planning and Analysis Collection, City Archives of New Orleans, New Orleans Public Library.

43 For a longer history of the Central City project, called Heritage Square, see French-Marcelin (2014).

44 See US Government 1977.

45 In front of the Senate Committee on Banking, Housing and Urban Affairs, city planning units lobbied for increased flexibility to make community development funds available to private-sector investment. Members of the Connecticut Community Development Association recommended that rather than enhancing measures targeting low-income areas, community development could be restructured to create "increased incentive for participation of the private sector." By 1977, this trend was widespread. Local mayors resisted the congressional call for more oversight and suggestions that provisions be added to protect low-income residents from displacement by urban renewal activities (US Senate, Committee on Banking Housing and Urban Affairs 1976).

46 US Government 1977, 3; see also Liebschutz 1983.

47 Announcement from Office of Urban Development Director Joseph McNeely on new Housing and Urban Development legislation, June 1, 1978, in possession of the author.

48 Mark Reutter, "30 Cities Asking HUD Grants for Hotel Projects," *Sun*, March 20, 1978, A1.

49 Presidential Commission on Neighborhoods, quoted in "UDAG Helps Distressed Cities," *Times-Picayune*, April 21, 1979, 14.

50 A request by city officials in Portsmouth, Virginia, called for more than $2.9 million to aid developers in the construction of luxury waterfront condominiums and retail space; officials in Utica, New York, asked for funds to build a pedestrian plaza linking a new Sheraton hotel to a parking center. Though some congresspeople and many activists balked at the notion that this type of development could do anything to aid the plight of low-income people in cities, HUD officials continued to insist that it would. Where activists claimed that this program should be used to invest in an economy that could provide mobility, not make "poor people become maids for ritzy people," the response of HUD was that it was better than not having a job at all. Reutter, "30 Cities Asking HUD Grants."

51 This strategy of prevention guided much of how the UDAG and CDBG programs came to be used across the country. Increasingly, fear mongering by growth advocates positioned blight as something that was pathogen-like, that would spread given the opportunity. See Report: Community Improvement Agency, "UDAG Grand Hotel Goals and Objec-

tives," 1977, box J14: Urban Development Action Grants, Ernest N. Morial Files, New Orleans City Archives, New Orleans Public Library.

52 "'Megalink' CBD Plan Announced," *Times-Picayune*, April 7, 1979, 1; Report: City of New Orleans, "UDAG Briefing Sheet," 1982, box J14: Urban Development Action Grants, Ernest N. Morial Files, New Orleans City Archives, New Orleans Public Library; "Moon, Morial to Urge Saks to Locate in N.O.," *Times-Picayune*, January 18, 1978, 4.

53 Conference Proceedings, Urban Development Action Grants, Public-Private Partnerships for New Orleans' Development, September 12, 1980, box 43, folder 463, Alma Young Collection, Earl K. Long Library, University of New Orleans.

54 Robert Doherty, "Midtown Centers Rival Suburban Malls," *Times-Picayune*, May 23, 1983, section 4, 11.

55 First Annual Report on UDAG, box 42, folder 459, Alma Young Collection, Earl K. Long Library, University of New Orleans.

56 Brooks and Young 1993, 257.

57 Metzger 2001, 44.

58 Brooks and Young 1993, 264.

59 Hirsch 1983, 109.

60 Whelan 1989, 227.

61 Cook and Lauria 1995, 539.

62 Quoted in Adam Clymer and Tracie Rozhon, "Progress Mingles with Past: New Orleans, a Paradox City," *Baltimore Sun*, September 19, 1975, A1. See also Bobo 1975, 26.

63 "Project Assist: Action Strategies for Implementing Social Transition," Assist, box 171, folder 7, Urban League of Greater New Orleans, Amistad Research Center, Tulane University.

64 Whelan, Young, and Lauria 1994, 22.

65 Report: Ernest N. Morial, "Report to the City Council on Federal Budget Reduction Proposals, March 26, 1981," L5: Federal Budget Cuts, Ernest N. Morial Collection, New Orleans City Archives, New Orleans Public Library; Booklet: Ernest Morial, "New Orleans 2001," 1980, box 41:450, Alma Young Collection, Earl K. Long Library, University of New Orleans; Morial and Whelan 2000, 215.

66 Morial and Whelan 2000, 215.

67 Cindy Rodriguez, "Some Public Housing Tenants Say Possible Rent Hike Is 'Class Warfare,'" WNYC blog, June 25, 2012, http://www.wnyc.org/story/218331-blog-public-housing-tenants-facing-rent-hikes/.

68 Megan French-Marcelin, "Gentrification's Ground Zero," *Jacobin*, August 28, 2015, https://www.jacobinmag.com/2015/08/katrina-new-orleans-arne-duncan-charters/.

12

What's Left for New Orleans?

The People's Reconstruction and the Limits of Anarcho-Liberalism

CEDRIC G. JOHNSON

The City That Care Forgot is a nickname for New Orleans that originated in advertisements for the St. Charles Hotel as early as 1910 and was popularized in a 1938 tourist guide produced by the Federal Writers' Project of the Works Progress Administration. It was intended to capture the city's "liberal attitude towards human frailties," and "live and let live" sociability, but the sobriquet has taken on a new, paradoxical meaning in the aftermath of the 2005 Hurricane Katrina disaster.[1] New Orleans has since been flooded with volunteers, celebrities, so-called YURPs (young urban rebuilding professionals), school reformers, and new residents, all promising to deliver a better New Orleans. This postdisaster movement of people and capital has revitalized the city's tourism industry and created new cultural hybrids and a blossoming film industry, but simultaneously deepened standing social contradictions, ushered in rent intensification, and renewed the dispossession and exploitation of the city's working class. And herein lies a central paradox of the new New Orleans. The city is flush with care and concern, but now, ten-plus years and six master plans later, many of the social problems that the city's boosters and residents hoped to remedy in the immediate aftermath of the Katrina disaster have in fact worsened.

The city is smaller, slightly whiter, wealthier, but still majority black. There are fewer children, and about one out of four children in the metropolitan area lives in poverty.[2] And yet the post-Katrina portrait is still more complex. According to 2015 US Census Bureau estimates, there were 95,625 fewer blacks in New Orleans proper than before Katrina. Corporate media's annual reports on the state of the city over the decade since Katrina often told a tale of two cities, emphasizing the more roseate story of economic revitalization, the hopes and joys of returning residents and transplants, and the renewal of traditions, but at other times portraying the stagnancy and hardship of the city's laboring classes.

The poverty rate in Orleans Parish decreased from 28 percent in 1999 to 23 percent in 2015, but still surpasses the national rate of 15 percent. During the same period, poverty in adjacent Jefferson Parish increased from 14 percent to 16 percent, and child poverty grew from 20 percent to 27 percent. And while some homeowners have fared well since the disaster—the number of homeowners without a mortgage increased from 35 percent in 2000 to 43 percent in 2015 and is higher than the national average throughout the greater New Orleans area—the story for renters has been more desperate. The median gross rent in Orleans Parish increased from $710 in 2004 to $947 in 2015, bringing the previously low-rent and still low-waged city proper and wider metropolitan region in line with the national median. The annual celebrations of progress and recovery have been marred by a persistent crime problem. There were 175 homicides in the city in 2016, the highest total since 2012.[3] Included in that grim 2016 death toll were former Saints defensive end Will Smith, who was shot to death in a road rage incident, and Demontris Toliver, a twenty-five-year-old Baton Rouge–based tattoo artist who was killed on Bourbon Street during Bayou Classic weekend. We can find these dynamics of rising housing costs and increasing poverty, crime, and social precarity in every American city. New Orleans is not exceptional. Within this broader milieu, however, New Orleans may well be the most neoliberal city in the United States.

In the immediate wake of the disaster, when New Orleans commanded the attention of the nation and the world, many hoped a more just city would materialize. In an essay penned the week after Katrina made landfall, left-progressive intellectual Naomi Klein called for such a bold, democratic reconstruction. Sensing the various cabals sizing up the opportunities for recovery during those early weeks after the flood, Klein wrote, "New Orleans could be reconstructed by and for the very people most victimized by the flood. Schools and hospitals that were falling apart before could finally have adequate resources; the rebuilding could create thousands of local jobs and provide massive skills training in decent paying industries."[4] "Rather than handing over the reconstruction to the same corrupt elite that failed the city so spectacularly," Klein continued, "the effort could be led by groups like the Douglass Community Coalition. . . . For a people's reconstruction process to become a reality (and to keep more contracts from going to Halliburton), the evacuees must be at the center of all decision-making." The Douglass Community Coalition was organized before Katrina by parents, students, and teachers to fight poverty and transform Frederick Douglass Senior High School, but its organizers would ultimately lose their fight. The school was closed through a right-sizing plan initiated by the Recovery School District, one of many casualties in the tidal wave of postdisaster privatization that Klein and others anticipated.

In the decade since Katrina, a spate of new organizations such as Common Ground Collective (CGC), the People's Hurricane Relief Fund (PHRF), the People's Organizing Committee, and the New Orleans Survivor Council were created in the hopes of developing a progressive alternative to the rebuilding designs of the city's ruling class. Other existing organizations like C3/Hands Off Iberville waged battles to save the city's public housing stock from demolition and create a material basis for the right of return for displaced, working-poor New Orleanians. The kind of people's reconstruction that Klein and many others envisioned, one that would have placed the voices and interests of native, working-class residents at the center of decision making and guaranteed the right to housing, education, and health care, did not materialize. Instead, the reconstruction of New Orleans has been an elite-driven affair where volunteers, homeowners, and activists have been mobilized around the rescue and expansion of the city's tourism-entertainment complex, and where the advancement of real estate development interests and privatization of public schools, health care, and public housing have taken center stage.[5]

Why was the left so unsuccessful in crafting a powerful alternative to the agenda of the city's business elite? A partial answer to this question can be found in the balance of class forces in the city after Katrina, where the very constituencies who might have written a different story of recovery—public workers, unionized teachers, and public housing residents—were banished from New Orleans. The city's construction and service economy workforce was reconstituted in the wake of the disaster through a reserve army of nonunionized and at times undocumented migrant laborers, a pro-capital context produced by the Bush administration's deregulatory actions in the weeks after the disaster.[6] And although less has been written about the economic impact of volunteer labor, the thousands of students, church members, and activists who donated free labor to debris removal, home repair, and reconstruction added more downward pressure on construction industry wage floors, adversely affecting an already vulnerable, contingent labor force.[7]

As crucial as the imbalance of class forces was, another major factor in the failure of the Left in New Orleans is the prevalence of anarcho-liberalism. This political tendency is suffused with concern for the various problems intrinsic to capitalism, but it does not directly contest the demands that capital imposes on society and the environment, favoring instead the creation of bottom-up, voluntarist political alternatives. This neologism is gleaned from Bhaskar Sunkara, who provides us with an appropriate descriptor for a prominent strain of post-Seattle left politics and its political limitations.[8] As Sunkara notes, anarcho-liberals share "an anti-intellectualism that manifest[s] in a rejection of 'grand narratives' and structural critiques of capitalism, abhorrence for the traditional forms of left-wing organization, a localist impulse, and an individualistic tendency to conflate lifestyle choices with political action." Like much American thinking of the age, anarcho-liberalism is haunted by Cold War antipathy toward socialism and by considerable amnesia regarding the place of centralized planning in the evolution of the US economy and the creation of the middle class after World War II.

Anarcho-liberals embrace a critique of capitalism's excesses, but they reject state intervention and social democracy in a manner that converges with neoliberal ideology. This tendency is defined by an antiauthoritarian posture suspicious of formal leadership and the use of state power to achieve social justice ends, favoring instead spontaneity, horizontalism, and counterculture. Faith in public institutions and the possibility of transforming the body politic were casualties of the Katrina disaster with long-term implications for the city and the nation. Rather than placing demands on the state for social housing, worker protections, and other measures that might have improved the conditions of the most vulnerable New Orleans residents, anarcho-liberal emphasis on independent, private, and grassroots-led efforts fit well within the market-driven recovery advanced by Democrats and Republicans alike in the city.

The turn to anarcho-liberal politics is not unique to New Orleans, and residents in other cities and states share the same critical view of the liberal democratic process as being overrun by wealthy donors, party insiders, and lobbying organizations. The city's reputation as a den of political corruption and graft, and the monumental failure of state institutions to guarantee basic protections to the most vulnerable New Orleanians during Katrina and the highly uneven recovery that followed, however, all fed cynicism toward government's capacity to deliver, lending credence to anarcho-liberal claims that only residents themselves could rebuild neighborhoods and lives. For many in New Orleans and across the US, the Katrina crisis provided ample evidence that government was inadequate, if not antagonistic, toward human needs.

This essay takes up the question of what form of governance might be most appropriate to achieving social justice in New Orleans and, against both neoliberal and anarcho-liberal market logics, opts for the renewal of a left politics focused on building popular power and advancing working-class interests through redistributive state interventions. Because New Orleans is but one node within a broader landscape of real and imaginary places where anarcho-liberalism draws inspiration and opportunities for action, this essay travels from the fictional world created by filmmaker Benh Zeitlin to Occupy Wall Street (OWS) encampments, the worker-run factories of Argentina, evacuating farming villages in Cuba, and back again to the roiling social struggles in the Crescent City.

The first section examines the origins of anarcho-liberalism and its resurgence by way of antiglobalization struggles at the start of the twenty-first century and evolution through OWS demonstrations. Here I engage manifestations of anarcho-liberal politics within post-Katrina New Orleans, analyzing ideological expressions in the writings and political prescriptions of Rebecca Solnit. The second section examines how grassroots mobilization worked with, not against, the broader elite-driven processes of rebuilding in the city. In practice, celebrations of voluntary disaster relief communities and calls for bottom-up reconstruction are forms of self-help that shore up neoliberalization by diminishing the potential for collective power over public decision making.

To sketch an alternative to anarcho-liberal politics, one that begins with the local, urban capitalist class relations that shape daily life, the concluding section of this essay takes up the slogan of the right to the city, first authored by French Marxist Henri Lefebvre, but revived in recent years by activists and intellectuals, most notably David Harvey and Peter Marcuse. The right to the city is understood here not as an individual right to access the city's resources but rather as the collective power to shape the processes of urbanization and the right to determine how the surplus created socially through urban productive relations should be distributed. Unlike the anarchist sensibility, this perspective is guided by a more direct critique of the dynamics of urban capital accumulation, a process that affects us all as wage laborers and city dwellers. Moreover, the right to the city frame as developed by Harvey,

Marcuse, and others encourages a politics that is squarely addressed to questions of building effective solidarity and social power, questions that must be answered by those who hope to craft a more just alternative to neoliberal urbanism in New Orleans and beyond.

The Origins and Limits of Anarcho-liberalism

Benh Zeitlin's 2012 fantasy film *Beasts of the Southern Wild* was a runaway art-house hit, and in many ways it conveyed the prevailing anarcho-liberal sensibility that had taken root in post-Katrina New Orleans. *Beasts of the Southern Wild* was widely acclaimed during the summer of 2012. Its fans included President Barack Obama and Oprah Winfrey, and it garnered a slew of awards on the film festival circuit. Such praise was largely due to the precocious performance of six-year-old Quvenzhané Wallis in her lead role as Hushpuppy, which garnered an Oscar nomination. The film is set in a fictional rural community, the Bathtub, which sits beyond the levee walls of a nearby city, where marshlands give way to the sea.[9] Perhaps inadvertently, the Bathtub recalls words of the antitax crusader Grover Norquist, who said he hoped to shrink the size of government to the point where it might be "drowned in a bathtub."[10] And like Norquist, the film celebrates the virtues of rugged individualism while vilifying government as invasive and ineffectual.

Like the other children in the Bathtub, Hushpuppy is taught to be fiercely independent. She and her father, Wink (played by local New Orleans bakery owner Dwight Henry) live in separate houses made of reclaimed materials, makeshift structures that evoke the slum aesthetic one might encounter in the informal settlements of Lagos or the hillside favelas of Rio de Janeiro. Hushpuppy's independence becomes all the more important as multiple disasters unfold—a major hurricane sweeps across the Bathtub; her father contracts a mysterious illness; and massive boar-like creatures called aurochs are unleashed by melting polar ice caps. This film is visually intriguing, and the folkloric dimensions are at times alluring, albeit underdeveloped. The strong performances by unknown, mostly black local actors lend an air of authenticity and believability to *Beasts of the Southern Wild*. These cinematic virtues, however, conceal the film's more cynical, reactionary politics.

Like those elements of the OWS demonstrations that demanded greater democracy and economic justice for the 99 percent but rejected the necessity of sustained organizing around a principled agenda, *Beasts of the Southern Wild* combines leftist social criticism with an antistatist politics that is essentially conservative. The film embodies an anarcho-liberal politics that is progressive in celebrating autonomy and popular protests, but hardly anticapitalist in any traditional sense. Revolutionary transformation of society is not a central aspiration, and, in practice, the localized forms of autonomy and protest that are encouraged are nonthreatening and fit comfortably within the established liberal democratic order.

The film celebrates wild freedom, but democratic government at a greater scale other than the primitive village form is demonized. As the film unfolds, and as Wink and Hushpuppy fight to maintain their lives and sense of home, emergency workers come to their aid, but such assistance is vigorously refused. And even after Wink is told that his life-threatening condition requires emergency surgery, Hushpuppy helps him and other residents to escape the storm shelter and return to the Bathtub. Those elements of the state designed to ensure social welfare, such as the national guard, flood control systems, hospitals, and emergency shelters, which all serve as critical lifelines in real disasters, are all depicted in *Beasts of the Southern Wild* as impersonal and corrupt, the enemies of the wild freedom that the Bathtub's residents enjoy. Even the physical landscape of the nearby city is depicted as ominous—the levees protect the city but flood the Bathtub.

The film offers a soft critique of the perils of modernization and invites introspection on the kind of world we as citizens of an advanced capitalist society have created and its pernicious effects for people who inhabit places like the Bathtub. The development of massive industrial cities and extensive infrastructure around the use of fossil fuels has caused great ecological ruin, but after viewing the film, one walks away with the sense that the solution to our current crises is to return to preindustrial, quaint ways of living—we can simply turn back the clock, reject modern technologies like the Bathtub's denizens, and live off the land (or sea) in small, autonomous communities. The forms of self-activity and independence that are cheered by fans of *Beasts of the Southern Wild*, however, are inadequate to address the looming environmental and social crises of our times. The film's antistatist posture and fetishization of communalism and horizontality reflect prevailing modes of left political critique and action in the post-Katrina landscape.

The anarcho-liberal tendency that has achieved popularity in the United States today is, in practice, a departure from international traditions of anarcho-syndicalism, Italian workerism, and the French notion of *autogestión* (which is roughly translated as workers' control over production) that were embedded in working-class struggles. By contrast, anarcho-liberalism's intellectual roots in the US, particularly its rejection of socialist statecraft and celebration of self-actualization, can be traced back to the New Left counterculture of the 1960s, though its more immediate sources reside in the anticapitalist politics that first crystallized against corporate globalization during Bill Clinton's presidency and resurged during OWS. The end of the Cold War and collapse of the USSR had a powerful effect on left politics during the 1990s, producing strands of anticapitalism leery of the socialism that was attempted throughout much of the twentieth century—the seizure of state power and initiation of nationalization and planning to abolish private property and redistribute social wealth.

We can see evidence of this antistatism in the ways that many OWS activists appropriated aesthetic and rhetorical elements of the left popular struggles that developed in response to Argentina's 2001–2 economic crisis. As an industrialized nation with a large middle class when the crisis took hold and plunged half of its population into poverty, Argentina provides a more a direct parallel with the US economic crisis than other Latin American nations. The pursuit of factory occupations and autogestión in that country's urban centers, however, was supported by a tumult of social forces that included the *piquetero* movement of the unemployed, some unions, existing cooperatives, Peronists, anarchists, communists, and various other left political parties as well as a mix of genuinely sympathetic and opportunistic politicians.[11] After the Argentine crisis, the popular slogan "¡Ocupar, Resistir, Producir!" referred to the active process of occupying shuttered factories and firms, resisting eviction, and restarting economic activity through cooperative ownership—a long and complicated process that, at its height, created some two hundred such recovered firms in places like Buenos Aires, Córdoba, and Neuquén.

Within the US context, "occupation" came to mean encampments in public parks and plazas rather than the takeover of productive property. The popular assemblies in Argentina were most often rooted in actual neighborhoods and involved ongoing deliberation and organizing among various social layers. In contrast, the human microphones in Manhattan's Zuccotti Park, Oakland's Ogawa Plaza, and other public spaces across the country were momentary spectacles of democracy. Such acts may have been powerful experiences for their participants, providing a moment of solidarity and in-gathering. In retrospect, however, Occupy failed to engage middle-income and working-class citizens in a sustained manner beyond activist networks and the coastal urban centers. Moreover, the demonstrations did not advance a specific policy agenda that might have addressed the insecurity and suffering so widely felt amid the housing foreclosure crisis and economic recession.

The Occupy demonstrations helped to momentarily open up more space for public criticism of capitalism, but the expressed aversion to politics—such as, "No demand is greater than any other demand," "We are our demands," and other such slogans—could not be expected to generate much more.[12] The language of the 1 percent versus the 99 percent was a vivid characterization of wealth inequality, but it fell short of providing an analysis of class relations that might have guided protracted political work and produced real solidarity. Most importantly, unlike Argentina, where popular responses to the economic crisis developed complex orientations toward the role of the state, which is multifaceted and can be repressive, instrumental, and benevolent, the Occupy demonstrations reflected a less discerning sensibility. Occupiers hoped to achieve societal transformation through counterculture and parallel institutions, rather than through the more arduous process of social struggle aimed at creating real popular power and pushing state practices in a more progressive democratic direction. Rebecca Solnit's writings on Katrina and disaster more generally may constitute the most representative illustration of this anarcho-liberal tendency and its limitations.

In her 2009 book *A Paradise Born in Hell*, Solnit celebrates the prosocial behaviors and altruism that flourish during moments of natural disaster and social crisis. Solnit's account of postdisaster sociality provides a necessary antidote to corporate media framing of the Katrina disaster that too often resorted to narratives of black criminality and mass chaos—a perspective that appealed to right-wing antiurban and racist fears. In contrast to the wild rumors of murder and mayhem that circulated in the weeks and months after the city's levee system failed, local residents responded in large measure with an outpouring of benevolence, sharing foraged food, medicine, and other supplies, improvising rescue squads, and shuttling elderly, young, and infirm residents to safety in makeshift flotillas of refrigerators, punching bags, doors, salvaged boats, and often on the backs of the able-bodied.[13] Solnit celebrates these spontaneous mutual aid communities and more formal organizations like Catholic Charities and Habitat for Humanity that responded to pressing need in the wake of Katrina.

Foremost among these post-Katrina formations, for Solnit, was the Common Ground Collective (CGC). This organization was founded in early September 2005 at the kitchen table of Algiers resident and former Black Panther Party member Malik Rahim, along with his partner, Sharon Johnson, a former Black Panther; a member of the Angola 3 political prisoners, Robert King Wilkerson; and two white Texas activists, anarchist Scott Crow and Brandon Darby (who was later revealed to be an FBI informant). In his endorsement of Crow's 2011 book *Black Flags and Windmills*, anarchist and key intellectual figure of the OWS demonstrations David Graeber later described CGC as "one of the greatest triumphs of democratic self-organization in American history."[14] The group was drawn together by the immediate need to combat racist vigilantes and help disaster victims. Solnit sees the various projects created by CGC, their initial first aid station and later health clinic, food distribution center, tool lending station, and so on, as descended from the Black Panthers' programs for "survival pending revolution," which included free breakfast for schoolchildren, free groceries to poor residents, medical screening, and so on.

Solnit is right to highlight these aspects of disaster sociality. The connection she draws between these disaster communities and the creation of a "beloved community," a more just social order envisioned by Martin Luther King Jr., however, is ill conceived and seems to forget that King and the thousands of citizens and activists who took part in postwar civil rights mobilizations saw federal intervention as central to their struggle to defeat Jim Crow segregation. Like others, Solnit rejects the older notions of left revolutionary change predicated on the seizure of state power and instead embraces the view that society might be transformed incrementally through the creation of parallel communities and institutions.[15] Solnit offers what is by now a familiar account of what went wrong during the Katrina disaster: "The original catastrophe of Katrina . . . was the result of the abandonment of social ties and investments. Yet despite the dire consequences of this social withdrawal, the answer to Katrina on the part of New Orleans Mayor Ray Nagin and many others has been more abandonment and privatization."[16] Solnit writes that Nagin and the city's governing elites used the disaster to fire public school teachers, transform the city's school district through charterization, making schools "less accountable to parents and taxpayers," and demolish public housing stock.[17] From this account of government failure, however, Solnit follows other actors in the post-Katrina milieu who do not call for a renewed struggle to create more effective governing institutions and a more just social order, but instead turn toward various forms of self-help as solutions to contemporary social problems.

Solnit's analysis of these disaster communities conflates self-actualization of volunteers with the creation of community, and it ignores how public policy—health care, schools, public safety, and so on—is also an expression of community values, care, and basic respect for human dignity. In contrast to King's vision of the beloved community, which sought state recognition and universal protection extended to black citizens throughout the nation,

Solnit's notion of the beloved community is limited in scale and temporality. She valorizes spontaneous and short-lived communities, while expressing deep cynicism about state power and bureaucratic organization, the antithesis of popular self-governance in her thinking.

Solnit does not seem to appreciate how the volunteer legions she celebrates were at times complicit in advancing the pro-capital recovery and reconstruction process. Her account does not discern in any critical way between the political motives and consequences of volunteerism in the region and the nature and objectives of progressive left organizing:

> The volunteers are evidence that it doesn't take firsthand experience of a disaster to unleash altruism, mutual aid, and the ability to improvise a response. Many of them were part of the subcultures, whether conservative churches or counterculture communities, that exist as something of a latent disaster community. . . . Such community exists among people who gather as civil society and who believe that we are connected, that change is possible, and who hope for a better earth and act on their beliefs.[18]

Solnit does not consider how undemocratic and exclusive these ostensibly empowering gatherings are in fact. She mentions some of the racial tensions that erupted between volunteers and local residents, as well as the ideological conflicts between interlopers who were committed to abstract anarchist values and those more settled activists and natives who needed to think through practical solutions and longer-term strategies. Still, her analysis misses the underlying class contradictions of volunteerism as a means of disaster management. Although there are always exceptions, volunteers are typically those with enough leisure, finances, and mobility to travel to disaster zones.[19]

Solnit characterizes the altruism that surges after disasters in terms of carnival, a familiar trope of post-Seattle anticapitalism, "a hectic, short-lived, raucous version of utopia" when social conventions and routines of everyday life are disrupted.[20] The carnivalesque—for which New Orleans is a celebrated and potent signifier—is not always good, just, or egalitarian. New Orleans's carnival traditions, far from ideal forms of democracy and openness, are rooted in long histories of class power, social hierarchy, racism, and at times violence. Moreover, the antiblack pogroms and routine lynchings of the Jim Crow era were characterized by a carnivalesque atmosphere where throngs of whites often donned Sunday attire, imbibed in social drink and good cheer, posed for family photographs, sometimes in front of a smoldering corpse, and created other macabre souvenirs of the fete. Popular control and unfettered freedom are not always consonant with radical democracy. Making inroads against lynching and black subjugation, indeed, creating King's beloved community, required more than moral suasion; it required state interventions like the mobilization of the National Guard to escort black students as they integrated Southern schools and federal marshals to open the ballot box to black voters. A more nuanced view of history and power relations would be helpful here, but these are deep flaws of the anarcho-liberal tendency.

To her credit, Solnit offers a glimpse of what effective disaster preparation and recovery looks like—a system that brings to bear the resources of the state while mobilizing elements of civil society. Her reading of the Cuban model, however, is rather selective. Solnit reports that during one 2008 hurricane, Cubans evacuated 2,615,000 people, as well as pets and livestock, through a system that combines "disaster education, an early-warning system, good meteorological research, emergency communications that work, emergency plans and civil defense systems—the whole panoply of possibilities to ensure that people survive the hurricanes that regularly scour the island."[21] Under the island's civil defense system's decentralized structure, neighborhood and village-level leaders are responsible for going door to door to make sure that all residents are accounted for and able to reach safe haven in advance of a coming storm.

Solnit celebrates the role of local people in coordinating evacuation but seems to forget that this effort is completely coordinated by the state and party apparatus. She also downplays the fact that the Cuban system features state-funded rebuilding, whereby residents with damaged or destroyed homes are provided with building materials and architectural plans for reconstruction. Such blueprints include a windowless safe room, located in the interior of the floor plan and constructed of a concrete shell able to withstand hurricane-force winds. Unlike the spontaneous disaster communities she touts, which are limited in scale and impact, and often reproduce social inequality by virtue of their volunteer dimension, the Cuban model uses state power to redistribute social resources nationally and guarantee some modicum of universal protection to its citizenry.

A People's Reconstruction Revisited

In her 2007 book *The Shock Doctrine*, Naomi Klein describes the phenomenon of disaster capitalism, concluding that "it has much farther-reaching tentacles than the military industrial complex that Dwight Eisenhower warned against," and that the "ultimate goal for the corporations at the center of the complex is to bring the model of for-profit government, which advances so rapidly in extraordinary circumstances, into the ordinary and day-to-day functioning of the state—in effect, to privatize government." Klein's analysis of the spread of neoliberalization is powerful, countering dominant narratives of consensual progress by recalling the actual historical violence of capital and the role of coup d'état and proxy wars in the advance of neoliberalism. As others have noted, though, her work overemphasizes shock and coercion at the expense of softer, more democratic political strategies employed by neoliberal reformers.[22]

Klein is one of the most influential left intellectuals of her generation, and her accessible writings have done much to popularize left critique of capitalism. But her overemphasis on White House patronage streams and the machinations of disaster profiteering firms like Bechtel, Halliburton, Blackwater, and the Shaw Group hides how, unlike in the war zones of Afghanistan and Iraq, in US domestic politics the imposition of the neoliberal model has been achieved through more consensual means. Like Solnit, Klein misses how altruism, goodwill, and even social protests are mobilized in the process of neoliberalization.

In New Orleans, short-run cleanup entailed disaster capitalism of the sort that Klein describes, but the longer-run reconstruction process has been characterized by more benign and even benevolent actors—grassroots organizations, civic associations, and charitable groups like Phoenix of New Orleans, the Good News Camp, Catholic Charities, Habitat for Humanity, and many others. In her ethnographic examination of the privatized recovery in post-Katrina New Orleans, Vincanne Adams concludes that "the acts of witnessing and the affective surplus" produced during moments of catastrophe "have become themselves part of an economy in which affect circulates as a source of market opportunity for profit. . . . The affect economy we live within today makes use of affective responses to suffering in ways that fuel structural relations of inequality, providing armies of free labor to do the work of recovery while simultaneously producing opportunities for new corporate capitalization on disasters."[23] Faith-based institutions largely drove the recovery. Catholics alone contributed at least $7 million in post-disaster assistance to over 700,000 survivors. And of the top ten private charities investing in post-Katrina relief, six were faith-based.[24] As part of a planned oral history project, historian Christopher Manning reported that within the first five years after Katrina, such organizations mobilized over a million volunteers, drawn from church congregations, civic organizations, high schools, and universities.

These actors have helped to facilitate a process that I've described elsewhere as grassroots privatization, where neoliberalization is legitimated and advanced through empowerment and civic mobilization.[25] These processes constitute, in fact, a people's reconstruction of a sort, but clearly one that lacks the left-oppositional character that Klein and many others called for in the aftermath of the Katrina disaster. Instead of a recovery and reconstruction process intimately shaped by the needs and interests of the great majority of New Orleanians and Gulf Coastal residents, the remaking of the region has featured the public and affective labors of volunteers, nonprofits, and activist organizations in a process driven by propertied interests, multinational hoteliers, private contractors, and real estate developers. What is left is the reality that anarcho-liberal critiques of capitalism's excesses (e.g., sweatshop conditions, soil and water pollution, mass layoffs, poverty, etc.) and the attending calls for more democracy all provide legitimation to dynamics of accumulation, insofar as these lines of criticism and action avoid directly challenging investor class power and the state-juridical structures that secure property relations.

Unlike the dispensation of contracts to Bush campaign contributors during the first months after Katrina, grassroots privatization did not garner the same popular outrage, but it followed a similar logic of governmental outsourcing and the process of accumulation by dispossession, where formerly public services and goods—sanitation, debris removal, education, housing, public safety, and health care—were enclosed for profit making.[26] Such activity furthers the reach of neoliberalization by cultivating consensus, often in unlikely corners of society. Occupiers, alienated citizens, liberationist clergy, New Urbanist planners, liberal academics, students, antipoverty activists, black nationalists, progressive architects and designers, and social conservatives have all embraced the allure of these strategies, but these measures lack the basic fairness, oversight, and wider economic impact that a public works approach to disaster relief and reconstruction might afford.

Grassroots privatization depoliticizes the process of reconstruction in a few notable ways. Volunteerism provides participants with an opportunity to express compassion without the risks associated with social protests or the depth of commitment required in protracted organizing campaigns. Volunteerism may lead to activism in some cases, but this is less likely within a context where problems that might be addressed through state power are routinely defined as personal or moral issues that can and should be rectified through individual initiative or technical and religious solutions. In her 1998 book *Avoiding Politics*, Nina Eliasoph examined the disappearance of the public sphere, understood here not as mass media but as what happens between people, the ways citizens talk about issues and discover common concern. Her ethnographic work focused on a suburban community in the Pacific Northwest and on spending time with her subjects in different social contexts—activist meetings, social activities, and volunteer settings—paying close attention to the character of everyday talk. What she found was strenuous disengagement. Her findings are disturbing, and her discussion of what happens in voluntarist settings speaks to the post-Katrina context. Although the act of volunteering most often brought citizens face-to-face with various social problems, the context of volunteerism repressed public-spirited conversation. Eliasoph found that volunteers "tried to shrink their concerns into tasks that they could define as unpolitical, unconnected to the wider world. . . . Volunteers shared faith in this ideal of civic participation, but in practice, paradoxically, maintaining this hope and faith meant curtailing political discussion: members sounded less publically minded and less politically creative in groups than they sounded individually."[27] I would add that the actions of volunteers are not then apolitical, but in fact politically conservative inasmuch as they preserve prevailing social relations.

Rather than confronting the processes of exploitation and uneven development at the center of the reconstruction process, volunteer-led rebuilding efforts coexist rather peacefully alongside local norms and power dynamics, in a manner that might be likened to theater actors who move from one scene to another, executing their lines faithfully while ignoring the heavy lifting and prop changes undertaken by stagehands. One clear illustration of this contradiction between volunteer moralism and progressive political action can be found in the first year after the disaster, when thousands of volunteers began pouring into places like St. Bernard Parish to do the work of debris removal, mucking and gutting homes, and providing emotional support to devastated residents. Many volunteers went about this work without engaging or contesting the blood-relative ordinance passed in St. Bernard that forbade residents from renting to anyone who was not kin, a measure that openly discriminated against blacks and Latino migrant workers in the largely white parish.[28] This measure was ultimately ruled unconstitutional, but it succeeded nonetheless in discouraging resettlement in the parish and limiting the housing options available to both returning minority residents and newcomers. Of course, some volunteers are awakened to such injustices through their visits, but many are able to evade these local political realities, focusing instead on innocuous microlevel forms of help freed from the thorny choices and risks that must be made whenever we take sides in a political fight.

Although volunteers were typically praised in periodic news coverage commemorating the disaster and marking the city's progress, the presence of a seemingly bottomless reservoir of unwaged labor undoubtedly devalued migrant wage labor in qualitative and relative terms. Why would homeowners want to employ wage laborers if mercurial students and devout church members could complete the same work for free? Donated labor was both free and devoid of the relations that might trouble the conscience of homeowners and triumphal narratives of recovery. In turn, volunteer laborers relished the homeowners' expressions of gratitude and tales of pluck and resiliency. For both homeowner and volunteer, this relationship holds great, mutually affective rewards, more desirous than the often publicized conditions of hyperexploitation and vulnerability associated with Latino male construction labor.

The use of secular and faith-based nonprofits to facilitate rebuilding also carries little guarantee of constitutional equal protection, and, as noted above, these arrangements most often facilitate the reproduction of social inequalities. As Adams makes clear, "The idea that citizens should have a right to recovery assistance just because they are citizens (and have paid insurance or taxes for this sort of recovery help) becomes easily replaced by the notion that disaster recovery is not itself a civil right but a moral choice, or even a measure of one's commitment to one's faith."[29] Additionally, post-disaster reconstruction undertaken by private, charitable groups has often benefited those sectors of the population who are more articulate, educated, and socially integrated. This is true for volunteers but also, in the case of New Orleans, for those recipients of nonprofit aid who are better positioned and able to negotiate the labyrinth of application procedures and subcultures of relevant nonprofit organizations.

The use of volunteer labor also bore negative consequences for working-class renters, since most NGO- and church-oriented recovery targeted single-family homes, reinforcing the bias toward homeowners reflected in the state of Louisiana's Road Home program and other initiatives. More troublesome still, the political elite's commitment to public housing demolition, a process that was conceived during the late 1980s in the city and well underway by the time of the Katrina crisis, made it more difficult for some residents to return, greatly diminished the availability of affordable housing stock, and contributed to the skyrocketing rents that came to define the city by the time of the tenth anniversary.[30] The common antiracist framing of the disaster and the dynamics of reconstruction that defined both liberal media coverage and much academic work in the ensuing years has largely failed to account for this discrete, local class conflict between public housing residents and private real estate interests, precisely because this struggle is not reducible to institutional racism or essentialist assumptions about black-white conflict.

The reconsolidation of the city's elite and the construction of new means of legitimacy out of a historical moment when the class contradictions of the city were so dramatically and painfully exposed is one of the more fascinating dimensions of Katrina's reconstruction. Although journalists and academics made much of the open expressions of class contempt and racism offered by the likes of restaurant owner and real estate broker Finis Shellnut and Louisiana congressman Richard Baker in the immediate wake of the Katrina disaster, such comments have overshadowed the more subtle interplay of elite prerogatives, racial brokering, and participative strategies that have defined the character, priorities, and trajectory of recovery and reconstruction in New Orleans.[31]

This process of reconsolidation has been fraught with internal political division, personal rivalries, economic competition, and public scandal, but elite consensus has congealed around a renewed agenda of neoliberalization and a revitalized tourist-entertainment industry. What has emerged is a multiracial recovery-growth regime, a historical bloc that advances the real estate interests of those like Shellnut, Joseph Canizaro, Pres Kabacoff, the restaurant and hospitality industries, and various other institutions and players that constitute the city's tourism zones, along with the varied interests of the more affluent and more organized neighborhoods, with postdisaster newcomers often playing a critical role.

Black public figures like jazz trumpeters Wynton Marsalis, Irvin Mayfield, and Kermit Ruffins, famed restaurateur Leah Chase, public officials like Ray Nagin, former HANO board chair Donald Babers, and one-time recovery czar Edward J. Blakely, among others, have been crucial at various junctures in projecting the image of multiracial, inclusive recovery. Most of these figures publicly demanded a racially just rebuilding process, asserted the centrality of the black presence to the city's culinary and musical traditions, and defended the right of return for all residents in the abstract, adding a sense of internal dynamism and a veneer of democratic inclusion to the neoliberal project. This combination of liberal notions of racial justice and neoliberal politics has been missed in some analyses of the post-Katrina milieu that do not appreciate the historical origins and role of black political leadership in the city since the end of Jim Crow.

Popular and academic treatments of New Orleans since Katrina have typically relied on potted narratives of racial segregation that miss the city's unique and complex social history and neglected the ways that black political incorporation during the 1960s and '70s not only ushered in four decades of local black rule but transformed the local tourism industry in ways that diversified the city's touristic identity and expanded black commercial elites' share of local economic growth. The process of postsegregation black incorporation was shaped by the Great Society interventions of the community action agencies, antipoverty programs that actively recruited and cultivated black politicos, and the nationwide demand for black power emanating from civil rights struggles, which encouraged the pursuit of black ethnic politics.[32] Despite internal class contradictions, historical tensions between Catholic Creoles and Protestant blacks, competing elite factions, neighborhood turf battles, ideological differences, and political intrigue, local blacks consolidated power during the early 1970s under the liberal, pro-integration regime of Moon Landrieu, and ultimately gained control of City Hall with the election of Ernest "Dutch" Morial in 1977.

During the same period of black incorporation, the renaming and development of the Municipal Auditorium site into a park honoring the late jazz trumpeter Louis Armstrong marked the beginnings of the liberal integration of the city's public tourist identity. The development of the park was met with opposition, especially by whites who detested bestowing such an honor on one of the city's most famous expatriates.[33] In the decades since the debates over Armstrong Park, the Tremé neighborhood, black parading and brass band traditions, Mardi Gras Indian subculture, and voodoo have all become some of the most identifiable aspects of the city marketed and commodified for tourist consumption. Under the leadership of Morial and subsequent black governing regimes, the city also saw the expansion of tourist niches tailored to black consumers, events such as the 1980s-era Budweiser Superfest tour and other major concerts, the annual Bayou Classic collegiate football game, the Essence Music Festival, and national conventions of black professional and social organizations. The commonly heard post-Katrina assertion that New Orleans is the most African city in America would have made little sense to visitors during the immediate post–World War II years and would have been rejected by those in power, because that postsegregation identity is the result of a decades-long transformation of who governs the city and who participates in its place branding.

As in other cities, black political elites in New Orleans have fallen silent during debates over the privatization of public housing and public schools and often have openly supported revanchist policy.[34] These voices alone, however, did not confer legitimacy on the neoliberal recovery-growth regime, especially given the widespread discontent and suspicion that permeated the post-Katrina environment. Rather, the support of NGOs and even some progressive activist organizations has been crucial to securing broad public support for privatized reconstruction.

As sociologist and longtime public housing advocate John Arena has noted, even those organizations expressly committed to a grassroots-led reconstruction have often succumbed to the overarching dynamics of corporate-centered recovery and reconstruction. The PHRF's executive director, Kali Akuno, submitted a grant proposal to the Venezuelan government in hopes of securing funds for the creation of a community bank and land trust in the Lower Ninth Ward. Arena notes that this attempt at advancing a "people's capitalism" reflects the accommodation of left progressive forces to the neoliberal recovery model. "The request was not about how the Bolivarian Republic could assist local groups to pressure and confront the state in the midst of its neoliberal restricting agenda," Arena writes, "but rather how to build a nonprofit alternative."[35]

For Arena, and others like myself, the true test of progressive left politics within the context of post-Katrina New Orleans centered on protecting and expanding those aspects of public policy that would have established the material bases for the right to return for all residents. The fights to protect existing public sector jobs and create transitional employment for returning residents through public works, to reopen Charity Hospital and continue its long tradition of accessible health care and service to New Orleanians, to save Iberville and the remaining Big Four public housing complexes from demolition, and to preserve and improve the city's system of K–12 public neighborhood schools each constituted crucial battlefronts in the post-Katrina context.

Within this context where the beneficent use of state power has been greatly diminished, private and collectivist alternatives like worker cooperatives and community land trusts seem especially appealing for many. Worker control over selected firms or individual factories or local community ownership of select buildings is certainly an advance over conditions of exploitation. These can have the immediate effect of improving the living conditions for those workers and tenants fortunate enough to have access to these collectivist projects, and they can also have a demonstration impact in cities, pointing the way to different postcapitalist modes of living, where the power of capital is supplanted by that of associated producers and planning guided by use values rather than profit making. If these alternative projects are not connected to broader popular struggles aimed at contesting capitalist power in other spheres of activity, they are bound to function as modalities of neo-liberalism, yet another niche within an elaborate and dynamic process of accumulation. Within the US context, carving out such spaces of economic autonomy has most often been launched by those who have lost faith in traditional union organizing and the possibility of achieving social justice by directly contesting the power of capital through statecraft and policy.

Sadly, many of the most outspoken progressive left activists in national media and on the ground in the city demurred on these critical fronts. It is still amazing and deeply unsettling that no major national demonstration was staged in solidarity with Katrina evacuees, nor any national mobilization of resources and bodies to defend the last remaining public housing complexes from demolition. On one level, the dearth of popular attention and mobilization can be attributed to the hegemony of antiwelfare sentiments and the difficulty that American publics have in perceiving more impersonal, systemic motors of inequality, especially when compared to racist offense.

These battlefronts entailed issues that would have secured the right of return for many working-class residents, but effectively confronting these very issues of public policy required a more nuanced, dialectical view of the American political process than the antistatist approach taken by anarcho-liberals. Within recent times, the state within the US has come to function largely, but not exclusively, as an executive committee of neoliberal reform, but when a longer, more international-historical view is taken, we see moments when working-class social movements have forced the state to reflect the popular democratic will, and when concrete social good was achieved through social democratic and socialist regimes. Though not without limitations, the renewed discourse of the right to the city, with its emphasis on popular democratic control over the urbanization process, may provide an alternative to the anarcho-liberal impasse because of its capacity to bridge the local character of political life and a left politics focused on building popular power and achieving redistributive policy.

The Right to the City and Anticapitalist Struggles

French Marxist Henri Lefebvre first coined the "right to the city" slogan amid the May 1968 events in Paris, where thousands of students and workers initiated a wave of university and factory occupations, public demonstrations, and general strikes that momentarily contested the power of the French ruling class. In his 1968 pamphlet *Le Droit à la Ville*, Lefebvre describes the right to the city as "a cry and a demand" that "cannot be conceived as a simple visiting right or as a return to traditional cities. It can only be formulated as a transformed and renewed *right to urban life*."[36] This slogan has experienced a rebirth within the past decade. Antieviction organizations such as the Right to the City Alliance have looked to Lefebvre's writings for inspiration, and a number of critical urban theorists have made good use of Lefebvre's work in their analysis of the contemporary urban malaise. The slogan, however, has also been appropriated by centrist and bourgeois political forces who have excised its anticapitalist content, adopting the slogan as a banner for poverty-reduction and slum-upgrading projects that have been in circulation for some time.

The United Nations and the World Bank have both adopted Right to the City platform planks, but as David Harvey warned at the 2010 World Urban Forum in Rio de Janeiro, "the concept of the right to the city cannot work within the capitalist system," a point that did not go over well with the reform-minded audience.[37] Such reformist appropriations of the right to the city run the risk of assimilating demands for social justice to market logics, and run counter to the left-critical position offered by Lefebvre, Harvey, Marcuse, and others asserting the slogan.

At the heart of their arguments is a more radical demand that citizens should have a collective right to shape urbanization, a popular democratic power that contradicts the current state of affairs where capital determines working conditions, wages, health care access, education, infrastructure, land use, housing and real estate value, leisure, and the character of everyday life. I agree with Harvey and others who wish to maintain the anticapitalist intentions of Lefebvre's initial formulation and see the right to the city as a useful way of orienting a working-class-led, left politics in a highly urbanized US society. American cities have been especially vulnerable to the volatility of neoliberal world making since they were both critical nodes of capitalist growth and federal investment during the Fordist-Keynesian era and, as a consequence, have been severely impacted by welfare state rollback and austerity.[38] Hence, urban space constitutes both the central battleground for struggles against neoliberalization and the site where left popular forces are most concentrated and organized and stand the greatest prospect of political success. If the slogan "right to the city" is to mean anything, then it must mean the difficult practice of contesting the very powers that now dominate the urbanization process, and, in contrast to the anarcho-liberal tendency, it must also mean taking up the equally daunting task of building more just forms of governance.

Harvey's extrapolation of the right to the city is firmly rooted in Karl Marx's labor theory of value and, as such, emphasizes the contradictions stemming from extensive social cooperation within highly urbanized, capitalist productive relations. Lefebvre characterizes the city as an oeuvre—a work in progress.[39] The contradiction here rests in the fact of broad-based social labor responsible for the city's continual remaking. The process is at once collective, because as workers, visitors, consumers, and citizens, we all contribute in manifold ways to the constant remaking of the urban form, its technological and social complexity, and economic and cultural wealth. And yet, at the same time, a small minority of politicians, investors, and developers shapes that future in ways that reproduce their power and the conditions of social precarity and exploitation essential to furthering the process of accumulation. Although the right to the city is presented in the liberal language of rights, Lefebvre, Harvey, and others are really calling for working-class power, the right of the great majority to determine urban processes through popular control.

Unlike Solnit's beloved community, which is predicated on self-actualization through small groups, the right to the city as articulated here celebrates the vast potential for creativity and freedom that is afforded only through the social complexity of metropolitan life. As the architecture critic and urbanist Lewis Mumford once wrote, "Within the city the essence of each type of soil and labor and economic goal is concentrated: thus arise greater possibilities for interchange and for new combinations not given in the isolation of their original inhabitants."[40] In a similar vein, Harvey notes that the right to the city is not merely the individual liberty to access urban resources. Rather, it is a "right to change ourselves by changing the city," and it is by definition "a common rather than an individual right since this transformation inevitably depends upon the exercise of a collective power to reshape the processes of urbanization."[41] This "freedom to make and remake our cities and ourselves is," according to Harvey, "one of the most precious yet most neglected of our human rights."[42] This concept shifts focus from recognition and inclusion within the established capitalist growth coalitions that govern most contemporary cities toward the possibility of an egalitarian urbanity where the interests and passions of living labor determine the course of public life, the shape of the built environment, and how the wealth produced through extensive cooperation is distributed and consumed. Unlike the anarcho-liberal tendency, the socialist right to the city outlined here insists on a return to politics and struggles over the distribution of social wealth and the development of policy that will ensure a freer, happier mode of existence for the greatest number.

Popular left forces in New Orleans were weakened during the immediate years after Katrina with the mass layoffs of public employees and public school teachers and the mass evictions of public housing tenants. In the intervening years, however, new bases of opposition have taken shape; older forces have regrouped, and there are promising signs of struggle throughout the city. In the wake of public housing demolitions, activists and residents have waged fights against rent intensification and for affordable housing. Others have sought to defend the rights of workers through traditional labor organizing. UNITE HERE Local 2262 and the Teamsters local successfully unionized nine hundred workers at Harrah's Hotel and Casino in 2014, and UNITE HERE more recently succeeded in organizing the Hilton Riverside.[43] Advocacy organizations like Women with a Vision and the Sex Workers Outreach Project have worked to create better conditions for sex workers, who constitute a central but socially dishonored labor force in tourist economies globally. In 2011, Women with a Vision succeeded in ending the draconian practice of placing convicted sex workers on the sex offenders' registry, a policy that further stigmatized the working class, minority, queer, and trans escorts and performers and undermined their right to gainful employment and civic life.[44] These struggles and others being waged against noise ordinances, stress policing, and rent intensification constitute the bases for a more just New Orleans, one that reflects the needs and interests of the working-class residents who make the tourist city run day in and day out.

Marking the first anniversary of the Katrina disaster, New Orleans native and political scientist Adolph Reed Jr. warned, "Unless current patterns change, the struggle for New Orleans's future may be a more extreme, condensed version of the future of many, many more people as the bipartisan neoliberal consensus reduces government to a tool of corporations and the investor class alone."[45] How much have we learned from the Katrina disaster and the intervening financial crisis of 2008? Some lessons have been taken to heart but not nearly enough. Public officials displayed considerably more savvy and urgency in managing late 2012s Hurricane Sandy crisis, but the 2017 south Louisiana floods that devastated communities from the Florida parishes across the greater Baton Rouge area and on westward to Acadiana proved once again that state and national approaches to flood protection, rescue, and rebuilding are woefully inadequate. Likewise, while the tragedy of Katrina sparked serious public debate and urgent planning to restore coastal wetlands lost to industrial pipelines and shipping channels, the political influence of the energy sector, the automotive industry, and other interests have undermined progressive reform and regulation. The experience of New Orleans should have also forever washed away that leftist canard that worsening social conditions alone will deliver the death blow to capitalism, and not the more difficult task of building popular support for alternatives. As Klein has brilliantly detailed, moments of crisis and social disruption can provide opportunities for capital to extend its power and produce even more dire conditions for many citizens.

Solnit contends that what "begins as opposition coalesces again and again into social invention, a revolution of everyday life rather than a revolt against the system. Sometimes it leads to the kind of utopian community that withdraws from the larger society; sometimes, particularly in recent decades, it has generated small alternatives—cooperatives, organic farms, health care projects, festivals—that become integral parts of this society."[46] "One of the fundamental questions of revolution," she continues, "is whether a change at the level of institutions and systemic power is enough or whether the goal is to change hearts, minds and acts of everyday life."[47] This is not a helpful question. It poses a false opposition between institutionalized power and quotidian life that obscures the complex interdependency, social relations, and bonds of trust that constitute contemporary societies. Governing institutions and systemic power have tremendous bearing on the character of daily life, that is, the quality of the built environment, basic water utilities and other infrastructure, ecological integrity, traffic, biomedical technology and health care access, and individual mobility in the literal and economic sense. What kind of society will the small alternatives touted by Solnit and many others actually generate? A society that looks very similar to what we already inhabit where some classes enjoy relative freedom, material comfort, healthy environs, longer lives, and personal security while others are left to fend for themselves.

A close examination of the experience of New Orleans should challenge those who abide the anarcho-liberal sensibility. The city's rebirth demonstrates that the kind of people's reconstruction we have seen is not enough. Like so many other well-intentioned projects, without substantive power, a bottom-up reconstruction can be appropriated and deployed to pro-capitalist ends, reproducing inequality in its wake. And perhaps most importantly, the experience of New Orleans might still force us to develop a revitalized leftist perspective on statist planning, one that does not succumb to the missteps of the past but is capable of abolishing poverty and producing a more just society, where care and altruism are not only expressed voluntarily within daily life but reflected as well in democratic public institutions.

Sincerest thanks to Thomas J. Adams, Matt Sakakeeny, and Sue Mobley for inviting me to participate in the 2014 "New Orleans as Subject: Against Authenticity and Exceptionalism" conference. Thank you for your camaraderie and intellectual engagement. Your passion for New Orleans is contagious, and I know my work is better because of your keen insights and intimate knowledge of the city. I would also like to thank Amanda Lewis, Ivan Arenas, and the Institute for Research on Race and Public Policy (IRRPP) at the University of Illinois at Chicago for their generous financial support of this project.

1   Works Progress Administration 1938, 20.

2   Vicki Mack and Elaine Ortiz, "Who Lives in New Orleans and the Metro Now?," Data Center, July 9, 2018, http://www.datacenterresearch.org/data-resources/who-lives-in -new-orleans-now/.

3   Ken Daley, "New Orleans Ends 2016 with 175 Murders, Most Since 2012," NOLA.com, January 1, 2017, http://www.nola.com/crime/index.ssf/2017/01/new_orleans_finishes _2016_with.html.

4   Naomi Klein, "Let the People Rebuild New Orleans," *Nation*, September 8, 2005.

5   Mike Davis, "The Predators of New Orleans," *Le Monde Diplomatique*, October 2005; Gotham 2007a; C. Johnson 2011; V. Adams 2013.

6   Trujillo-Pagán 2011; Fussell 2009.

7   V. Adams 2013; C. Johnson 2015.

8   Bhaskar Sunkara, "The Anarcho-Liberal," *Dissent* 28 (September 2011), http://www .dissentmagazine.org/blog/the-anarcho-liberal.

9   The film was actually shot in the town of Montegut in southern Terrebonne Parish.

10 Grover Norquist interview, Mara Liasson, "Conservative Advocate," *Morning Edition*, NPR, May 25, 2001, http://www.npr.org/templates/story/story.php?storyId=1123439.

11 Monteagudo 2008; Vieta 2010; Sitrin 2006.

12 See Khatib, Killjoy, and McGuire 2012.

13 In one of the first histories of the disaster, Douglass Brinkley (2007, 372–81) makes reference to the Cajun Navy, those volunteers from the suburbs of New Orleans and the countryside of Acadiana who descended upon the city with pirogues and recreational motorboats in tow to rescue residents and offer emergency care and relief. Brinkley's account captures one dimension of grassroots disaster relief but neglects others, especially the work of black working-class residents. Their unsung heroism was captured brilliantly by Upper Ninth Ward resident Kim Rivers Roberts's handheld video footage of the flooding and used in the 2008 film *Trouble the Water* by Tia Lessin and Carl Deal. See also Ancelet, Gaudet, and Lindahl 2013.

14 Crow 2011.

15 Holloway 2002.

16 Solnit 2009b, 302.

17 Solnit 2009b, 302.

18 Solnit 2009b.

19 V. Adams 2013.

20 Solnit 2009b, 166–67.

21 Solnit 2009b, 265. Oxfam International, an antipoverty NGO, provided a thorough report on the Cuban civil defense system which detailed specific lessons that US policy
makers and citizens might glean from the Cuban model, a report that was published
and circulated incidentally the year before Katrina struck. Oxfam America, *Weathering
the Storm: Lessons in Risk Reduction from Cuba*, 2004, https://www.oxfamamerica.org
/static/oa3/files/OA-Cuba_Weathering_the_Storm-2004.pdf

22 See Arena 2012, 148; Doug Henwood, "Awe, Shocks," *Left Business Observer*, March
2008, 117; Alexander Cockburn, "On Naomi Klein's *The Shock Doctrine*," *Counterpunch*,
September 23, 2007; C. Johnson 2011, xxxii–xxxiii.

23 V. Adams 2013, 10.

24 The Salvation Army raised $336 million; Catholic Charities USA contributed $142.2
million; United Methodist Committee on Relief raised $69.6 million; while Inter-
national Aid (a Christian relief/mission organization) raised $50.5 million. Feed the
Children (an Oklahoma City–based Christian relief nonprofit) contributed $47.1 mil-
lion, and Habitat for Humanity (Baptist Crossroads) raised $82 million (see V. Adams
2013, 134).

25 C. Johnson 2011.

26 Harvey 2003, 137–82; Lipmann 2011.

27 Eliasoph 1998, 23; see also Eliasoph 2013.

28 Bill Quigley, "The Right of Return to New Orleans," *Counterpunch*, February 26, 2007,
https://www.counterpunch.org/2007/02/26/the-right-to-return-to-new-orleans/.

29 V. Adams 2013, 150.

30 Rochon and Associates 1988; Arena 2012.

31 Christopher Cooper, "Old-Line Families Plot the Future," *Wall Street Journal*, September 8, 2005, A1; Matthias Gebauer, "Will the Big Easy Become White, Rich and Republican?," *Der Spiegel*, September 20, 2005, http://www.spiegel.de/international/a-375496
.html.

32 Germany 2007.

33 Wealthy white businessman and local art patron Edward Benjamin called it "preposterous" to dedicate the Municipal Auditorium parcel in honor of Armstrong, adding that
"his best riffs were jungle sound as compared with many magnificent hours of sight and
sound over the two hundred year old history of music, opera, ballet, and theatre." For a
detailed discussion of the fight over Armstrong Park, see Crutcher 2010, 66–81.

34 See Arena 2011b; Reed 2016.

35 Arena 2011a, 172.

36 Lefebvre (1968) 1996, 158, emphasis in original.

37 "A Tale of Two Forums," Urban Social Forum, March 29, 2010, http://usf2010.wordpress
.com.

38 Peck, Theodore, and Brenner 2009.

39 Lefebvre (1968) 1996, 149.

40 Mumford 1970, 4.

41 Harvey 2008, 23.

42 Harvey 2008.

43 Robert McClendon, "Hospitality Union, Teamsters, Quietly Negotiating Contract

with Harrah's after Employees Unionize," *Times-Picayune*/NOLA.com, September 26, 2014, http://www.nola.com/business/index.ssf/2014/09/hospitality_union_teamsters _qu_1.html; Jennifer Larino, "Hilton Riverside Workers Picket: 'Without Us, the City Can't Move,'" *Times-Picayune*/NOLA.com, January 29, 2016, http://www.nola.com /politics/index.ssf/2016/01/workers_picket_hilton_riversid.html.

44 Jordan Flaherty, "Sex Offender Registration for Sex Workers Ends in Louisiana," *Huffington Post* (blog), August 29, 2011, http://www.huffingtonpost.com/jordan-flaherty /louisiana-prostitution-_b_887317.html; Dewey and St. Germain 2015.

45 Adolph Reed Jr., "Undone by Neoliberalism," *Nation*, September 18, 2006.

46 Solnit 2009b, 285–86.

47 Solnit 2009b, 286.

13

Neoliberal Futures

Post-Katrina New Orleans, Volunteers, and the Ongoing Allure of Exceptionalism

VINCANNE ADAMS

Volunteering and civic engagement are the cornerstone of a strong nation.... Our report found that 62.8 million adults (25.3 percent) volunteered through an organization in 2014. Altogether, Americans volunteered nearly 7.9 billion hours last year. The estimated value of this volunteer service is nearly $184 billion, based on the Independent Sector's estimate of the average value of a volunteer hour.

—Corporation for National and Community Service,
"Volunteering in America"

In one of her many inspiring books, *Cities on a Hill*, published in 1981, Frances Fitzgerald reminds us that one of the original American narratives of exceptionalism was articulated around the possibility of experiencing a communitarian authenticity. The Puritans, she writes, following John Winthrop, envisioned themselves as forming a "city on a hill"—a community wherein "large numbers of people decided to forget their past and start all over again."[1] This theme of rebirth was repeated by Rebecca Solnit in relation to communities rebuilding postdisaster. Community in both cases was aspirational, egalitarian, experientially present, built on authentic relationships, but most importantly, it was formed in response to social upheavals that called upon members to "restitch [or, in the case of the Pilgrims, to create] the fabric of American life" for themselves.[2]

In these accounts, the ideals of communitarianism, egalitarianism, presentism, and authenticity are built into a distinctive American mythos of exceptional achievement. This is a story many Americans like to tell about themselves. The ethos here is built from a collection of emotional sentiments that knit aspiration to social opportunity with moral certainty. It forms what I call an affective sublime. With these sentiments in mind, it should thus be unremarkable that, today, exceptionalism and neoliberalism are happy bedfellows.[3] Nowhere is this connection more visible than in post-Katrina New Orleans, where the allure of and aspiration to communitarianism, egalitarianism, and authenticity was enabled in and through the nonprofit and NGO charity sector as the city began to rebuild with volunteer labor.[4] In this chapter, I explore how the ethos of exceptionalism and its associated affective sublime work in ways that simultaneously critique and empower neoliberal agendas.

Exceptionalism in the Successful Rebuilding of New Orleans

The notion that New Orleans successfully recovered from Hurricane Katrina and its subsequent flooding is built on several competing narratives. Some see a city that pulled itself up by its own bootstraps through hard work, perseverance, community spirit, and volunteer labor.[5] Others point to the radically altered racial, class, and environmental demography of the city, arguing that recovery success was neither fair nor complete. In many ways, both bootstrap recovery and the displacements provoked by incomplete recovery could be seen as outcomes of neoliberal political and economic policies that utilize notions of exceptionalism. For sure, neoliberal reforms were set in motion long before the storm, but the storm augmented the visibility of their inherent failures.[6] What is interesting is how both versions of recovery in New Orleans share an underlying commitment to iterations of exceptionalism that serve neoliberal policies, for better and for worse.

In one account, exceptionalism is found in the communitarian processes of recovery. A corrective to victim blaming that arose in the aftermath of storm, floods, and delayed rebuilding, this narrative suggests that because of its history of community organizing, its particular race, class, and ethnic composition, and its long history of exclusion within the US socio-polity, New Orleans's experience and recovery were exceptional within the US.[7] This is a desirable exceptionalism, and one that recalls the grand narrative of American exceptionalism more generally, like that described by Fitzgerald and Solnit. By being exceptional, New Orleans was able to eventually rebuild from the ground up on its own—offering evidence of a society that came together and rebuilt its community through egalitarian-tending, authentic, shared, and presentist iterations of an affective sublime.

Exceptionalism here reproduces neoliberal thinking by legitimizing the idea that recovery and rebuilding in New Orleans occurred by way of the exceptional and entrepreneurial spirit of the people who lived there. They succeeded against all odds (much as the Pilgrims might have) by bonding together and raising their city from the mud, in this case with help from outsiders who joined in the spirit of volunteer giving. To foreshadow my analysis, this narrative of exceptionalism dances in step with neoliberal views of how disaster recovery should work in a highly functioning twenty-first-century neoliberal political economy. In this economy, the safety net is largely orchestrated through the nonprofit, volunteer charity sector.

In the account of failed recovery, in contrast, exceptionalism works in a slightly different way in relation to neoliberalism. Affirming our deepest suspicions about neoliberal social policies in times of disaster, a normalized logic of worthiness versus unworthiness was used to deny state and federal recovery assistance to large categories of residents. Lack of access to wealth, property, and market participation became huge obstacles to recovery for many because recovery resources were left in the hands of mostly for-profit institutions (from the for-profit subcontractors of the Road Home Program to the insurance companies and the Small Business Administration loan programs).[8] These for-profit contractors used logics of exclusion in relation to market worthiness (and race) to deny large swaths of the New Orleans public a chance to return, rebuild, or recover, a story I have documented elsewhere.[9]

In this view, neoliberal policies build in a recurring exceptionalism as normative to economic success; those who fall outside the safety net are exceptional (not structural). In postdisaster times in the US today, the catchment for exceptionalism is drawn large as safety-net institutions become increasingly privatized and subcontracted to market-driven, for-profit corporations. Exceptionalism here also has an ethos filled with affective sentiments that are articulated around notions of fiscal worthiness versus moral hazard. In this account, New Orleans is not exceptional but exemplary of a larger US political economic predicament, but the predicament of failed recovery arises, in fact, because of neoliberalism's built-in reliance on the logic and affective ethos of exceptionalism.

One could talk, again, about how these two forms of exceptionalism and their affective appeals operate in tandem. The exceptionalism that denies large sectors of the public access to safety-net resources, in the case of

New Orleans, left a lot of people without the funds they needed to rebuild. Hence, the rise of a volunteer-charity-NGO economy can be read as an opportunity arising in response to neoliberalism's inherently exceptionalist architecture.

In sum, exceptionalism can cut both ways as a celebratory achievement of the American spirit and as a cause of second-order catastrophes built into the mechanics of neoliberal social policies in times of great need. To be sure, exceptionalism has worked in varied ways as a kind of lever in the process of New Orleans's recovery. And, as narrative, ethos, and affect, exceptionalism can be used in arguments for and against neoliberal policies. In part because of its multiplicities, it is sometimes hard to locate a critical political position in regard to exceptionalism at all. This murkiness and doubling is my point of departure.

To jump into the treacherous dead-end politics of exceptionalism in post-Katrina New Orleans prompts me to explore two things: first, how the exceptionalism that informs charity and volunteer activities has become a driver of the neoliberal economy, and second, how, because of its aspirational appeal to an affective sublime, exceptionalism has also become a stumbling block for an engaged politics of resistance to neoliberal policies.

The Growth of the Philanthropy-Charity Economy

Many have written carefully about the shift to privatized, nonprofit, community-based social welfare infrastructures in New Orleans as a subset of larger trends across the US.[10] The longer history of charitable choices in the US, particularly in and through religious groups, has created social safety nets of mixed effectiveness for many decades.[11] As social service safety nets that had been in place since Roosevelt's New Deal became retooled in ways that limited support in the 1980s,[12] so too did the charity sector grow in response.[13]

Today the trends toward not just charitable choices but also a wide range of nonprofit volunteer-based institutions, grassroots social movements, and partnerships between public and private safety-net resources reflect a larger dismantling and/or restructuring of public sector infrastructures for taking care of long-term social problems, including recovery from disasters. To restate what Michael Watts identified for the global development aid economy, we witness in these trends a tendency toward "the privatization of everything," including government itself.[14] Charitable choices are not just allowed by government; the government has used charity to privatize the safety net.

The history here is in some ways brief. The growth and flourishing of the charitable choices agenda that began in the 1980s was augmented with George Bush Sr.'s call in 1989 for a "thousand points of light" of charity to rise up and take care of the needy in America. This policy shift grew a very large and powerful set of public-private institutions that today still aim to grow charity labor as a public good.[15] These policies provided a scaffolding for the blurring of secular/faith as well as public/private efforts. To stimulate the national engines of volunteering and other service as part of this (and far beyond the reach of churches), in 1990 Bush Sr. converted the federal government's National Volunteer Center (begun in 1970) into the Points of Light Foundation, set up as a nonprofit foundation that received federal and private funding. By 2007, the Points of Light Foundation (by then called the Points of Light Institute) had merged with HandsOn Network (which had been started by citizens in Atlanta in 1989 to connect volunteers with nonprofits).

Today, Points of Light is the largest organization of its kind in America (now called simply Points of Light, with HandsOn continuing as a subsidiary organization), but it serves as a model for neoliberal forms of provisioning the safety net through privatized appendages of the government. It alone boasts mobilizing 30 million hours of voluntary service valued at $635 million and pledges of skill-based voluntary services worth $1.9 billion.[16] Through these organizations, volunteers and unskilled youth are sent to fill even the most egregious gaps in our public education, national health care, and social services institutions.

These neoliberal models for ensuring the social compact cut across political parties. Public-private partnerships for the safety net were early on supported by the formation (under President Bill Clinton) of the Corporation for National and Community Service (CNCS). Note that CNCS is called a corporation within the federal government that funds a wide range of nonprofit, volunteer-based service efforts, including deployments for postdisaster recovery but also for very large programs such as AmeriCorps, Senior Corps, Social Innovation Fund, Teach for America, and even organizations such as Big Brothers and Big Sisters, and the Boy Scouts of America. The public-private-ness of these partnerships is found in their being sustained by federal funding as well as private (corporate and individual) contributions, and by the fact that they support programs that are themselves both public and private, including many private charities but also the Points of Light/HandsOn Network that, again, was also set up as a semiprivatized government corporation. Large for-profit corporations (under the allure of philanthrocapitalism) are also getting involved in the building of this na-tional infrastructure in multiple ways, pointing to the ironic fact that charity NGOs are now a growing sector of the for-profit economy.[17]

Celebrated by neoliberals and true liberals alike, these charity infrastruc-tures promote more and more private sector involvement in, and funding for, dealing with public sector problems. For this reason, they are often seen by many as a win-win scenario.[18] However, the aspirations in these institu-tions (particularly in faith-based institutions) are filled with other kinds of moral and ideological promises that sometimes sit comfortably with neolib-eral ideals and sometimes go against them.[19]

What interests me is how an affective ethos of exceptionalism works here, specifically in relation to volunteering postdisaster.[20] To this end, I see local organizations that grew from the ground up in response to Hurricane Katrina as end points of the trickle-down of federal policies that have been growing the charity sector of the economy for decades. As evidence that New Orleans's experience was typical of the larger trend in the US, and that both local and national sites of charity are increasingly connected by policy and in practice, the HandsOn Network held its annual conference in New Orleans in 2011, which we will hear more about below. My argument is that one of the key drivers of the charity infrastructure/assemblage is the affective allure that re-enlivens and derives from an iteration of American exceptionalism.

How then does exceptionalism emerge in and through forms of volunteer labor that produce sentiments of communitarian authenticity, egalitarian-ism, and presentism in ways that are problematic not because they fail but because they succeed? Whether or not these arrangements work to ame-liorate social (or safety net) problems is not my primary concern, as clearly there are both winners and losers on this front. Rather, my concern is with how the affective sublime aroused by the exceptionalism at work in these labors renders illegible, impossibly blurs, the distinction between social justice, equality, or other structural improvements on the one hand and, on the other, the feelings of authentic belonging and community that are aroused by this work and that justify ongoing arrangements of neoliberal deprivation.

Affective Labor in a Charity Economy

In New Orleans, volunteers were seen by many residents as the primary rea-son they were able to move forward toward recovery at all. Take the story of William Foster, a fifty-three-year-old single white man who was living in his

FEMA trailer on the front lawn of his home in Gentilly when I first met him in 2008. My research assistant from New Orleans had already met him once. She thought I should hear his story directly, and so we headed to his trailer.

His story was typical of many returning residents. His single-story shotgun-style house, which we could see a mere twenty feet from his trailer, was still completely unlivable. It had been gutted and stripped to studs that were still moldy. Whatever wiring remained in the walls was exposed, and there were a few remnants of bathroom fixtures, sinks, and countertops in rooms that had yet to be completely reamed out.

William was waiting to hear back from the Road Home Program about his request for help. Insurance had only paid for damage to his roof, a paltry $5,000. He figured he would need another $80,000 to $100,000 to rebuild, and even though he was frustrated by the long wait, he was hopeful that funding would come through from the state program, and he'd be back in his house by the end of the year. Sitting in his little trailer, with piles of correspondence nearly covering his available counter space and the ledges behind the built-in dining seat, he started to talk about how hard it was to deal with all the losses.

"It's crowded in here," he said. "Can you imagine having a family of four living in one of these?" I couldn't.

The tiny bathroom at one end, with a toilet wedged between a shower stall and a sink, was hardly big enough for one person. The bed filled up the other end of the trailer, so that there was virtually no real space to live in save a few feet near the front door. Sitting at the table that filled up the midsection of the trailer, I worried about how he would dig out of this predicament.

"Two years now," he said. "I'm going on two years now in this trailer."

William was quick to tell us that the only people who really helped him after Katrina were the "church folks, the volunteers." He said they had come through sometime around February 2007. It was a group of African American kids from a church in Florida. They were "big guys." They looked like a football team, he said.

"I was so relieved. They just came in and started to empty it out." Wearing masks and gloves, "they just dug in," he said. "They ripped it all down to the studs, those guys. I couldn't believe it. I was so grateful to them."

I asked if he remembered anything about the church they came from. He said no, he didn't recall anything particular about it. But they left a Bible for him. He wasn't particularly religious, but he told us he kept that Bible because it reminded him of those kids and their generosity.

"I keep it right near my bed," he said, "in eyesight when I wake up in the morning. It gives me hope."

A year later, we tried to visit William again. He canceled our visit when we first got in touch, telling us it was "one of those days"—the kind of day when he thought he might not be able to talk to us without crying. But then he changed his mind and let us come over. He was embarrassed, he said, to still be living like this, to have made no progress. Like many others still trying to rebuild in years three and four posthurricane, he was living day to day, wondering if he would make it. He had been denied money from the Road Home Program and was fairly sure that his appeals to reconsider his case would go nowhere based on what others in his neighborhood had experienced.

William talked about leaving New Orleans for good, selling the house (or what remained of it) and starting over somewhere else. We talked with him for about an hour and told him that there were folks working in other parts of the city who might be able to help.

After we left William, we contacted Caroline, the head of a grassroots rebuilding NGO. Her group had rebuilt her neighborhood almost entirely through support from volunteers, and that area was now looking like one of the early successes. They were now branching out to other neighborhoods. We asked if she could help William. She had volunteers, support, but, most importantly, she had the evidence that rebuilding was possible. She had helped others like him before, and many of those people were back in their homes now. William needed to hear this from someone. Caroline said she'd look into his situation.

Volunteers like those who came to help William were part of an informal collection of people who initially showed up on their own to help and later came by way of churches and larger (sometimes national) nongovernmental charity organizations. Many different kinds of nonprofit NGO charities were at work in New Orleans, and to be sure most of them early on operated entirely outside of the infrastructures of the large public-private organizations or corporations that had support from federal programs. Over time, grassroots efforts formalized into formal nonprofit institutions. Sometimes these organizations competed for funding from larger national entities or government programs, an irony given that they emerged in some sense in response to failures on the part of the large federal and state rebuilding programs.

The Road Home Program that had been set up by the state government to receive federal money to help fund rebuilding of private homes helped some people early on, for instance. Their responsiveness and effectiveness quickly dropped off within the first year, leaving huge gaps and creating huge delays in recovery—in some part, a consequence of their being subcontracted to large for-profit companies, like ICF International, who managed to promote shareholder value despite abysmal performance in helping homeowners to rebuild.[21] These failures generated a huge amount of affective sentiment, of betrayal, abandonment, and anger.

In contrast, and in response to both actions and feelings generated by these failures, the small grassroots and charity organizations came to the rescue, often with funding from the volunteers themselves, from churches, from individual donors, and eventually from larger national and federal organizations. More important than the resources they provided, these small organizations created a counter affect—an opportunity to heal and to feel cared for. Residents talked about how these organizations brought people in need together with people who could help. In making these connections, these NGOs created emotional experiences that were recalled later, by people like William, as the "only reason they survived."

William's sense of having been uplifted by the churchgoing football players from Florida, and his gratitude after he received volunteer help for rebuilding—help that enabled him to stay in New Orleans—was not very different from that of his neighbor Gerald, who told us how he was also helped by volunteers:

> I'd just come here every day and my jaw would hit the ground watching these people. That sidewall where the window is? It was blown out. Some guys from Wisconsin, professional contractors-carpenters, came in and rebuilt the wall. Every day I'd come here, I'd be in awe. And there was an article in one of the newspapers [about the volunteers who helped]. They were presenting me with the keys—that placard right up there [pointing to a framed set of keys]. What else? A loaf of bread, a Bible. And there was like 150 people out in front of my house. Man, I broke down like a baby. I went and hugged everybody. I'm getting a rush right now thinking about it. I just broke down. "What do I have to pay you all? I have no money." They said, "We don't want money. Pay it forward."[22]

The call to aid others who were in need circulated in and through the charity economy and asked people not only to give of their time and money but also to share in an experience of authentic community. For many, there was an assumption that the types of communities created by this need, and sustained by experiences of volunteering, would be endlessly capable of expansion, of giving until all needs were met, and impacting people in ways that even far exceeded their immediate needs.

Residents talked about receiving help in ways that were consistent with this expansive affective frame of reference. Volunteers described feeling as if they had become part of the New Orleans community, not just part of the volunteer community who came together (often at their own expense) to help. The volunteer experience generated in them an expanded sense of connectedness, of being made spiritually whole by the experience much the same way recipients talked about receiving volunteer assistance. Volunteering and receiving aid helped knit together groups of people who previously had no connection; it gave them a shared sense of moral integrity and moral certainty. Communities created in the wake of volunteering were imagined to cross over and destroy social boundaries that previously kept people apart: between regions of the US, races and ethnicities, religious affiliations, and social classes.[23]

Volunteering and charity work created communities that were imagined to be as far and wide as the nation itself, built from what was seen as a distinctive can-do American spirit that could, as Solnit described, rise from the ashes of ruin and become whole again. In this sense, one could see elements of the same kind of exceptionalism that Fitzgerald describes for the founding fathers and repeated in intentional communities across the US, where altruism, egalitarianism, and a kind of rebirth are all seen as not only possible but foundational to what makes for American greatness.

Receiving help was described as like having a spiritual experience, as efforts that helped restore residents' faith in humanity. Indeed, these experiences tapped into the kinds of affective sentiments that are promoted by faith-based charities more specifically that Bartkowski and Regis describe in relation to faith-based charity: "the special repository of resources cultivated within the faith communities—a robust sense of mission, high standards of moral integrity, close-knit relationships among co-religionists, holistic views of personhood and a connectedness to local communities in which religious adherents are situated."[24] Similar sentiments were generated among volunteers post-Katrina, but for whom the ethos of community was ecumenical or at least cross- or nondenominational, and very often secular and egalitarian.

The affect I am speaking of here attends to the emotional pull and sentimental reasoning that came from personal experience and that undergirded normative rationalizations for recovery action. The life-giving, life-affirming potency of volunteer work in New Orleans after Hurricane Katrina formed a basis for the affective sublime that was tied to feelings of being exceptional in multiple ways. Exceptionalism was forged in the experiential moments of being saved and of feeling like one belonged to a community that was larger than oneself, that was egalitarian, presentist, authentic, and expansive. Lives that were marked by neglect and abandonment were being saved by the exceptional things other people did, each reminding each other of familiar narratives Americans told themselves about being exceptional. These sentiments where shared by volunteers and those who received help from volunteers.

Exceptionalism was also fostered through a kind of spiritual awakening of one's connections to things larger than oneself. Volunteers talked about being uplifted to be more than they otherwise would be: the fellow in Seattle who gave $4,000 to rebuild Mr. Bradlieu's roof and felt closer to God because of this ("by doing God's work"); the yoga teacher from Chicago who came every year for a month and gutted, cleaned, and rebuilt homes in the Lower Ninth Ward and talked about her personal journey from depression to exultation in her newfound work, of having a renewed sense of "purpose in life"; the multitudes of young volunteers who came to New Orleans to help and then fell in love with the city and decided to make it their home, feeling that they had been welcomed as part of a city itself undergoing rebirth.

My point here is that the exceptionalism affirmed by charity was a cultural aspiration made real by way of the work that got done through both volunteering and receiving help, but also by way of the affective impulses that drove it. This iteration of exceptionalism was fed and fueled by larger sentiments of American exceptionalism, again, by the idea that this is what made America and Americans great.

Exceptionalism Blurs Neoliberal Problems

Exceptionalism here worked to actually accomplish much in the recovery process, from rebuilding homes and communities to rebuilding lives and senses of self-worth. At the same time, these sentiments of exceptionalism were also forged as oppositional to the failures of America, or specifically to the failure of public and privatized recovery institutions, and thus they fueled the idea that citizens were better off rebuilding on their own, pulling themselves up by their own bootstraps, so to speak.

Here, exceptionalism narratives that could be seen in post-Katrina New Orleans and their affective allure worked in tandem with neoliberal policies. Specifically, I would argue that they helped render illegible the connections between the disaster capitalism that produced failure on the one hand, and the support for (if not celebration of) the volunteer-based safety net on the other. The exceptionalism that was mobilized through the affective sublime of volunteering, that is, perhaps gets in the way of a recognition of volunteering's critical role in neoliberal formations.

The exceptionalism that bubbled up in and through acts of charity postdisaster in New Orleans was fueled by larger transformations occurring on a national level in neoliberal policy making over the safety net. The sentiments that fueled volunteer solutions in both places were and are, however, much the same. We see this in campaigns like that of Points of Light and HandsOn that called, and call, on Americans to rise up and take care of those in need through service work and charity. Again, these organizations are not just orchestrated by an ethos of charity; they are a tangible response to neoliberal agendas that continue to allow for-profit companies to get government subcontracts for recovery work but then leave the bulk of the work of recovery to the volunteers and residents themselves.

The grassroots and volunteer efforts of charity seen postdisaster in New Orleans are not in this sense exceptional at all. They are exemplary of the privatization of everything, including our postdisaster safety net. The exceptionalism narratives they arouse, however, help cement the blurring of lines between public and private, for-profit and charity, volunteer service and underpaid labor.

In New Orleans, what was marginal and invisible became, after Hurricane Katrina, not only visible but also applauded as an innovative solution to a set of intractable problems—using volunteers and charity to fill in the gaping holes of the government safety net. The celebrated intentions of grassroots recovery, in their own way, reinforce neoliberal efforts to keep these lines and their authorizing politics blurry. In a new twist, this blurring now fuels the growth of large for-profit corporations that are in the business of both supporting and using these grassroots efforts to grow an economy built on volunteerism, service, and charity. Narratives of exceptionalism are at the heart of this blurring, and the affective pull generated from the experience of volunteering and receiving its charity helps this sector of the economy to thrive. These narratives of exceptionalism are thus worth exploring in more detail as a new national commitment.

Volunteering in America

Getting people to respond to the call for action, to give their time, money, and skills to help others, is orchestrated by a nearly uncountable number of grassroots charitable organizations in the US. Over the last decades, this effort has also been supported by federal efforts. Again, exemplary among these are CNCS and Points of Light. These organizations make use of the same affective surpluses that arise from the experience of both those who are needy and those who give. As feelings of sadness and loss, but also hope and gratitude, are corralled into motivations for helping others and/or receiving aid, so too do the activities of volunteering (or giving) create a basis for authentic community, fueling the engines of a charity economy.

Muehlebach, writing about the growth of the volunteer sector in Italy, describes motivations for volunteering as being based on the idea that this work generates feelings of social connectedness and belonging that have all but disappeared in a post-Fordist society where waged work is no longer a means to this end. Popular advocates of volunteer or underpaid safety-net work in the US traffic in sentiments that are similar to these but also slightly different.[25] They suggest that America's greatness is built on the commitment to communitarianism exemplified in and through the kind of labor that is surplus to, if not beyond, economics. Again, the result is an imagined community that extends to the limits of the nation itself (or beyond). Volunteering, and the affect that motivates it, like philanthropic giving, are seen as not only consummately American but also as key to American greatness or, in a word, exceptional. These, it is imagined, will provide solutions to our deeply entrenched structural problems as well as our more temporary responses to those in need from disasters.

When Points of Light's subsidiary volunteer organization, HandsOn, selected New Orleans as the location of its annual conference in 2011, it first reached out to local grassroots organizations and asked selected leaders to come showcase their work at the highly publicized event. They were specifically asked to provide testimonials about the power of harnessing Americans' collective sense of charity. They referred to New Orleanians' collective experience as exemplary of the effectiveness and value of volunteer and charity work in the US more widely.

Organizations like these have continued to use testimonials as a means of arousing in others a willingness to give either labor or money to the charity sector. Note how the CNCS markets itself with testimonials that appeal to the patriotic version of the affective sublime: "Volunteering is a core American value. Americans who volunteer enrich our communities and keep our nation strong. . . . As citizens, there are so many ways we can make a difference for those who are in need. . . . Helping others who are in need and working together to strengthen our communities is an important American tradition that helps make our nation so resilient." Another says, "Volunteering is a critical component of civic life.... When people are involved in their communities through service, giving, political involvement, and other civic actions, our country is stronger and more prosperous.... But volunteering goes beyond helping other people; studies have shown that the volunteers themselves benefit, whether through increased job prospects, better health, or even better overall well-being."[26] The story told in and through these organizations about how service and volunteering make America exceptional is crafted in careful use of accounts like these. Many of them establish the links not only between American sensibilities of good citizenship and charity, but also between patriotism and volunteering. One young man named Johann who volunteered for Teach for America said, at a later national event at Gettysburg:

> I am so proud of the students I have helped and so happy with the great impact that I have had on my community. Feeling this much pride and happiness is something that no paycheck can replace; it is something I will have with me for the rest of my life. I also get to see Gettysburg a place that I have on my list of places to see before I can no longer see. I couldn't be more excited to be here making this testimonial. It is an honor and privilege. I hope that over time, more and more people will get to feel this pride and serve their country as a national service member.[27]

Volunteering in America is in these efforts presented as an opportunity to be patriotic and a good citizen, but also to experience authentically what all Americans are supposed to value: it is crafted as a response to, or as subversive of, the structural qualities of American life that constantly threaten to tear us apart. Volunteering will enable us to envision that we are part of one national community across our many divides; it will reweave the "fabric of American Democracy": "As the most civic minded and politically independent generation since the Greatest Generation, millennials have a tall task: It's up to us to repair politics. A shared commitment to national service is essential to reweaving the fabric of American democracy and ameliorating polarization."[28] Again, the recurring suggestion that these activities are capable of creating a better America by stitching us all back together into a single cloth is accompanied by the recurring suggestion that such activities are outside of the contemptible failures of today's political economy. Volunteering is not only a direct response to an economy that needs inexpensive labor; it will potentially replace the cash economy altogether. This is visible in comments like those of Gerald (above), who was told he could not pay his volunteers but he could pay it forward in generosity to others, or in the words of Johann (above) who says that no paycheck could replace the value of his service.

Volunteering is seen as in some sense oppositional to the system of regular employment, where transactions of money define the value of work. Johann's logic implies that the job of teaching should be determined not in relation to remuneration but spiritual or affective rewards, subtly implying that teachers who demand higher paychecks have misplaced or questionable values. These transactions of affect-propelled labor are seen as undoing the class hierarchy of America rather than exacerbating it. This is in part because of the actual work that gets done but also because of the affective bonds that are created by such (usually) unpaid labor.

The idea that volunteering provides an antidote to the problems of poverty, homelessness, and huge disparities in socioeconomic class in America emerges as a cornerstone of the affective-value edifice built around volunteering. Today, this upending of socioeconomic inequality through volunteering is mapped out in the same way that volunteering is seen as upending age-old battles between the public and private sector safety nets. In fact, the two potentialities are often woven together.

Of course, the notion that volunteer (and low-paid internship) labor like that promoted through AmeriCorps is outside of the market (or the political economy) belies the obvious fact that there are huge socioeconomic prerequisites and outcomes of this work. One has to be financially secure enough to take time off to volunteer (or have sponsors who will pay for your cost of volunteering). Volunteer labor in the long run displaces jobs that could be filled by skilled workers. Charities and for-profit companies earn huge sums of money (and pay their executives well) even though they pay nothing to (or vastly underpay) these workers (not to mention avoiding tax burdens associated with for-profit corporations). Finally, labor in the volunteer economy is largely unpaid, or vastly underpaid, creating large swaths of poverty frequently among the youngest ranks of the labor force. I have elsewhere called this assemblage a "poverty factory."[29]

Charities, NGOs, and the engines of volunteering in America now provide the low-cost labor for many of the sectors of our economy that have suffered from the distorting effects of privatization of the safety net. In fact, it is this sense of accomplishment that ends up ascribing monetary claims back onto the work of volunteering, as when CNCS reminds us that nearly 63 million Americans volunteered nearly 7.9 billion hours last year [and that the] estimated value of this volunteer service is nearly $184 billion," or when Points of Light also makes great publicity of the dollar value of their mobilized volunteer labor.[30] Here, the work that sets itself apart from the world of corporate and market profiteering is brought back into these neoliberal logics. Perhaps neoliberalism is itself redeemed here, made to seem as if absolved of its destructive potential in and through the work of volunteering.

The Affective Sublime and Neoliberal Social Problems

What I have argued in this chapter is that the specific affect of exceptionalism that circulates in and through a volunteer economy sutures us to the possibility of redemption through neoliberal policies. The promise of authentic communitarianism, a collective rejoicing in/celebration of shared exceptionalism, produces an affective sublime that has deep roots in America. This constellation of emotion and sentiment is the opposite of abjection and alienation. It is fulfillment on a grand scale. In the philosophical sense, it is transcendent.

This version of exceptionalism, however, serves the engines of neoliberalism by masking the real culprit in a neoliberal economy, concealing all kinds of exploitative economic things: more volunteer work, undermining tax-based revenues (from charities), and turning publicly run programs for social welfare into for-profit businesses, not to mention the profiting by government contractors who are given this work in disaster recovery situations. Turning over the work of ensuring a safety net to the charity private sector has an allure that is not just based on the economics of this architecture; its appeal is also found in the sense of community that things like volunteering and charity arouse. I would argue that it is precisely this affective experience that gets in the way of seeing the spoils of neoliberal policies.

Neoliberal regimes are, by design, drawn toward a breaking of the rules, toward finding the exceptions to the rules.[31] In postdisaster situations like post-Katrina New Orleans, neoliberal strategies of recovery create supposedly out-of-the-box (exceptional) problem solving. Charity in the form of public-private partnerships and their volunteer opportunities (not to mention the for-profit philanthropy partnerships) do just that. They break the rules to solve problems. We can see this repeated across the US today, not only after disasters but as normal responses to entrenched social problems. Social bond measures that create investment opportunities for private investor funds are used to mobilize the wealthy to invest in nonprofit organizations working on solving problems of poverty, the crisis in our prisons, teen pregnancy, and addiction.[32] One would not want to dismiss these tactics outright. Sometimes these strategies do solve problems. Their margin of efficacy is in part what makes them hard to critique, but so does their affective allure.

The affective sublime of exceptionalism pushes forward the notion that we Americans continue to not just find but to actually become exceptions to the rule. Thus it becomes even more challenging to gain a critical foothold on or about charity and volunteer work, to see how this labor draws us into its grasp, enabling us to form communities, into feeling good about this as a final solution to our ongoing problems of an inadequate safety net.

An interrogation of the links between exceptionalism and neoliberalism might start here then, with these affective authorizations. Delving into this place may enable us to see enactments of exceptionalism as both achievements in their own right and as successes that have effects far beyond those seen in a rebuilt home, a fledgling NGO, a charity that uses state resources to make private profits. We might see them, in other words, as authorizations of ongoing neoliberal failures.

I am not the first to suggest that affective sentiments divert us from dealing with the true sources of structural oppression.[33] I have tried to build on this perspective by calling attention to the ways in which volunteer activities augment and satisfy the search for authentic community as an aspiration that draws upon a particular version of American exceptionalism. We are, in and through volunteer charity work, drawn toward John Winthrop's vision of that city on a hill where "we delight in each other, seek to make others' condition our own, rejoice together, labor and suffer together, always having before our eyes our community as members of the same body."[34] But what we have not been mapping carefully is how these affective sentiments of exceptionalism find their way back into the structural arrangements of our neoliberal economy in ways that are problematic. Today these sentiments are sources of profit, as opportunities to grow new kinds of charity businesses, for better or worse, continue to be seen as the solution to our social inequalities.

Not only does volunteering form a large and very inexpensive labor pool that fills in gaps that form in the aftermath of disasters, it also displaces previous (and often more highly compensated) forms of labor and opportunity. It now also services an economy that makes profits on the business of charity. Ultimately, the allure of exceptionalism authorizes forms of charity that not only are predicated on but also contribute to the persistence of the very inequalities that charity is mobilized to address.

Notes

Epigraph: Corporation for National and Community Service, "Volunteering in America," June 2014, https://www.nationalservice.gov/impact-our-nation/research-and-reports/volunteering-in-america.

1 Cited in Solnit 2009b.

2 Solnit 2009b, 390.

3 Charles Murray (2013) suggests an American exceptionalism based on fundamental notions of freedom and innovation. Ong (2006) argues that neoliberalism enables capitalism to become global by creating and accommodating exceptions to their own rules. Ferguson (2006) notes that neoliberalism offers exceptional solutions to classic political economic problems (poverty, social justice, unemployment, etc.).

4 There is a long list of critiques pointing to the shortcomings of the partnership between neoliberal social policy and charity (see Cnaan et al. 2002; Bartkowski and Regis 2003; Wuthnow 2004; Hackworth 2012). The growth of what Cedric Johnson (2011, xvii–l) calls grassroots privatization can undermine both a conscientious politics of social justice and collective and institutional activisms (based on class, race, or other inequalities) that could challenge neoliberal formations. See also Arena (2012) on this point.

5 See Solnit 2009b; Flaherty 2010; V. Adams 2013; Ancelet, Gaudet, and Lindahl 2013.

6 See BondGraham 2011; C. Johnson 2011; Arena 2012.

7 New Orleanian exceptionalism is also sometimes incorporated into victim blaming, as when local corruption at state and city levels is blamed for the failures and delays of recovery. A number of scholars have suggested that the grassroots and social justice character of rebuilding was uniquely New Orleanian (see Flaherty 2010). Early on, Luft (2009) argued against this version of exceptionalism.

8 On obstacles to recovery, see C. Johnson 2011; V. Adams 2013. One could also explore how the logic of a state of emergency was invoked to justify these exclusions (Agamben 1998).

9 V. Adams 2013.

10 Cf. Luft 2009; Johnson 2011.

11 Bartkowski and Regis 2003; Hackworth 2012.

12 Dauber 2005.

13 Wolch 1990; Cnaan et al. 2002; Wuthnow 2004; Hackworth 2012.

14 Watts 1994.

15 Bartkowski and Regis 2003.

16 "End of Year Appeal," Points of Light, 2012, http://www.pointsoflight.org/sites/default/files/site-content/files/pol_endofyearappeal_5x8_webversion.pdf.

17 The creation and use of advisors and business models from successful private sector corporations is now commonplace as a method for titrating philanthropic giving to private charities. For-profit companies are increasingly tapped to provide fiscal and administrative support for running large philanthropic, charity, and service institutions. Those who run charities are taught by MBAs and CEOs how to use business principles to create fiscally sustainable institutions (e.g., Preston 2013). Not only do these executives get large compensation packages, they are also rewarded for successful capitalization

campaigns that seek to generate not just sustainable income but also financial profit from charity work.

18 See Bishop and Green (2010), and just about any of the articles in the *Chronicle of Philanthropy* by Caroline Preston (e.g., 2013).

19 Bartkowski and Regis (2003) note mixed results and associate this with Clinton's vow to "end welfare as we know it." Hackworth (2012), Kohl-Arenas (2015), and Wolch (1990) offer more useful insights on the political failures and dependencies of charity institutions.

20 For good work on NGOs in New Orleans, see Luft (2009) and Arena (2012). On the numbers that were faith based, see Sparks (2009); Carol J. De Vita and Fredrica D. Kramer, "The Role of Faith-Based and Community Organizations in Providing Relief and Recovery Services after Hurricanes Katrina and Rita," Urban Institute, January 22, 2009, http://www.urban.org/publications/1001244.html; and BondGraham (2011).

21 V. Adams 2013.

22 V. Adams 2013, 91–92.

23 In contrast, Bartkowski and Regis (2003) describe problems of fragmentation by denominational boundaries.

24 Bartkowski and Regis 2003, 5.

25 Muehlebach 2011.

26 First quote from Wendy Spencer, CEO of CNCS; second from Ilir Zherka, executive director of National Conference on Citizenship: "New Federal Report Finds 1 in 4 Americans Volunteer," *CNCS* (blog), December 16, 2013, http://www.nationalservice .gov/newsroom/press-releases/2013/new-federal-report-finds-1-4-americans-volunteer.

27 An AmeriCorps (Teach for America) member shares the impact of his service year on the children he has tutored—and his own life: Johann Shockency, "The Pride and Joy of Serving Others," *CNCS* (blog), June 20, 2014, http://nationalservice.tumblr.com/post /89362447712/the-pride-and-joy-of-serving-others.

28 Eric Zenisek and Mike Stinnett, "Why Millennials Should Ditch Corporate Jobs for Public Service," *Fortune*, June 16, 2014, http://fortune.com /2014/06/16/why -millennials-should-ditch-corporate-jobs-for-public-service/.

29 V. Adams 2015.

30 Cited in the epigraph for this chapter.

31 Ong 2006; Ferguson 2010.

32 In these arrangements, companies are asked to pay for nonprofit social interventions that have emerged in the absence of effective government programs. Under these arrangements, if the nonprofit succeeds in its mission, it generates profits that are then paid by the government to the hedge fund investors with a percentage profit.

33 C. Johnson (2011) provides an insightful and slightly different thorough description of how volunteer labor post-Katrina undermined collective action for social justice.

34 Winthrop, quoted in Joseph 1995, 19.

14

The Myth of Authenticity and Its Impact on Politics—in New Orleans and Beyond

ADOLPH REED JR.

As I reflected on the charge for this essay, I repeatedly returned to the question, "Why should we care about the prevalence of tropes of authenticity and exceptionalism in discussions of New Orleans anyway?"

From one angle, grappling with the exceptionalism question is really simple. Every place is exceptional, or can be, by definition. It is a matter of where one sets the analytical lens: the more closely one looks at the specificities of a given place or group or set of relations, the more exceptional it will appear; the more one looks for general properties, the less exceptional it will seem. In that sense there is a purposive dimension to the question of the appropriateness of exceptionalist premises: What does a focus on New Orleans's putatively exceptional characteristics throw into relief? What does it obscure? Most of all, what ends and which interests does such a focus serve?

The authenticity issue is somewhat dicier because it is a more expansive notion. As several of this book's chapters indicate, authenticity can refer to quite different sorts of claims—from the ultimately commodified, countertouristic touristic discourse propelled by pursuit of the genuinely genuine, definitive New Orleans experience to the competing notions of cultural authenticity propounded in heritage tourism and closely linked preservationist redevelopment ideology and programs on one side and anti-gentrification discourse, which asserts political authenticity through claims to aboriginal occupancy and community on the other.

A different discourse of authenticity, one that has its conceptual roots in self-realization psychology, nineteenth-century mind cure, and various strains of communitarianism, has played out in New Orleans in the aftermath of Katrina. Chapter 13, by Vincanne Adams, examines the ways in which volunteers in recovery efforts, in concert with those whom they helped, constructed at least simulacra (my qualification, not necessarily hers) of authentic ties of interpersonal affect or community. She notes astutely that these solidaristic relations, precisely because they are authentic or experienced as such, can provide an institutional legitimation of the neoliberal discourse and program of privatization. Cedric Johnson's formulation of grassroots privatization, although focused on a different node in NGO work—the local or neighborhood groups that function as agents of privatized social service activity—similarly draws attention to the deeper problem of the place of the ideology of authenticity in redefining progressive social action in line with the devaluation and erasure of the sphere of the public that is consonant with neoliberalism. As Johnson argues forcefully, that redefinition is equally represented in the antistatist, voluntarist politics he characterizes as "anarcho-liberalism," a political posture an earlier generation of leftists would have described as left in form, right in essence.

Then there is the ubiquitous discourse of racial/cultural authenticity that has become a key trope in local black politics, which as a political program reduces to jockeying for position in the interest-group dynamics of publicly mediated allocation of resources in the era of touristic ideology's hegemony. Thus appeals to the rich African/Creole/African American heritage, neighborhoods, and practices as vital contributions to New Orleans's distinctive culture have long since become pro forma in debates over who gets what, when, and how—as political scientist Harold Lasswell succinctly summarized the substance of politics in a time when its meaning and point had not yet been obscured by generations of academics' ideological mystification.[1]

As several of the chapters here note, national as well as local debates over post-Katrina recovery intensified the rhetoric of New Orleans's cultural exceptionalism and authenticity. Most people who paid attention at the time can recall the pattern of response to proposals that the city not be rebuilt, or at least not be rebuilt at all like it had been before August 29, 2005. National and international figures, as well as local ones, argued that New Orleans—not unlike a white Siberian tiger—was too special and distinct a place to let perish. For example, that was certainly the project that the abundantly well-intentioned David Simon sought to advance with the HBO series *Treme*.

In all those expressions, claims to the authentic constitute elements of a moral economy that hinges on a presumption that authenticity confers a sort of political standing. A problem, though, is that all such claims—unless they are claims to represent a specific constituency with names and addresses (or identification with locations that make them reachable) and demonstrated capacity to ratify or reject claims to speak on their specific behalf—are bogus. One plausibly can be, that is, an authentic representative of the Zulu Social Aid and Pleasure Club, the Knights of Peter Claver, Council District C, or International Brotherhood of Electrical Workers Local 130; one cannot have a paramount proprietary claim as an authentically aboriginal resident of Tremé or to represent the really, really, really genuine, authentic New Orleans, or a singular black community of New Orleans.

Moreover, as this argument may suggest, the problem with authenticity claims is not simply that they are mystifications, though they generally are. The deeper and greater problem is why they seem to have power to those who make or seek them. Authenticity claims stem from a mind-set and interpretation of the world that on examination is generally familiar but incompatible with, if not antithetical to, a left-egalitarian politics. Perhaps an allegory can elucidate that criticism.

When I was a kid, my father often gave me what were in effect little impromptu social theory tutorials. Sometimes he would deliver them when driving me to serve early morning weekday Mass; sometimes he would do it at Mulé's in the Seventh Ward, while he drank a goblet of draft beer and I ate a hot sausage sandwich and begged for quarters to play the jukebox. That reference to Mulé's is, of course, a nod to one strain of New Orleans nostalgia. It may even seem suspiciously like a cheap authenticity claim itself. The reason I mention it, though, is that one of those little tutorials centered on the great muckraker Lincoln Steffens's observation about the Garden of Eden story. Steffens reports having been asked by an Episcopalian bishop at a public meeting to identify the Edenic sources of the current system of inequality. He replied, "Most people, you know, say it was Adam. But Adam, you remember, he said that it was Eve, the woman; she did it. And Eve said, no, no, it wasn't she; it was the serpent. And that's where you clergy have stuck ever since. You blame the serpent, Satan. Now I come and I am trying to show you that it was, it is, the apple," by which he meant property.[2]

Steffens comes to mind because the more I have reflected on the problems created by the ideologies of authenticity and exceptionalism, especially the more I have thought about them with respect to their political significance in the contemporary United States in general and in New Orleans in particular, the clearer it has seemed to me that what is most problematic, if not pernicious, about these two related ideological discourses has to do with how they connect with reified ideas of culture. I want to argue that in the context of making sense of the political and ideological mischief that authenticity and exceptionalism support, culture is the equivalent of Steffens's apple.

We understand culture in two ways that ultimately conflict, and general failure to distinguish them creates confusion and, worse, is politically counterproductive, when not retrograde. Going back to Franz Boas's pre–World War I challenge to conventional notions of racial evolution, egalitarian discourse distinguished culture from nature—biology—as a more plastic framework for understanding apparent variation among human populations. Anthropologists increasingly have seen culture as fluid and pragmatic, sets of open-ended, syncretic practices and *mentalités* that do not yield sharp, uncrossable boundaries between populations. From that perspective, culture is dynamic and processual and spreads by diffusion. However, culture also has been understood as a distinctive characteristic, or a property, of peoples. That version of the culture idea reinscribes the essentialism that is the core of the race idea.

Taxonomically, the fundamental unit of classification in the one notion of culture is mentalités, ideas, and practices. One might be interested in establishing similarity or patterns of diffusion, for example, how one expression of monotheism relates either synchronically or diachronically to others or how lute and oud evolved. In this view, locating points of origination is an element of charting trajectories of diffusion and adaptation rather than establishing propietorship, which would be antithetical to this understanding of culture. Ontologically, this approach affirms the cultural unity and continuity of the species.

The other understanding of culture proceeds from taxonomies of people rather than mentalités and practices. The fundamental unit is the group; it classifies populations into groups defined by distinctive traits and characteristics. In identifying populations with specific practices or attitudes and dispositions, this view of culture is the one that underwrites notions of authenticity. Despite demurrals from many who embrace it, this notion of culture is equivalent to race, without, as Walter Benn Michaels put it, "the embarrassments of blood."[3] Culture in this view can signify durable, ambiguously essential differences that affect the social performance and characteristics of natural populations. In fact, such an understanding was always available in the culture idea, even when it was deployed as an explicit challenge to biological race theories. The great American historian of anthropology George Stocking Jr. notes, writing about the birth of the culture idea in the early race theory:

> "Culture," in its [Victorian] anthropological sense, provided a functionally equivalent substitute for the older idea of "race temperament." It explained all the same phenomena, but did so in strictly non-biological terms, and indeed its full efficacy as an explanatory concept depended on the rejection of the inheritance of acquired characters.... For "race" read "culture" or "civilization," for "racial heritage" read "cultural heritage," and the change had taken place. From implicitly Lamarckian "racial instincts" to an ambiguous "centuries of racial experience" to a purely cultural "centuries of tradition" was a fairly easy transition—especially when the notion of "racial instincts" had in fact been largely based on centuries of experience and tradition.[4]

In the groupist view, cultural practices live as essences within the primordial groups with which they are identified and to which the practices therefore are held to belong. Claims of origination carry a different ontological significance: in purporting to line up practices with the groups to which they really belong, they reinforce the folk tendency to divide our species into nonexistent subdivisions separated by distinctive, effectively innate characteristics. (Ironically, this particular folk common sense, like primordialism in general, is the naturalized residue of earlier race theory that has forgotten its conceptual foundations.) This groupist notion of culture is the context within which cultural authenticity seems plausible. Conceptually, Michaels argues, "although the move from racial identity to cultural identity appears to replace essentialist criteria of identity (who we are) with performative criteria (what we do), the commitment to pluralism [in my terms here, primordialist groupism] requires in fact that the question of who we are continue to be understood as prior to questions about what we do." That is, only if we see existing populations as given, essentially and irreducibly distinct groups, as natural populations, can culture become the definitive culture of the X, and only from such an essentialist understanding is it possible to assert what qualifies as authentically expressing the X's culture.

Michaels is concerned principally with examining the ideological work that pluralism performs in preserving the race idea under the rubric of culture. Pluralism, he argues, "invokes the identity of the group as the grounds for justification of the group's practices"; to that extent, "it is only for the pluralist that identity is absolutely crucial since only the pluralist, striving to see the different as neither better nor worse, must like it or dislike it on the basis of its difference alone." Thus, "it is precisely this pluralism that transforms the substitution of culture for race into the preservation of race" because pluralism reifies culture by fastening it to group identity.[5] And that reified understanding of culture undergirds notions of proprietorship and appropriation. He argues,

> in pluralism, our preference for our own practices can only be justified by the fact that they are ours; our desire to do the things our "community" does can only be justified by the fact that they are ours. . . . So the assertion of cultural identity depends upon an identity that cannot be cultural—we are not Jews because we do Jewish things, we do Jewish things because we are Jews. . . . Cultural pluralism is thus committed in principle to identity essentialism, which is to say that in cultural pluralism, culture does not constitute identity, it reflects or, more precisely, expresses it.[6]

Both groupist and practical notions of culture are modern inventions, as is the idea of authenticity itself, and Michaels points out that the pluralist, substantively racialist one emerged from the modernist intellectual project of the 1920s and 1930s. And to return to Steffens's indictment of the apple, the idea that cultural practices in some way belong to specific groups became common sense so easily because that intellectual project presumed bourgeois property relations and read them into nature. This undergirds characterization of cultural diffusion in terms that assume the logic of double-entry bookkeeping, both in the more sanguine form as "cultural borrowing" and in the more pejorative current phrase influenced by the history of (Western) imperialist and colonial looting of artifacts, "cultural appropriation." It is significant in this regard that the contemporary racial/cultural discourse of reparations for black Americans, also propelled by critique of cultural appropriation, is similarly premised on a notion of justice that naturalizes bourgeois property relations.[7]

Concerns about cultural appropriation resonate with a particular strain of the history and lore of racial hierarchy in the United States. As chattel, slaves were factors of production owned by their masters; owning a slave meant owning her labor power and product, by definition. Eliding that fact is one of the hazards of representing American slavery as having been about, in historian Barbara Fields's pithy observation, the production of white supremacy rather than cotton, sugarcane, and rice. For example, the standard moral of the venerable lore that the cotton gin was invented by one of Eli Whitney's slaves rather than Whitney himself, who held the patent for it, is to note that recognition of black inventiveness has been suppressed, not to comment on the nature of chattel slavery as a system of property. Through the Jim Crow era blacks commonly did not receive public recognition or reward for accomplishments outside of certain stereotyped endeavors, and whites were likely to receive acclaim and to reap material benefits for innovations that blacks had pioneered.

A mass culture industry emerged as a national phenomenon in the twentieth century within a context of presumptive racial inequality, and, unsurprisingly, blacks were marginalized as performers, functionaries, and profit takers within it. The music industry is an area well-known for particularly egregious illustrations of whites' adoption and marketization of blacks' artistic production without adequate recognition or compensation, from the boosting of white musicians as avatars of early jazz in the 1920s to the many tragic stories of black artists in postwar rock 'n' roll and R&B who unwittingly signed away rights to royalties or who found record companies and radio stations promoting ultimately more lucrative covers of their original material by white artists. (And, yes, in the rock 'n' roll era especially, the practice of generating covers by white artists was bound up with sexualized fears of possible white moral degeneration at a moment when political and social pressures on racial segregation were mounting. Covers were likely to be watered down and sanitized; however, while that fact gives an aesthetic edge to the critique of appropriation, it is not the main objection.) That history is no doubt especially vivid in New Orleans, given the city's pride of place in originating jazz and its prominence in the postwar race music scene.[8]

The country's history of racial subordination makes it seem reasonable to interpret recurring marginalization and mistreatment as stemming from a persisting inclination, even ontological commitment, among whites to denigrate black people or negate their humanity. But if we consider that "black" in the United States has been a shorthand for poor, vulnerable, and relatively powerless and therefore indicative of availability for victimization, then a more mundane perspective on expropriation in the culture industry may be nearer the mark. From that perspective, the injustice is not that the products of black culture are appropriated out of some elaborate psychologistic combination of "love and theft" but that the labor of vulnerable producers is exploited intensely.[9] If anything, the discourse of cultural appropriation, like the more general tendency to shoehorn inequality into a language of racial disparity, sacrifices concrete grievances on the altar of declaiming on the depth, persistence, and pervasiveness of a generic racism.[10] A racialized notion of culture, that is, obscures the workings of political economy.

For example, blacks are hardly the only workers badly exploited in the culture industry. Recognizing that its exploitative structures are not reducible simply to racism might help broaden the base of support for popular challenges by encouraging pursuit of solidarities rooted on common conditions of exploitation. Doing so also might help to craft more popular and egalitarian ways—less driven by corporate market imperatives—to organize the industry and provide popular access to cultural production, perhaps even to generate and preserve space for alternatives to the saturation of mass entertainment by the glittering banalities pumped out of Hollywood and the recording industry. By contrast, the discourse of cultural appropriation in the contemporary United States is by and large blind to grievances generated through the routine operations of the industry's market imperatives. Its ideal of justice centers on racial parity in the distribution of recognition and remuneration and compensatory acknowledgment of past injustices. As Walter Benn Michaels and Kenneth Warren observe regarding reparations discourse, "The very idea that justice consists in restoring to people what they would have had if the labor market or the housing market or the loan market hadn't taken it away from them is just another version of the reforms we're presented with every day, reforms that identify fairness with the supposedly efficient functioning of the market." They conclude, "That's what it means to call identity politics not an alternative to but a form of class politics—a politics for those who already belong to the upper class and for those whose most fervent political aspiration is to join it."[11] Nothing illustrates that point more clearly than the annual controversies over group parity in awards of Oscars, Grammies, and other accolades as the equivalent of burning social justice issues of the moment—as though we all would somehow share in acclaim for Ava DuVernay, Nate Parker, or Rihanna.

Critiques of cultural appropriation commonly dress up what are ultimately complaints about encroachment on presumed market preserves as moral offenses falling somewhere on a continuum of groupist transgressions that runs from petty ethnocentric insensitivity to genocide. But what counts as protectable group property in the context of a mass culture industry is very problematic. Was Iggy Azalea, who is, or was, a pure product of the hip-hop industry, appropriating something called black culture when she performed—with the crafting and encouragement of her Svengali, the rapper T.I.—a compendium of the disparaging class and racial stereotypes that flood the airwaves and cyberspace every day? Her transgression apparently was realizing fame and material gain from having performed them, on the premise that she invaded a protected racial market and violated an actual or potential proprietary relation. Yet how is it possible to isolate such a niche in a mass entertainment market? Less dramatic and closer to home, are white people who participate in black social clubs' second lines appropriating black culture? Are they doing so if they organize their own second lines, say, down Henry Clay from Magazine to St. Charles? And, most consequentially, who says what is authentic culture and when it is improperly appropriated and when not?

Similarly, objections to white, or presumably other non-coethnic, actors playing parts written as Asian, Latino, or black characters reduce fundamentally to a guild issue that, given industry prejudices, actors of color face a restricted universe of parts for which they are deemed castable, while white actors, because they are considered normative, can be cast as anything. As a guild matter, that objection is certainly defensible on its own terms. However, without inflation through the moral language of cultural appropriation, it is not clear why those of us who are not part of the guild or affected by its structures in any direct way should elevate the issue to a priority for political concern—not more than, say, the persisting practice among NBA teams of unofficially preserving roster spots for white players or sports chatterers' hyperjudgmental dispositions regarding black professional quarterbacks and hyperbolic praise of white ones, especially those who "look like" quarterbacks.

The furor over Rachel Dolezal's embrace of an identity as black was an especially striking illustration of the extent to which concern about appropriation is rooted in concerns about protection of market niches in the vast field of diversity engineering.[12] The vitriol and contumely that met Dolezal's public exposure seemed far out of proportion to her putative transgression, particularly because (a) many of those who savaged her at the same time defended and lauded Republican (as I argue, that is the one public identity continuous between Bruce and Caitlyn) Jenner's embrace of transgender identity, and (b) Dolezal's identity seemed to be linked to her civil rights and social justice activism, for which she had been recognized and lauded in Spokane, Washington, where she lived. Instructively, critics strained, commonly to the point of outright fabrication, to accuse her of having adopted black identity for material gain. Even if she did not derive any material benefit from her willed identity, critics explicitly denounced her representation of herself as black as an encroachment on recognition in principle set aside for (officially?) black people. Even her wearing hairstyles recognized as black and doing them for others was to critics an act of offensive appropriation no less than her having attended Howard University or her acceptance of the unpaid presidency of the Spokane NAACP chapter or occasional adjunct teaching of a black studies course. That response to Dolezal speaks eloquently of the fact that concern for policing the boundaries of authenticity in identity claims has a material foundation, that is, the extent to which identity politics is embedded in and reproduces a political economy of race relations administration through which the neoliberal regime of social justice as group parity is legitimized and policed.

Distinguishing culture as sets of practices from culture as racial property can help to sort through the complexities of how a rhetoric of authenticity operates in New Orleans politics and its moral and political economy. Over the last half century, New Orleans has evolved into what Kevin Fox Gotham describes as a "touristic culture," that is, "a process by which tourist modes of staging, visualization, and experience increasingly frame meanings and assertions of local culture, identity, authenticity, and collective memory."[13] Racial transition in New Orleans politics evolved and consolidated contemporaneously and in dialectical relation with that development into touristic culture. As in other cities, a nascent black political class aligned with a pro-growth, modernizing tendency that was insurgent within the governing elite. As elsewhere, the emerging black political class's constitution through an alliance with pro-growth development interests obscured how the class dynamics that drive local politics and policy also defined the forms, scope, and limits of racial transition, including the composition of what has been considered the black political agenda.[14] In New Orleans, the coincidence of black incorporation and the increasing centrality of commitment to cultural heritage tourism as an engine of development may have strengthened black elites' position in the alliance because so much of the heritage is bound up with the city's current and historical black presence. And blacks' position in the governing coalition no doubt has contributed to the touristic culture's stress on the city's diversity.

Mayor Moon Landrieu rightly is credited with having initiated significant black political incorporation into municipal government and contracting during his mayoralty from 1970 to 1978. Landrieu governed as a genuine and committed civil rights liberal. However, he was able to make the strides that he did because white elite resistance to black political assertiveness had begun to soften somewhat during the later 1960s, under his predecessor,

Victor H. Schiro. Mayor Schiro's career illustrates the shift that took place in local politics; for his first mayoral race on the heels of the city's 1960–61 school desegregation controversy, he ran as a segregationist. In his second term, he sought to distinguish himself as a fair-minded racial moderate.[15] His change in posture reflected an astute politician's ability to read the changing political environment at least as much as a personal conversion. And facets of that changing environment included, in addition to increased black voting and federal enforcement of civil rights legislation, implications of the local growth-oriented elite's commitment to intensified encouragement of tourism in general and pursuit of a professional sports franchise in particular.

The contradiction between acceptance of racial segregation and pursuit of big-league sports came to a head dramatically when the city made a successful bid to host the 1965 All-Star Game of the American Football League, then the upstart rival to the National Football League. Hosting the All-Star Game was an audition for being awarded a new franchise, and with a projected record attendance of sixty thousand the city would have been practically a shoo-in. It was all undone, though, when black players encountered systematic discrimination in the city—from cab drivers even on coming in from the airport, in French Quarter establishments, and elsewhere. The black players had so many bad experiences that they voted—despite desperate urging, pleading, and cajoling, as well as considerable criticism and denunciation—to boycott the game if it were played in New Orleans. The league responded by relocating the event to Houston, an outcome that local boosters feared would tarnish the city's reputation and be a major setback.[16]

Black political elites recognized the contradiction and saw that aligning with the development interests advocating tourism could be a source of leverage for advancing black agendas. As a stratagem, stressing the harm that racial discrimination could do to economic development aspirations was parallel to appeals to Cold War imperatives that represented racism as unpatriotic. At the same time, blacks were no less likely than other New Orleanians to support acquisition of a professional sports franchise and intensified tourism development as desirable on their own terms. Over the following decades, the loose, initially often conflictual, alliance formed in the mid-1960s congealed as a new regime of local governance based on shared commitments to racial equity—at least as an abstract principle—and the growth agenda centered on promotion of tourism and rent-intensifying redevelopment. Moon Landrieu's administration formalized black participation in governance and, as John Arena points out, solidified the regime's material foundation in the redevelopment agenda as well as commitment to racial equity.[17] In the four decades since Moon left office, the regime has become only more tightly hegemonic and more seamlessly interracial under thirty-two years of black-led administrations and eight years led by Moon's son, Mitch.

The larger point here is that from the mid-1960s forward, black and white political classes in New Orleans increasingly have been constituted in relation to each other around those common commitments. Significantly, cultural heritage tourism and the rhetorical celebration of its commitment to diversity as "America's most interesting city" became vehicles for grounding the regime both symbolically and materially. Felipe Smith's essay (chapter 4) chronicles the evolving racial character of the city's governing regime through examination of the history of the Zulu parade—historically the only black representation on the Mardi Gras parade schedule—and Zulu's place in the pantheon of Carnival krewes, particularly its relation to Rex, the nominal ruler of Carnival day. Now King Zulu and King Rex meet on the riverfront on Lundi Gras (the day before Mardi Gras) to share a toast and acknowledge each other's pride of place.

In part, the increasingly interracial character of the governing class is the outcome of a straightforward sociological dynamic enabled and accelerated by the defeat of racial segregation. As race has become less potent as the dominant metaphor, or blanket shorthand, through which class hierarchy is lived, and as black and white elites increasingly live in the same neighborhoods, interact socially as individuals and families, attend the same schools and functions, consume the same class-defining commodities and pastimes, and participate in the same civic and voluntary associations, they increasingly share a common sense not only about frameworks of public policy but also about the proper order of things in general. They share a sensibility and worldview and a reservoir of their class's cultural experiences, aspirations, quotidian habits, and values, as well as the material interests that unite them as a stratum.[18] Despite the fact that grievances or competition within the consensual framework of governance still may be expressed in more or less muted racial terms, perception that deep racial cleavage remains the key fault line around which elites align is a badly out-of-date vestige of the tense politics and structural conflict that were especially salient during the period of racial transition.

From this perspective, the histrionics that captivated so much of the black and antiracist commentariat when Mitch Landrieu was elected mayor in 2010 along with a white majority on the city council—or when other whites have been elected, or nearly elected, to mayoralties of cities that had been governed by black executives for decades—were naive. Those who fretted about loss of black political power misunderstood the extent to which the governing classes in those cities that have had black-led governments are by now integrated racially. While talk of rebuilding New Orleans on a smaller footprint understandably stoked black anxieties about surreptitious plans to alter the city's racial demography radically, it became clear before long—or should have become clear to those willing to read the signs—that the local ruling class had no particular interest in upsetting the settled governing arrangements. It was clear by 2015 that Landrieu's successor would likely as not be black, and, as of 2018, blacks and whites each held three city council seats, while the seventh was held by a Vietnamese American. A 2012 charter amendment mandating that the two at-large council posts be elected independently of each other also increases the likelihood that one of the two will be black, because the new procedure facilitates informally negotiated elite agreements about candidates, as symbolized in the Zulu and Rex Lundi Gras ritual.[19] The notion that a deep racial divide separates black and white governing elites rests on a presumption that explicitly racial subordination remains the dominant ideological framework for the maintenance of class power. It does not.

The 2017 municipal election bore this out. LaToya Cantrell, a black woman, defeated Desirée Charbonnet, another black woman, to become mayor; like Mitch Landrieu, Cantrell won majorities of both blacks' and whites' votes. Although Cantrell had long been considered the most likely next mayor, in the summer of 2017, Charbonnet, a former judge and member of a multigenerationally prominent Downtown political family, entered the mayoral race as a potential front-runner. Cantrell defeated her handily in the runoff election, garnering 60 percent of the mayoral vote. The new city council includes three blacks, two whites, a Latina, and a Vietnamese American.[20]

I have argued elsewhere that the inclination to interpret patterns of inequality and dispossession in simplistically racial terms has undercut efforts to challenge the reactionary neoliberal forces that have intensified inequality in New Orleans post-Katrina. Egalitarian interests have been spectacularly unsuccessful at even slowing down charterization of public schools, the attack on public housing for poor people, privatization of public goods and services, and the steadily deepening crisis in availability of affordable housing.[21] Of course, the deck is stacked against such interests by definition in a regime of asymmetrical power. It is striking, however, that in fights in which the objective fault lines—etched through Marx's famous heuristic, "Cui bono?"—are so clear, egalitarian critics have not been able to gain any appreciable public traction whatsoever. One reason for that failure is crit-ics' insistence on a racial frame of reference for critique and action. When blacks are prominent among architects and perpetrators of injustice as well as among its victims, arguments that racism is the source of the injustice and, especially, that antiracism is the necessary political response are intrinsically incoherent and fail to mobilize opposition. Salvaging commitment to the racism/antiracism paradigm under such circumstances requires appeal to ra-cial authenticity—who really represents black perspectives and interests—as a basis for political judgment, and such judgments are inevitably arbitrary and self-interested.

Race reductionism and claims to authenticity come together, for example, in the conventional terms of debate over gentrification that characterize dis-placement for rent-intensifying redevelopment as a cultural issue folded into overarching narratives of aboriginality and (racial) authenticity (see chapter 6, this volume). This orientation leads to demands for inclusion, often cast in pluralist terms as recognition, not redistribution, and distances the issue of dis-placement from the machinations of the publicly supported real estate market. It also reflects how the discourse of cultural authenticity and exceptionalism, which is a core component of the fetish system that drives and sustains the local political economy and culture of tourism, also grounds and circumscribes the neoliberal moral economy in contemporary New Orleans. So, for example, the black actor Wendell Pierce and black business operative and former may-oral candidate Troy Henry defined their fight with another development in-terest over disposition of a property on the cusp of trendy neighborhoods in terms pitting themselves as embodying the aboriginal, authentic, and local (black) against (white) inauthentic hipsters and outsiders.[22] This is only one of many ways post-Katrina New Orleans illustrates how what we think of as black politics is embedded in a political common sense that is not merely compatible with urban neoliberalism but is a dynamic element in its institu-tional and organizational, as well as ideological, reproduction.[23]

The race-reductionist politics is sustained more by ontological commit-ment than sober analysis of the dynamics of contemporary inequality. That is why it is impervious to the mounting evidence of its practical failure. It is anchored to a circular narrative that posits white racism as the transhistorical source of injustices that black people experience and then insists that any in-justice befalling blacks or other nonwhites in the present is also the product of white supremacy. A particular expression of that narrative vis-à-vis New Orleans, which was rehearsed repeatedly during the 2017 controversy over removal of the odious monuments to Confederates Robert E. Lee, Jefferson

Davis, P. G. T. Beauregard, and the 1874 attempted white supremacist putsch against the city's Reconstruction government, is that the city has been ruled since the antebellum period by a hereditary uptown upper class bound together by a commitment to white supremacy.[24]

Some activists associated with the Take 'Em Down NOLA group that formed to protest the monuments contend that their public condemnations of white supremacy then and now will facilitate building a mass challenge to interracial neoliberal hegemony in the city. A self-selected Peoples' Assembly associated with Take 'Em Down NOLA met after the monuments were removed (Take 'Em Down NOLA claims credit for the removal) and adopted a set of "Goals for New Orleans and LA."[25] There is, however, no apparent reason we should expect either that the race-reductionist politics that has failed consistently to generate any political momentum in response to the neoliberal onslaught in the wake of Katrina would succeed now or that this grouping of primarily freelance activists with no viable claims to represent any constituencies (except perhaps charter schools) will be able to develop the political capacity necessary to pursue effectively any of the items on what is for all intents and purposes their wish list of reforms. We know as well that Take 'Em Down NOLA's agenda is focused on removal of every monument to a slaveholder or Confederate and changing all offending street names and school names—that is, purely symbolic politics, and symbolic politics wrapped in a therapeutic language of trauma at that. Among the group's core demands was that "we not be forced to pay taxes for the maintenance of public symbols that demean us and psychologically terrorize us." Not only is this contention absurdly hyperbolic; it also throws into relief the fact that even a militantly ideological antiracism can nest naturally within a neoliberalizing political and economic order. Indeed, the Peoples' Assembly goals call not for restoring public education but to "pressure charter schools to hire more African American teachers who live in Orleans Parish. Charters can rebuild the middle class that was destroyed by Katrina. New Orleans needs the structure and tax base of families with teachers in the communities." The shriveled political vision indicated in this goal stands in stark contrast to the flamboyance in denunciations of abstract white supremacy; it may also reflect the fact that one of Take 'Em Down NOLA's principal spokespersons is a career charter school administrator and at least one other is a charter functionary.

If racism is ontological and cannot be overcome by changing political relations and institutions but only through the equivalent of epiphany and conversion, or baptism, then what takes the place of political action is exposé and demands for recognition of the oppressed and symbolic displays of atonement. But how are recognition and atonement to be expressed? Through giving space to the voices and perspectives of the oppressed, that is, as a pragmatic matter, accepting the interpretive authority of those who purport to speak for them and their interests. And who does the recognizing and accepting? It is the elites who govern and make the rules of the regime who have the power to ratify claims to speak for the oppressed groups. In New Orleans, that politics of representation dovetails conveniently with both the reigning discourse that touts cultural heritage and diversity and a local political economy based on redevelopment and marketing through invention of cultural authenticity—it's no accident that the city now boasts a traditional festival nearly every weekend and a second line every day—and shaped through competition over recognition and standing for grants and contracts.

No matter how elaborately adorned with nostalgic trappings of 1960s and 1970s black militancy or rhetorical evocations of mass struggle, this antiracism is a petition politics that accepts the governing framework and is limited in its vision to defining and pursuing objectives within it. It depends on moral suasion buttressed by the pageantry of protest, and it can work only to the extent that it operates within a moral economy that reduces the ideal of equality to racial parity in the distribution of goods and bads, costs and benefits within a system grounded on transfer from the many to the few. To the extent that it centers on pursuit of recognition and representation—a seat at the table—rather than altering patterns of regressive redistribution, this race politics is a class politics pegged to the perspectives and interests of strata either embedded in or aspiring to niches within that moral economy articulated through management of groupist diversity within neoliberal inequality.

Notes

1 Lasswell 1936.
2 Steffens 1931, 574.
3 Michaels 1997, 13.
4 Stocking 1982, 265–66. The Lamarckian view of inheritance, which presumed the heritability of characteristics acquired after birth, undergirded a major strain within late Victorian race theory. Those neo-Lamarckians saw biology and culture as inseparably intertwined in a way that reduced, in Stocking's characterization, to a "vague sociobiological indeterminism." Lamarckian race theorists were likely to be more open in principle to the potential for racial equality than were their biological reductionist contemporaries. However, in enabling what Franz Boas's former student A. L. Kroeber described

as a "'blind and bland' shuttling between race and civilization," the Lamarckian view of inheritance confounded scientific evaluation of theories of racial difference and thus obscured contradictions at the core of race theory's origins in folk ideology. The Boasians considered strategically that separating biology and culture was a necessary step to subjecting theories of racial hierarchy to rigorous scrutiny and critique. Having challenged biology as a possible foundation for manifest differences in social standing, the Boasian critique, as an ideological project, stressed the essential equality of human capacities across all racial groups. Stocking 1982, 265. Also see V. Williams 1996.

5   Michaels 1997, 14–15. "Since, in pluralism, what we do can be justified only by reference to who we are, we must, in pluralism, begin by affirming who we are; it is only once we know who we are that we will be able to tell what we should do; it is only when we know what race we are that we can tell which culture is ours. . . . Pluralism makes this disconnection [of one's culture from one's actual beliefs and practices] possible by *deriving* one's beliefs and practices *from* one's cultural identity instead of *equating* one's beliefs and practices *with* one's cultural identity. It thus produces the possibility of a discrepancy between the two; because your culture cannot simply be equated with whatever you actually do and believe, it now becomes something that can be lost or stolen, reclaimed or repudiated" (14–16). He concludes, in an assessment directed as much toward contemporary advocates of nominally progressive identitarianism as to judgment of 1920s modernist intellectuals, "The problem with cultural pluralism, in other words, is not that it is insufficiently pluralistic and therefore serves only to mask a commitment to European culture; the problem is that, insofar as it is *genuinely* pluralistic, it expresses a commitment to the irrevocability of cultural differences and therefore to their basis in race" (146n26).

6   Michaels 1997, 139–40. Michaels indicates that even Lothrop Stoddard, one of the most prominent American nativists and racists of the interwar years and protégé of Madison Grant, by 1927 rejected "theorizing about superiors and inferiors" in arguing for immigration control and proposed getting "down to the bedrock of *difference*" (1997, 14). Stoddard even proclaimed that "America welcomes diversity—but diversity within limits." He argued that natural difference was what justified the color line even for the "genuine negro [*sic*]" who "realizes that he is different from the white man and is usually content with the society of his fellows" (1927, 297). In Stoddard's view, the source of racial friction emerged from the unnatural social position of the mulatto, as both "genuine" blacks and whites naturally recognized their essential difference and acted accordingly; see his discussion of "bi-racialism" (Stoddard 1927, 284–325).

7   Walter Benn Michaels and Kenneth Warren, "Reparations and Other Right-Wing Fantasies," *Nonsite.org*, February 11, 2016, http://nonsite.org/editorial/reparations-and -other-right-wing-fantasies.

8   Souther 2003b; Hannusch 1985; Berry, Foose, and Jones 2009.

9   Lott 1993; Roediger 1991, 65–165.

10   Reed and Chowkwanyun 2012.

11   Michaels and Warren 2016, n.p.

12   Adolph Reed Jr., "From Jenner to Dolezal: One Trans Good, the Other Not So Much," *Common Dreams*, June 15, 2015, https://www.commondreams.org/views/2015/06/15

/jenner-dolezal-one-trans-good-other-not-so-much; Brubaker 2016a, 2016b; Dolezal 2017.

13 Gotham 2007b, 2012.

14 Reed 1999, 79–178.

15 Haas 2014, 92–190.

16 Souther 2003a.

17 Arena 2012, 1–54.

18 The literature on the sociology of class formation is vast. Regarding the specific dynamics of formation and reproduction of governing-class dominance in postwar American urban politics, Clarence N. Stone's early 1980s accounts remain especially clear and useful (see Stone 1980, 1982).

19 Frank Donze, "New Orleans City Council Runoff May Be Test of Trends in the City's Racial Politics," *Times-Picayune*, April 19, 2012, http://www.nola.com/politics/index.ssf/2012/04/new_orleans_city_council_runof_5.html.

20 Of the black council members, Jason Williams was reelected to his at-large post, and Jared Brossett was reelected from District D. Jay Banks, a recent King Zulu and longtime Democratic political operative associated with BOLD, the largely uptown black political organization, defeated a white candidate by just over a hundred votes to succeed Cantrell in District B; Banks carried endorsements from Governor John Bel Edwards and the *Times-Picayune*, as well as labor and much of the political establishment. The two whites elected are Joseph "Joe" Giarrusso III, scion of a prominent political family, who won the open seat in District A, and Kristen Gisleson Palmer, who narrowly—also just over a hundred votes—defeated black incumbent Nadine Ramsey in District C. Palmer had held the seat 2010–14 but chose not to seek reelection. Helena Moreno, a Mexican American former local news anchor, was elected in 2010 as a Democrat to the state legislature from House District 93, which is roughly 63 percent black and includes much of Central City, the Seventh Ward, Tremé, the Central Business District, and a bit of Coliseum Square. She won the House seat with support from much of the black political establishment against a black relative political novice who was, incidentally, married to media personality and then Tulane professor Melissa Harris Perry. In the city council race, Moreno received support from prominent black political organizations (including BOLD), labor, good government, and liberal organizations. Cyndi Nguyen, a Vietnam-born social service functionary and activist, defeated a black incumbent, who had been tarred by scandal, in District E, which is more than 80 percent black and home to a large and vibrant Vietnamese community. Nguyen won a majority of black votes.

21 Reed 2016.

22 Katherine Sayre, "On a Gentrifying Corner of New Orleans, Celebrity vs. Neighborhood Fight Emerges," *Times-Picayune*, July 28, 2015, http://www.nola.com/business/index.ssf/2015/07/st_claude_auto_parts_gas_stati.html. As if to punctuate the larger shift in black politics, Henry is grandson of the legendary local labor leader Clarence "Chink" Henry, president of International Longshoremen's Association Local 1419, which was a prominent node in local politics from the 1940s through the 1960s.

23 Jay Arena, "A People's Reconstruction," *Jacobin*, August 28, 2015, https://www.jacobinmag.com/2015/08/hurricane-katrina-ten-year-anniversary-charter-schools/; Megan French-

Marcelin, "Gentrification's Ground Zero," *Jacobin*, August 28, 2015, https://www.jacobinmag.com/2015/08/katrina-new-orleans-arne-duncan-charters/; and Thomas Jessen Adams, "How the Ruling Class Remade New Orleans," *Jacobin*, August 29, 2015, https://www.jacobinmag.com/2015/08/hurricane-katrina-ten-year-anniversary-charter-schools/.

24 Adolph Reed Jr., "Don't Be Duped: The Clamor to Take Down the Monuments Falls Short of a Truly Radical Movement," *The Lens*, June 3, 2017, http://thelensnola.org/2017/06/03/dont-be-duped-take-em-down-nola-falls-short-of-a-truly-radical-movement/.

25 Jeff Thomas, "Goals for New Orleans and LA," New Orleans Peoples' Assembly, April 8, 2017, http://peoplesassemblyneworleans.org/goals-for-new-orleans-and-la.

References

Abbott, Lynn, and Doug Serroff. 2002. *Out of Sight: The Rise of African American Popular Music, 1889–1895*. Jackson: University Press of Mississippi.

Abbott, Lynn, and Doug Serroff. 2007. *Ragged but Right: Black Traveling Shows, "Coon Songs," and the Dark Pathway to Blues and Jazz*. Jackson: University Press of Mississippi.

Adams, Thomas Jessen. 2014. "The Political Economy of Invisibility in Twenty-First-Century New Orleans: Security, Hospitality, and the Post-Disaster City." In *Hurricane Katrina in Transatlantic Perspective*, edited by Romain Huret and Randy J. Sparks, 121–36. Baton Rouge: Louisiana State University Press.

Adams, Thomas Jessen. 2015. "A Tale of Two Katrinas." HuffPost, August 29. https://www.huffingtonpost.com/thomas-j-adams/a-tale-of-two-katrinas_b_8057710.html ?ir=Australia.

Adams, Vincanne. 2013. *Markets of Sorrow, Labors of Faith: New Orleans in the Wake of Katrina*. Durham, NC: Duke University Press.

Adams, Vincanne. 2015. "The Poverty Factory." In *Territories of Poverty*, edited by Ananya Roy and Emma Shaw Crane, 151–72. Athens: University of Georgia Press.

Adorno, Theodor W. 1973. *The Jargon of Authenticity*. Evanston, IL: Northwestern University Press.

Adorno, Theodor W. 1997. *Aesthetic Theory*. London: Bloomsbury.

Agamben, Giorgio. 1998. *Homo Sacer: Sovereign Power and Bare Life*. Stanford, CA: Stanford University Press.

Airriess, Christopher. 2002. "Creating Vietnamese Landscapes and Place in New Orleans." In *Geographical Identities of Ethnic America: Race, Space, and Place*, edited by Kate A. Berry and Martha L. Henderson, 228–54. Reno: University of Nevada Press.

Airriess, Christopher A., and David L. Clawson. 1994. "Vietnamese Market Gardens in New Orleans." *Geographical Review* 84 (1): 16.

Airriess, Christopher A., Wei Li, Karen J. Leong, Angela Chia-Chen Chen, and Verna M. Keith. 2008. "Church-Based Social Capital, Networks and Geographical Scale: Katrina Evacuation, Relocation, and Recovery in a New Orleans Vietnamese American Community." *Geoforum* 39 (3): 1333–46.

Allen, Carolyn. 2002. "Creole: The Problem of Definition." In *Questioning Creole: Creolisation Discourses in Caribbean Culture*, edited by Verene A. Shepherd and Glen L. Richards, 47–63. Kingston, Jamaica: Ian Randle.

Alleyne-Detmers, Patricia Tamara. 2002. "Black Kings: Aesthetic Representation in Carnival in Trinidad and London." *Black Music Research Journal* 22 (2): 241–58.

Alpers, Paul. 1996. *What Is Pastoral?* Chicago: University of Chicago Press.

Ancelet, Barry, Jean Marcia Gaudet, and Carl Lindahl, eds. 2013. *Second Line Rescue: Improvised Responses to Katrina and Rita.* Jackson: University Press of Mississippi.

Arena, Jay. 2013. "Foundations, Nonprofits, and the Fate of Public Housing: A Critique of the Right to the City Alliance's 'We Call These Projects Home' Report." *Cities* 35: 379–83.

Arena, John. 2011a. "Black and White, Unite and Fight? Identity Politics and New Orleans's Post-Katrina Public Housing Movement." In *The Neoliberal Deluge: Hurricane Katrina, Late Capitalism, and the Remaking of New Orleans*, edited by Cedric Johnson. Minneapolis: University of Minnesota Press.

Arena, John. 2011b. "Bringing In the Black Working Class: The Black Urban Regime Strategy." *Science and Society* 75 (2): 153–79.

Arena, John. 2012. *Driven from New Orleans: How Nonprofits Betray Public Housing and Promote Privatization.* Minneapolis: University of Minnesota Press.

Arnesen, Eric. 1994. *Waterfront Workers of New Orleans: Race, Class, and Politics, 1863–1923.* Urbana: University of Illinois Press.

Arnold, Matthew. (1869) 1909. *Culture and Anarchy: An Essay in Political and Social Criticism.* London: Smith, Elder.

Arthur, Stanley Clisby. 1933. *The Story of the Kemper Brothers: Three Fighting Sons of a Baptist Preacher Who Fought for Freedom When Louisiana Was Young.* St. Francisville, LA: n.p.

Asbury, Herbert. 1936. *The French Quarter: An Informal History of the New Orleans Underworld.* New York: A. A. Knopf.

Banet-Weiser, Sarah. 2012. *Authentic^{TM}: The Politics of Ambivalence in a Brand Culture.* New York: New York University Press.

Bankston, Carl L. 2000. "Vietnamese-American Catholicism: Transplanted and Flourishing." *U.S. Catholic Historian* 18 (1): 36–53.

Barber, John W., and Elizabeth G. Barber. 1850. *Historical, Poetical and Pictorial American Scenes.* New Haven, CT: J. W. Barber.

Barker, Hugh, and Yuval Taylor. 2007. *Faking It: The Quest for Authenticity in Popular Music.* New York: Norton.

Barnes, Riché J. Daniel. 2016. *Raising the Race: Black Career Women Redefine Marriage, Motherhood, and Community.* New Brunswick, NJ: Rutgers University Press.

Barrios, Roberto. 2011. "If You Did Not Grow Up Here, You Cannot Appreciate Living Here: Neoliberalism, Space-Time, and Affect in Post-Katrina New Orleans." *Human Organization* 70 (2): 118–27.

Barrow, Kai Lumumba. 2015. "Ten Years Post-Katrina, Black Feminists Imagine a New New Orleans." *Gallery of the Streets*, May 30. http://galleryofthestreets.org/ten-years-post-katrina/.

Bartkowski, John P., and Helen A. Regis. 2003. *Charitable Choices: Religion, Race, and Poverty in the Post Welfare Era.* New York: New York University.

Bauer, Ralph, and José Antonio Mazzotti, eds. 2009. *Creole Subjects in the Colonial Americas: Empires, Texts, Identities.* Chapel Hill: University of North Carolina Press.

Bechet, Sidney. 1960. *Treat It Gentle: An Autobiography*. New York: Twayne.

Becker, Cynthia, Rachel Breunlin, and Helen A. Regis. 2013. "Performing Africa in New Orleans." *African Arts* 46 (2): 12–21.

Bendix, Regina. 1997. *In Search of Authenticity: The Formation of Folklore Studies*. Madison: University of Wisconsin Press.

Benjamin, Walter, Hannah Arendt, and Harry Zohn. 1968. *Illuminations*. New York: Harcourt, Brace and World.

Benjamin, Walter, and Rolf Tiedemann. 1999. *The Arcades Project*. Cambridge, MA: Belknap.

Berman, Marshall. 1970. *The Politics of Authenticity: Radical Individualism and the Emergence of Modern Society*. New York: Atheneum.

Berry, Jason. 1995. *The Spirit of Black Hawk: A Mystery of Africans and Indians*. Jackson: University Press of Mississippi.

Berry, Jason, Jonathan Foose, and Tad Jones. 2009. *Up from the Cradle of Jazz: New Orleans Music since World War II*. Lafayette: University of Louisiana at Lafayette Press.

Bérubé, Allan. 1990. *Coming Out under Fire: The History of Gay Men and Women in World War II*. Chapel Hill: University of North Carolina Press.

Bishop, Matthew, and Michael Green. 2010. *Philanthrocapitalism: How Giving Can Save the World*. London: Crown.

Blassingame, John. 1973. *Black New Orleans: 1860–1880*. Chicago: University of Chicago Press.

Blaufarb, Rafe. 2005. *Bonapartists in the Borderlands: French Refugees and Exiles on the Gulf Coast, 1815–1835*. Birmingham: University of Alabama Press.

Blesh, Rudi. 1946. *Shining Trumpets: A History of Jazz*. New York: Alfred A. Knopf.

Bobo, James R. 1975. *The New Orleans Economy: Pro Bono Publico?* New Orleans: Division of Business and Economic Research, College of Business Administration, University of New Orleans.

Bogado, Aura. 2013. "How One Immigrant Community Secured Itself." *Colorlines*, September 3. https://www.colorlines.com/articles/how-one-immigrant-community -secured-itself.

Boll, Andrea. 2009. *The Parade Goes On without You*. New Orleans: NOLA Fugees Press.

BondGraham, Darwin. 2011. "Building the *New* New Orleans: Foundations and NGO Power." *Review of Black Political Economy* 38 (11): 279–309.

Bourdieu, Pierre, and Loïc Wacquant. 2001. "Newliberal Speak: Notes on the New Planetary Vulgate." *Radical Philosophy* 105 (2): 2–5.

Boyette, Gene W. 1976. "Money and Maritime Activities in New Orleans during the Mexican War." *Louisiana History* 17 (4): 413–29.

Brading, D. A. 1991. *The First America: The Spanish Monarchy, Creole Patriots, and the Liberal State, 1492–1867*. Cambridge: Cambridge University Press.

Breunlin, Rachel, and Graham Button. 2000. "Oy! Such a Home: The Art of Masking Jieuxish in New Orleans." *Mardi Gras Traditions*. https://mardigrastraditions.com /l-j-goldstein/.

Breunlin, Rachel, and Ronald W. Lewis. 2009. *The House of Dance and Feathers: A Museum by Ronald W. Lewis*. New Orleans: Neighborhood Story Project, UNO Press.

Breunlin, Rachel, and Helen A. Regis. 2009. "Can There Be a Critical Collaborative Ethnography? Community and Activism in the Seventh Ward, New Orleans." *Collaborative Anthropologies* 2: 115–46.

Brinkley, Douglass. 2007. *The Great Deluge: Hurricane Katrina, New Orleans, and the Mississippi Gulf Coast*. New York: HarperCollins.

Brooks, Jane S., and Alma H. Young. 1993. "Revitalizing the Central Business District in the Face of Decline: The Case of New Orleans 1973–1993." *Town Planning Review* 64 (3): 251–71.

Brothers, Thomas. 1999. *Louis Armstrong in His Own Words: Selected Writings*. Oxford: Oxford University Press.

Brothers, Thomas David. 2006. *Louis Armstrong's New Orleans*. New York: Norton.

Brown, Cecil. 2003. *Stagolee Shot Billy*. Cambridge, MA: Harvard University Press.

Brubaker, Rogers. 2016a. "The Dolezal Affair: Race, Gender, and the Micropolitics of Identity." *Ethnic and Racial Studies* 39 (3): 414–48.

Brubaker, Rogers. 2016b. *Trans: Gender and Race in an Age of Unsettled Identities*. Princeton, NJ: Princeton University Press.

Brunn, H. O. 1960. *The Story of the Original Dixieland Jazz Band*. Baton Rouge: Louisiana State University Press.

Bryan, Violet Harrington. 1993. *The Myth of New Orleans in Literature: Dialogues of Race and Gender*. Knoxville: University of Tennessee Press.

Butler, Judith. 2005. *Giving an Account of Oneself*. New York: Fordham University Press.

Cable, George Washington. 1886. "The Dance in Place Congo." *Century* 31: 517–32.

Cacho, Lisa Marie. 2012. *Social Death: Racialized Rightlessness and the Criminalization of the Unprotected*. Nation of Newcomers: Immigrant History as American History. New York: New York University Press.

Campanella, Richard. 2007. "An Ethnic Geography of New Orleans." *Journal of American History* 94 (3): 704–15.

Campanella, Richard. 2008. *Bienville's Dilemma: A Historical Geography of New Orleans*. Lafayette: University of Louisiana at Lafayette Press.

Campanella, Richard. 2013. "Gentrification and Its Discontents: Notes from New Orleans." *New Geography*, March 1. http://www.newgeography.com/content/003526 -gentrification-and-its-discontents-notes-new-orleans.

Campanella, Richard. 2014. *Bourbon Street: A History*. Baton Rouge: Louisiana State University Press.

Campanella, Richard, and Marina Campanella. 1999. *New Orleans Then and Now*. Gretna, LA: Pelican.

Canonge, Placide. 1850. *France et Espagne ou la Louisiane en 1768 et 1769*. New Orleans.

Carpenter, Donald H. 2014. *Man of a Million Fragments: The True Story of Clay Shaw*. N.p.: Donald H. Carpenter.

Carter, Rebecca Louise. 2014. "Valued Lives in Violent Places: Black Urban Placemaking at a Civil Rights Memorial in New Orleans." *City and Society* 26 (2): 239–61.

Caulfield, Ruby Van Allen. 1998. *The French Literature of Louisiana*. Gretna, LA: Pelican.

Chamberlain, Charles. 2009. "A Synopsis." In *From Tramps to Kings: 100 Years of Zulu*.

Louisiana State Museum Exhibit Catalog, 2009–10. https://www.crt.state.la.us /Assets/Museum/onlineexhibits/zulu/Zulu_History.pdf.

Chartier, Roger. 1994. *The Order of Books: Readers, Authors, and Libraries in Europe between the Fourteenth and Eighteenth Centuries.* Translated by Lydia G. Cochrane. Stanford, CA: Stanford University Press.

Chauncey, George. 1994. *Gay New York: Gender, Urban Culture, and the Making of the Gay Male World, 1890–1940.* New York: Basic Books.

Checkoway, Barry. 1980. "Large Builders, Federal Housing Programmes, and Postwar Suburbanization." *International Journal of Urban and Regional Research* 4 (1): 21–45.

Chiang, S. Leo, dir. 2009. *A Village Called Versailles.* Walking Iris Films.

Chopin, Kate. (1899) 1984. *The Awakening.* New York: Penguin.

Christopherson, Susan, and Jennifer Clark. 2009. *Remaking Regional Economies: Power, Labor and Firm Strategies in the Knowledge Economy.* London: Routledge.

Clark, Emily. 2013. *The Strange History of the American Quadroon: Free Women of Color in the Revolutionary Atlantic World.* Chapel Hill: University of North Carolina Press.

Clark, John Garretson. 1970. *New Orleans, 1718–1812: An Economic History.* Baton Rouge: Louisiana State University Press.

Clark, Richard D. 2009. "City of Desire: A History of Same-Sex Desire in New Orleans, 1917–1997." PhD diss., Tulane University.

Cnaan, Ram A., with Stephanie C. Boddie, Femida Handy, Gaynor Yancey, and Richard Schneider. 2002. *The Invisible Caring Hand: American Congregations and the Provision of Welfare.* New York: New York University Press.

Cole, Catherine M. 1996. "Reading Blackface in West Africa: Wonders Taken for Signs." *Critical Inquiry* 23 (1): 183–215.

Collens, T. Wharton. 1836. *The Martyr Patriots; or, Louisiana in 1769, an Historical Tragedy, in Five Acts.* New Orleans: Dillard.

Colten, Craig E. 2005. *An Unnatural Metropolis: Wresting New Orleans from Nature.* Baton Rouge: Louisiana State University Press.

Comaroff, John L., and Jean Comaroff. 2009. *Ethnicity, Inc.* Chicago: University of Chicago Press.

Connerton, Paul. 2008. "Seven Types of Forgetting." *Memory Studies* 1 (1): 59–71.

Cook, Christine C., and Mickey Lauria. 1995. "Urban Regeneration and Public Housing in New Orleans." *Urban Affairs Quarterly* 30 (4): 538–57.

Countryman, Matthew. 2006. *Up South: Civil Rights and Black Power in Philadelphia.* Philadelphia: University of Pennsylvania Press.

Cowen, Scott S., and Betsy Seifter. 2014. *The Inevitable City: The Resurgence of New Orleans and the Future of Urban America.* New York: St. Martin's Griffin.

Crow, Scott. 2011. *Black Flags and Windmills: Hope, Anarchy, and the Common Ground Collective.* Oakland, CA: PM Press.

Crutcher, Michael E. 2010. *Tremé: Race and Place in a New Orleans Neighborhood.* Athens: University of Georgia Press.

Cullen, C. L. 1900. *Tales of Ex-Tanks.* New York: Grosset and Dunlap.

Curtis, Wayne. 2009. "Houses of the Future." *The Atlantic,* November. https://www .theatlantic.com/magazine/archive/2009/11/houses-of-the-future/307708/.

Dantas, Luisa, dir. 2011. *Land of Opportunity*. DVD. 97 mins. Produced by Luisa Dantas and Rebecca Snedeker. New Orleans: JoLu Productions.

Dauber, Michele Landis. 2005. "The Sympathetic State." Forum: Overtaken by a Great Calamity: Disaster Relief and the Origin of the American Welfare State. *Law and History Review* 23: 387–442.

Davis. 2014. *Ex Machina*. Produced by Davis Rogan and Andrew Bohren. New Orleans: Cafard Music.

Davis, Mike. 1992. *City of Quartz: Excavating the Future in Los Angeles*. New York: Vintage.

Davis, William C. 2006. *The Pirates Laffite: The Treacherous World of the Corsairs of the Gulf*. New York: Mariner.

Dawdy, Shannon Lee. 2007. "La Nouvelle-Orléans au XVIIIe siècle: Courants d'échanges dans le monde caraïbe." *Annales* 62 (3): 663–85.

Dawdy, Shannon Lee. 2008. *Building the Devil's Empire: French Colonial New Orleans*. Chicago: University of Chicago Press.

Dawdy, Shannon Lee. 2016. *Patina: A Profane Archaeology*. Chicago: University of Chicago Press.

De Bow, J. D. B. 1852. "The Spanish Rule in Louisiana." *De Bow's Review* 13 (4): 383–90.

de Caro, Frank. 2010. "Emerging New Orleans Mardi Gras Traditions: The St. Joan of Arc Parade and the Red Beans Krewe." *Louisiana Folklore Miscellany* 20: 1–29.

de Marigny, Bernard [Un Créole, pseud.]. 1827. "Aux electeurs de l'etat de la Louisiane: Réponse du Créole au dernier pamphlet du Citoyen Naturalisé." New Orleans: n.p.

de Marigny, Bernard. 1853. *To His Fellow Citizens*. New Orleans: n.p.

D'Emilio, John. 1998. *Sexual Politics, Sexual Communities: The Making of a Homosexual Minority in the United States, 1940–1970*. Chicago: University of Chicago Press.

Denham, James M. 1994. "New Orleans, Maritime Commerce, and the Texas War for Independence, 1836." *Southwestern Historical Quarterly* 97 (3): 510–34.

Dent, Tom. 2018. *New Orleans Griot: The Tom Dent Reader*. Edited by Kalamu ya Salaam. New Orleans: University of New Orleans Press.

Derrida, Jacques. 2008. "Freud and the Scene of Writing." In *Writing and Difference*, translated by Alan Bass, 246–91. New York: Routledge.

Dessens, Nathalie. 2007. *From Saint-Domingue to New Orleans: Migration and Influences*. Gainesville: University Press of Florida.

Dessens, Nathalie. 2015. *Creole City: A Chronicle of Early American New Orleans*. Gainesville: University Press of Florida.

Dewey, Susan, and Tonia P. St. Germain. 2015. "Sex Workers/Sex Offenders: Exclusionary Criminal Justice Practices in New Orleans." *Feminist Criminology* 10 (3): 211–34.

DiBiase, Ted, and Tom Caiazzo. 2008. *Ted DiBiase: The Million Dollar Man*. London: Simon and Schuster.

Dolezal, Rachel. 2017. *In Full Color: Finding My Place in a Black and White World*. Dallas–Ft. Worth: BenBalla.

Domínguez, Virginia R. 1986. *White by Definition: Social Classification in Creole Louisiana*. New Brunswick, NJ: Rutgers University Press.

Donaldson, Gary A. 1984. "A Window on Slave Culture: Dances at Congo Square in New Orleans, 1800–1862." *Journal of Negro History* 69 (2): 63–72.

Duany, Andres. 2009. "Restoring the Real New Orleans." *New Geography*, March 18. http://www.newgeography.com/content/00673-restoring-real-new-orleans.

Duchein, Mary Scott. 1934. "Research on Charles Etienne Arthur Gayarré." Master's thesis, Louisiana State University.

Duneier, Mitchell. 1992. *Slim's Table: Race, Respectability, and Masculinity*. Chicago: University of Chicago Press.

Eaton, Clement. 1969. *The Waning of the Old South Civilization*. New York: Pegasus.

Ebeyer, Pierre Paul. 1944. *Paramours of the Creoles: A Story of New Orleans and the Method of Promiscuous Mating between White Creole Men and Negro Colored Slaves and Freewomen*. New Orleans: Windmill.

Eckstein, Barbara J. 2005. *Sustaining New Orleans: Literature, Local Memory, and the Fate of a City*. New York: Routledge.

ECOHYBRIDITY Collective. 2015. "Ecohybridity: Love Song for NOLA, a Visual [Black] Opera in 5 Movements, August 28–30." Video posted by *Gallery of the Streets*, May 30. http://galleryofthestreets.org/ten-years-post-katrina/.

Eliasoph, Nina. 1998. *Avoiding Politics: How Americans Produce Apathy in Everyday Life*. Cambridge: Cambridge University Press.

Eliasoph, Nina. 2013. *The Politics of Volunteering*. Malden, MA: Polity.

Emerson, Ralph Waldo. 1909. *Essays and English Traits*. Cambridge, MA: Harvard Classics.

Espiritu, Yen Le. 2014. *Body Counts: The Vietnam War and Militarized Refuge(es)*. Berkeley: University of California Press.

Evans, Freddi Williams. 2011. *Congo Square: African Roots in New Orleans*. Lafayette: University of Louisiana at Lafayette Press.

Fairclough, Adam. 1995. *Race and Democracy: The Civil Rights Struggle in Louisiana, 1915–1972*. Athens: University of Georgia Press.

Faulkner, William. 1958. *New Orleans Sketches*. Edited by Carvel Collins. New Brunswick, NJ: Rutgers University Press.

Ferguson, James. 2010. "The Uses of Neoliberalism." *Antipode* 41 (1): 166–84.

Fertel, Rien T. 2014. *Imagining the Creole City: White Creole Print Culture, Community, and Identity Formation in Nineteenth-Century New Orleans*. Baton Rouge: Louisiana State University Press.

"Festival Program Book." 1979. New Orleans: New Orleans Jazz & Heritage Festival. Jazz & Heritage Foundation Archive.

Fishman, Richard P. 1975. "Title I of the Housing and Community Development Act of 1974: New Federal and Local Dynamics in Community Development." *Urban Lawyer* 7 (2): 189–214.

Fitzgerald, Frances. 1981. *Cities on a Hill*. New York: Simon and Schuster.

Fitzmorris, Jim. 2015. *Be a New Orleanian: The Book*. New Orleans: Dirty Coast.

Flaherty, Jordan. 2010. *Floodlines: Community and Resistance from Katrina to the Jena Six*. Chicago: Haymarket.

Flanagan, Richard M. 1997. "The Housing Act of 1954: The Sea Change in National Urban Policy." *Urban Affairs Review* 33 (2): 265–86.

Flew, Terry. 2011. *The Creative Industries: Culture and Policy*. London: Sage.

Florida, Richard. 2002. *The Rise of the Creative Class: And How It's Transforming Work, Leisure, Community, and Everyday Life*. New York: Basic Books.

Floyd, Samuel. 1991. "Ring Shout! Literary Studies, Historical Studies, and Black Music Inquiry." *Black Music Research Journal* 11 (2): 265–87.

Fortier, Edward J. 1915. *Les Lettres françaises en Louisiane*. Québec: Imprimerie L'Action sociale limitée.

Frankenberg, Ruth. 2001. "The Mirage of Unmarked Whiteness." In *The Making and Unmaking of Whiteness*, edited by Birgit Brander Rasmussen, Eric Kineberg, Irene J. Nexica, and Matt Wray, 72–86. Durham, NC: Duke University Press.

French-Marcelin, Megan. 2014. "Community Underdevelopment : Federal Aid and the Rise of Privatization in New Orleans." PhD diss., Columbia University.

French-Marcelin, Megan. 2015. "If You Blight It, They Will Come: Moynihan, New Orleans, and the Making of the Gentrification Economy." *Nonsite*, no. 17. http://nonsite.org/article/if-you-blight-it-they-will-come.

Freund, David R. 2007. *Colored Property*. Chicago: University of Chicago Press.

Fussell, Elizabeth. 2009. "Hurricane Chasers in New Orleams: Latino Immigrants as a Source of a Rapid Response Labor Force." *Hispanic Journal of Behavioral Sciences* 31 (3): 375–94.

Gayarré, Charles. 1848. *Romance of the History of Louisiana: A Series of Lectures*. New York: D. Appleton.

Gayarré, Charles. (1854) 1974. *History of Louisiana*, vol. 1: *The French Domination*. Gretna, LA: Pelican.

Gayarré, Charles. 1888. "The New Orleans Bench and Bar in 1823." *Harper's New Monthly Magazine*, November.

Gayarré, Charles. 1890. "Literature in Louisiana." *Belford's Magazine*, August.

Germany, Kent B. 2007. *New Orleans after the Promises: Poverty, Citizenship, and the Search for the Great Society*. Athens: University of Georgia Press.

Geschiere, Peter. 2009. *The Perils of Belonging: Autochthony, Citizenship, and Exclusion in Africa and Europe*. Chicago: University of Chicago Press.

Gill, James. 1997. *Lords of Misrule: Mardi Gras and the Politics of Race in New Orleans*. Jackson: University Press of Mississippi.

Gill, Rosalind, and Andy Pratt. 2008. "In the Social Factory? Immaterial Labour, Precariousness and Cultural Work." *Theory, Culture and Society* 25 (7–8): 1–30.

Gilmore, James H., and B. Joseph Pine. 2007. *Authenticity: What Consumers Really Want*. Boston: Harvard Business School Press.

Gilroy, Paul. 2000. *Against Race: Imagining Political Culture beyond the Color Line*. Cambridge, MA: Harvard University Press.

Gipson, Jennifer. 2014. "Lafcadio Hearn, Hurricane Katrina and Mardi Gras: A Nineteenth-Century Folklorists New Life in New Orleans." *Western Folklore* 73 (2/3): 173–94.

Gomez, Gay M. 2006. "Publicizing a Vast New Land: Visual Propaganda for Attracting Colonists to Eighteenth-Century Louisiana." In *Printmaking in New Orleans*, edited by Jessie J. Poesch, 52–68. New Orleans: Historic New Orleans Collection.

Gotham, Kevin Fox. 2002. *Race, Real Estate, and Uneven Development: The Kansas City Experience, 1900–2000*. Albany: State University of New York Press.

Gotham, Kevin Fox. 2007a. *Authentic New Orleans: Tourism, Culture, and Race in the Big Easy*. New York: New York University Press.

Gotham, Kevin Fox. 2007b. "Selling New Orleans to New Orleans: Tourism Authenticity and the Construction of Community Identity." *Tourist Studies* 7 (3): 317–39.

Gotham, Kevin Fox. 2010. "Resisting Urban Spectacle: The 1984 Louisiana World Exposition and the Contradictions of Mega Events." *Urban Studies* 48 (1): 197–214.

Gotham, Kevin Fox. 2012. "Tourism and Culture." In *Handbook of Cultural Sociology*, edited by John R. Hall, Laura Grindstaff, and Ming-Chen Lo, 608–16. New York: Routledge.

Gotham, Kevin Fox, and Miriam Greenberg. 2014. *Crisis Cities: Disaster and Redevelopment in New York and New Orleans*. New York: Oxford University Press.

Grazian, David. 2003. *Blue Chicago: The Search for Authenticity in Urban Blues Clubs*. Chicago: University of Chicago Press.

Gross, Ariela, and Alejandro de la Fuente. 2013. "Slaves, Free Blacks, and Race in the Legal Regimes of Cuba, Louisiana, and Virginia: A Comparison." *North Carolina Law Review* 91 (5): 1699–1756.

Gross, Robert A., and Mary Kelley, eds. 2010. *A History of the Book in America*, vol. 2: *An Extensive Republic: Print, Culture, and Society in the New Nation, 1790–1840*. Chapel Hill: University of North Carolina Press.

Gruesz, Kirsten S. 2006. "The Gulf of Mexico System and the 'Latinness' of New Orleans." *American Literary History* 18 (3): 468–95.

Gundewardena, Nandini, and Mark Schuller, eds. 2008. *Capitalizing on Catastrophe: Neoliberal Strategies in Postdisaster Reconstruction*. Lanham, MD: AltaMira Press.

Haas, Edward F. 1974. *DeLesseps S. Morrison and the Image of Reform: New Orleans Politics, 1946–1961*. Baton Rouge: Louisiana State University Press.

Haas, Edward F. 2014. *Mayor Victor H. Schiro: New Orleans in Transition, 1961–1970*. Jackson: University Press of Mississippi.

Hackworth, Jason. 2012. *Faith Based: Religious Neoliberalism and the Politics of Welfare in the United States*. Athens: University of Georgia Press.

Hair, William Ivy. 1976. *Carnival of Fury: Robert Charles and the New Orleans Race Riot of 1900*. Baton Rouge: Louisiana State University Press.

Hall, Gwendolyn Midlo. 1992a. *Africans in Colonial Louisiana: The Development of Afro-Creole Culture in the Eighteenth Century*. Baton Rouge: Louisiana State University Press.

Hall, Gwendolyn Midlo. 1992b. "The Formation of Afro-Creole Culture." In *Creole New Orleans: Race and Americanization*, edited by Arnold Hirsch and Joseph Logsdon, 58–87. Baton Rouge: Louisiana State University Press.

Halttunen, Karen. 1982. *Confidence Men and Painted Women: A Study of Middle-Class Culture in America, 1830–1870*. New Haven, CT: Yale University Press.

Hamilton, Marybeth. 2009. *In Search of the Blues*. New York: Basic Books.

Hannusch, Jeff. 1985. *I Hear You Knockin': The Sound of New Orleans Rhythm and Blues*. Ville Platte, LA: Swallow.

Hardy, Arthur. 2007. *Mardi Gras in New Orleans: An Illustrated History*. Mandeville, LA: Arthur Hardy Enterprises.

Harold, Claudrena. 2007. *The Rise and Fall of the Garvey Movement in the Urban South, 1918–1942*. New York: Routledge.

Harvey, David. 2003. *The New Imperialism*. Oxford: Oxford University Press.

Harvey, David. 2008. "The Right to the City." *New Left Review* 53: 23–40.

Hearn, Lafcadio. (1877) 2001. *Inventing New Orleans: Writings of Lafcadio Hearn*. Edited by S. Frederick Starr. Jackson: University Press of Mississippi.

Heath, James E. 1834. "Southern Literature." *Southern Literary Messenger* 1 (1): 1–3.

Hegel, Georg Wilhelm Friedrich. 1899. *The Philosophy of History*. New York: Colonial Press.

Hendrix, Michael. 2015. "In New Orleans, Entrepreneurship Paves the Path to Change." US Chamber of Commerce Foundation, May 14. https://www .uschamberfoundation.org/blog/post/new-orleans-entrepreneurship-paves-path -change/43177.

Herskovits, Melville J. 1941. *The Myth of the Negro Past*. New York: Harper and Brothers.

Hickey, Dennis, and Kenneth C. Wylie. 1993. *An Enchanting Darkness: The American Vision of Africa in the Twentieth Century*. East Lansing: Michigan State University Press.

Himelstein, Abram. 2015. "I Moved Here and Ruined the Scene." Next City, August 20. https://nextcity.org/features/view/new-orleans-hurricane-katrina-local-stories -housing-gentrification-race.

Hirsch, Arnold R. 1983. "New Orleans: Sunbelt in the Swamp." In *Sunbelt Cities: Politics and Growth since World War II*, edited by Richard M. Bernard and Bradley R. Rice, 100–137. Austin: University of Texas Press.

Hirsch, Arnold R. 1990. "Race and Politics in Modern New Orleans: The Mayoralty of Dutch Morial." *Amerikastudien* 35: 461–84.

Hirsch, Arnold R. 1992. "Simply a Matter of Black and White: The Transformation of Race and Politics in Twentieth-Century New Orleans." In *Creole New Orleans: Race and Americanization*, edited by Arnold R. Hirsch and Joseph Logsdon, 262–319. Baton Rouge: Louisiana State University Press.

Hirsch, Arnold R. 2000b. "Searching for a 'Sound Negro Policy': A Racial Agenda for the Housing Acts of 1949 and 1954." *Housing Policy Debate* 11 (2): 393–441.

Hirsch, Arnold R. 2000a. "Race and Renewal in the Cold War South: New Orleans, 1947–1968." In *The American Planning Tradition*, edited by Robert L. Fishman, 219–38. Baltimore: Johns Hopkins University Press.

Hirsch, Arnold R. 2007. "Fade to Black: Hurricane Katrina and the Disappearance of Creole New Orleans." *Journal of American History* 94 (3): 752–61.

Hirsch, Arnold R., and Joseph Logsdon, eds. 1992. *Creole New Orleans: Race and Americanization*. Baton Rouge: Louisiana State University Press.

Holloway, John. 2002. *Change the World without Taking Power*. London: Pluto.

Horkheimer, Max, and T. W. Adorno. 1972. *Dialectic of Enlightenment*. Translated by John Cumming. New York: Herder and Herder.

Horton, Scott. 2007. "How Walter Scott Started the American Civil War." *Harper's*

Magazine Online, July 29. https://harpers.org/blog/2007/07/how-walter-scott
-started-the-american-civil-war/.

Hurston, Zora. 1931. "Hoodoo in America." *Journal of American Folklore* 44 (174): 317–417.

Hutchinson, C. A. 1956. "Valentin Gomez Farias and the 'Secret Pact of New Orleans.'" *Hispanic American Historical Review* 36 (4): 471–89.

Hyra, Derek S. 2017. *Race, Class, and Politics in the Cappuccino City*. Chicago: University of Chicago Press.

Jackson, Antoinette T. 2011. "Diversifying the Dialogue Post-Katrina: Race, Place, and Displacement in New Orleans, USA." *Transforming Anthropology* 19 (1): 3–16.

Jackson, John L. 2001. *Harlemworld: Doing Race and Class in Contemporary Black America*. Chicago: University of Chicago Press.

Jackson, Kenneth T. 1985. *Crabgrass Frontier: The Suburbanization of the United States*. New York: Oxford University Press.

James, Joy. 1996. *Resisting State Violence: Radicalism, Gender, and Race in U.S. Culture*. Minneapolis: University of Minnesota Press.

Johnson, Cedric. 2007. *Revolutionaries to Race Leaders: Black Power and the Making of African American Politics*. Minneapolis: University of Minnesota.

Johnson, Cedric, ed. 2011. *The Neoliberal Deluge: Hurricane Katrina, Late Capitalism, and the Remaking of New Orleans*. Minneapolis: University of Minnesota Press.

Johnson, Cedric. 2015. "Working the Reserve Army: Proletarianization in Revanchist New Orleans." *Nonsite*, no. 17. http://nonsite.org/article/working-the-reserve-army.

Johnson, Jerah. 1991. "New Orleans's Congo Square: An Urban Setting for Early Afro-American Culture Formation." *Louisiana History* 32 (2): 117–57.

Johnson, Walter. 1999. *Soul by Soul: Life inside the Antebellum Slave Market*. Cambridge, MA: Harvard University Press.

Jordan, Rosan Auguta, and Frank de Caro. 1996. "'In This Folk-Lore Land': Race, Class, Identity, and Folklore Studies in Louisiana." *Journal of American Folklore* 109 (431): 31–59.

Joseph, Miranda. 2002. *Against the Romance of Community*. Minneapolis: University of Minnesota Press.

Jung, Moon-Ho. 2006. *Coolies and Cane: Race, Labor, and Sugar in the Age of Emancipation*. Baltimore: Johns Hopkins University Press.

Kato, Yuki, Catarina Passidomo, and Daina Harvey. 2013. "Political Gardening in a Post-Disaster City: Lessons from New Orleans." *Urban Studies* 51 (9): 1833–49.

Keith, Charles. 2012. *Catholic Vietnam: A Church from Empire to Nation*. Berkeley: University of California Press.

Kelley, Robin D. G. 1993. "We Are Not What We Seem: Re-thinking Black Working Class Opposition in the Jim Crow South." *Journal of American History* 80 (1): 75–112.

Kelman, Ari. 2006. *A River and Its City: The Nature of Landscape in New Orleans*. Berkeley: University of California Press.

Khatib, Kate, Margaret Killjoy, and Mike McGuire, eds. 2012. *We Are Many: Reflections on Movement Strategy from Occupation to Liberation*. Chico, CA: AK Press.

Kim, Claire Jean. 1999. "The Racial Triangulation of Asian Americans." *Politics and Society* 27 (1): 105–38.

Kinser, Samuel. 1990. *Carnival American Style: Mardi Gras at New Orleans and Mobile.* Chicago: University of Chicago Press.

Kittler, Friedrich. 1999. *Gramophone, Film, Typewriter.* Translated by Geoffery Winthrop-Young and Michael Wutz. Stanford, CA: Stanford University Press.

Klein, Greg. 2012. *King of New Orleans: How the Junkyard Dog Became Wrestling's First Black Superstar.* Toronto: ECW Press.

Klein, Naomi. 2008. *The Shock Doctrine: The Rise of Disaster Capitalism.* New York: Picador.

Kmen, Henry Arnold. 1966. *Music in New Orleans: The Formative Years, 1791–1841.* Baton Rouge: Louisiana State University Press.

Kmen, Henry Arnold. 1972. "The Roots of Jazz in Place Congo: A Re-appraisal." *Inter-American Musical Research Yearbook* 8: 5–17.

Kohl-Arenas, Erica. 2015. "The Self-Help Myth: Towards a Theory of Philanthropy as Consensus Broker." *American Journal of Economics and Sociology* 74 (4): 796–825.

Koptiuch, Kristin. 1991. "Third-Worlding at Home." *Social Text* 28: 87–99.

Krasner, David. 1997. *Resistance, Parody, and Double Consciousness in African American Theatre, 1895–1910.* New York: St. Martin's.

Ku, Robert Ji-Song, Martin F. Manalansan IV, and Anita Mannur. 2013. "An Alimentary Introduction." In *Eating Asian America: A Food Studies Reader,* edited by Robert Ji-Song Ku, Martin F. Manalansan IV, and Anita Mannur, 1–9. New York: New York University Press.

Labouisse, M. 1974. "Architecture: The Ironical History of Louis Armstrong Park." *New Orleans,* July, 74–75.

Lasch, Christopher. 1978. *The Culture of Narcissism: American Life in an Age of Diminishing Expectations.* New York: Norton.

Lasswell, Harold. 1936. *Politics: Who Gets What, When, How.* New York: McGraw-Hill.

Laussat, Pierre Clément de. (1831) 1978. *Memoirs of My Life.* Edited by Robert D. Bush. Translated by Agnes-Josephine Pastwa. Baton Rouge: Louisiana State University Press.

LaViolette, Forrest E. 1960. "The Negro in New Orleans." In *Studies in Housing and Minority Groups,* edited by Nathan Glazer and Davis McEntire, 110–34. Berkeley: University of California Press.

Leach, William. 1993. *Land of Desire: Merchants, Power, and the Rise of a New American Culture.* New York: Pantheon.

Lears, T. J. Jackson. 1981. *No Place of Grace: Antimodernism and the Transformation of American Culture, 1880–1920.* New York: Pantheon.

Lee, Spike, dir. 2006. *When the Levees Broke: A Requiem in Four Acts.* HBO Documentary Films.

Lefebvre, Henri. (1968) 1996. "The Right to the City." In *Writing on Cities,* edited by E. Kofman and E. Labas, 63–81. Oxford: Blackwell.

Lejeune, Philippe. 1989. *On Autobiography*. Translated by Katherine Leary. Minneapolis: University of Minnesota Press.

Lessin, Tia, and Carl Deal, dirs. 2008. *Trouble the Water*. Zeitgeist Films.

Ley, David. 2003. "Artists, Aestheticisation and the Field of Gentrification." *Urban Studies* 40 (12): 2527–44.

Li, Wei, Christopher Airriess, Angela Chia-Chen Chen, Karen J. Leong, Verna M. Keith, and Karen Adams. 2008. "Surviving Katrina and Its Aftermath: Evacuation and Community Mobilization by Vietnamese Americans and African Americans." *Journal of Culture Geography* 25 (3): 263–86.

Liebschutz, Sarah F. 1983. "Neighborhood Conservation: Political Choices under the Community Development Block Grant Program." *Publius* 13 (3): 23–37.

Lightweis-Goff, J. 2014. "'Peculiar and Characteristic': New Orleans's Exceptionalism from Olmsted to the Deluge." *American Literature* 86 (1): 147–69.

Lipmann, Pauline. 2011. *The New Political Economy of Urban Education: Neoliberalism, Race, and the Right to the City*. New York: Routledge.

Lipsitz, George. 2011. *How Racism Takes Place*. Philadelphia: Temple University Press.

Loda, Robyn. 2010. "Inventing and Reinventing Tradition: The Jefferson City Buzzards: The Oldest Marching Group in New Orleans." *Beat Street Magazine* 2 (2): 13–15.

Logsdon, Joseph, and Caryn Cossie Bell. 1992. "The Americanization of Black New Orleans." In *Creole New Orleans: Race and Americanization*, edited by Arnold R. Hirsch and Joseph Logsdon, 201–61. Baton Rouge: Louisiana State University Press.

Loichot, Valérie. 2011. "*Créolité* Nineteenth Century Style: Lafcadio Hearn's Vision." *Canadian Review of Comparative Literature/Revue Canadienne de Littérature Comparée* 38 (1): 57–69.

Lomax, Alan. 1950. *Mister Jelly Roll: The Fortunes of Jelly Roll Morton, New Orleans Creole and "Inventor of Jazz."* New York: Duell, Sloan and Pearce.

Lomax, John, and Alan Lomax. 1934. *American Ballads and Folk Songs*. New York: Macmillan.

Long, Alecia P. 2004. *The Great Southern Babylon: Sex, Race, and Respectability in New Orleans, 1865–1920*. Baton Rouge: Louisiana State University Press.

Lott, Eric. 1993. *Love and Theft: Blackface Minstrelsy and the American Working Class*. New York: Oxford University Press.

Loughran, Trish. 2007. *The Republic in Print: Print Culture in the Age of U.S. Nation Building, 1770–1870*. New York: Columbia University Press.

Luft, Rachel. 2009. "Beyond Disaster Exceptionalism: Social Movement Developments in New Orleans after Hurricane Katrina." *American Quarterly* 61 (3): 499–527.

Lussan, Auguste. 1839. *Les Martyrs de la Louisiane*. Donaldsonville, LA: E. Martin and F. Prou.

Lye, Colleen. 2008. "The Afro-Asian Analogy." *PMLA* 123 (5): 1732–36.

Mah, Alice. 2014. *Port Cities and Global Legacies: Urban Identity, Waterfront Work, and Radicalism*. New York: Palgrave.

Marler, Scott P. 2013. *The Merchants' Capital: New Orleans and the Political Economy of the Nineteenth-Century South*. Cambridge: Cambridge University Press.

Marx, Leo. 1964. *The Machine in the Garden: Technology and the Pastoral Ideal in America*. London: Oxford University Press.

Mason, Wyatt. 2010. "The HBO Auteur." *New York Times Magazine*, March 17, 26.

Masquelier, Adeline. 2006. "Why Katrina's Victims Aren't Refugees: Musings on a 'Dirty' Word." *American Anthropologist* 108 (4): 735–43.

Matteson Associates. 1966. *Dimensions and Solutions of New Orleans' Financial Dilemma: Report of a Reconnaissance Study*. New Orleans: Bureau of Governmental Research.

Mayer, Vicky. 2017. *Almost Hollywood, Nearly New Orleans: The Lure of the Local Film Economy*. Berkeley: University of California Press.

Mbembe, Achille. 2009. "African Contemporary Art: Negotiating the Terms of Recognition. A Conversation with Vivian Paulissen." *Chimurenga*. http://www.chimurenga.co.za/page-127.html.

M'Caleb, Thomas, ed. 1894. *The Louisiana Book: Selections from the Literature of the State*. New Orleans: R. F. Straughan.

Meeker, Martin. 2006. *Contacts Desired: Gay and Lesbian Communications and Community, 1940s–1970s*. Chicago: University of Chicago Press.

Meltzer, Dave. 2001. *Tributes: Remembering Some of the World's Greatest Wrestlers*. Etobicoke, Ontario: Winding Stair Press.

Metzger, John T. 2001. "The Failed Promise of a Festival Marketplace: South Street Seaport in Lower Manhattan." *Planning Perspectives* 16 (1): 25–46.

Michaels, Walter Benn. 1997. *Our America: Nativism, Modernism, and Pluralism*. Durham, NC: Duke University Press.

Michaels, Walter Benn. 1998. *The Gold Standard and the Logic of Naturalism*. Berkeley: University of California Press.

Michaels, Walter Benn, and Kenneth Warren. 2016. "Reparations and Other Right-Wing Fantasies." *Nonsite*, February 11. https://nonsite.org/editorial/reparations-and-other-right-wing-fantasies.

Mitchell, Mary Niall. 2000. "'A Good and Delicious Country': Free Children of Color and How They Learned to Imagine the Atlantic World in Nineteenth-Century Louisiana." *History of Education Quarterly* 40 (2): 123–44.

Mitchell, Reid. 1995. *All on a Mardi Gras Day: Episodes in the History of New Orleans Carnival*. Cambridge, MA: Harvard University Press.

Mizell-Nelson, Michael. 2009. "Interracial Unionism Meets the Open Shop Drive: African American Membership in the Carmen's Union, 1918–1926." In *Working in the Big Easy: The History and Politics of Labor in New Orleans*, edited by Thomas Jessen Adams and Steve Striffler. Lafayette: University of Louisiana at Lafayette Press.

Monteagudo, Graciela. 2008. "The Clean Walls of a Recovered Factory: New Subjectivities in Argentina's Recovered Factories." *Urban Anthropology* 37 (2): 175–210.

Moore, Leonard N. 2010. *Black Rage in New Orleans: Police Brutality and African American Activism from World War II to Hurricane Katrina*. Baton Rouge: Louisiana State University Press.

Morial, Marc H., and Robert K. Whelan. 2000. "Privatizing Government Services in

New Orleans." In *Making Government Work: Lessons from America's Governors and Mayors*, edited by Paul J. Andrisani, Simon Hakin, and Eva Leeds, 211–22. New York: Rowman and Littlefield.

Morton, Jelly Roll. 2005. *Jelly Roll Morton: The Library of Congress Recordings*. Cambridge, MA: Rounder Records.

Mosher, Anne E., Barry D. Keim, and Susan A. Franques. 1995. "Downtown Dynamics." *Geographical Review* 85 (4): 497–517.

Motley, Constance Baker. 1955. *Some Theories upon Which a Legal Attack on Racial Discrimination in FHA Mortgage Insured Housing May Be Predicated*. New York: NAACP Legal Defense Fund.

Muehlebach, Andrea. 2011. "On Affective Labor in Post-Fordist Italy." *Cultural Anthropology* 26 (1): 59–82.

Mumford, Lewis. 1970. *The Culture of Cities*. New York: Harcourt Brace.

Murray, Catherine, and Mirjam Gollmitzer. 2012. "Escaping the Precarity Trap: A Call for Creative Labour Policy." *International Journal of Cultural Policy* 18 (4): 419–38.

Murray, Charles. 2013. *American Exceptionalism: An Experiment in History*. Washington, DC: AEI Press.

Narrett, David E. 2012. "Geopolitics and Intrigue: James Wilkinson, the Spanish Borderlands, and Mexican Independence." *William and Mary Quarterly* 69 (1): 101–46.

Nathan, Richard P., Paul R. Dommel, Sarah F. Liebschutz, and Milton D. Morris. 1977. "Monitoring the Block Grant Program for Community Development." *Political Science Quarterly* 92 (2): 219–44.

Naughton, Aoife, and Wes Wallace. 2006. "Day Laborers in the Reconstruction of New Orleans." *Callaloo* 29 (4): 1372–88.

Ngai, Mae M. 2004. *Impossible Subjects: Illegal Aliens and the Making of Modern America*. Princeton, NJ: Princeton University Press.

Nguyen, Marguerite. 2013. "'Like We Lost Our Citizenship': Vietnamese Americans, African Americans, and Hurricane Katrina." In *Asian Americans in Dixie: Race and Migration in the South*, edited by Jigna Desai and Khyati Y. Joshi, 264–88. Urbana: University of Illinois Press.

Nguyen, Marguerite. 2015. "Vietnamese American New Orleans." *Minnesota Review* 84: 114–28.

Nguyen, Vien, and Charles Henry Rowell. 2006. "Father Vien Nguyen with Charles Henry Rowell." *Callaloo* 29 (4): 1071–81.

Nguyen, Viet Thanh. 2012. "Refugee Memories and Asian American Critique." *positions: east asia cultures critique* 20 (3): 911–42.

Nguyen, Viet Thanh. 2016. *Nothing Ever Dies: Vietnam and the Memory of War*. Cambridge, MA: Harvard University Press.

Nguyen-Marshall, Van. 2005. "The Moral Economy of Colonialism: Subsistence and Famine Relief in French Indo-China, 1906–1917." *International History Review* 27 (2): 237–58.

Nine Times Social and Pleasure Club. 2006. *Coming Out the Door for the Ninth Ward*. New Orleans: Neighborhood Story Project.

Nyerges, Aaron. 2014. "Immemorial Cinema: Film, Travel, and Faulkner's Poetics of Space." In *Faulkner and Film*, edited by Peter Lurie and Ann Abadie, 47–70. Jackson: University Press of Mississippi.

Nystrom, Justin A. 2010. *New Orleans after the Civil War: Race, Politics, and a New Birth of Freedom*. Baltimore: Johns Hopkins University Press.

O'Brien, Michael. 2004. *Conjectures of Order: Intellectual Life and the American South, 1810–1860*. Chapel Hill: University of North Carolina Press.

Odum, Howard Washington, and Guy Benton Johnson. 1925. *The Negro and His Songs: A Study of Typical Negro Songs in the South*. Chapel Hill: University of North Carolina Press.

Omi, Michael, and Howard Winant. 2014. *Racial Formation in the United States*. 3rd ed. New York: Routledge.

Ong, Aihwa. 2006. *Neoliberalism as Exception: Mutations in Citizenship and Sovereignty*. Durham, NC: Duke University Press.

Orgel, Stephen. 1981. *The Jonsonian Masque*. New York: Columbia University Press.

Orleck, Annelise. 2005. *Storming Caesars Palace: How Black Mothers Fought Their Own War on Poverty*. Boston: Beacon.

Parsons, Elaine Frantz. 2005. "Midnight Rangers: Costume and Performance in the Reconstruction-Era Ku Klux Klan." *Journal of American History* 92 (3): 811–36.

Patillo-McCoy, Mary. 1999. *Black Picket Fences: Privilege and Peril among the Black Middle Class*. Chicago: University of Chicago Press.

Pavelle, Emily C. 2011. "The Flavor of Ethnicity: Taco Truck Regulations and Border Construction in Greater New Orleans." Master's thesis, University of Chicago.

Peck, Jamie. 2006. "Liberating the City: Between New York and New Orleans." *Urban Geography* 27 (8): 681–713.

Peck, Jaime, Nik Theodore, and Neil Brenner. 2009. "Neoliberal Urbanism: Models, Moments, Mutations." *SAIS Review* 29: 49–66.

Pfolh, Kaite A. 2015. *Mexico in New Orleans: A Tale of Two Americas*. Baton Rouge: Louisiana State Museum of Art.

Pickett, Albert James. 1847. *Eight Days in New-Orleans in February, 1847*. Montgomery: A. J. Pickett.

Pierson, George Wilson. (1938) 1996. *Tocqueville in America*. Baltimore: Johns Hopkins University Press.

Piliawsky, Monte. 1985. "The Impact of Black Mayors on the Black Community: The Case of New Orleans' Ernest Morial." *Review of Black Political Economy* 13: 5–23.

Povinelli, Elizabeth. 2002. *The Cunning of Recognition: Indigenous Alterities and the Making of Australian Multiculturalism*. Durham, NC: Duke University Press.

Powell, Lawrence N. 1999. "Reinventing Tradition: Liberty Place, Historical Memory, and Silk-Stalking Vigilantism in New Orleans Politics." *Slavery and Abolition* 20: 127–49.

Powell, Lawrence N. 2012. *The Accidental City: Improvising New Orleans*. Cambridge, MA: Harvard University Press.

Prashad, Vijay. 2006. "Foreword: 'Bandung Is Done'—Passages in Afroasian Epistemology." In *Afroasian Encounters: Culture, History, Politics*, edited by Heike Raphael-Hernandez and Shannon Steen, xi–xxiii. New York: New York University Press.

Pratt, Lloyd. 2007. "New Orleans and Its Storm: Exception, Example, or Event?" *American Literary History* 19 (1): 251–65.

Preston, Caroline. 2013. "Using Hollywood to Teach People about Disaster Giving." *Chronicle of Philanthropy*, January 10. https://www.philanthropy.com/article/Using -Hollywood-to-Teach/227765.

Quigley, Bill. 2013. "Why I Stand with the Immigrant Workers Who Rebuilt New Orleans." *Times-Picayune*, November 15. http://www.nola.com/opinions/index.ssf /2013/11/why_i_stand_with_the_immigrant.html.

Raeburn, Bruce Boyd. 2009a. *New Orleans Style and the Writing of American Jazz History*. Ann Arbor: University of Michigan Press.

Raeburn, Bruce Boyd. 2009b. "Stars of David and Sons of Sicily: Constellations beyond the Canon in Early New Orleans Jazz." *Jazz Perspectives* 3 (2): 123–52.

Ramsey, Frederic, Jr., and Charles Edward Smith, eds. 1939. *Jazzmen: The Story of Hot Jazz Told in the Lives of the Men Who Created It*. New York: Harcourt Brace.

Rasmussen, Daniel. 2011. *American Uprising: The Untold Story of America's Largest Slave Revolt*. New York: Harper.

Real Estate Research Corporation. 1974. *Recommendations for Community Development Planning*. Washington, DC: Government Printing Office.

Reed, Adolph, Jr. 1999. *Stirrings in the Jug: Black Politics in the Post-segregation Era*. Minneapolis: University of Minnesota Press.

Reed, Adolph, Jr. 2016. "The Post-1965 Trajectory of Race, Class, and Urban Politics in the United States Reconsidered." *Labor Studies Journal* 41 (3): 260–91.

Reed, Adolph, Jr., and Merlin Chowkwanyun. 2012. "Race, Class, Crisis: The Discourse of Racial Disparity and Its Analytical Discontents." *Socialist Register* 48: 149–75.

Reed, John Shelton. 2012. *Dixie Bohemia: A French Quarter Circle in the 1920s*. Baton Rouge: Louisiana State University Press.

Regis, Helen A. 2009a. "Skeletons." In *The House of Dance and Feathers: A Museum by Ronald W. Lewis*, edited by Rachel Breunlin and Ronald W. Lewis, 178–81. New Orleans: Neighborhood Story Project/UNO Press.

Regis, Helen A. 2009b. "Social Aid and Pleasure Clubs." In *The House of Dance and Feathers: A Museum by Ronald W. Lewis*, edited by Rachel Breunlin and Ronald W. Lewis, 126–31. New Orleans: Neighborhood Story Project/UNO Press.

Regis, Helen A. 2011. "Davis, the Irritant: Whiteness in Black Spaces. Critical Exchange on David Simon's Treme." *Contemporary Political Theory* 10 (3): 399–406.

Regis, Helen A. 2013. "Producing Africa at the New Orleans Jazz and Heritage Festival." *African Arts* 46 (2): 70–85.

Regis, Helen A., and Shana Walton. 2008. "Producing the Folk at the New Orleans Jazz and Heritage Festival." *Journal of American Folklore* 121 (482): 400–440.

Reilly, Tom. 1982. "A Spanish-Language Voice of Dissent in Antebellum New Orleans." *Louisiana History* 23 (4): 325–39.

Reynolds, Donald. 1964. "The New Orleans Riot of 1866, Reconsidered." *Louisiana History* 5 (1): 5–17.

Rightor, Henry, ed. 1900. *Standard History of New Orleans, Louisiana*. Chicago: Lewis.

Ripley, Eliza. 1889. *From Flag to Flag: A Woman's Adventures and Experiences in the South during the War, in Mexico, and in Cuba*. New York: D. Appleton.

Roach, Joseph R. 1996. *Cities of the Dead: Circum-Atlantic Performance*. New York: Columbia University Press.

Roberts, John W. 1989. *From Trickster to Badman: The Black Folk Hero in Slavery and Freedom*. Philadelphia: University of Pennsylvania Press.

Robertson, Campbell. 2015. "10 Years after Katrina." *New York Times*, August 26. http://www.nytimes.com/interactive/2015/08/26/us/ten-years-after-katrina.html?_r=0.

Robick, Brian David. 2011. "Blight: The Development of a Contested Topic." PhD diss., Carnegie Mellon University.

Rochon and Associates. 1988. *A Housing Plan for New Orleans*. New Orleans: Rochon and Associates.

Rodgers, Daniel T. 2011. *Age of Fracture*. Cambridge, MA: Belknap.

Roediger, David. 1991. *The Wages of Whiteness: Race and the Making of the American Working Class*. New York: Verso.

Rogers, Kim Lacy. 1993. *Righteous Lives: Narratives of the New Orleans Civil Rights Movement*. New York: New York University Press.

Rose, Al. 1974. *Storyville, New Orleans: Being an Authentic, Illustrated Account of the Notorious Red-Light District*. Tuscaloosa: University of Alabama Press.

Rosowski, Susan. 1979. "The Novel of Awakening." *Genre* 12: 313–32.

Rothman, Adam. 2005. *Slave Country: American Expansion and the Origins of the Deep South*. Cambridge, MA: Harvard University Press.

Rothman, Hal. 2002. *Neon Metropolis: How Las Vegas Started the Twenty-First Century*. New York: Routledge.

Roumillat, Shelene. 2013. "From the 'Hour of Her Darkest Peril' to the 'Brightest Page of Her History': New Perspectives on the Battle of New Orleans." PhD diss., Tulane University.

Rouselle, Bill. 2009. "Oral History Interview with Kevin McCaffery." January 28. Past Presidents Collection. New Orleans Jazz and Heritage Foundation Archive.

Ryan, Mary. 1997. *Civic Wars: Democracy and Public Life in the American City during the Nineteenth Century*. Berkeley: University of California Press.

S. T. G. 1852. "Early History of Louisiana." *Southern Literary Messenger* 18 (5): 311–12.

Sakakeeny, Matt. 2011a. "New Orleans, Louisiana, USA." *Perspectives on Politics* 10 (3): 723–26.

Sakakeeny, Matt. 2011b. "New Orleans Music as a Circulatory System." *Black Music Research Journal* 31 (2): 291–325.

Sakakeeny, Matt. 2013. *Roll With It: Brass Bands in the Streets of New Orleans*. Durham, NC: Duke University Press.

Saville, Julie. 1996. *The Work of Reconstruction: From Slave to Wage Laborer in South Carolina*. New York: Cambridge University Press.

Saxon, Lyle. 1988. *Fabulous New Orleans*. Reprint. Gretna, LA: Pelican.

Saxon, Lyle, Edward Dreyer, and Robert Tallant. (1945) 1988. *Gumbo Ya-Ya: A Collection of Louisiana Folk Tales*. Gretna, LA: Pelican.

Schafer, Judith. 2009. *Brothels, Depravity, and Abandoned Women: Illegal Sex in Antebellum New Orleans*. Baton Rouge: Louisiana State University Press.

Schindler, Henri. 1997. *Mardi Gras: New Orleans*. Paris: Flammarion.

Scott, Allen J. 2005. *On Hollywood: The Place, the Industry*. Princeton, NJ: Princeton University Press.

Scott, James C. 1990. *Domination and the Arts of Resistance: Hidden Transcripts*. New Haven, CT: Yale University Press.

Scott, Rebecca J., and Jean M. Hébrard. 2012. *Freedom Papers: An Atlantic Odyssey in the Age of Emancipation*. Cambridge, MA: Harvard University Press.

Seidman, Karl F. 2013. *Coming Home to New Orleans: Neighborhood Rebuilding after Katrina*. Oxford: Oxford University Press.

Sexton, Jared. 2010. "Proprieties of Coalition: Blacks, Asians, and the Politics of Policing." *Critical Sociology* 36 (1): 87–108.

Shafer, Jack. 2005. "Don't Refloat." *Slate*, September 7. http://www.slate.com/articles /news_and_politics/press_box/2005/09/dont_refloat.html.

Shange, Savannah. 2015. "Project Description." *Gallery of the Streets*, May 30. http:// galleryofthestreets.org/ten-years-post-katrina/.

Shepherd, Samuel C., Jr. 1985. "A Glimmer of Hope: The World's Industrial and Cotton Centennial Exposition, New Orleans, 1884–1885." *Louisiana History* 26 (3): 271–90.

Shoemaker, David. 2013. *The Squared Circle: Life, Death, and Professional Wrestling*. New York: Gotham.

Sitrin, Marina. 2006. *Horizontalism: Voices of Popular Power in Argentina*. Oakland, CA: AK Press.

Siwek, Stephen E. 2013. "Copyright Industries in the U.S. Economy: The 2013 Report." Washington, DC: International Intellectual Property Alliance. http://www.iipa .com.

Sluyter, Andrew, Case Watkins, James P. Cheney, and Annie M. Gibson. 2015. *Hispanic and Latino New Orleans: Immigration and Identity since the Eighteenth Century*. Baton Rouge: Louisiana University Press.

Smith, Felipe. 2003. "Coming of Age in Creole New Orleans: An Ethnohistory." In *Problematizing Blackness: Self-Ethnographies by Black Immigrants to the United States*, edited by Percy Claude Hintzen and Jean Muteba Rahier, 113–29. New York: Routledge.

Smith, Sidonie, and Julia Watson. 2010. *Reading Autobiography: A Guide for Interpreting Life Narratives*. 2nd ed. Minneapolis: University of Minnesota Press.

Solnit, Rebecca. 2009a. "If Gardens Are the Answer, What Is the Question?" Lecture presented at UC Berkeley Forum on the Humanities and the Public World, Berkeley, CA.

Solnit, Rebecca. 2009b. *A Paradise Built in Hell: The Extraordinary Communities That Arise in Disaster*. New York: Penguin.

Solnit, Rebecca, and Rebecca Snedeker. 2013. *Unfathomable City: A New Orleans Atlas*. Berkeley: University of California Press.

Sontag, Susan. 2013. *Regarding the Pain of Others*. London: Hamish Hamilton.

Souther, J. Mark. 2003a. "Into the Big League: Conventions, Football, and the Color Line in New Orleans." *Journal of Urban History* 29 (6): 694–725.

Souther, J. Mark. 2003b. "Making the 'Birthplace of Jazz': Tourism and Musical Heritage Marketing in New Orleans." *Louisiana History* 44 (1): 39–73.

Souther, J. Mark. 2006. *New Orleans on Parade: Tourism and the Transformation of the Crescent City*. Baton Rouge: Louisiana State University Press.

Souther, J. Mark. 2008. "Suburban Swamp: The Rise and Fall of Planned New-Town Communities in New Orleans East." *Planning Perspectives* 23 (2): 197–219.

Spain, Daphne. 1979. "Race Relations and Residential Segregation in New Orleans: Two Centuries of Paradox." *Annals of the American Academy of Political and Social Science* 441: 82–96.

Sparks, Randy J. 2009. "'An Anchor to the People': Hurricane Katrina, Religious Life, and Recovery in New Orleans." After the Storm: A Special Issue on Hurricane Katrina, *Journal of Southern Religion*. http://jsreligion.org/Katrina/Sparks.pdf.

Spear, Jennifer M. 2003. "Colonial Intimacies: Legislating Sex in French Louisiana." *William and Mary Quarterly* 60 (1): 75–98.

Spear, Jennifer M. 2009. *Race, Sex, and Social Order in Early New Orleans*. Baltimore: Johns Hopkins University Press.

Spitzer, Nicholas R. 2003. "Monde Creole: The Cultural World of French Louisiana Creoles and the Creolization of World Cultures." *Journal of American Folklore* 116 (459): 57–72.

Spivak, Gayatri. 1999. *Critique of Postcolonial Reason*. Cambridge, MA: Harvard University Press.

Stanonis, Anthony J. 2006. *Creating the Big Easy: New Orleans and the Emergence of Modern Tourism, 1918–1945*. Athens: University of Georgia Press.

Starr, S. Frederick. 2001. "Introduction." In *Inventing New Orleans: Writings of Lafcadio Hearn*, edited by S. Frederick Starr. Jackson: University Press of Mississippi.

Steffens, Lincoln. 1931. *Autobiography*. Berkeley, CA: Heyday.

Stewart, Susan. 1984. *On Longing: Narratives of the Miniature, the Gigantic, the Souvenir, the Collection*. Baltimore: Johns Hopkins University Press.

Stocking, George W., Jr. 1982. *Race, Culture, and Evolution: Essays in the History of Anthropology*. Chicago: University of Chicago Press.

Stoddarrd, Lothrop. 1927. *The Rising Tide of Color against White World-Supremacy*. New York: Charles Scribner's Sons.

Stone, Clarence N. 1980. "Systemic Power in Community Decision Making: A Restatement of Stratification Theory." *American Political Science Review* 74 (4): 978–90.

Stone, Clarence N. 1982. "Social Stratification, Nondecision-Making, and the Study of Community Power." *American Politics Research* 10 (3): 275–302.

Storper, Michael. 2009. *Keys to the City: How Economics, Institutions, Social Interaction, and Politics Shape Development*. Princeton, NJ: Princeton University Press.

Sublette, Ned. 2008. *The World That Made New Orleans: From Spanish Silver to Congo Square*. Chicago: Lawrence Hill.

Sublette, Ned. 2010. *The Year before the Flood: A Story of New Orleans.* Chicago: Lawrence Hill.

Szwed, John. 2010. *Alan Lomax: The Man Who Recorded the World.* New York: Penguin.

Tallant, Robert. 1950. *The Romantic New Orleanians.* New York: Dutton.

Tallant, Robert, Lyle Saxon, and Edward Dreyer. 1945. *Gumbo Ya-Ya: A Collection of Louisiana Folk Tales.* Boston: Houghton Mifflin.

Tang, Eric. 2006. "Boat People." *Colorlines: News for Action,* March 21. http://www.colorlines.com/articles/boat-people.

Tang, Eric. 2011. "A Gulf Unites Us: The Vietnamese Americans of Black New Orleans East." *American Quarterly* 63 (1): 117–49.

Tate, Katherine. 1993. *From Protest to Politics: The New Black Voters in American Elections.* Cambridge, MA: Harvard University Press.

Testut, Charles. 1849. *Les Veillés louisianaises, série de romans historiques sur la Louisiane.* 2 vols. New Orleans: Imprimerie de H. Méridier.

Thomas, Lynnell L. 2014. *Desire and Disaster in New Orleans: Tourism, Race, and Historical Memory.* Durham, NC: Duke University Press.

Thompson, Mark L. 2008. "Locating the Isle of Orleans: Atlantic and American Historiographical Perspectives." *Atlantic Studies* 5 (3): 305–33.

Thompson, Robert Farris. 1988. "Recapturing Heaven's Glamour: Afro-Caribbean Festivalizing Arts." In *Caribbean Festival Arts: Each and Every Bit of Difference,* edited by John W. Nunley and Judith Betelheim, 17–29. Seattle: University of Washington Press.

Tinker, Edward Larocque. 1932. *Les Écrits de langue française en Louisiana.* Paris: Libraire Ancienne Honoré Champion.

Tinker, Edward Larocque. 1933. *The Palingenesis of Craps.* New York: Press of the Wooly Whale.

Toledano, Roulhac, and Mary L. Christovich. 1980. *New Orleans Architecture: Faubourg Tremé and the Bayou Road.* Gretna, LA: Pelican.

Tregle, Joseph G., Jr. 1992. "Creoles and Americans." In *Creole New Orleans: Race and Americanization,* edited by Arnold R. Hirsch and Joseph Logsdon, 131–88. Baton Rouge: Louisiana State University Press.

Tregle, Joseph G., Jr. 1999. *Louisiana in the Age of Jackson: A Clash of Cultures and Personalities.* Baton Rouge: Louisiana State University Press.

Trillin, Calvin. 1964. "A Reporter at Large: The Zulus." *New Yorker,* June 20, 41–119.

Trilling, Lionel. 1972. *Sincerity and Authenticity.* Cambridge, MA: Harvard University Press.

Trouillot, Michel-Rolph. 1991. "The Savage Slot." In *Recapturing Anthropology: Working in the Present,* edited by Richard G. Fox, 17–44. Santa Fe, NM: School of American Research Press.

Truitt, Allison. 2012. "The Viet Village Urban Farm and the Politics of Neighborhood Viability in Post-Katrina New Orleans." *City and Society* 24 (3): 321–38.

Truitt, Allison. 2015. "Not a Day but a Vu Lan Season: Celebrating Filial Piety in the Vietnamese Diaspora." *Journal of Asian American Studies* 18 (3): 289–311.

Trujillo-Pagán, Nicole. 2011. "Hazardous Constructions: Mexican Immigrant Masculinity and the Rebuilding of New Orleans." In *The Neoliberal Deluge: Hurricane*

Katrina, Late Capitalism and the Remaking of New Orleans, edited by Cedric Johnson, 327–53. Minneapolis: University of Minnesota Press.

Trujillo-Pagán, Nicole. 2012. "Neoliberal Disasters and Racialisation: The Case of Post-Katrina Latino Labour." *Race and Class* 53 (4): 54–66.

Tuck, Richard. 2001. *The Rights of War and Peace: Political Thought and the International Order from Grotius to Kant*. New York: Oxford University Press.

Twain, Mark. 1883. *Life on the Mississippi*. Boston: James R. Osgood.

Tylor, Edward B. 1871. *Primitive Culture: Researches into the Development of Mythology, Philosophy, Religion, Art, and Custom*. London: J. Murray.

Tyrrell, Ian. 1991. "American Exceptionalism in an Age of International History." *American Historical Review* 96 (4): 1031–55.

US Government. 1977. *Summary of the Housing and Community Development Act of 1977*. Washington, DC: Department of Housing and Urban Development.

US Senate, Committee on Banking Housing and Urban Affairs. 1976. *Community Development Block Grant Program: Hearings before the Committee on Banking, Housing and Urban Affairs*, 94th Congress, 2nd sess. Washington, DC: US Government Printing Office.

Usner, Daniel. 1992. *Indians, Settlers, and Slaves in a Frontier Exchange Economy: The Lower Mississippi Valley before 1783*. Chapel Hill: University of North Carolina Press.

Uzée, Philip D. 1943. "An Analysis of the Histories of Charles E. A. Gayarré." *Proceedings of the Louisiana Academy of Sciences* 7 (April): 120–28.

VanLandingham, Mark Jennings. 2017. *Weathering Katrina: Culture and Recovery among Vietnamese Americans*. New York: Russell Sage.

Vennman, Barbara. 1993. "Boundary Faceoff: New Orleans Civil Rights Law and Carnival Tradition." *TDR* 37 (3): 76–109.

Vidal, Cécile, ed. 2014. *Louisiana: Crossroads of the Atlantic World*. Philadelphia: University of Pennsylvania Press.

Vieta, Marcelo. 2010. "Social Innovations of Autogestión in Argentina's Worker-Recuperated Enterprises: Cooperatively Reorganizing Productive Life in Hard Times." *Labour Studies* 35 (3): 295–321.

Volpp, Leti. 2005. "Divesting Citizenship: On Asian American History and the Loss of Citizenship through Marriage." *UCLA Law Review* 53 (2): 405–83.

Von Hoffman, Alexander. 2000. "A Study in Contradictions: The Origins and Legacy of the Housing Act of 1949." *Housing Policy Debate* 11 (2): 299–325.

Wagner, Bryan. 2009. *Disturbing the Peace: Black Culture and the Police Power after Slavery*. Cambridge, MA: Harvard University Press.

Wallace, McHarg, Roberts, and Todd. 1975. *Central Area New Orleans Growth Management Program: Technical Report Containing the Proposed CBD Community Improvement Plan and Program, 1974 to the Year 2000*. Philadelphia: Bureau of Governmental Research.

Walters, Ronald G. 1973. "The Erotic South: Civilization and Sexuality in American Abolitionism." *American Quarterly* 25 (2): 177–201.

Warner, Chantelle. 2009. "Speaking from Experience: Narrative Schemas, Deixis, and

Authenticity Effects in Verena Stefan's Feminist Confession Shedding." *Language and Literature: Journal of the Poetics and Linguistics Association* 18 (1): 7–23.

Warren, Harris Gaylord. 1943. *The Sword Was Their Passport: A History of American Filibustering in the Mexican Revolution*. Baton Rouge: Louisiana State University Press.

Watson, Charles S. 1970. "A Denunciation on the State of Spanish Rule: James Workman's Liberty in Louisiana." *Louisiana History* 11 (3): 245–58.

Watts, Bill, and Scott Williams. 2006. *The Cowboy and the Cross: The Bill Watts Story. Rebellion, Wrestling and Redemption*. Chicago: ECW Press.

Watts, Lewis, and Eric Porter. 2013. *New Orleans Suite: Music and Culture in Transition*. Berkeley: University of California Press.

Watts, Michael. 1994. "Development II: The Privatization of Vverything?" *Progress in Human Geography* 18: 371–84.

Weheliye, Alexander G. 2005. *Phonographies: Grooves in Sonic Afro-Modernity*. Durham, NC: Duke University Press.

Weinstein, Richard. 1996. "The First American City." In *The City: Los Angeles and Urban Theory at the End of the Twentieth Century*, edited by Allen Scott and Edward Soja, 22–46. Berkeley: University of California Press.

Weise, Julie M. 2015. *Corazón de Dixie: Mexicanos in the U.S. South since 1910*. Chapel Hill: University of North Carolina Press.

Wheeler, Mary. 1944. *Steamboatin' Days: Folk Songs of the River Packet Era*. Baton Rouge: Louisiana State University.

Whelan, Robert K. 1989. "New Orleans: Public-Private Partnerships and Uneven Development." In *Unequal Partnerships: The Political Economy of Urban Redevelopment in Postwar America*, edited by Gregory D. Squires, 222–39. New Brunswick, NJ: Rutgers University Press.

Whelan, Robert K., Alma H. Young, and Mickey Lauria. 1994. "Urban Regimes and Racial Politics in New Orleans." *Journal of Urban Affairs* 16 (1): 1–21.

Wiese, Andrew. 2004. *Places of Their Own*. Chicago: University of Chicago Press.

Williams, Raymond. 1958. *Culture and Society, 1780–1950*. New York: Columbia University Press.

Williams, Vernon J. 1996. *Rethinking Race: Franz Boas and His Contemporaries*. Lexington: University of Kentucky Press.

Wilson, Samuel, Mary Louise Christovich, and Roulhac Toledano, eds. 1971. *New Orleans Architecture*. Gretna, LA: Pelican.

Wolch, Jennifer R. 1990. *The Shadow State: Government and Voluntary Sector in Transition*. New York: Foundation Center.

Wolfinger, James. 2012. "The American Dream for All Americans: Race, Politics, and the Campaign to Desegregate Levittown." *Journal of Urban History* 38 (3): 430–51.

Woods, Clyde. 2017. *Development Drowned and Reborn: The Blues and Bourbon Restorations in Post-Katrina New Orleans*. Edited by Jordan T. Camp and Laura Pulido. Athens: University of Georgia Press.

Woodward, Ralph Lee, Jr. 2003. "Spanish Commercial Policy in Louisiana, 1763–1803." *Louisiana History* 44 (2): 133–64.

Works Progress Administration. 1938. *New Orleans City Guide*. Boston: Houghton Mifflin.

Wuthnow, Robert. 2004. *Saving America? Faith-Based Services and the Future of Civil Society*. Princeton, NJ: Princeton University Press.

Yeager, Gene. 1977. "Porfirian Commercial Propaganda: Mexico in the World Industrial Expositions." *The Americas* 34 (2): 230–43.

Yungai, Muhammed. 2015. Oral History Interview with Helen Regis and Rachel Lyons, March 30. New Orleans Jazz and Heritage Foundation Archive.

Contributors

THOMAS JESSEN ADAMS is lecturer in history and American studies at the University of Sydney and director of the United States Study Center.

VINCANNE ADAMS is professor and vice chair of medical anthropology in the Department of Anthropology, History and Social Medicine at the University of California, San Francisco. She is author of seven books, including *Metrics: What Counts in Global Health* and *Markets of Sorrow, Labors of Faith: New Orleans in the Wake of Katrina* (both Duke University Press).

VERN BAXTER is professor emeritus of sociology at the University of New Orleans. His research interests cover the broad areas of social organization, social theory, and urban sociology. Recent publications include *Left to Chance: A Story of Disaster in Two New Orleans Neighborhoods* (2015) and articles on the environmental consequences of urban development and the role of honor in economic exchange. A current project investigates slave finance and urban development in 1830s New Orleans.

MARIA CELESTE CASATI ALLEGRETTI holds a master of arts in sociology (2014) from the University of New Orleans. Her early research interests revolved around intersectionality, social inequality, and urban sociology. More recently, her interests have come to include early trauma and infant mental health. Casati currently works at Tulane University, providing parenting interventions to families involved with the child welfare system.

SHANNON LEE DAWDY is professor of anthropology and social sciences in the College at the University of Chicago. She teaches classes in historical anthropology, archaeology of the contemporary, and informal economies. She is the author of *Building the Devil's Empire: French Colonial New Orleans* (2008) and *Patina: A Profane Archaeology* (2016). Her current research focuses on the materiality of American funeral practices.

RIEN FERTEL is a writer, historian, and itinerant teacher. He is the author of *Imagining the Creole City* (2014), *The One True Barbecue* (2016), and *Southern Rock Opera* (2018) in the 33⅓ music series. He lives in New Orleans.

MEGAN FRENCH-MARCELIN serves as the campaign coordinator for JustLeadership-USA's A Working Future campaign, which seeks to dismantle barriers to employment and other collateral consequences of mass incarceration for people with criminal records. As the ACLU's policy research manager, she oversaw a broad portfolio of advocacy-driven criminal justice research. Megan holds a PhD in US history from Columbia University. She is the author of several scholarly articles on the origins of neoliberalism and economic inequality, including the forthcoming "Doing Business New Orleans Style: Racial Progressivism and the Politics of Uneven Development," to be published in Thomas Sugrue and Andrew Diamond's forthcoming book on urban neoliberalism. She has written for journalistic publications as well, including *Jacobin*, *Nonsite*, and *Jadalyyia*.

CEDRIC G. JOHNSON is associate professor of African American studies and political science at the University of Illinois at Chicago. He is the author of *Revolutionaries to Race Leaders: Black Power and the Making of African American Politics* (2007) and editor of *The Neoliberal Deluge: Hurricane Katrina, Late Capitalism, and the Remaking of New Orleans* (2011). His writings have appeared in *Catalyst*, *Nonsite*, *Historical Materialism*, *Jacobin*, *New Labor Forum*, *Labor Studies*, and *SOULS*. He is an assembly representative for UIC United Faculty Local 6456.

ALECIA P. LONG is the John R. Loos and Paul and Nancy Murrill Professor in the Department of History at Louisiana State University. She is the author of *The Great Southern Babylon: Sex, Race, and Respectability in New Orleans, 1865–1920* (2004), coeditor with LeeAnn Whites of *Occupied Women: Gender, Military Occupation, and the American Civil War* (2009), and *Louisiana: Our History, Our Home* (2015), a textbook designed for use in Louisiana history courses. Her current book project is titled *Crimes against Nature: Sex, Violence, and the Search for Conspirators in the Assassination of JFK*. The book connects Clay Shaw's 1969 conspiracy trial in the assassination of JFK to the longer history of homosexuality in New Orleans and reveals Shaw's overlooked role in the national movement for gay and lesbian civil rights.

VICKI MAYER is professor of communication at Tulane University. She writes on media production, the political economies of media and communications industries, and the cultures of media producers and consumers. She is author of three books, including *Almost Hollywood, Nearly New Orleans: The Lure of the Local Film Economy* (2017) and *Below the Line: Television Producers and Production Studies in the New Economy* (Duke University Press, 2011).

TOBY MILLER is a visiting professor at the Universidad del Norte. His latest of over forty books is *El trabajo cultural* (2018).

SUE MOBLEY is a New Orleans–based urbanist, organization, and advocate. She is director of advocacy at Colloqate Design, a nonprofit urban design firm with a racial and social justice framework, and codirector of the Paper Monuments project. Her primary research interests are in urban studies, public space, and public history, with a near-obsessive focus on race, class, and gender. She holds a BA in anthropology from Loyola University New Orleans and an MA in political science from the American University in Cairo.

MARGUERITE NGUYEN is associate professor of English at Wesleyan University. She is the author of *America's Vietnam: The Longue Durée of U.S. Literature and Empire* (2018) and coeditor of *Refugee Cultures: Forty Years after the Vietnam War* (2016). She is currently at work on a project titled "Refugee Ecologies," which examines narratives of forced displacement in New Orleans through an ecocritical lens.

AARON NYERGES is a lecturer in American studies at the US Studies Centre at the University of Sydney. His articles have appeared in *Textual Practice, Sound Studies, Australasian Journal of American Studies*, and *Journal of Popular Culture*. He has edited several special issues of scholarly journals, including one for *Occassion*—on the "Pop West" and comparative regionalism. He is currently completing a book manuscript titled "The Modernist States of America: Literature and the Mass Production of National Geography." The book provides a cultural geography of American modernism that emphasizes the expansion of the US imperial state in the early twentieth century. It contextualizes canonical American and less familiar non-US authors via an archive of "mass geography," a term that describes the mechanical reproducibility of space and its impact on the literary fantasy of the nation.

ADOLPH REED JR. is professor of political science at the University of Pennsylvania. He is the editor of *Race, Politics, and Culture: Critical Essays on the Radicalism of the 1960s* (1986) and *Without Justice for All: The New Liberalism and Our Retreat from Racial Equality* (1999), author of *The Jesse Jackson Phenomenon: The Crisis of Purpose in Afro-American Politics* (1986), *W. E. B. Du Bois and American Political Thought: Fabianism and the Color Line* (1997), *Stirrings in the Jug: Black American Politics in the Post-segregation Era* (1999), and *Class Notes: Posing as Politics and Other Essays on the American Scene* (2000), and coauthor of *Renewing Black Intellectual History: The Ideological and Material Foundations of African American Thought* (2010). He is currently completing a book on the decline and transformation of the US left since World War II.

HELEN A. REGIS is a cultural anthropologist in the Department of Geography and Anthropology at Louisiana State University. A board member and series editor at the Neighborhood Story Project, Regis has written a series of articles at the intersections of culture and commerce, focusing on public space, uneven policing, parading, festivity, and tourism. She is the author, with John Bartkowski, of *Charitable Choices: Religion, Race, and Poverty in the Post-welfare Era*. Her projects include *Seventh Ward Speaks, Paseos por New Orleans*, the exhibit *Creating Congo Square: Jazz Fest and Black Power*, and *Subsistence in Coastal Louisiana* (forthcoming, with Shana Walton). She has published in *African Arts, Cultural Anthropology, American Ethnologist*, and *Collaborative Anthropology*. She is currently completing an ethnography of the New Orleans Jazz and Heritage Festival.

MATT SAKAKEENY is associate professor of music at Tulane University. He is the author of *Roll With It: Brass Bands in the Streets of New Orleans* and coeditor of *Keywords in Sound* (both Duke University Press).

HEIDI SCHMALBACH is the executive director of the Arts Council New Orleans and a PhD candidate in city, culture, and community at Tulane University. She has over a decade of experience imagining and implementing projects at the intersection of the arts, urban planning, and community development. Heidi has worked in a diversity of contexts and communities, from New Orleans and Austin to rural Texas and southern Appalachia.

In her current role, she leads the Arts Council's programmatic efforts, including public art processes, creative youth development, arts and cultural advocacy, and policy initiatives. Her research focuses on arts-based community development, spatial justice and land use, and emergent social imaginaries. Heidi holds a master's degree in community and regional planning from the University of Texas at Austin School of Architecture.

FELIPE SMITH is a retired associate professor of English, formerly in the Department of English at Tulane University. His 1998 book, *American Body Politics: Race, Gender, and Black Literary Renaissance*, interrogates pervasive American theories and representations of race in turn-of-the-twentieth-century modern African American literature. In his essay, "Things You'd Imagine Zulu Tribes to Do: The Zulu Parade in New Orleans Carnival," Smith discusses the interesting history of the Zulu Social Aid and Pleasure Club, an African American, originally working-class organization that has paraded annually in, New Orleans for over a century, dressed in its early history as "jungle savages" in confirmation of white audience racial beliefs. The transformation of the Zulu parade from fringe spectacle into a can't-miss Carnival event underscores the transformative possibilities presented by Zulu's simultaneous fidelity to its black working-class origins, on one hand, and its reputation as an outsider organization, on the other hand, certifying its indispensability to the carnivalesque play and counterplay of racial disguise.

BRYAN WAGNER is associate professor in the English Department at the University of California, Berkeley. His books include *Disturbing the Peace: Black Culture and the Police Power after Slavery* (2009), *The Tar Baby: A Global History* (2017), and *The Life and Legend of Bras-Coupé: The Fugitive Slave Who Fought the Law, Ruled the Swamp, Danced at Congo Square, Invented Jazz, and Died for Love* (2019).

Index